# FINAL FANTASY®
ファイナルファンタジー　ロスト・ストレンジャー
## LOST STRANGER

6 Volume Six

Story: Hazuki Minase
Art: Itsuki Kameya



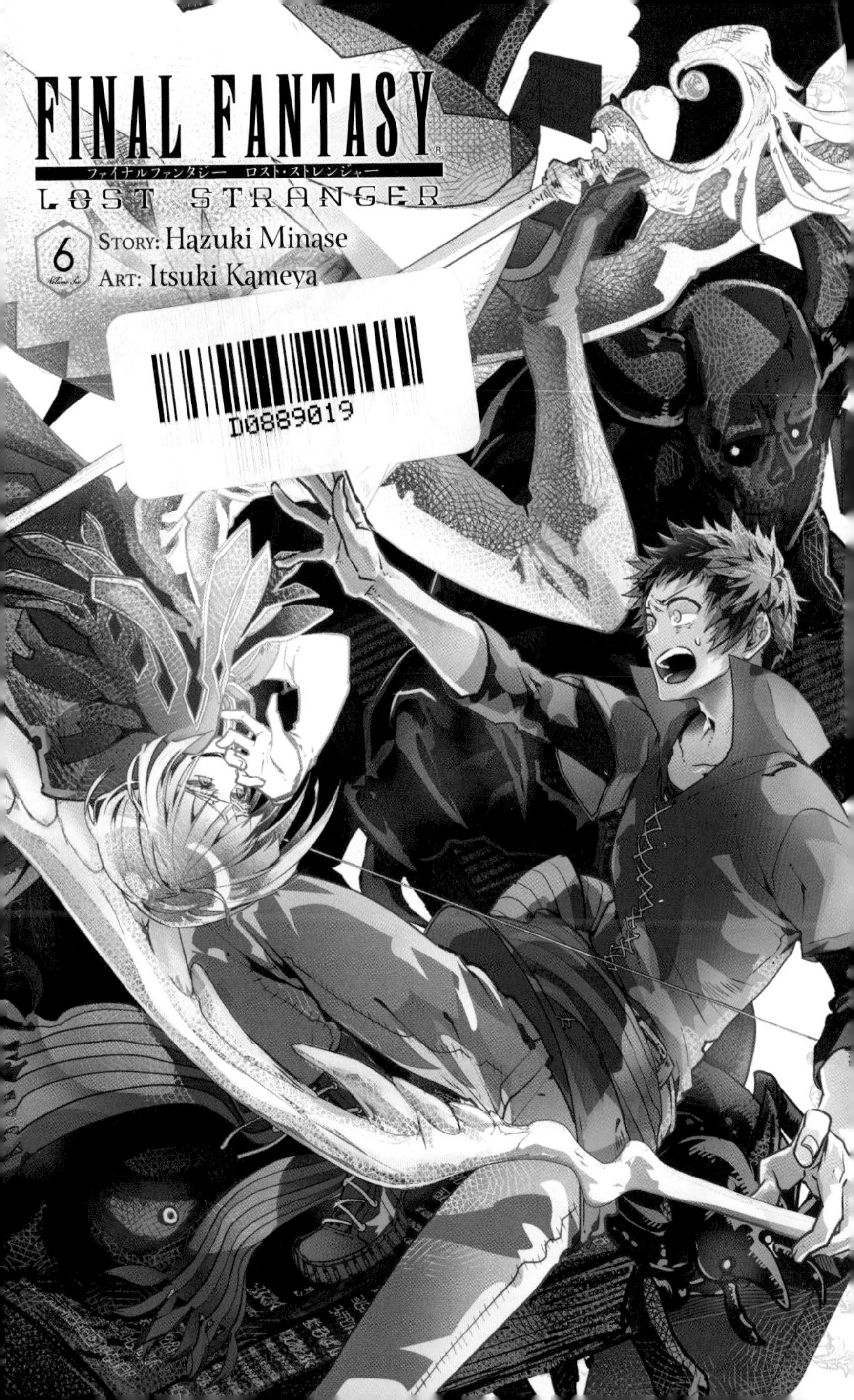

# Contents

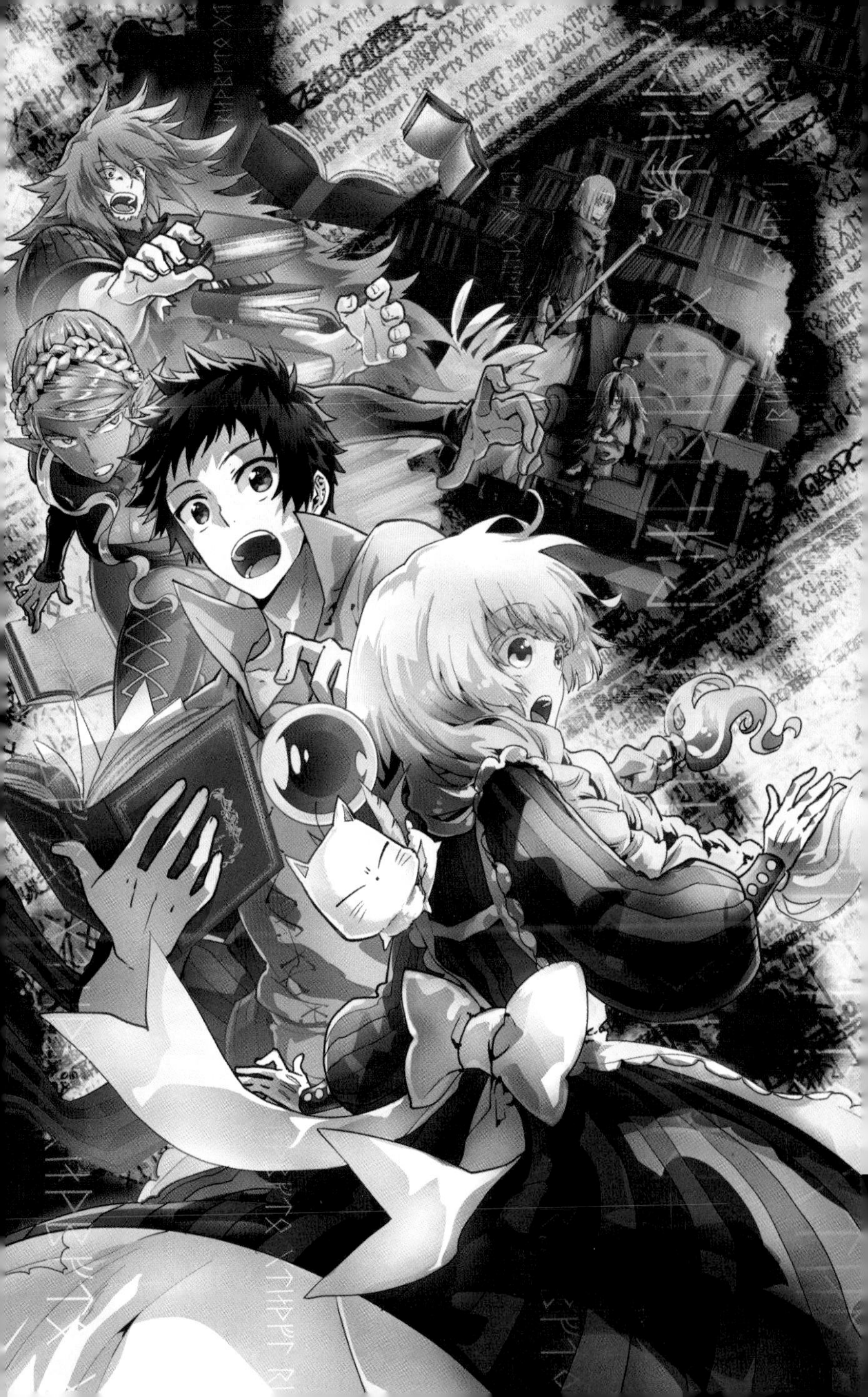

# FINAL FANTASY®

ファイナルファンタジー　ロスト・ストレンジャー

# LOST STRANGER

## STORY & CHARACTERS

Shogo and his little sister Yuko are SE employees. After awakening from their run-in with a truck, they found themselves in the *FF* world they'd always longed for...! Much like in the games, Shogo and Yuko had fun exploring the area, but tragedy would soon befall them. The ultimate fantasy awaits—a forbidden tale of reincarnation in another world with an *FF* twist!!

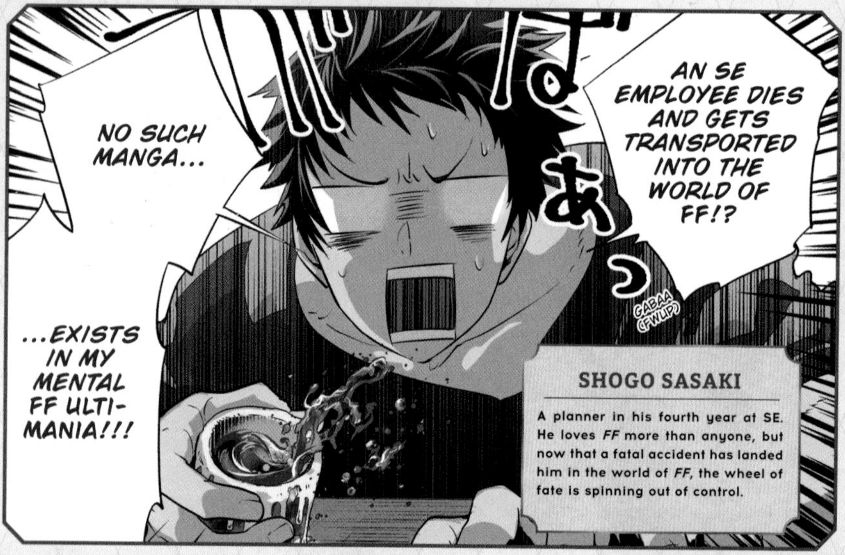
AN SE EMPLOYEE DIES AND GETS TRANSPORTED INTO THE WORLD OF FF!?
GABAA (FWUP)
NO SUCH MANGA...
...EXISTS IN MY MENTAL FF ULTI-MANIA!!!

**SHOGO SASAKI**

A planner in his fourth year at SE. He loves *FF* more than anyone, but now that a fatal accident has landed him in the world of *FF*, the wheel of fate is spinning out of control.

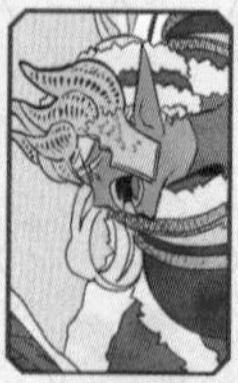

**REI HAGAKURE**

An Elrein Warrior who is loyal to Sharu to a fault.

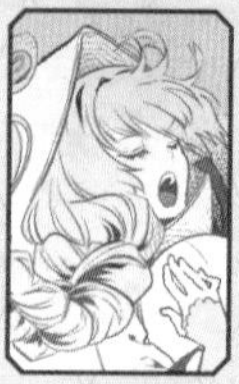

**SHARURU LINKINGFEATHER**

A kindhearted White Mage who eagerly treats all who are injured.

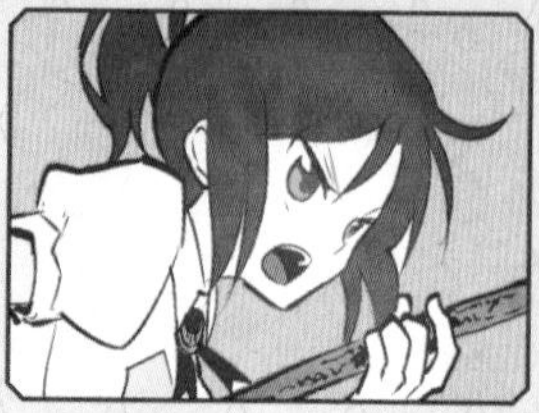

**YUKO SASAKI**

A second-year sales department employee at SE. She was transported alongside her brother Shogo but was killed saving a little girl from a dragon. Her soul was turned into a crystal.

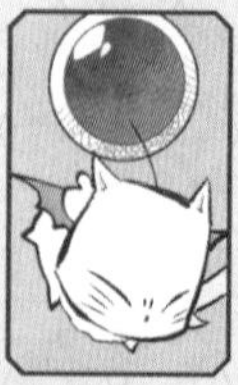

**MOG MOGCAN**

A moogle who travels with Sharuru's party.

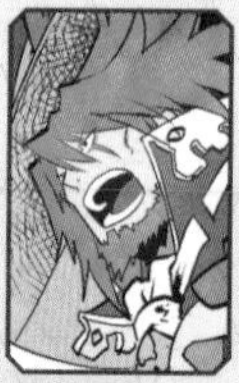

**DUSTON VOLTA**

A burly Black Mage of the Hyuuj race who also cooks.

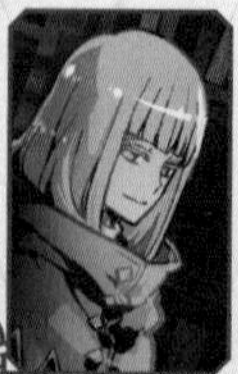

**ALUS**

A young man with blond hair and aquamarine eyes. Wields powerful spells such as "Reflect."

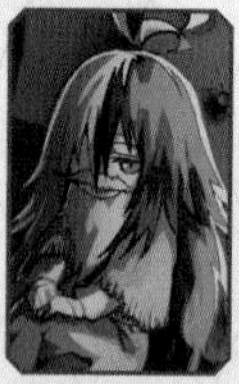

**G-SENPAI**

A mysterious elderly man the party met in the Great Library. Well versed in the library's secrets.

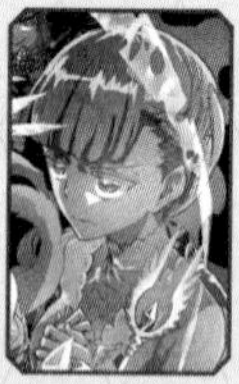

**SARA MYSIDIAN**

Princess of the Mysidian Kingdom. Concerned for her nation's future, she teams up with Shogo and company.

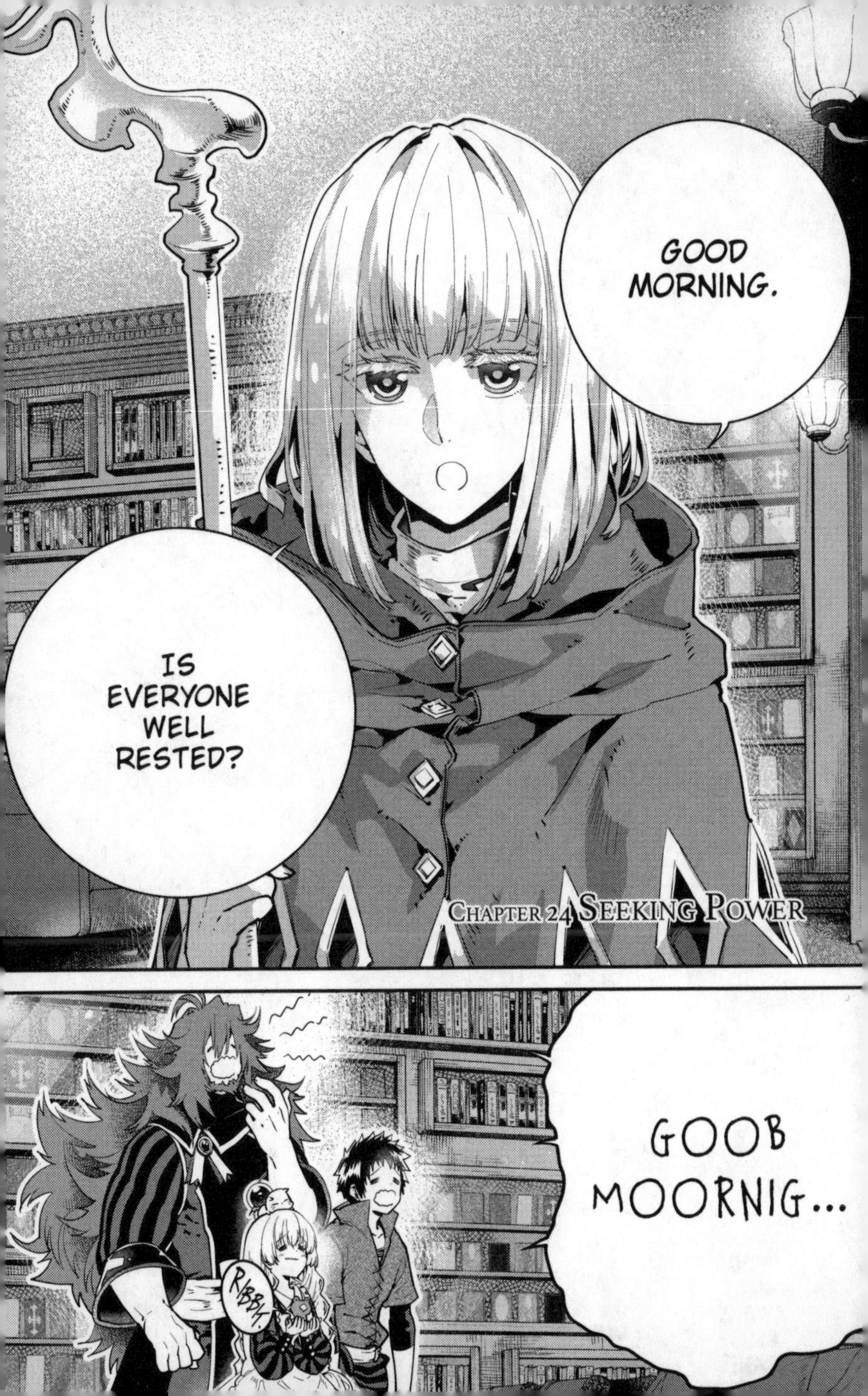
GOOD MORNING.
IS EVERYONE WELL RESTED?
CHAPTER 24 SEEKING POWER
GOOB MOORNIG...
RIBBIT.

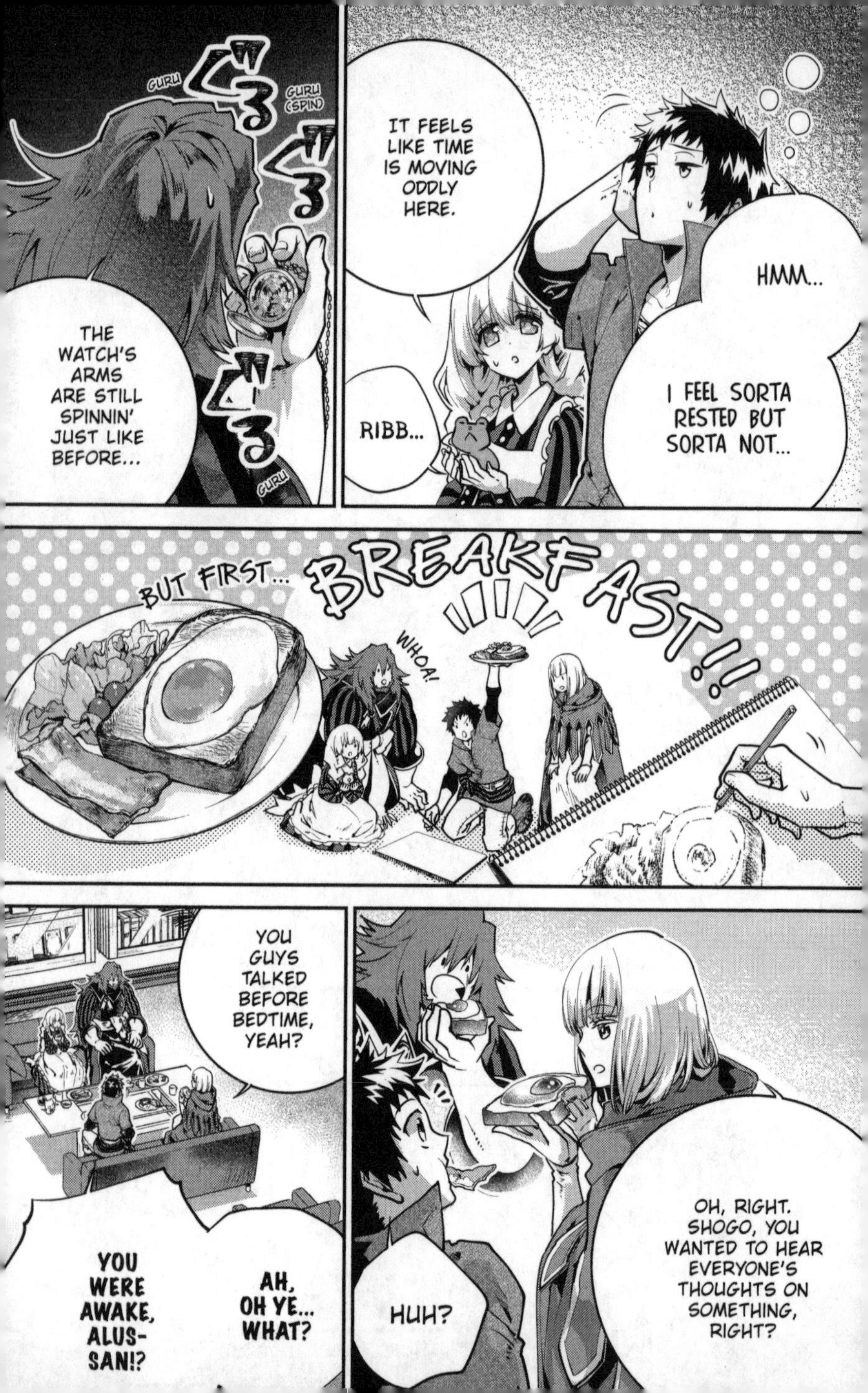
HMM...
I FEEL SORTA RESTED BUT SORTA NOT...
IT FEELS LIKE TIME IS MOVING ODDLY HERE.
RIBB...
GURU
GURU (SPIN)
THE WATCH'S ARMS ARE STILL SPINNIN' JUST LIKE BEFORE...
GURU
BUT FIRST... BREAKFAST!!
WHOA!
OH, RIGHT. SHOGO, YOU WANTED TO HEAR EVERYONE'S THOUGHTS ON SOMETHING, RIGHT?
HUH?
YOU GUYS TALKED BEFORE BEDTIME, YEAH?
AH, OH YE... WHAT?
YOU WERE AWAKE, ALUS-SAN!?

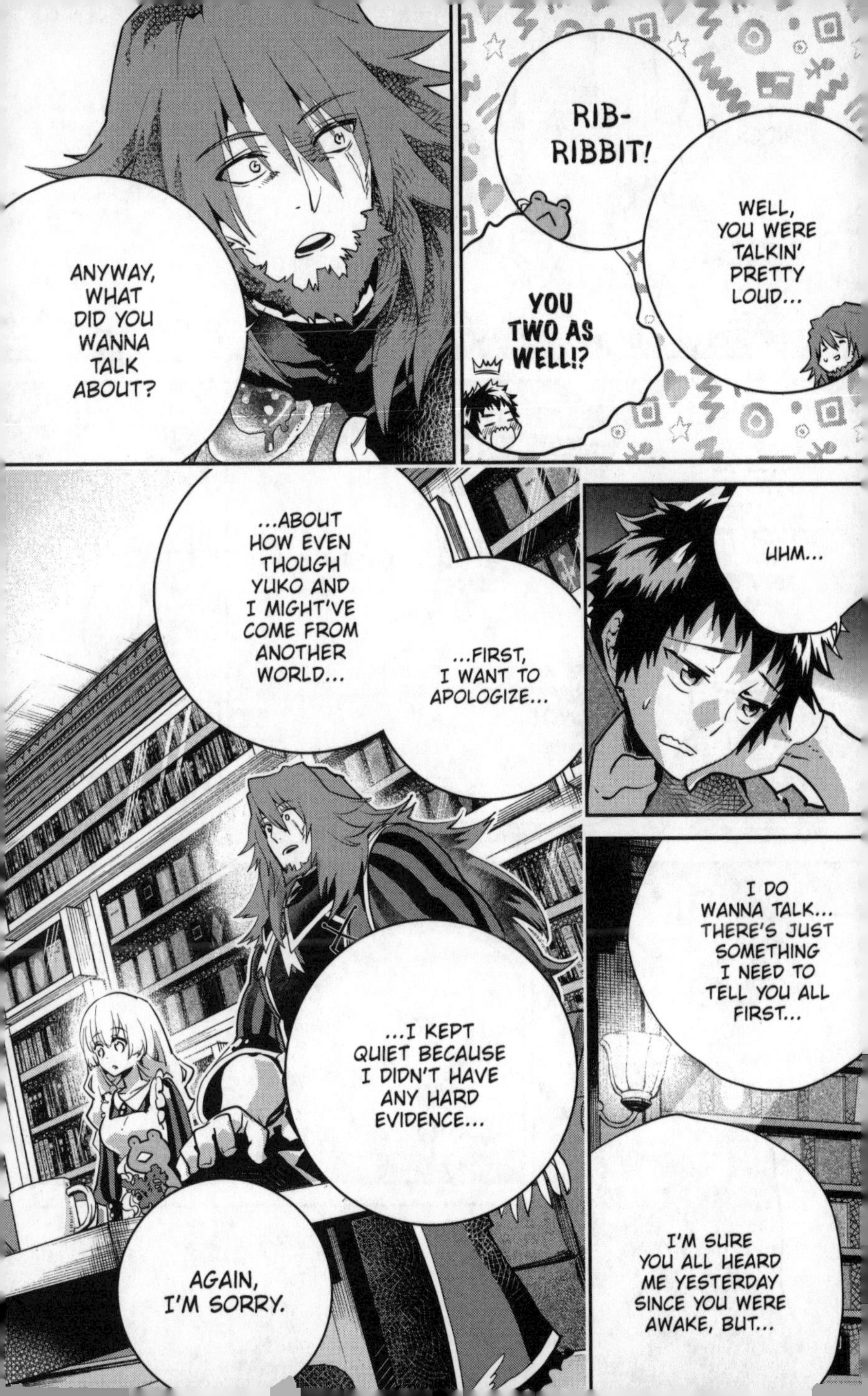
RIB- RIBBIT!
WELL, YOU WERE TALKIN' PRETTY LOUD...
YOU TWO AS WELL!?
ANYWAY, WHAT DID YOU WANNA TALK ABOUT?
UHM...
I DO WANNA TALK... THERE'S JUST SOMETHING I NEED TO TELL YOU ALL FIRST...
I'M SURE YOU ALL HEARD ME YESTERDAY SINCE YOU WERE AWAKE, BUT...
...FIRST, I WANT TO APOLOGIZE...
...ABOUT HOW EVEN THOUGH YUKO AND I MIGHT'VE COME FROM ANOTHER WORLD...
...I KEPT QUIET BECAUSE I DIDN'T HAVE ANY HARD EVIDENCE...
AGAIN, I'M SORRY.

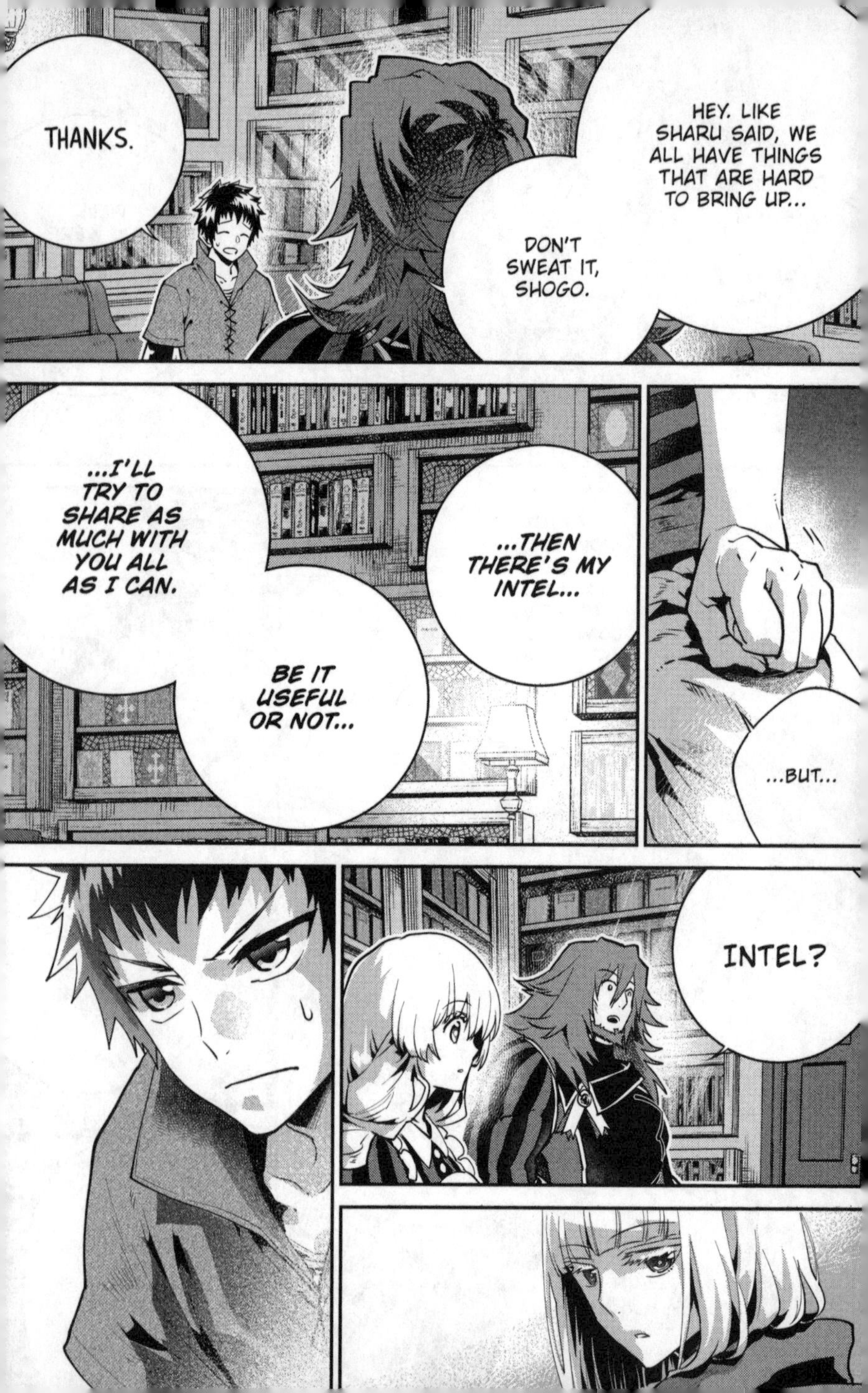
HEY. LIKE SHARU SAID, WE ALL HAVE THINGS THAT ARE HARD TO BRING UP...
DON'T SWEAT IT, SHOGO.
THANKS.
...BUT...
...THEN THERE'S MY INTEL...
BE IT USEFUL OR NOT...
...I'LL TRY TO SHARE AS MUCH WITH YOU ALL AS I CAN.
INTEL?

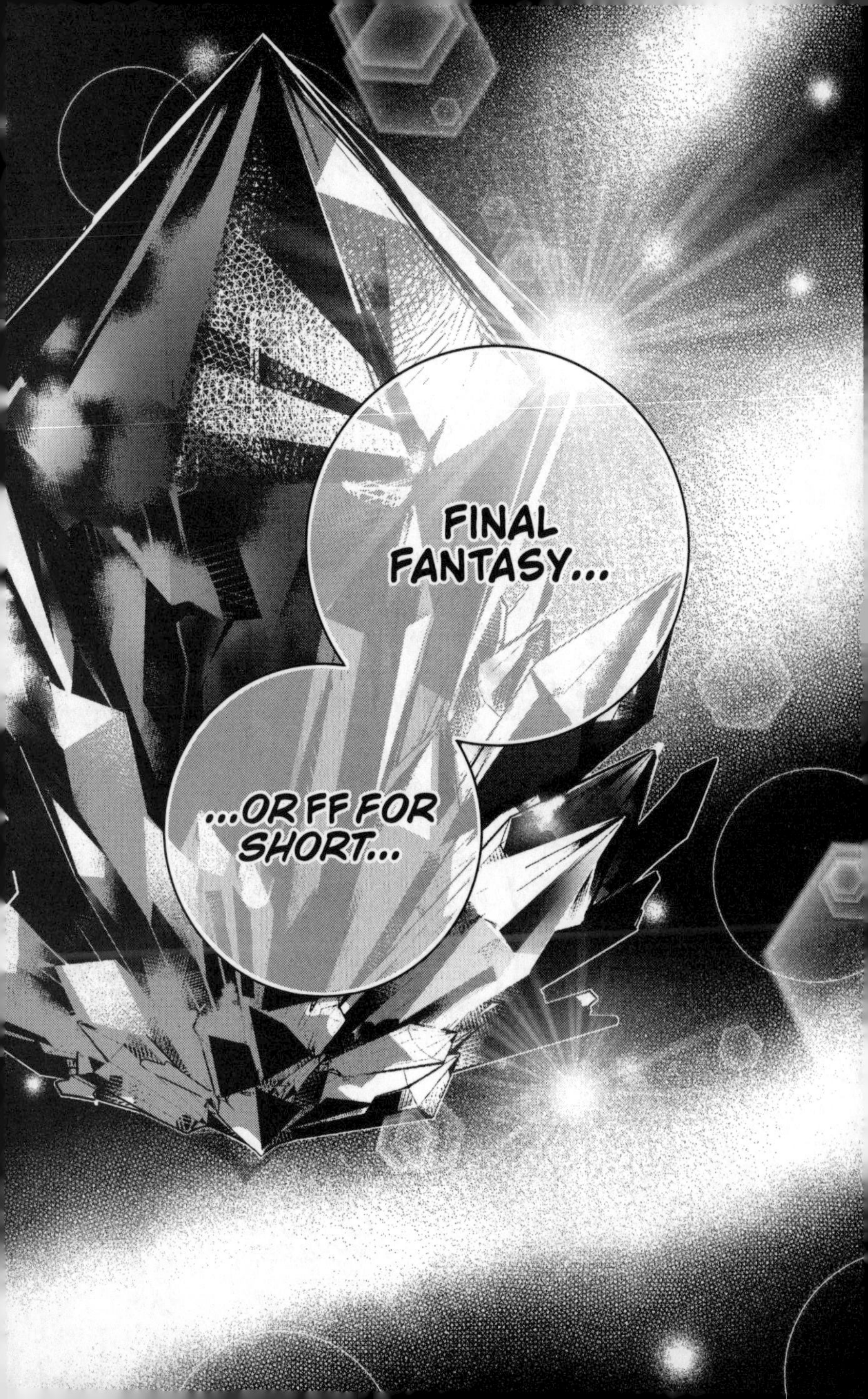
FINAL FANTASY...
...OR FF FOR SHORT...

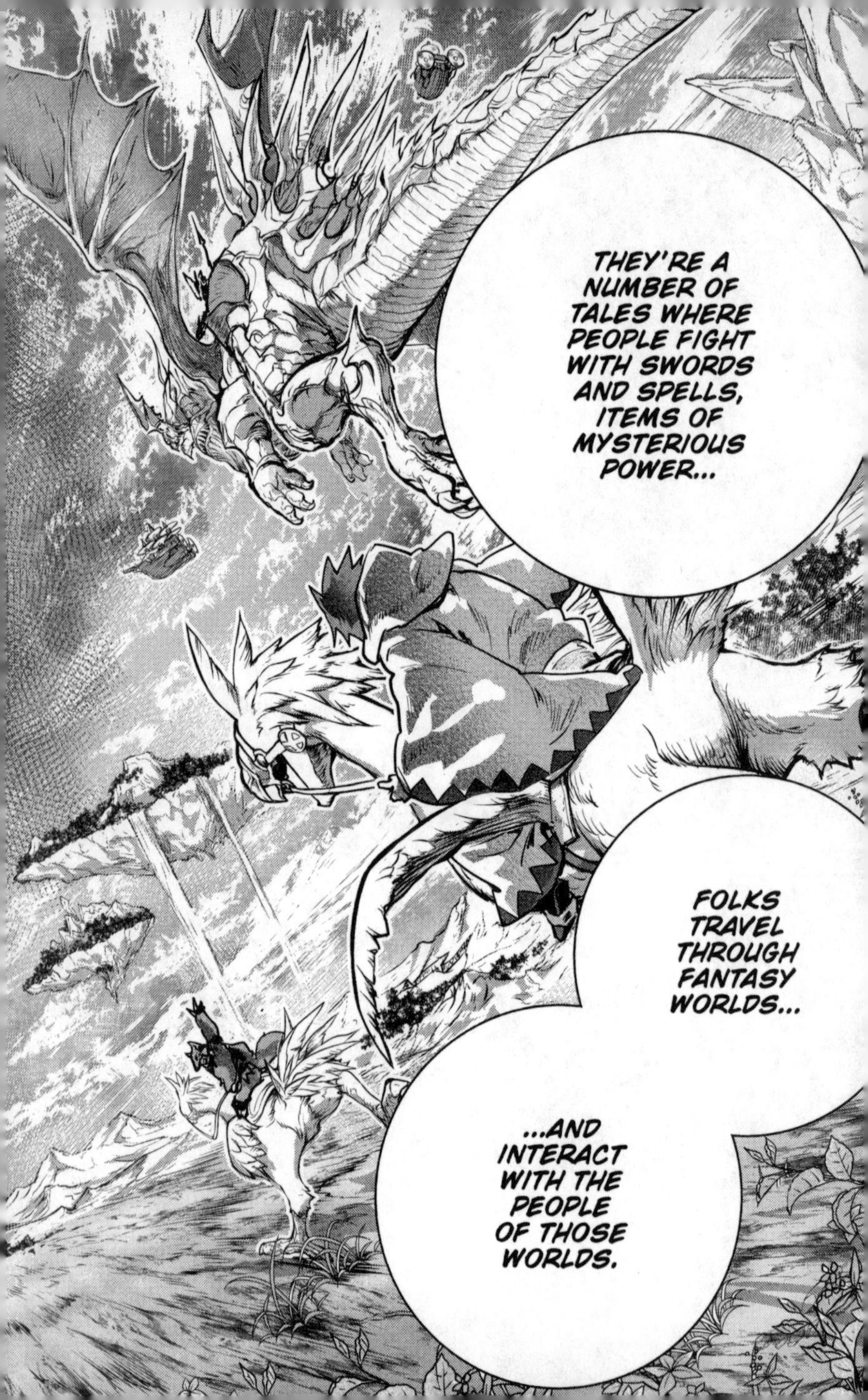
THEY'RE A NUMBER OF TALES WHERE PEOPLE FIGHT WITH SWORDS AND SPELLS, ITEMS OF MYSTERIOUS POWER...
FOLKS TRAVEL THROUGH FANTASY WORLDS...
...AND INTERACT WITH THE PEOPLE OF THOSE WORLDS.

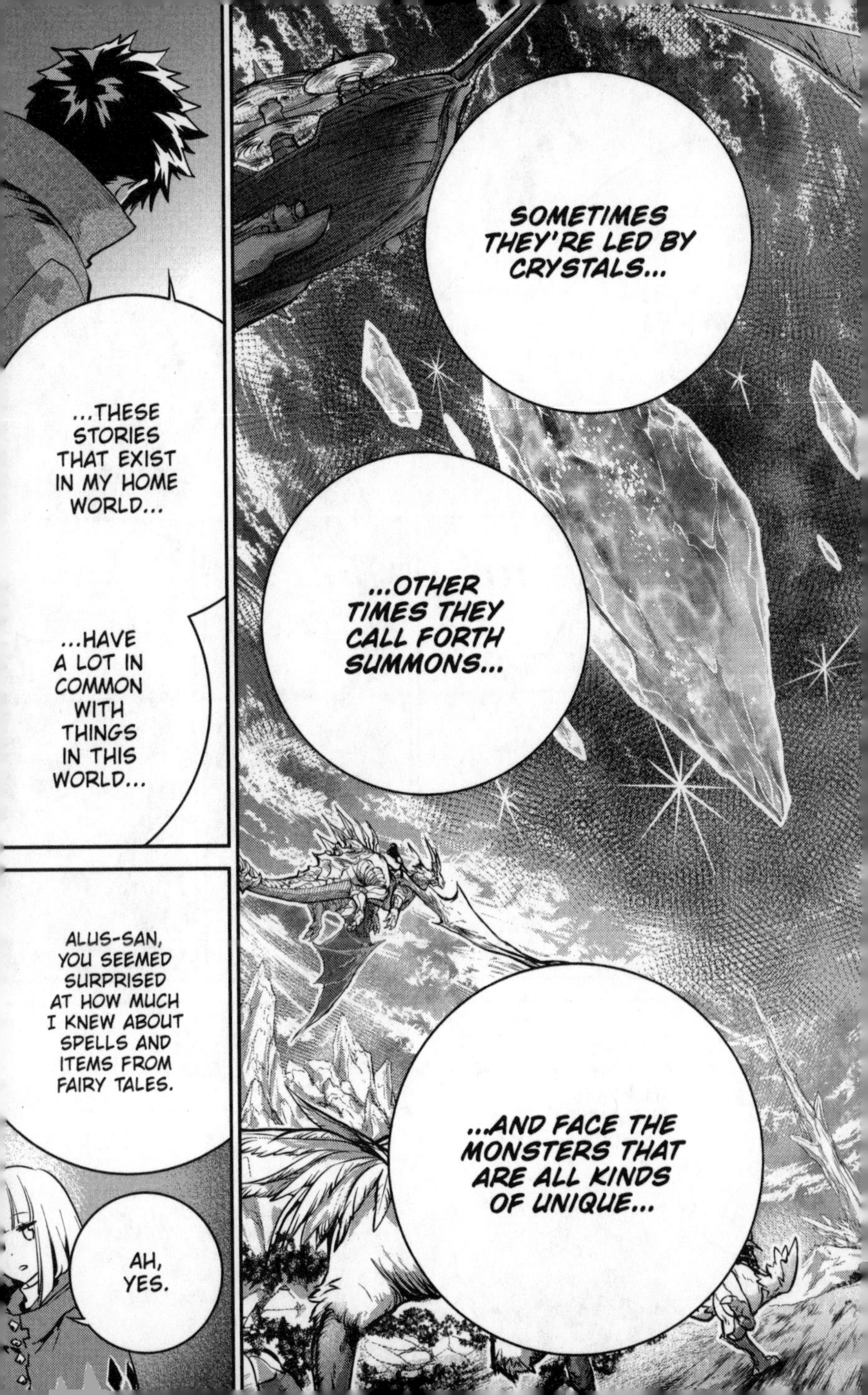
SOMETIMES THEY'RE LED BY CRYSTALS...
...OTHER TIMES THEY CALL FORTH SUMMONS...
...AND FACE THE MONSTERS THAT ARE ALL KINDS OF UNIQUE...
...THESE STORIES THAT EXIST IN MY HOME WORLD...
...HAVE A LOT IN COMMON WITH THINGS IN THIS WORLD...
ALUS-SAN, YOU SEEMED SURPRISED AT HOW MUCH I KNEW ABOUT SPELLS AND ITEMS FROM FAIRY TALES.
AH, YES.

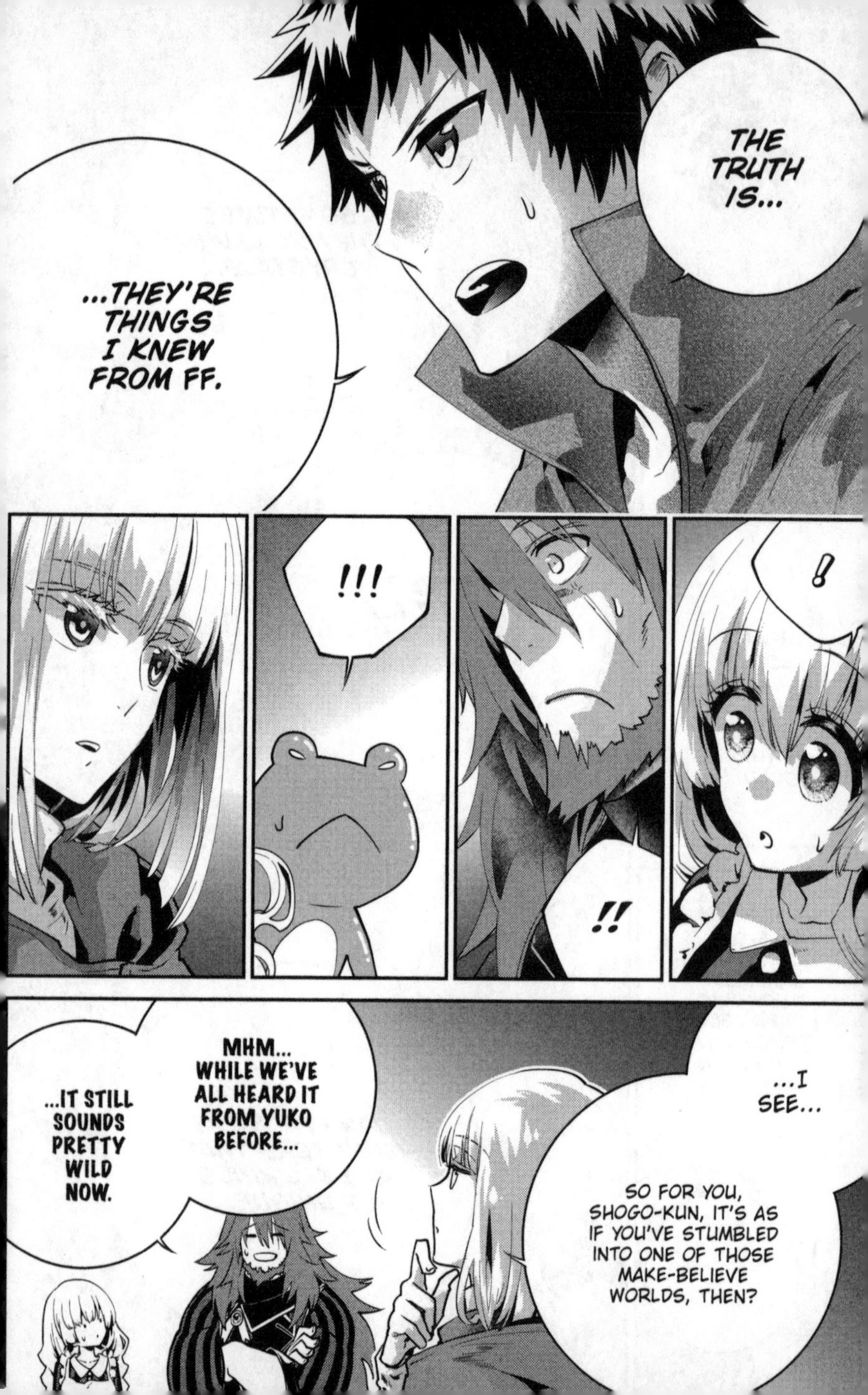
THE TRUTH IS...
...THEY'RE THINGS I KNEW FROM FF.
!
!!
!!!
...I SEE...
SO FOR YOU, SHOGO-KUN, IT'S AS IF YOU'VE STUMBLED INTO ONE OF THOSE MAKE-BELIEVE WORLDS, THEN?
MHM... WHILE WE'VE ALL HEARD IT FROM YUKO BEFORE...
...IT STILL SOUNDS PRETTY WILD NOW.

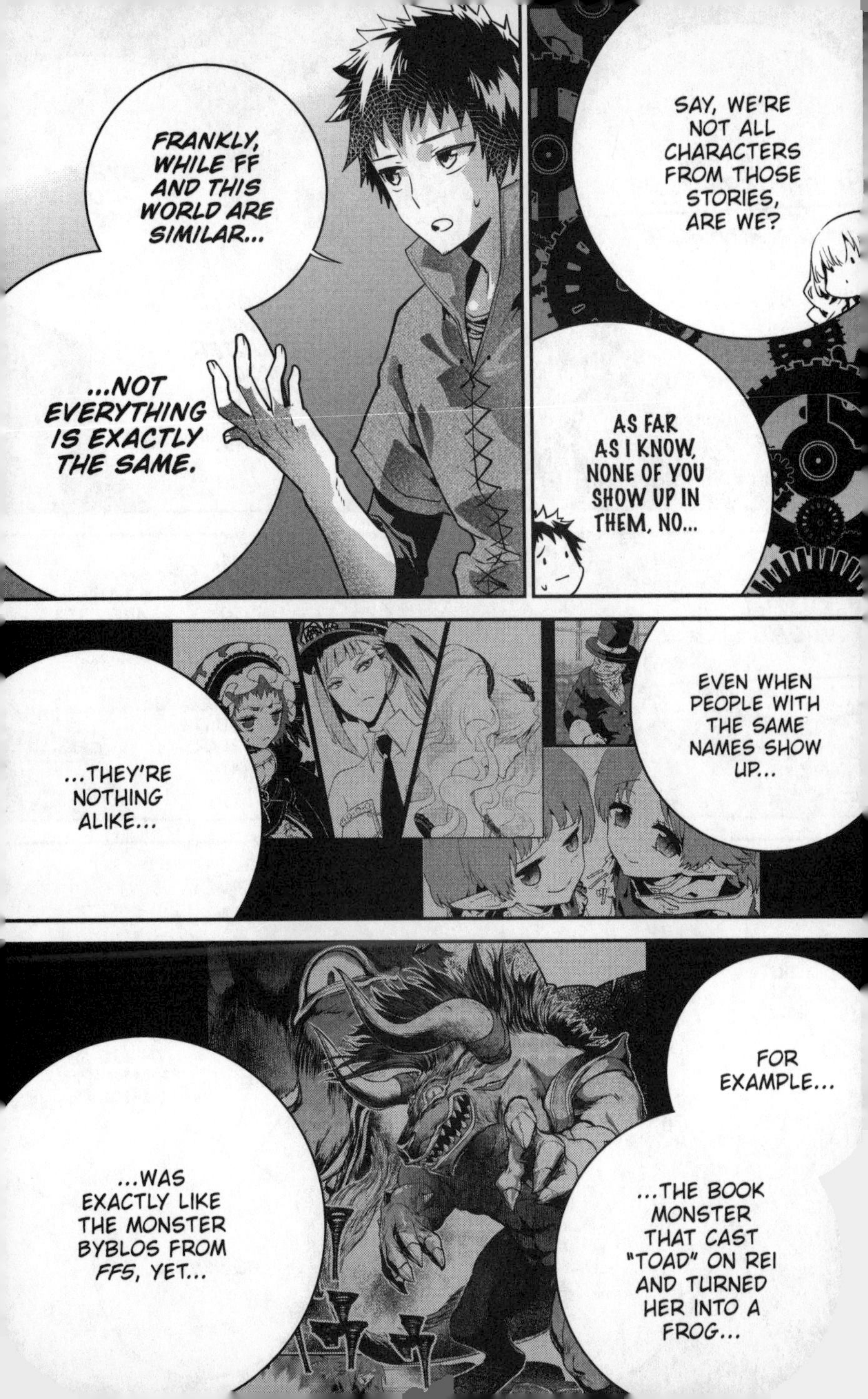
SAY, WE'RE NOT ALL CHARACTERS FROM THOSE STORIES, ARE WE?
AS FAR AS I KNOW, NONE OF YOU SHOW UP IN THEM, NO...
FRANKLY, WHILE FF AND THIS WORLD ARE SIMILAR...
...NOT EVERYTHING IS EXACTLY THE SAME.
EVEN WHEN PEOPLE WITH THE SAME NAMES SHOW UP...
...THEY'RE NOTHING ALIKE...
FOR EXAMPLE...
...THE BOOK MONSTER THAT CAST "TOAD" ON REI AND TURNED HER INTO A FROG...
...WAS EXACTLY LIKE THE MONSTER BYBLOS FROM FF5, YET...

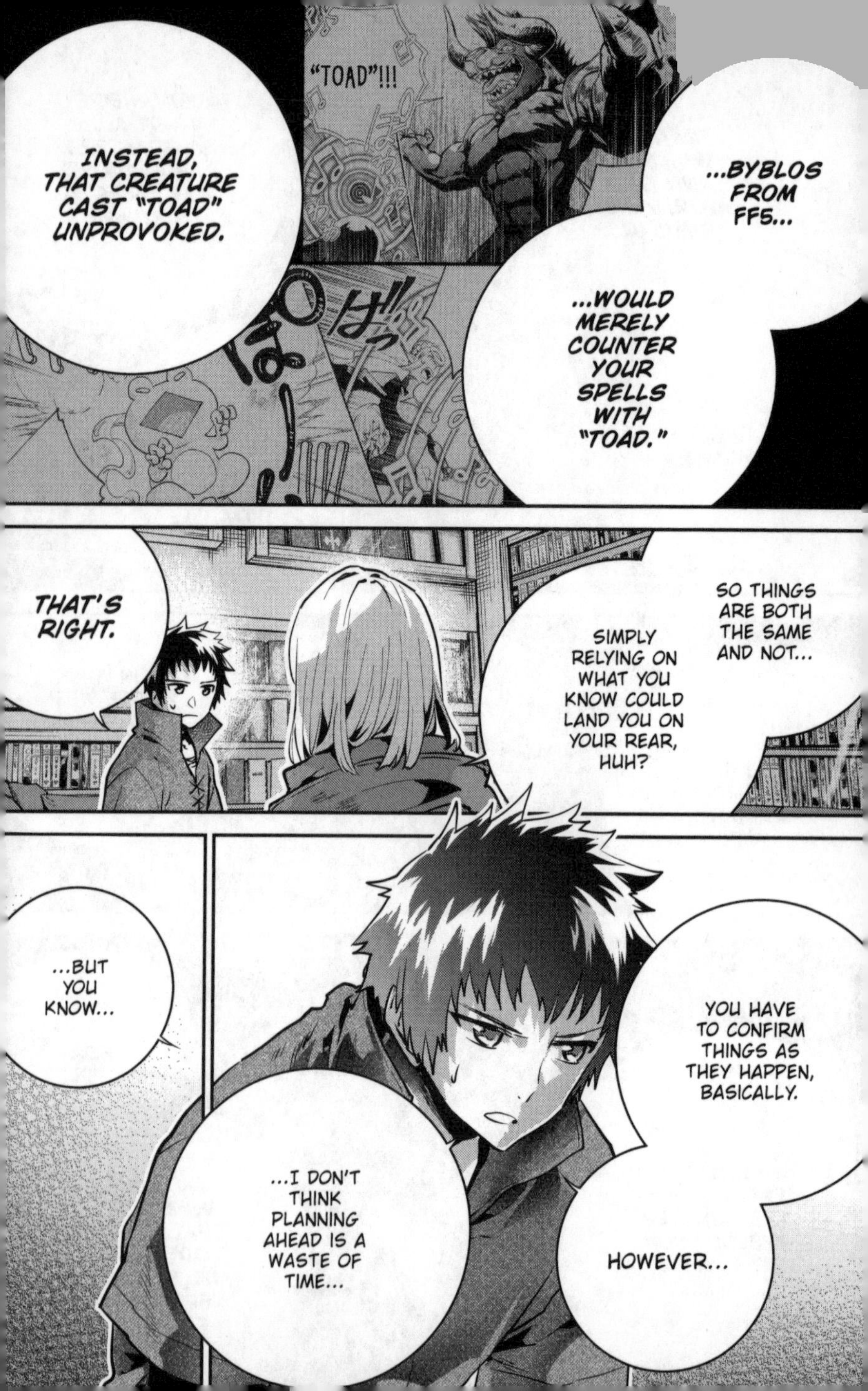
...BYBLOS FROM FF5...
...WOULD MERELY COUNTER YOUR SPELLS WITH "TOAD."
"TOAD"!!!
INSTEAD, THAT CREATURE CAST "TOAD" UNPROVOKED.
SO THINGS ARE BOTH THE SAME AND NOT...
SIMPLY RELYING ON WHAT YOU KNOW COULD LAND YOU ON YOUR REAR, HUH?
THAT'S RIGHT.
YOU HAVE TO CONFIRM THINGS AS THEY HAPPEN, BASICALLY.
HOWEVER...
...BUT YOU KNOW...
...I DON'T THINK PLANNING AHEAD IS A WASTE OF TIME...

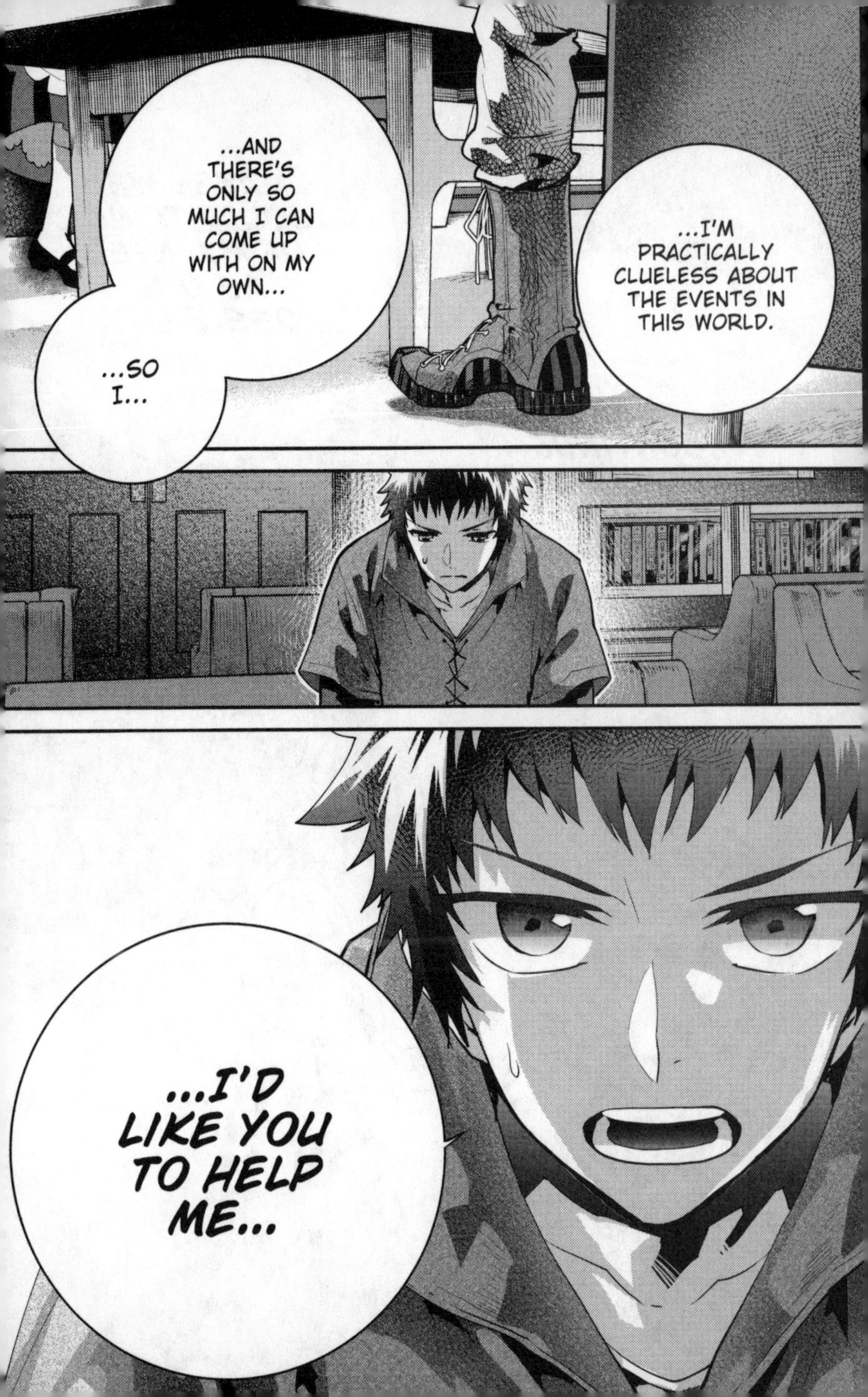
...I'M PRACTICALLY CLUELESS ABOUT THE EVENTS IN THIS WORLD.
...AND THERE'S ONLY SO MUCH I CAN COME UP WITH ON MY OWN...
...SO I...
...I'D LIKE YOU TO HELP ME...

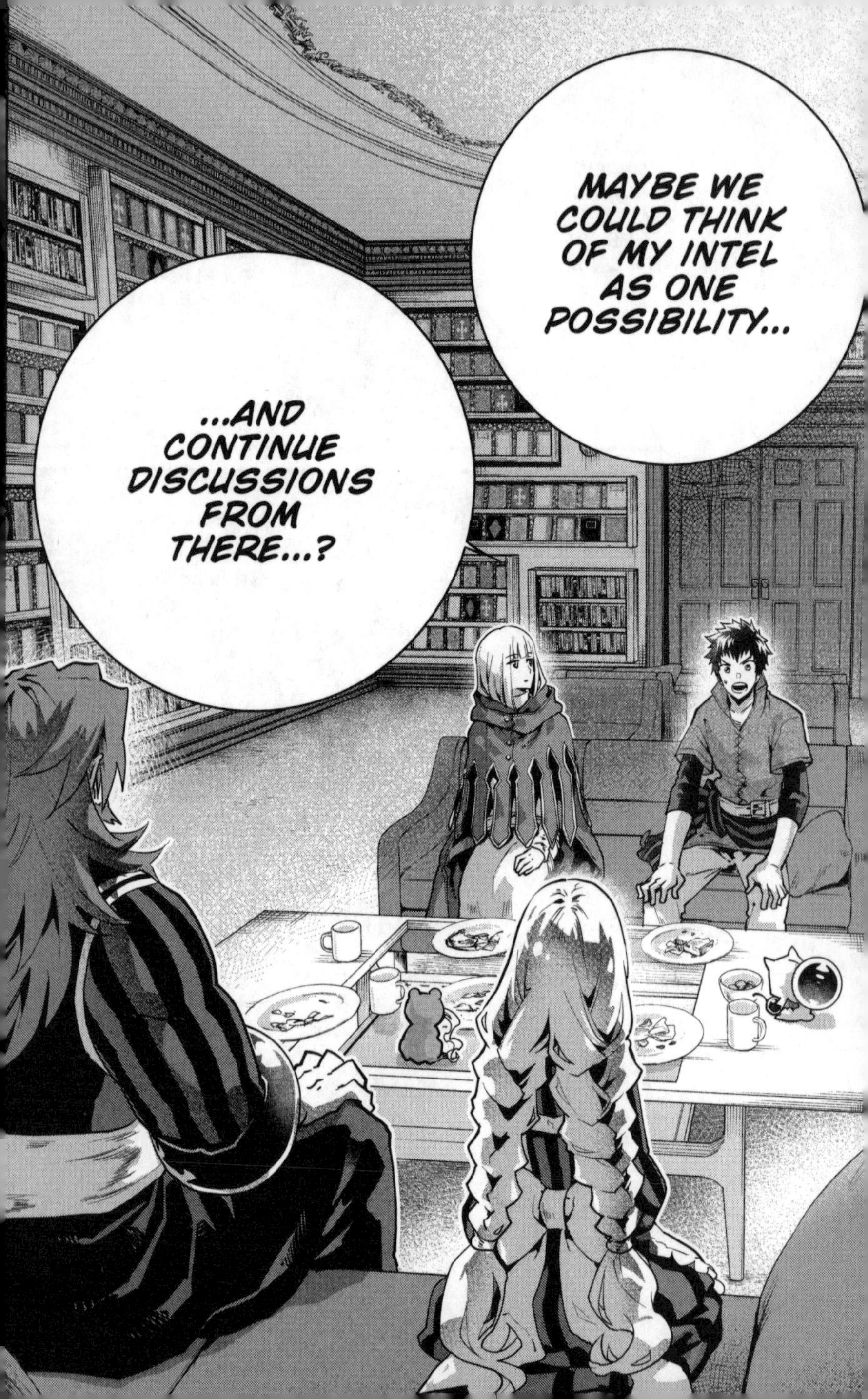
MAYBE WE COULD THINK OF MY INTEL AS ONE POSSIBILITY...
...AND CONTINUE DISCUSSIONS FROM THERE...?

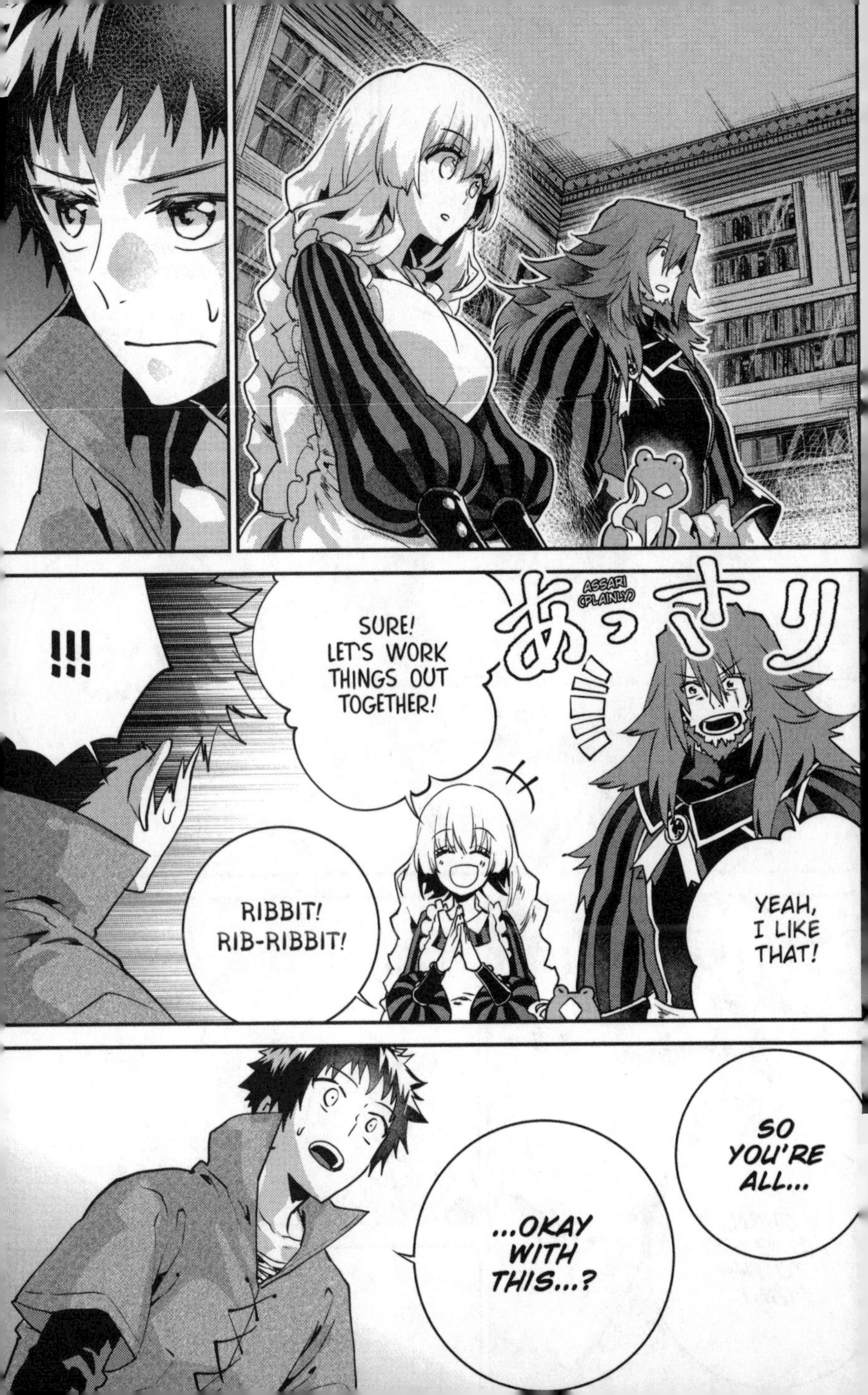
あっさり
ASSARI (PLAINLY)
YEAH, I LIKE THAT!
SURE! LET'S WORK THINGS OUT TOGETHER!
RIBBIT! RIB-RIBBIT!
!!!
SO YOU'RE ALL...
...OKAY WITH THIS...?

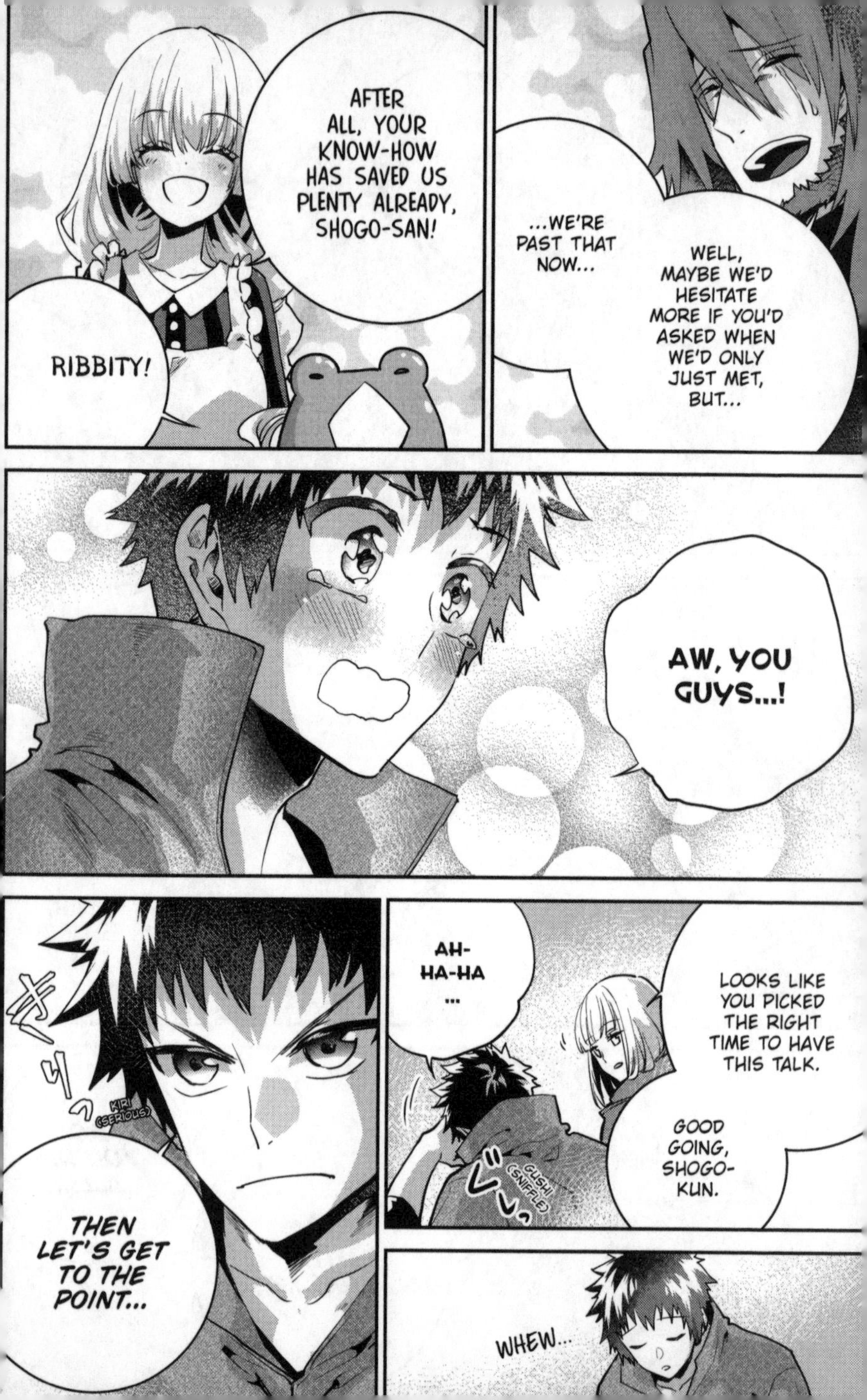
WELL, MAYBE WE'D HESITATE MORE IF YOU'D ASKED WHEN WE'D ONLY JUST MET, BUT...
...WE'RE PAST THAT NOW...
AFTER ALL, YOUR KNOW-HOW HAS SAVED US PLENTY ALREADY, SHOGO-SAN!
RIBBITY!
AW, YOU GUYS...!
LOOKS LIKE YOU PICKED THE RIGHT TIME TO HAVE THIS TALK.
GOOD GOING, SHOGO-KUN.
AH-HA-HA...
GUSHI (SNIFFLE)
WHEW...
KIRI (SERIOUS)
THEN LET'S GET TO THE POINT...

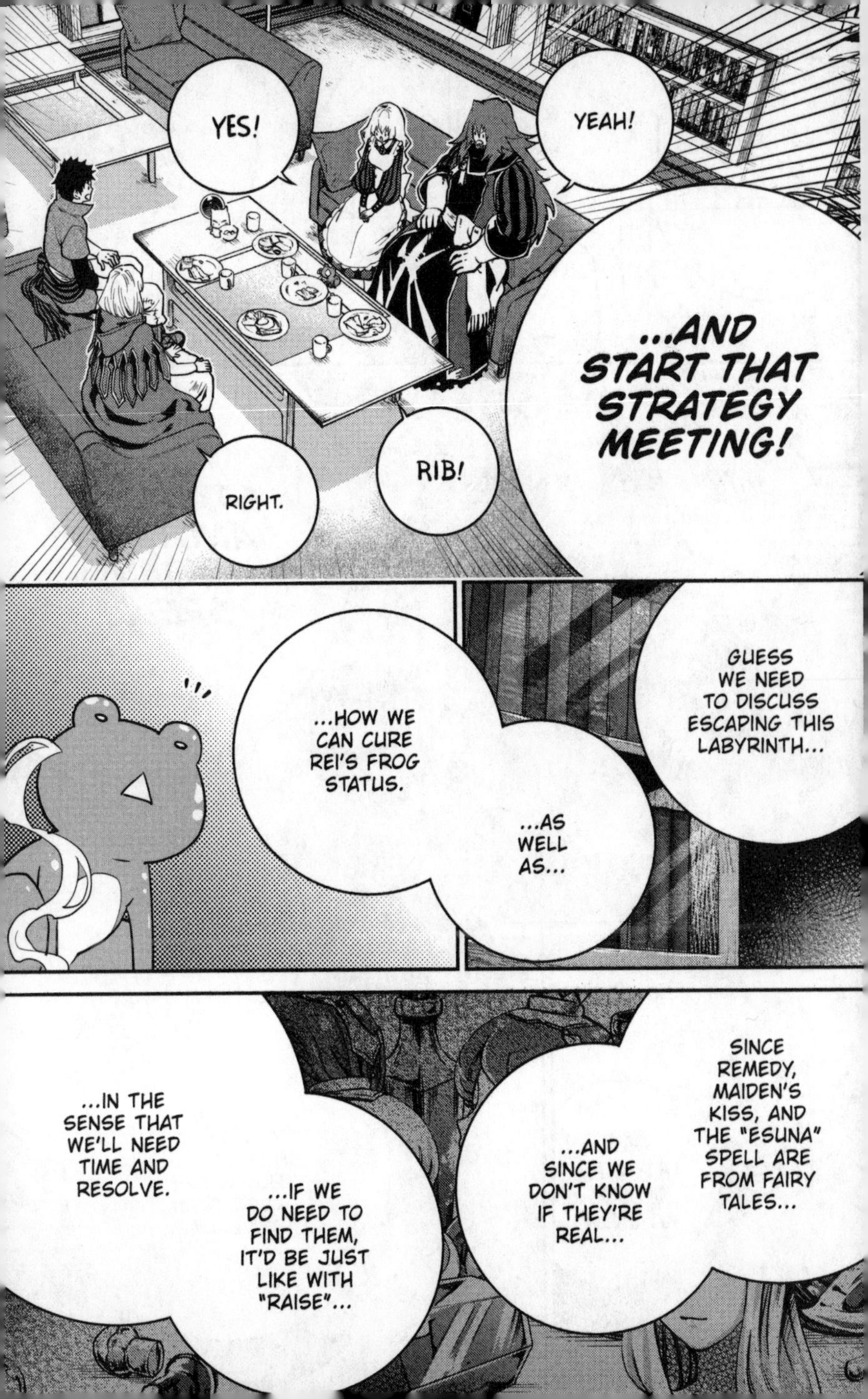
...AND START THAT STRATEGY MEETING!
YEAH!
YES!
RIB!
RIGHT.
GUESS WE NEED TO DISCUSS ESCAPING THIS LABYRINTH...
...AS WELL AS...
...HOW WE CAN CURE REI'S FROG STATUS.
SINCE REMEDY, MAIDEN'S KISS, AND THE "ESUNA" SPELL ARE FROM FAIRY TALES...
...AND SINCE WE DON'T KNOW IF THEY'RE REAL...
...IF WE DO NEED TO FIND THEM, IT'D BE JUST LIKE WITH "RAISE"...
...IN THE SENSE THAT WE'LL NEED TIME AND RESOLVE.

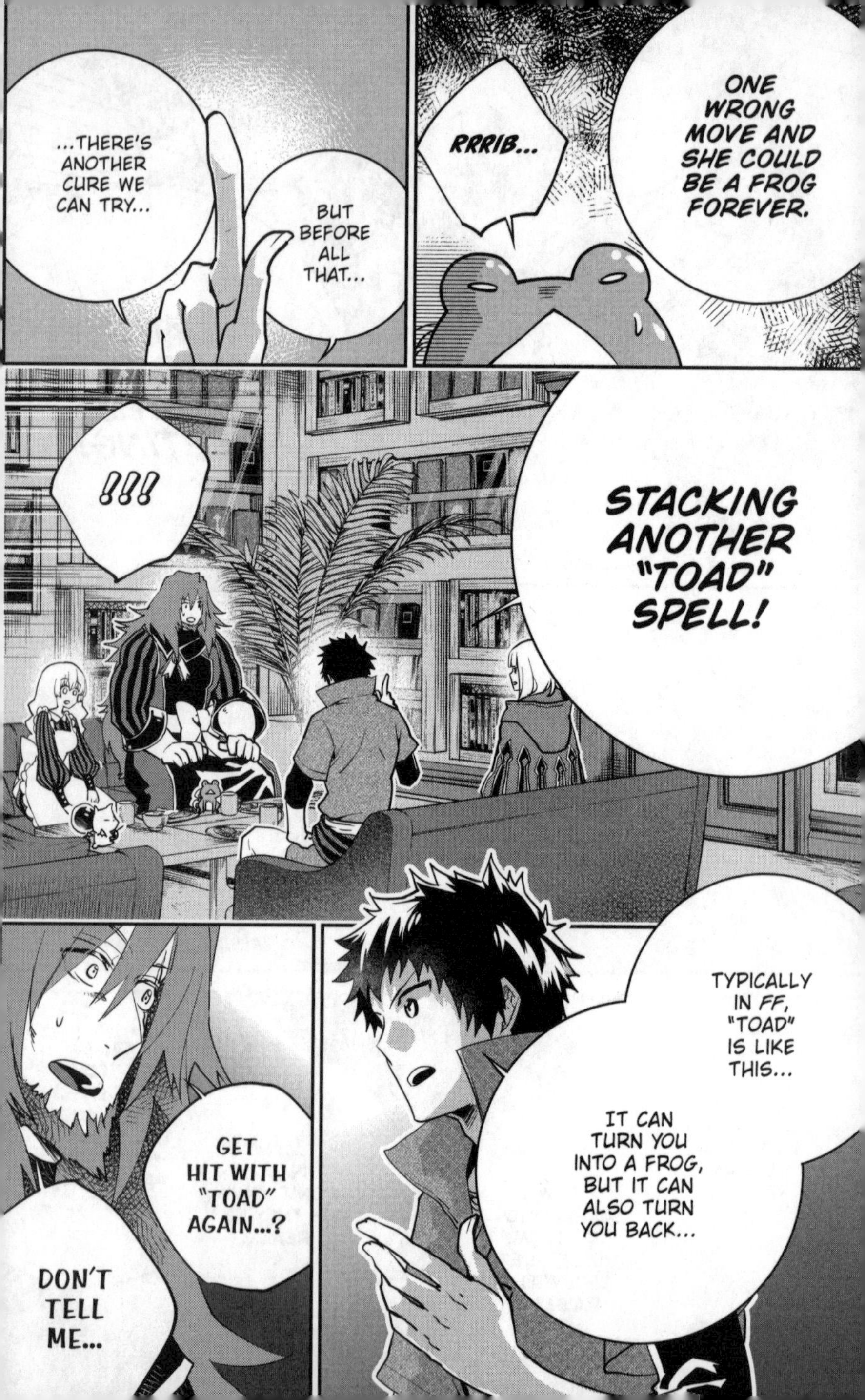
ONE WRONG MOVE AND SHE COULD BE A FROG FOREVER.
RRRIB...
...THERE'S ANOTHER CURE WE CAN TRY...
BUT BEFORE ALL THAT...
STACKING ANOTHER "TOAD" SPELL!
!!!
TYPICALLY IN *FF*, "TOAD" IS LIKE THIS...
IT CAN TURN YOU INTO A FROG, BUT IT CAN ALSO TURN YOU BACK...
GET HIT WITH "TOAD" AGAIN...?
DON'T TELL ME...

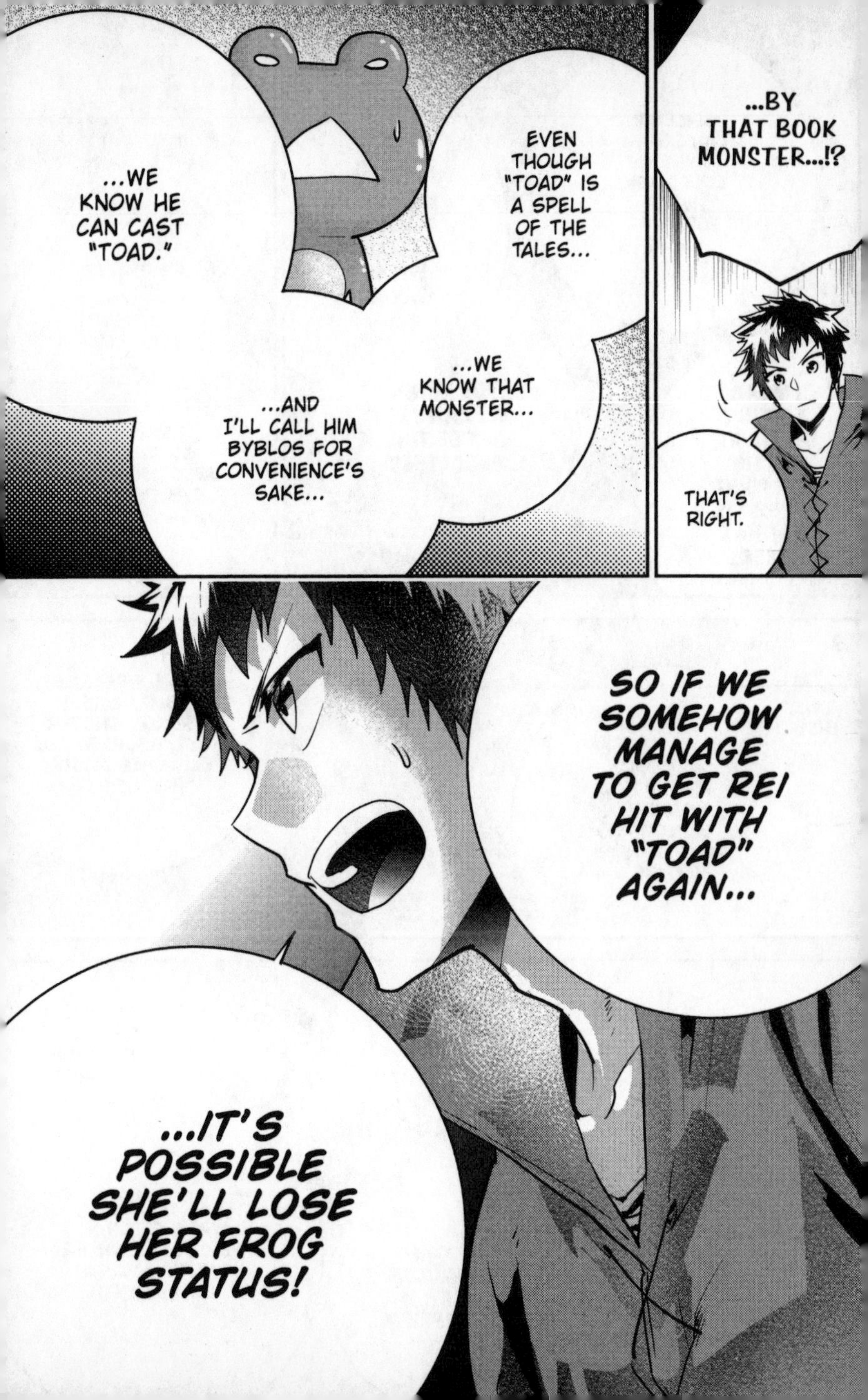
...BY THAT BOOK MONSTER...!?
THAT'S RIGHT.
EVEN THOUGH "TOAD" IS A SPELL OF THE TALES...
...WE KNOW HE CAN CAST "TOAD."
...WE KNOW THAT MONSTER...
...AND I'LL CALL HIM BYBLOS FOR CONVENIENCE'S SAKE...
SO IF WE SOMEHOW MANAGE TO GET REI HIT WITH "TOAD" AGAIN...
...IT'S POSSIBLE SHE'LL LOSE HER FROG STATUS!

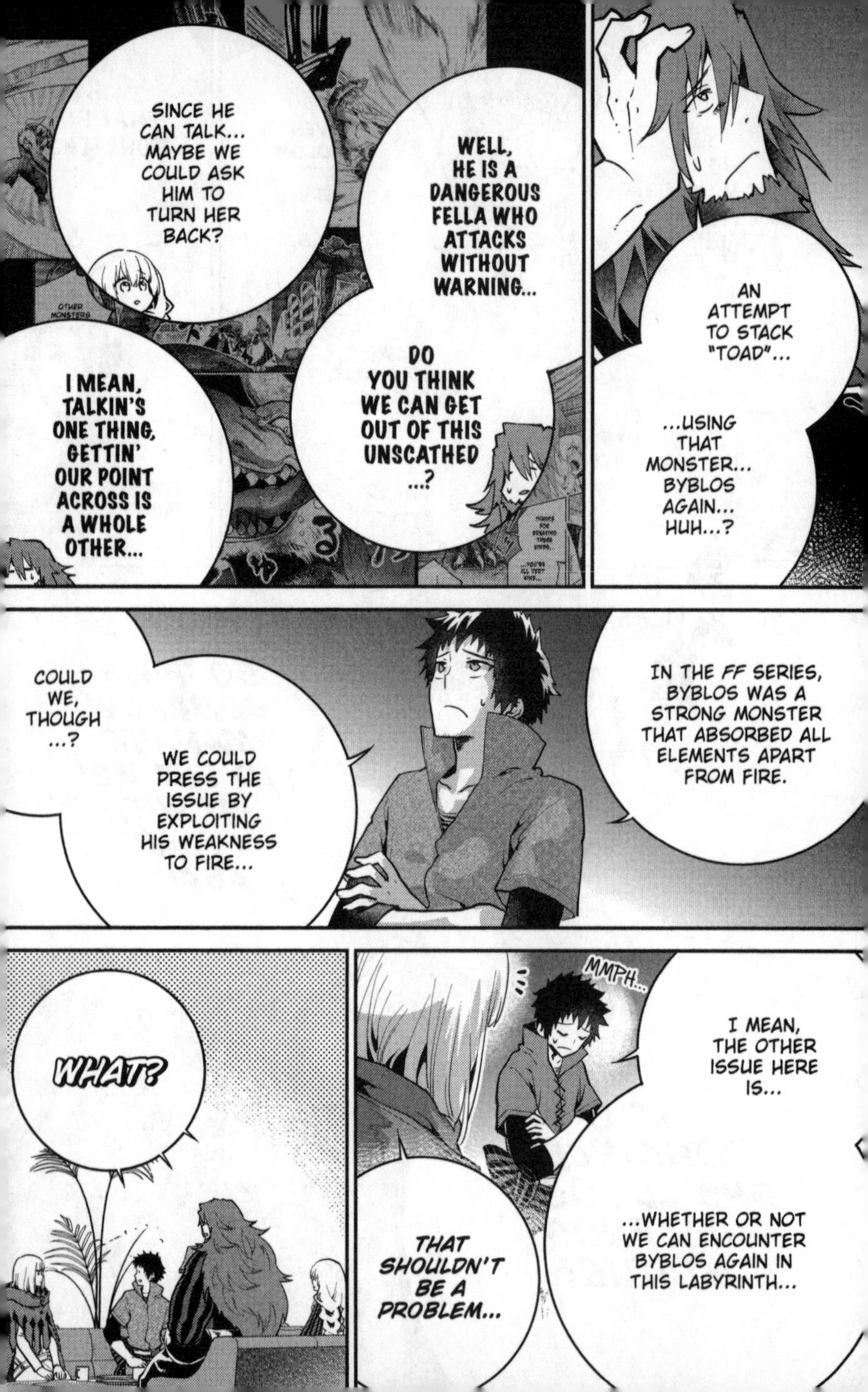
AN ATTEMPT TO STACK "TOAD"...
...USING THAT MONSTER... BYBLOS AGAIN... HUH...?
SINCE HE CAN TALK... MAYBE WE COULD ASK HIM TO TURN HER BACK?
OTHER MONSTERS
I MEAN, TALKIN'S ONE THING, GETTIN' OUR POINT ACROSS IS A WHOLE OTHER...
WELL, HE IS A DANGEROUS FELLA WHO ATTACKS WITHOUT WARNING...
DO YOU THINK WE CAN GET OUT OF THIS UNSCATHED ...?
IN THE *FF* SERIES, BYBLOS WAS A STRONG MONSTER THAT ABSORBED ALL ELEMENTS APART FROM FIRE.
WE COULD PRESS THE ISSUE BY EXPLOITING HIS WEAKNESS TO FIRE...
COULD WE, THOUGH ...?
MMPH...
I MEAN, THE OTHER ISSUE HERE IS...
...WHETHER OR NOT WE CAN ENCOUNTER BYBLOS AGAIN IN THIS LABYRINTH...
THAT SHOULDN'T BE A PROBLEM...
WHAT?

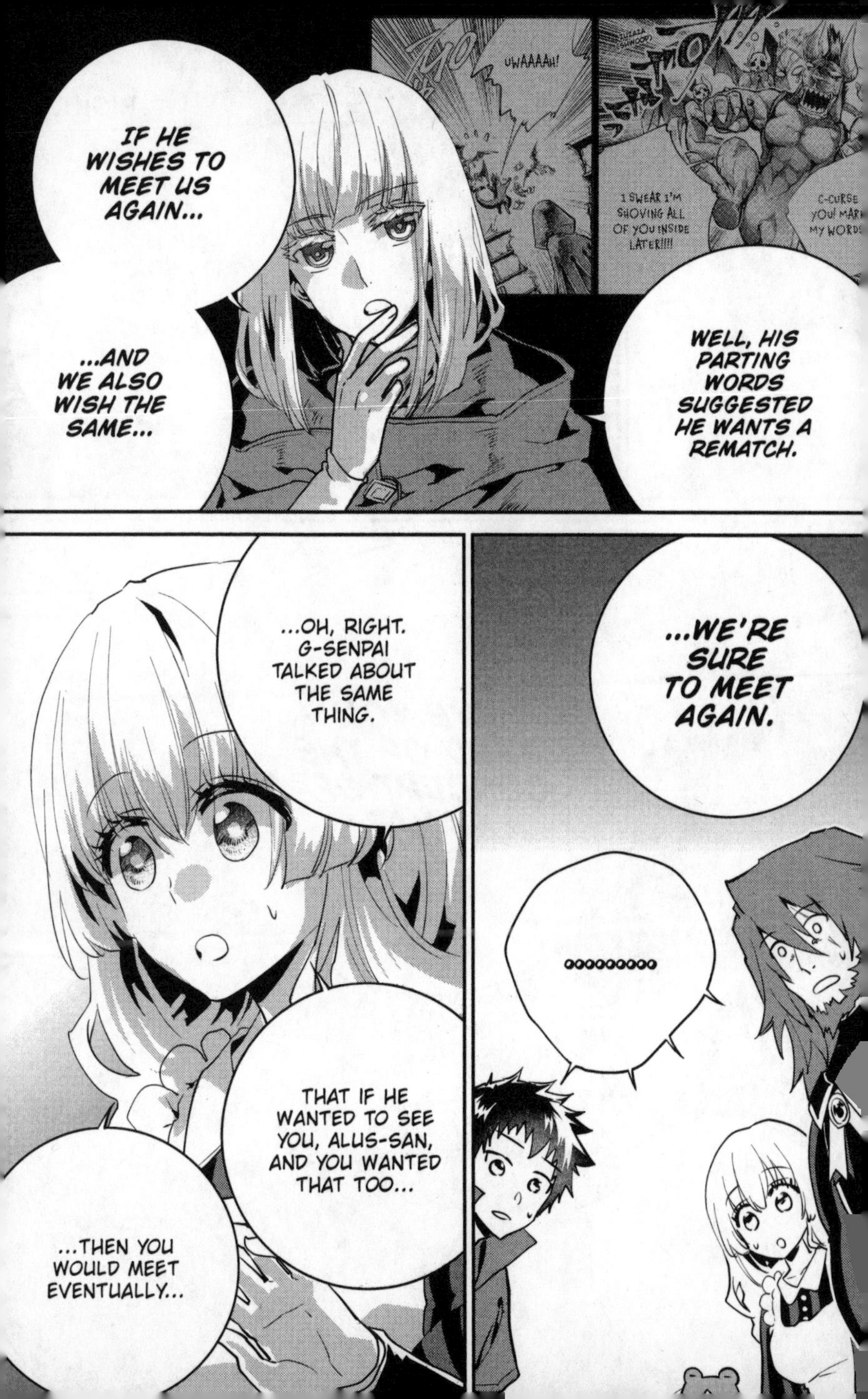
ZUZAZA (SHWOOP)
C-CURSE YOU! MARK MY WORDS
I SWEAR I'M SHOVING ALL OF YOU INSIDE LATER!!!!
UWAAAAH!
WELL, HIS PARTING WORDS SUGGESTED HE WANTS A REMATCH.
IF HE WISHES TO MEET US AGAIN...
...AND WE ALSO WISH THE SAME...
...WE'RE SURE TO MEET AGAIN.
.........
...OH, RIGHT. G-SENPAI TALKED ABOUT THE SAME THING.
THAT IF HE WANTED TO SEE YOU, ALUS-SAN, AND YOU WANTED THAT TOO...
...THEN YOU WOULD MEET EVENTUALLY...

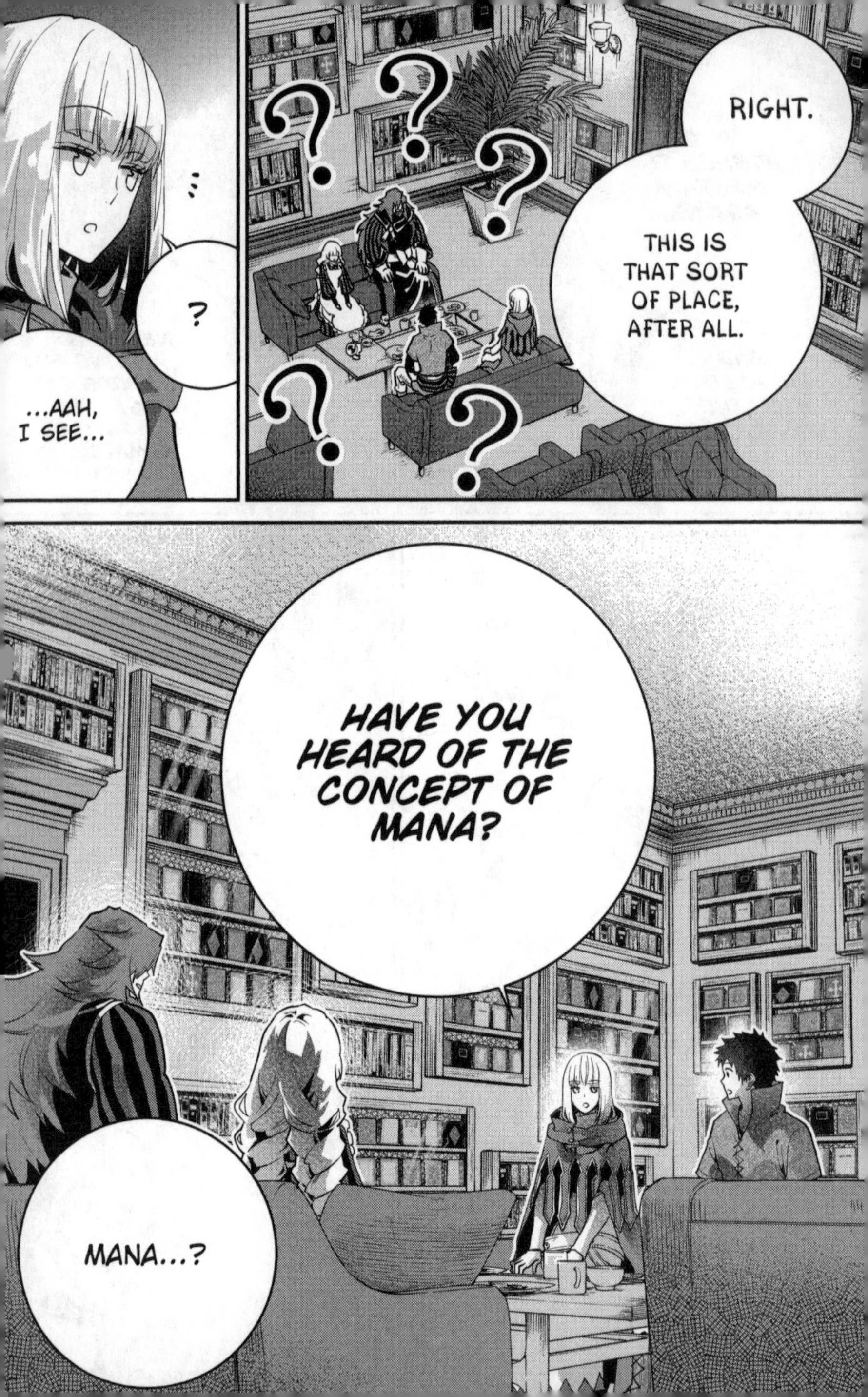
RIGHT.
THIS IS THAT SORT OF PLACE, AFTER ALL.
?
...AAH, I SEE...
HAVE YOU HEARD OF THE CONCEPT OF MANA?
MANA...?

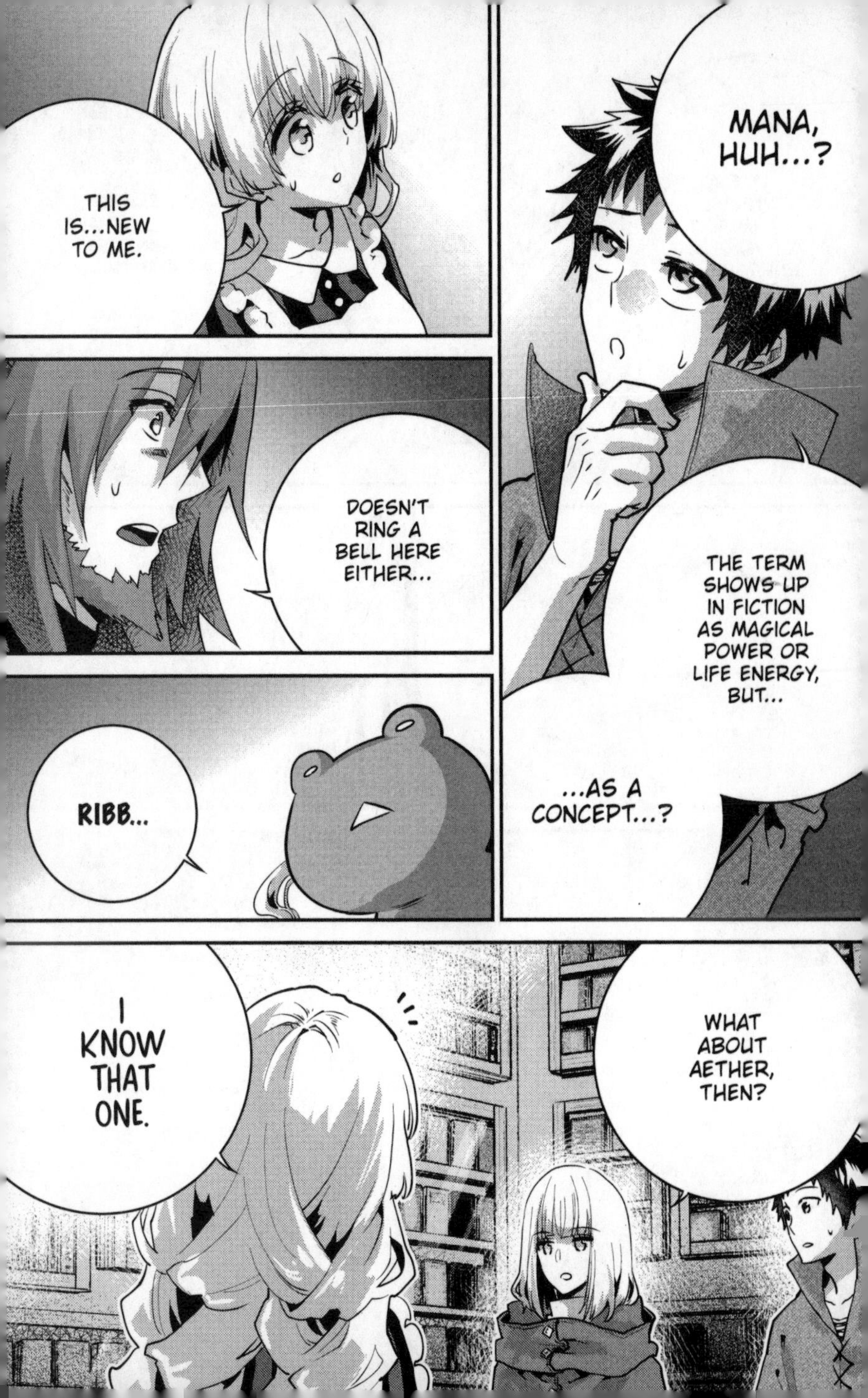
MANA, HUH...?
THE TERM SHOWS UP IN FICTION AS MAGICAL POWER OR LIFE ENERGY, BUT...
...AS A CONCEPT...?
THIS IS...NEW TO ME.
DOESN'T RING A BELL HERE EITHER...
RIBB...
WHAT ABOUT AETHER, THEN?
I KNOW THAT ONE.

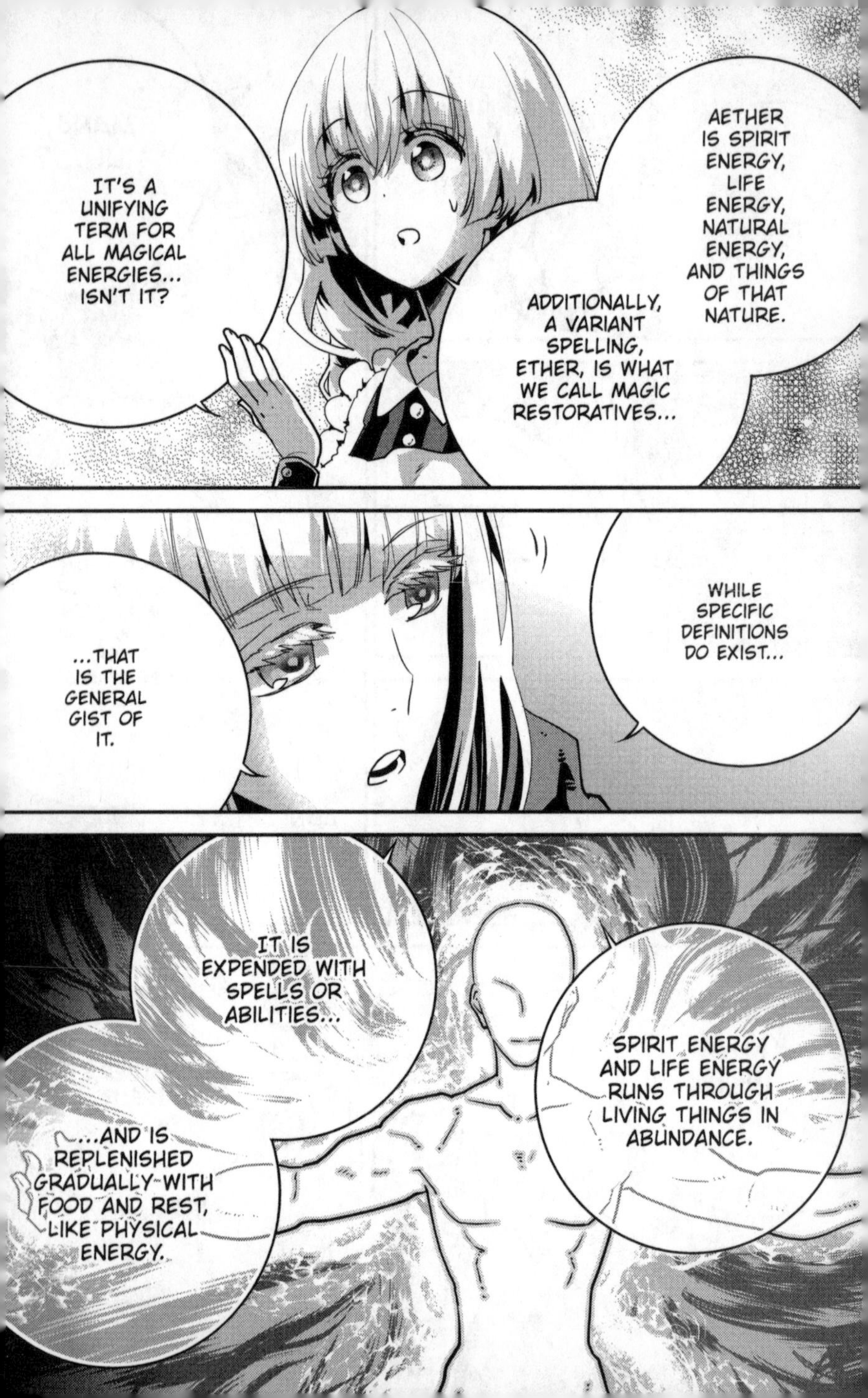
AETHER IS SPIRIT ENERGY, LIFE ENERGY, NATURAL ENERGY, AND THINGS OF THAT NATURE.
ADDITIONALLY, A VARIANT SPELLING, ETHER, IS WHAT WE CALL MAGIC RESTORATIVES...
IT'S A UNIFYING TERM FOR ALL MAGICAL ENERGIES... ISN'T IT?
WHILE SPECIFIC DEFINITIONS DO EXIST...
...THAT IS THE GENERAL GIST OF IT.
SPIRIT ENERGY AND LIFE ENERGY RUNS THROUGH LIVING THINGS IN ABUNDANCE.
IT IS EXPENDED WITH SPELLS OR ABILITIES...
...AND IS REPLENISHED GRADUALLY WITH FOOD AND REST, LIKE PHYSICAL ENERGY.

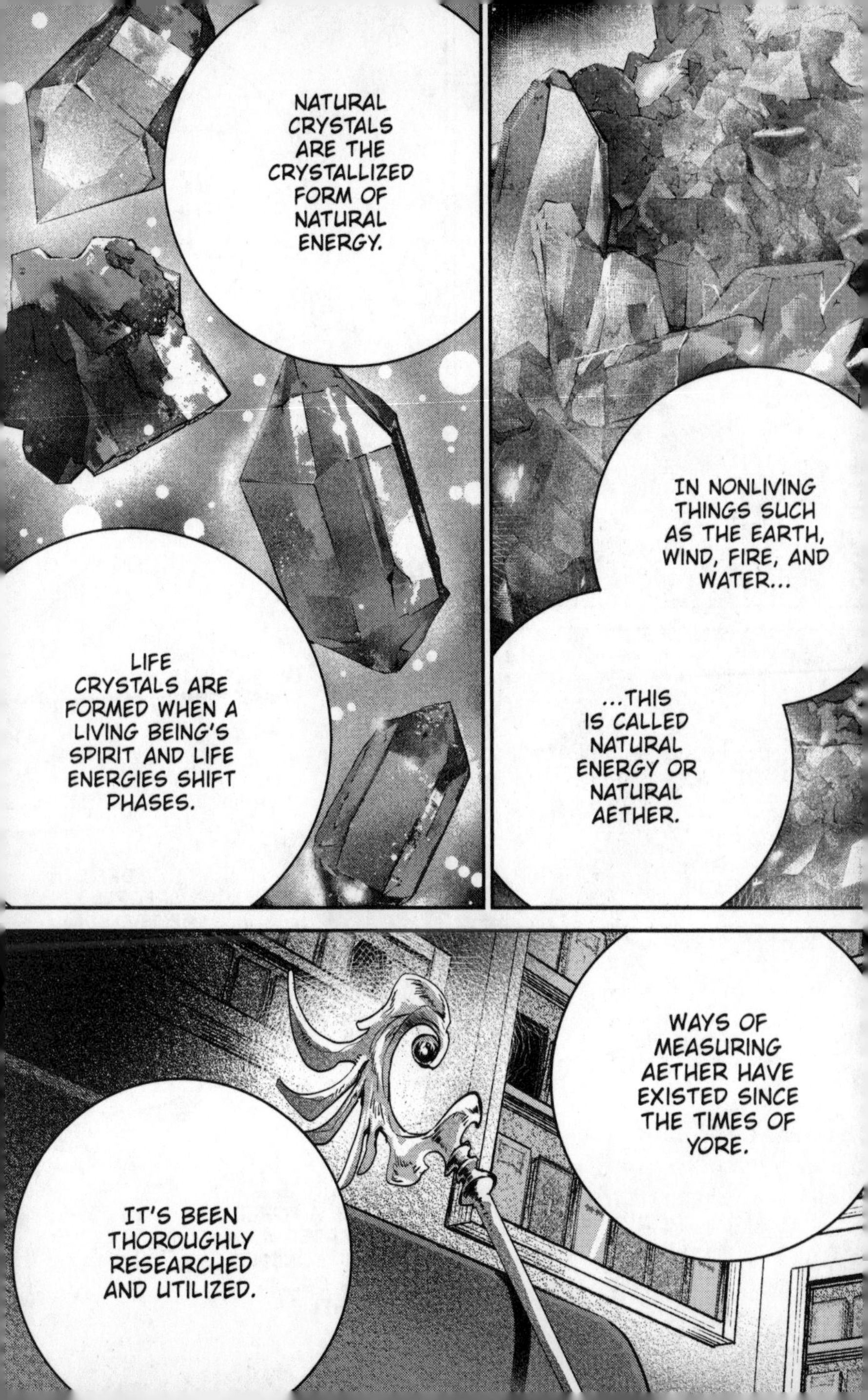
IN NONLIVING THINGS SUCH AS THE EARTH, WIND, FIRE, AND WATER...
...THIS IS CALLED NATURAL ENERGY OR NATURAL AETHER.
NATURAL CRYSTALS ARE THE CRYSTALLIZED FORM OF NATURAL ENERGY.
LIFE CRYSTALS ARE FORMED WHEN A LIVING BEING'S SPIRIT AND LIFE ENERGIES SHIFT PHASES.
WAYS OF MEASURING AETHER HAVE EXISTED SINCE THE TIMES OF YORE.
IT'S BEEN THOROUGHLY RESEARCHED AND UTILIZED.

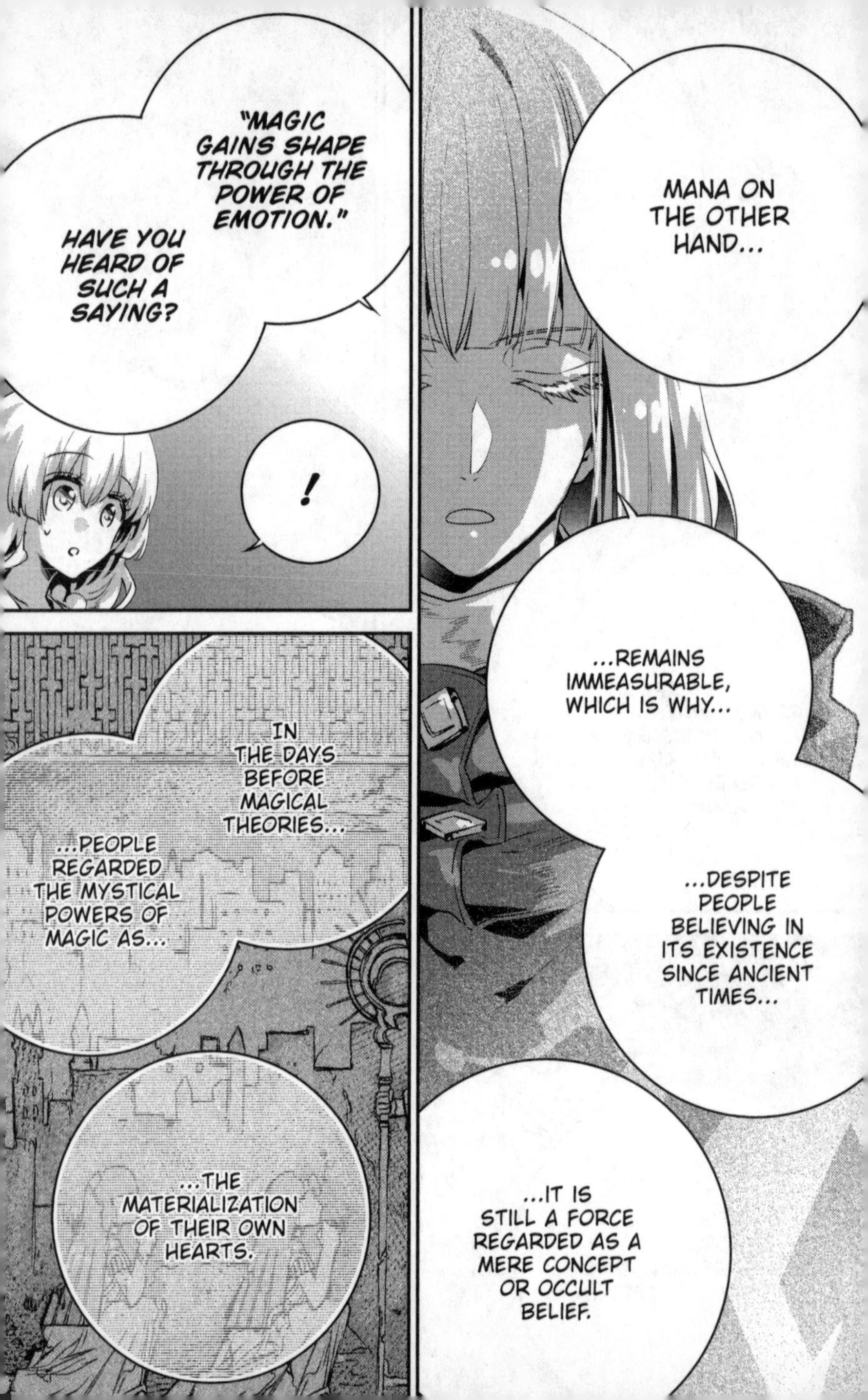
"MAGIC GAINS SHAPE THROUGH THE POWER OF EMOTION."
HAVE YOU HEARD OF SUCH A SAYING?
!
IN THE DAYS BEFORE MAGICAL THEORIES...
...PEOPLE REGARDED THE MYSTICAL POWERS OF MAGIC AS...
...THE MATERIALIZATION OF THEIR OWN HEARTS.
MANA ON THE OTHER HAND...
...REMAINS IMMEASURABLE, WHICH IS WHY...
...DESPITE PEOPLE BELIEVING IN ITS EXISTENCE SINCE ANCIENT TIMES...
...IT IS STILL A FORCE REGARDED AS A MERE CONCEPT OR OCCULT BELIEF.

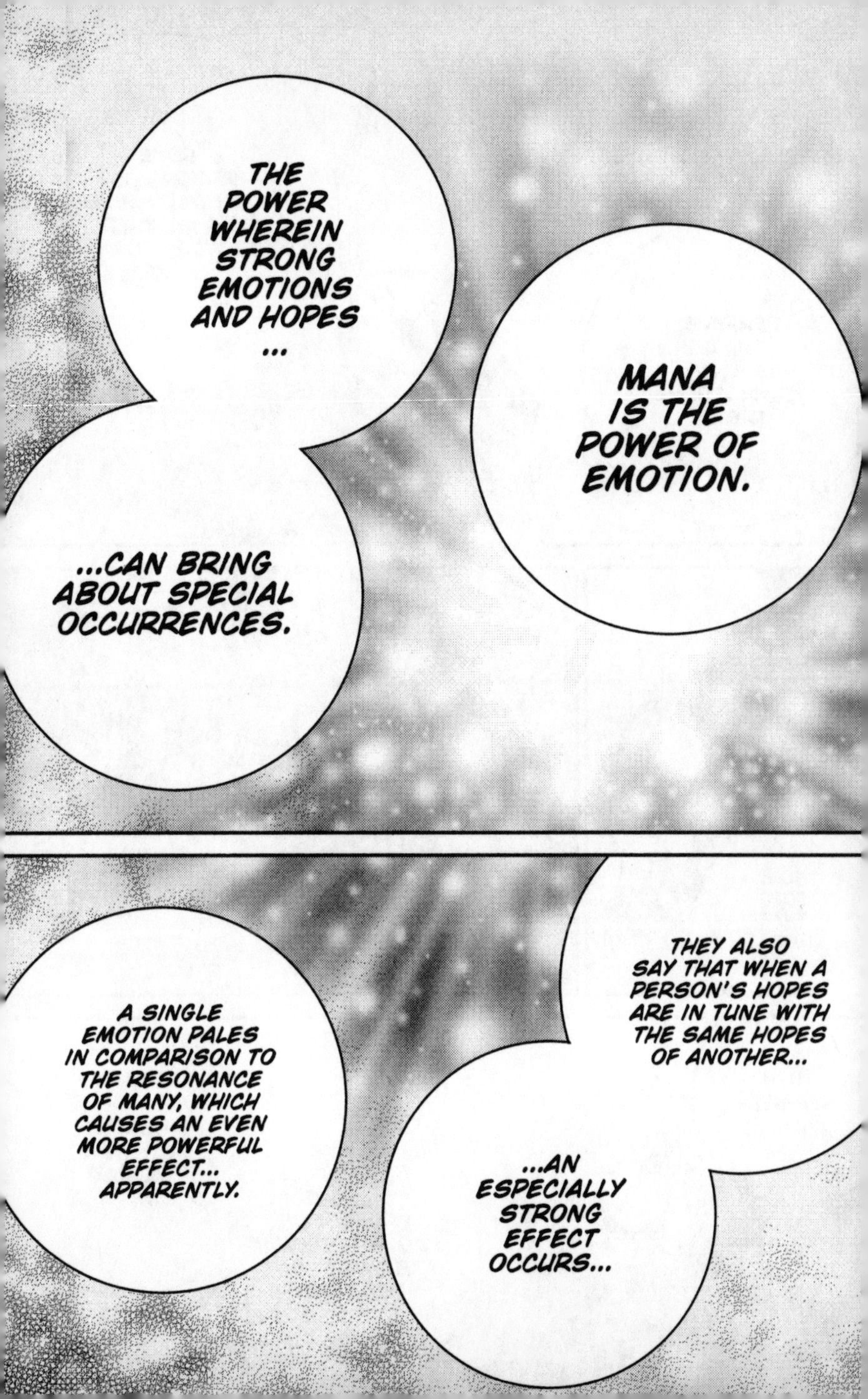
MANA IS THE POWER OF EMOTION.
THE POWER WHEREIN STRONG EMOTIONS AND HOPES ...
...CAN BRING ABOUT SPECIAL OCCURRENCES.
THEY ALSO SAY THAT WHEN A PERSON'S HOPES ARE IN TUNE WITH THE SAME HOPES OF ANOTHER...
...AN ESPECIALLY STRONG EFFECT OCCURS...
A SINGLE EMOTION PALES IN COMPARISON TO THE RESONANCE OF MANY, WHICH CAUSES AN EVEN MORE POWERFUL EFFECT... APPARENTLY.

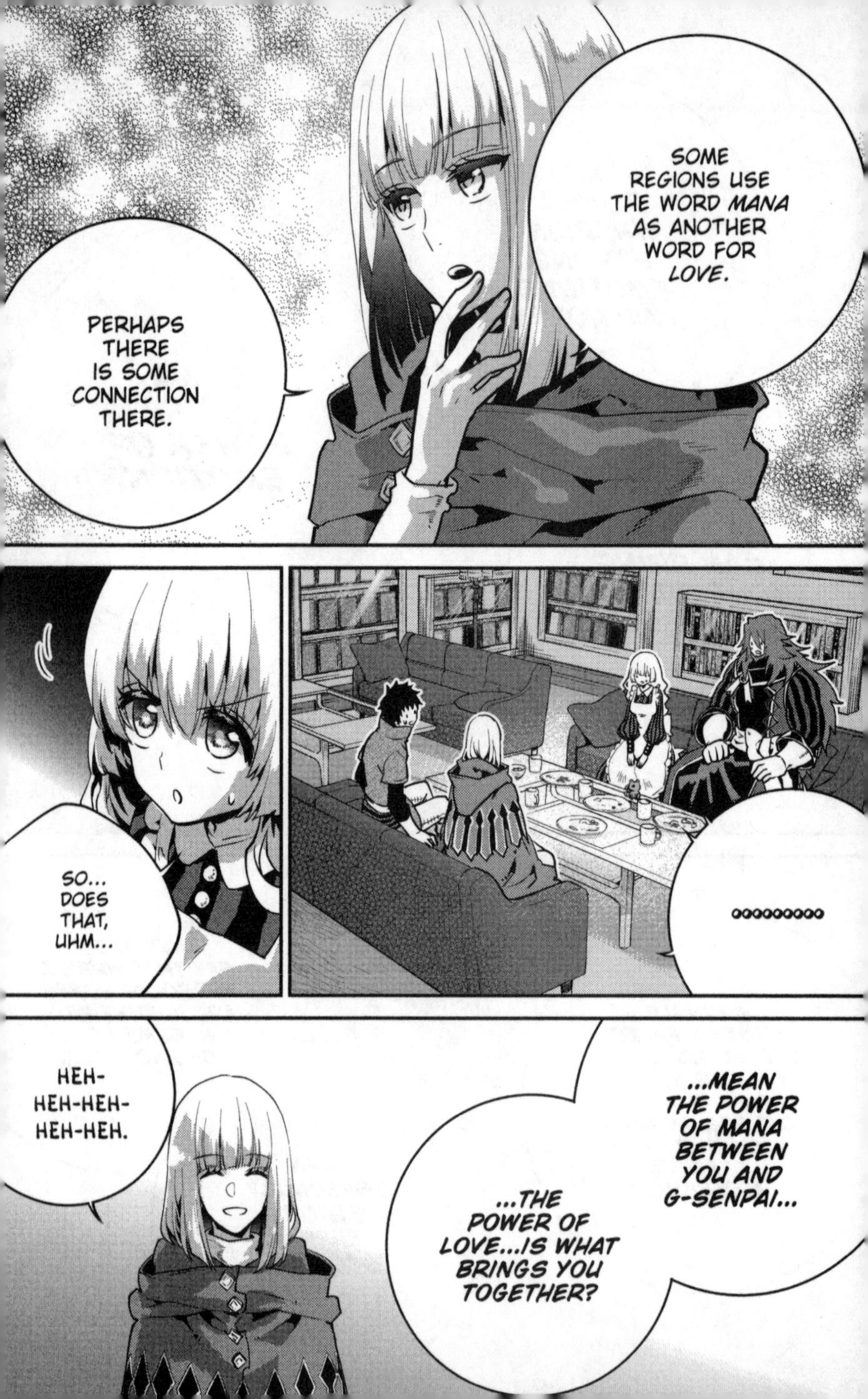
SOME REGIONS USE THE WORD *MANA* AS ANOTHER WORD FOR *LOVE*.
PERHAPS THERE IS SOME CONNECTION THERE.
.........
SO... DOES THAT, UHM...
...MEAN THE POWER OF MANA BETWEEN YOU AND G-SENPAI...
...THE POWER OF LOVE...IS WHAT BRINGS YOU TOGETHER?
HEH-HEH-HEH-HEH-HEH.

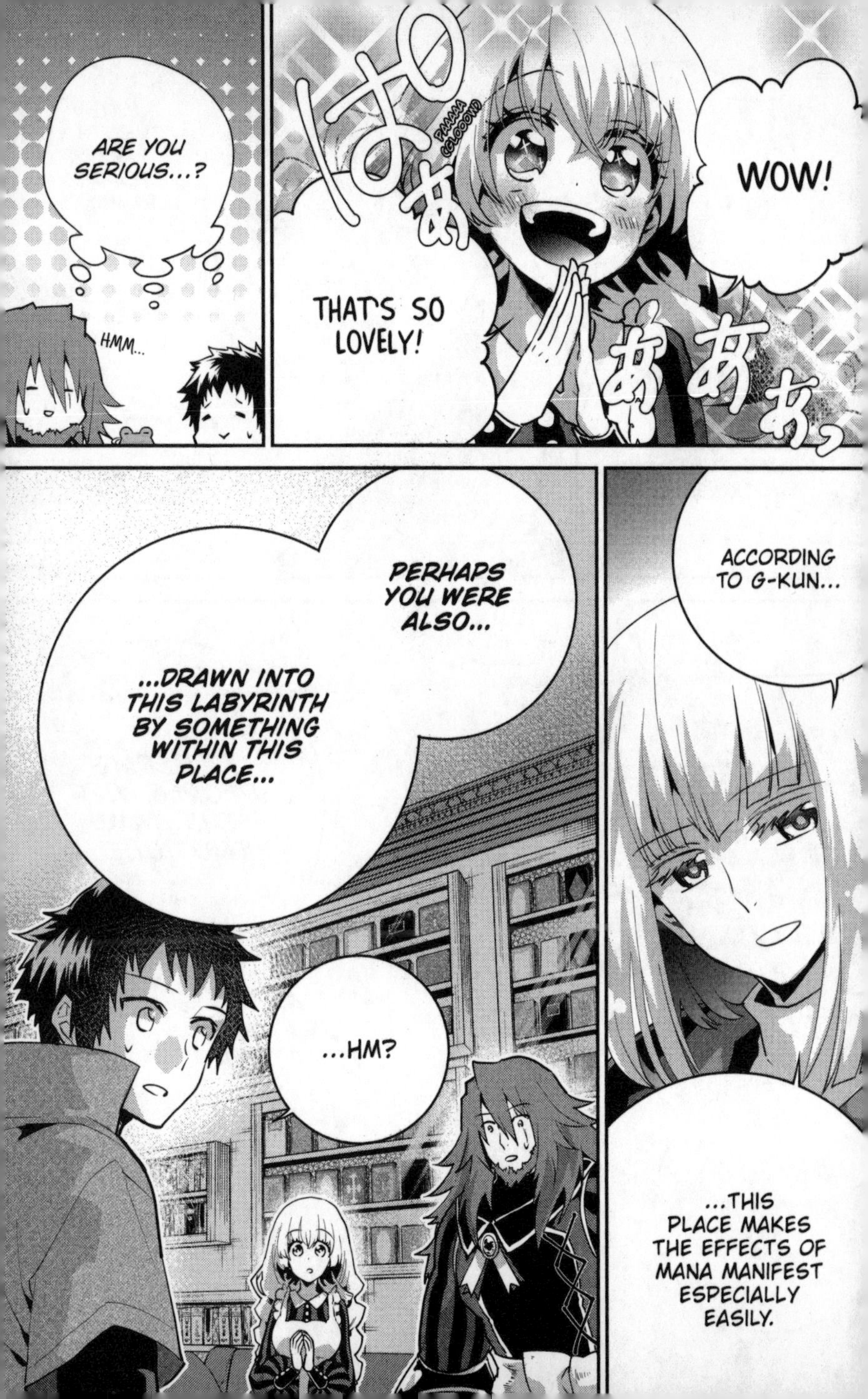
WOW!
PAAAAA (GLOOOW)
ぱぁあああ
THAT'S SO LOVELY!
ARE YOU SERIOUS...?
HMM...
ACCORDING TO G-KUN...
...THIS PLACE MAKES THE EFFECTS OF MANA MANIFEST ESPECIALLY EASILY.
PERHAPS YOU WERE ALSO...
...DRAWN INTO THIS LABYRINTH BY SOMETHING WITHIN THIS PLACE...
...HM?

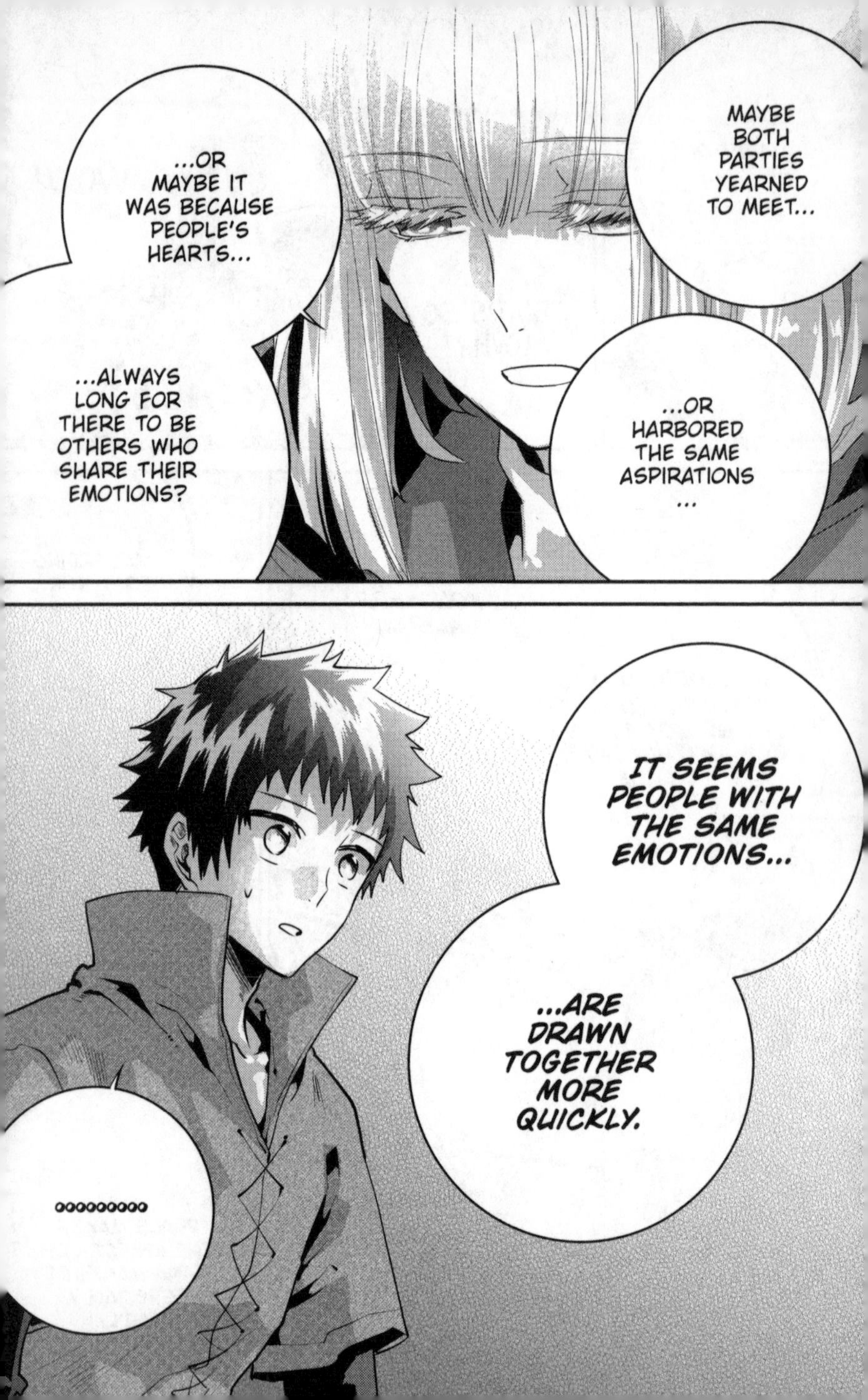
MAYBE BOTH PARTIES YEARNED TO MEET...
...OR HARBORED THE SAME ASPIRATIONS...
...OR MAYBE IT WAS BECAUSE PEOPLE'S HEARTS...
...ALWAYS LONG FOR THERE TO BE OTHERS WHO SHARE THEIR EMOTIONS?
IT SEEMS PEOPLE WITH THE SAME EMOTIONS...
...ARE DRAWN TOGETHER MORE QUICKLY.
.........

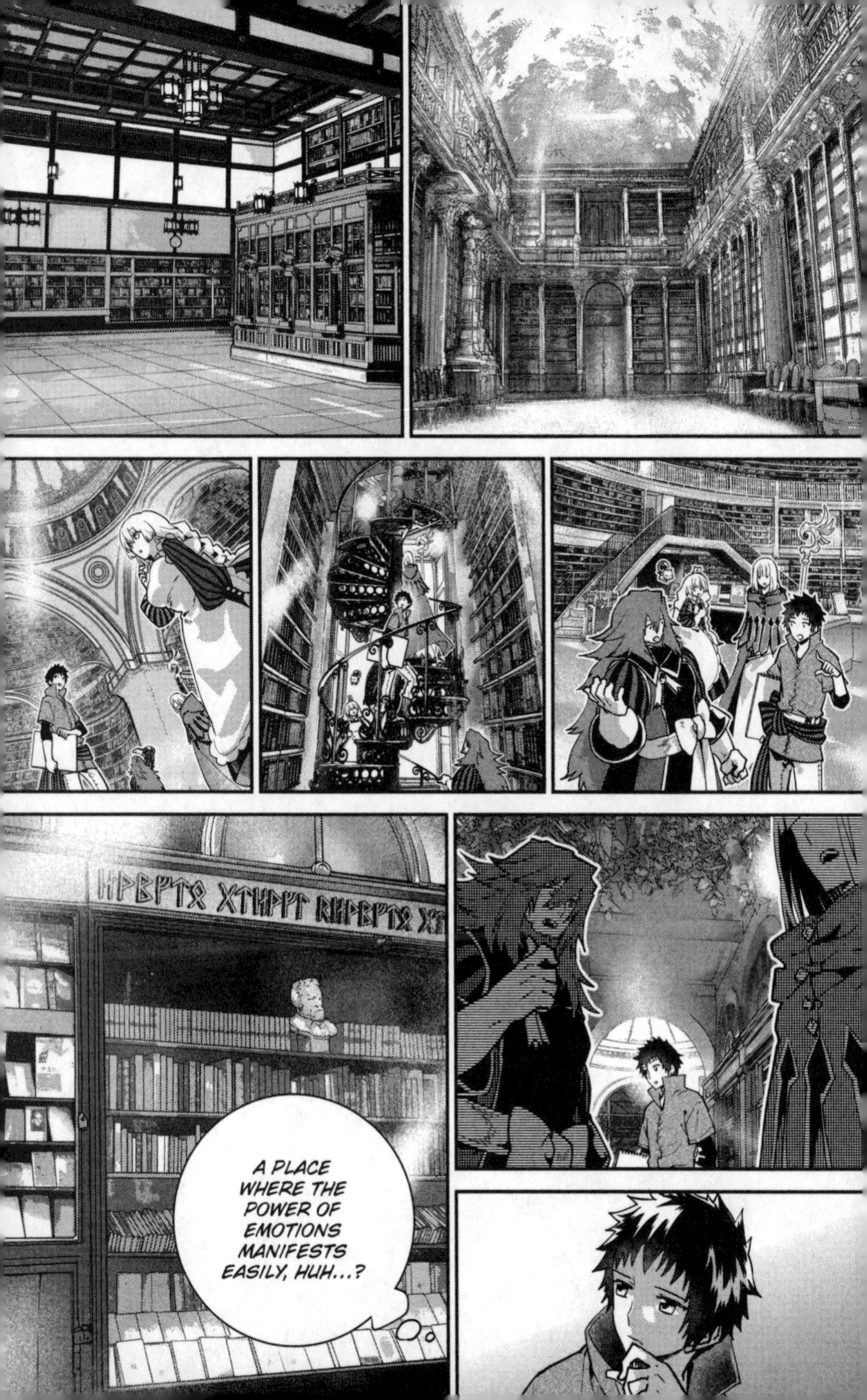
A PLACE WHERE THE POWER OF EMOTIONS MANIFESTS EASILY, HUH...?

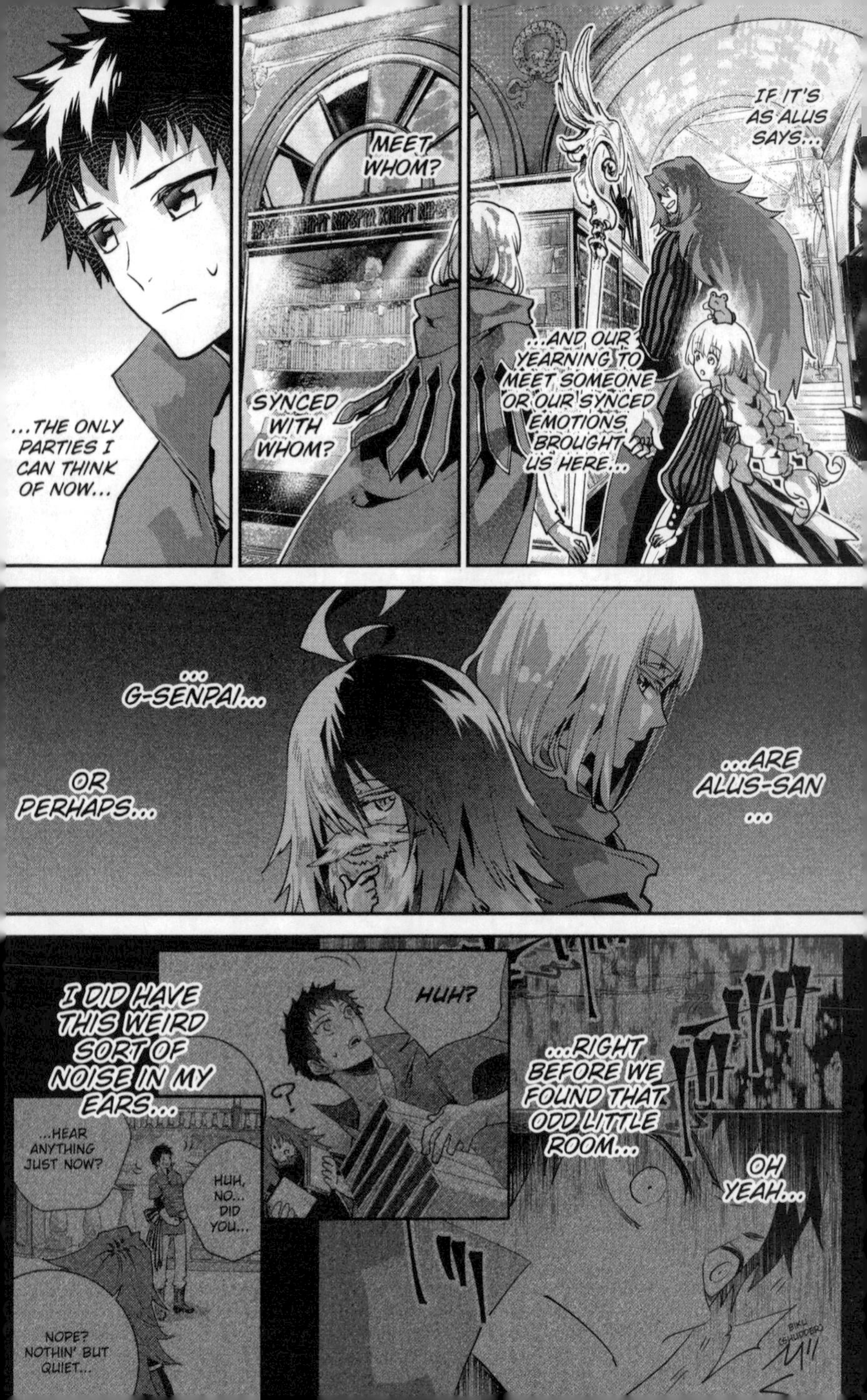
IF IT'S AS ALUS SAYS...
...AND OUR YEARNING TO MEET SOMEONE OR OUR SYNCED EMOTIONS BROUGHT US HERE...
MEET WHOM?
SYNCED WITH WHOM?
...THE ONLY PARTIES I CAN THINK OF NOW...
...ARE ALUS-SAN...
...G-SENPAI...
OR PERHAPS...
OH YEAH...
...RIGHT BEFORE WE FOUND THAT ODD LITTLE ROOM...
BIKU (SHUDDER)
I DID HAVE THIS WEIRD SORT OF NOISE IN MY EARS...
HUH?
...HEAR ANYTHING JUST NOW?
HUH, NO... DID YOU...
NOPE? NOTHIN' BUT QUIET...

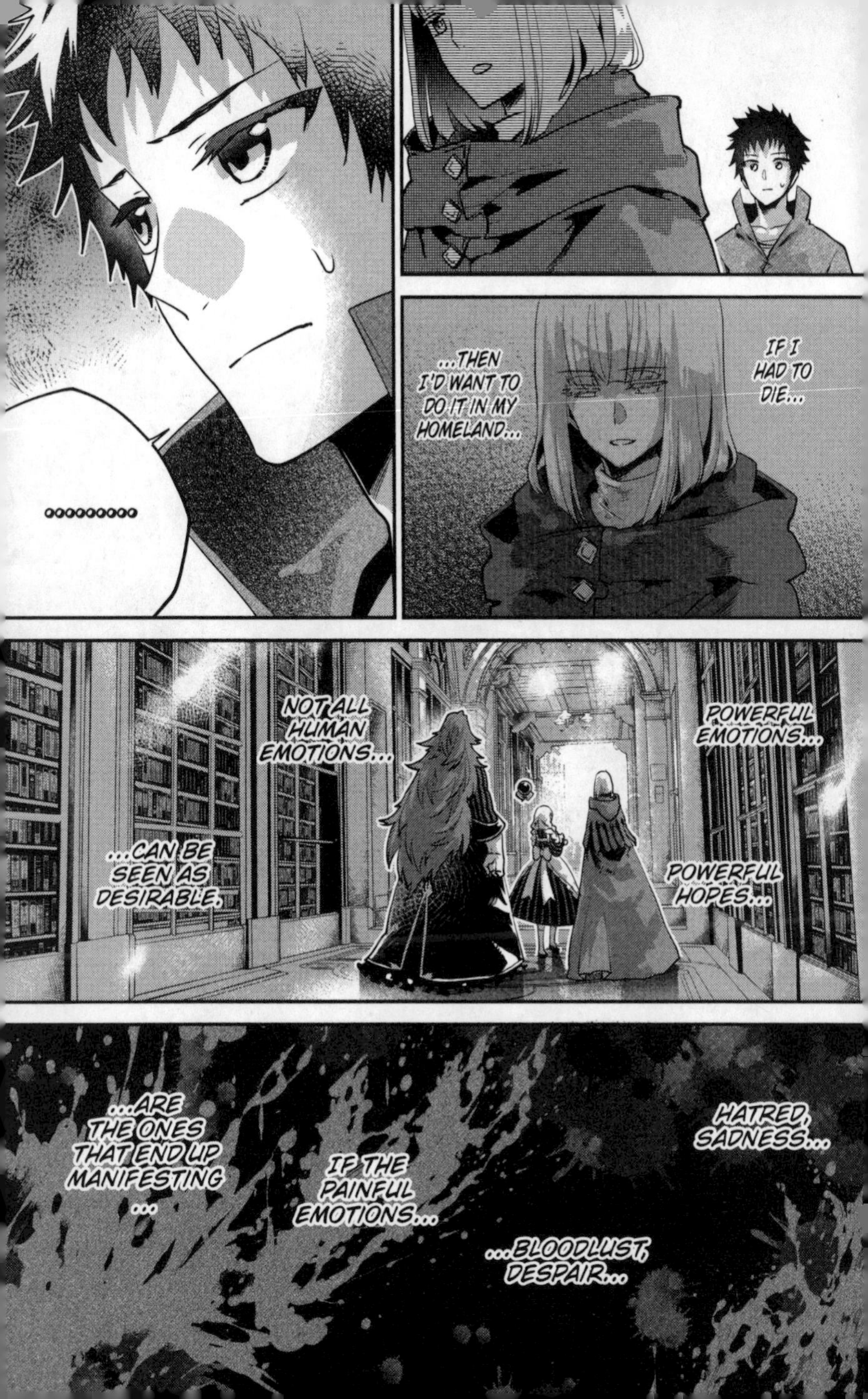
IF I HAD TO DIE...
...THEN I'D WANT TO DO IT IN MY HOMELAND...
.........
POWERFUL EMOTIONS...
POWERFUL HOPES...
NOT ALL HUMAN EMOTIONS...
...CAN BE SEEN AS DESIRABLE.
HATRED, SADNESS...
...BLOODLUST, DESPAIR...
IF THE PAINFUL EMOTIONS...
...ARE THE ONES THAT END UP MANIFESTING...

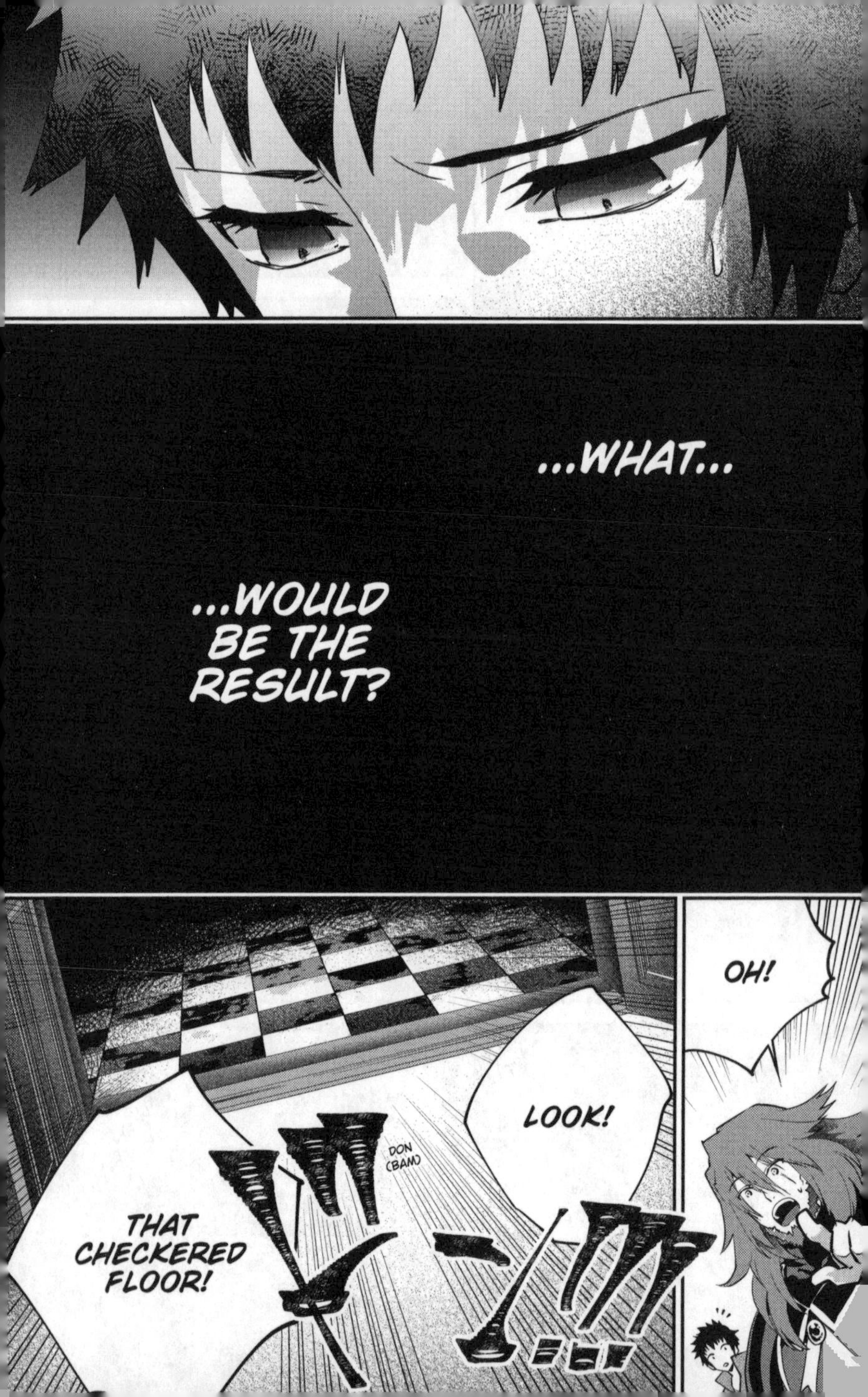
...WHAT...
...WOULD BE THE RESULT?
OH!
LOOK!
DON (BAM)
THAT CHECKERED FLOOR!

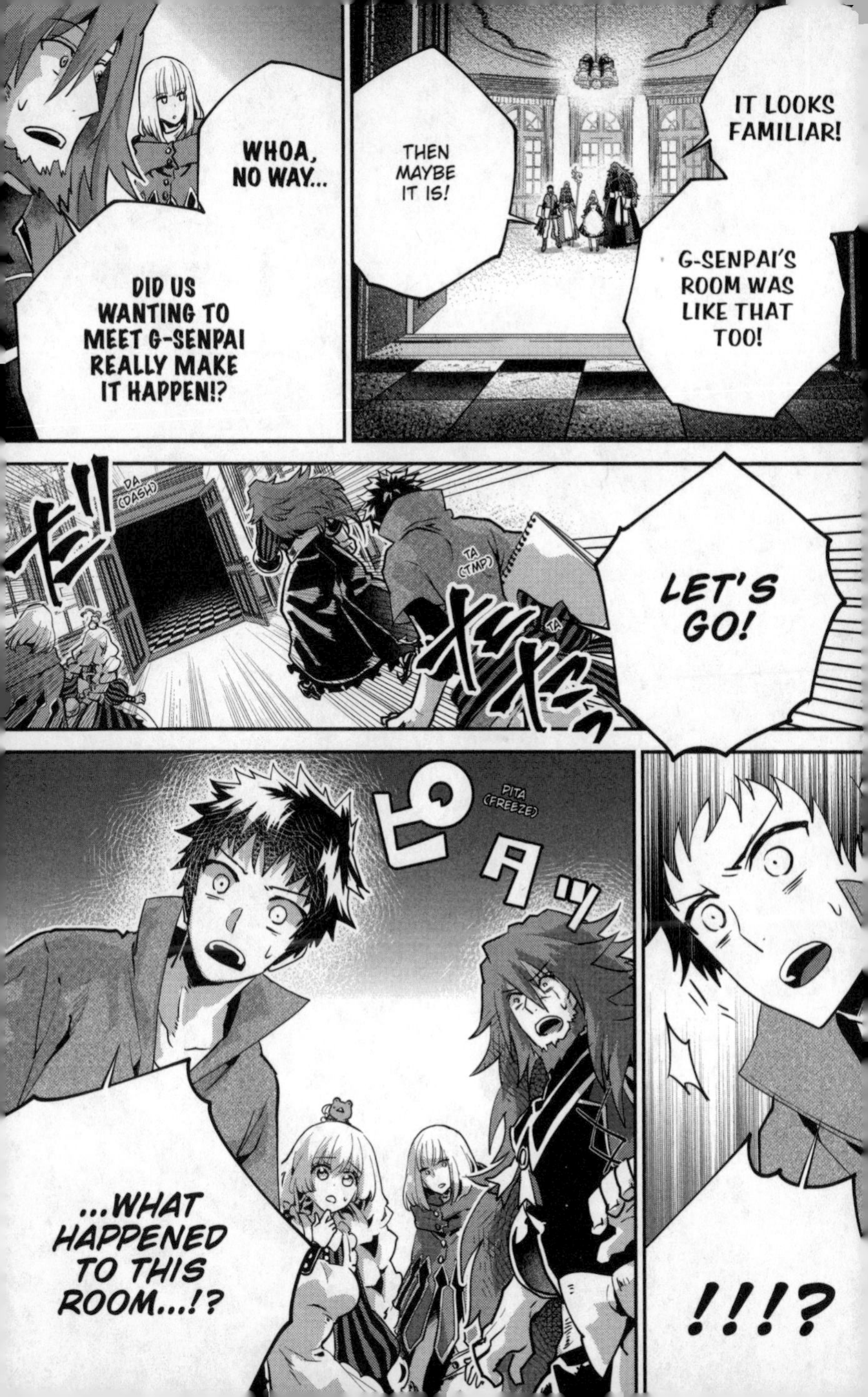
IT LOOKS FAMILIAR!
G-SENPAI'S ROOM WAS LIKE THAT TOO!
THEN MAYBE IT IS!
WHOA, NO WAY...
DID US WANTING TO MEET G-SENPAI REALLY MAKE IT HAPPEN!?
LET'S GO!
TA (TMP)
TA
DA (DASH)
!!!?
PITA (FREEZE)
...WHAT HAPPENED TO THIS ROOM...!?

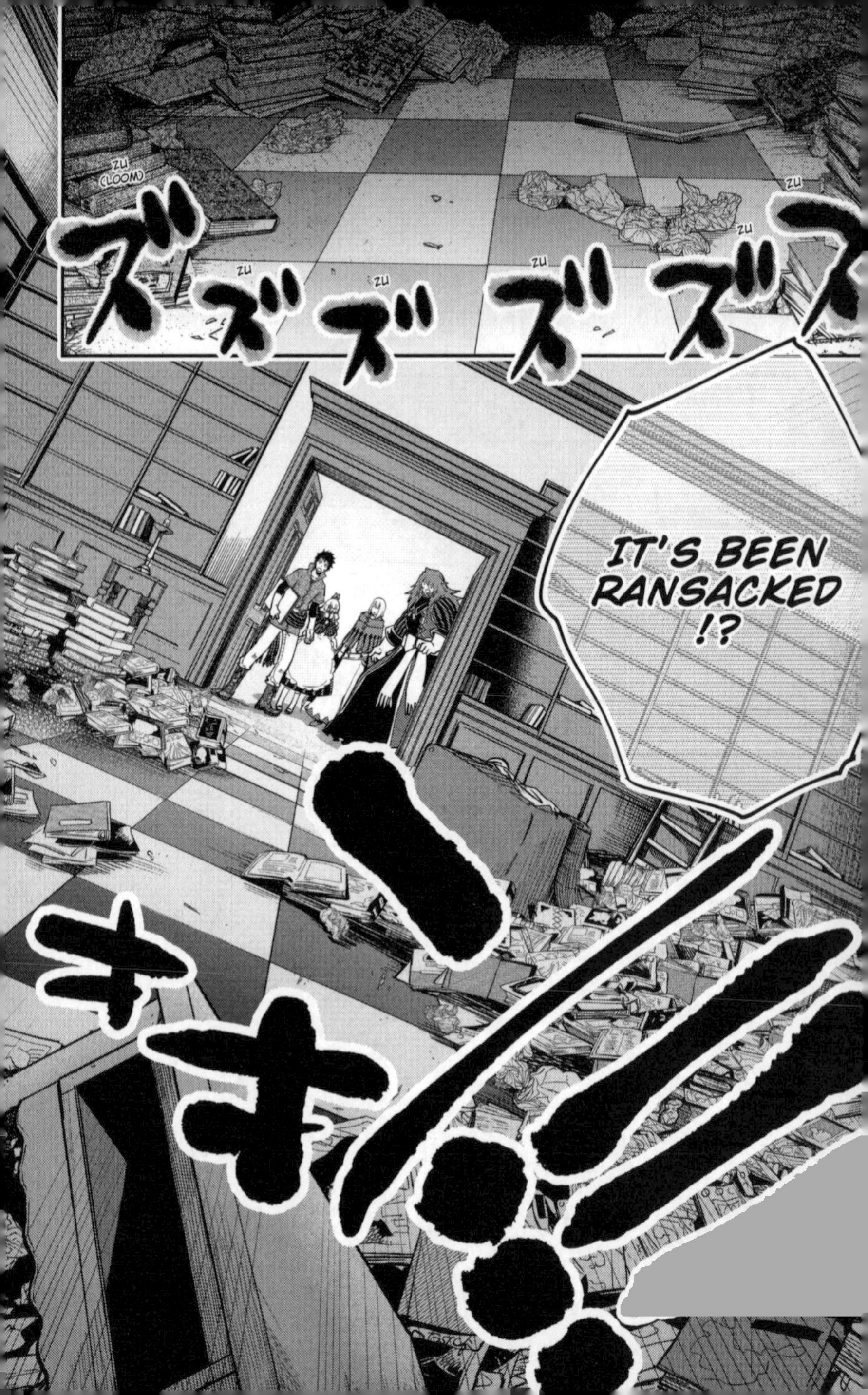

ズズズズズ
ZU (LOOM)
ZU
ZU
ZU
ZU
ZU
IT'S BEEN RANSACKED !?

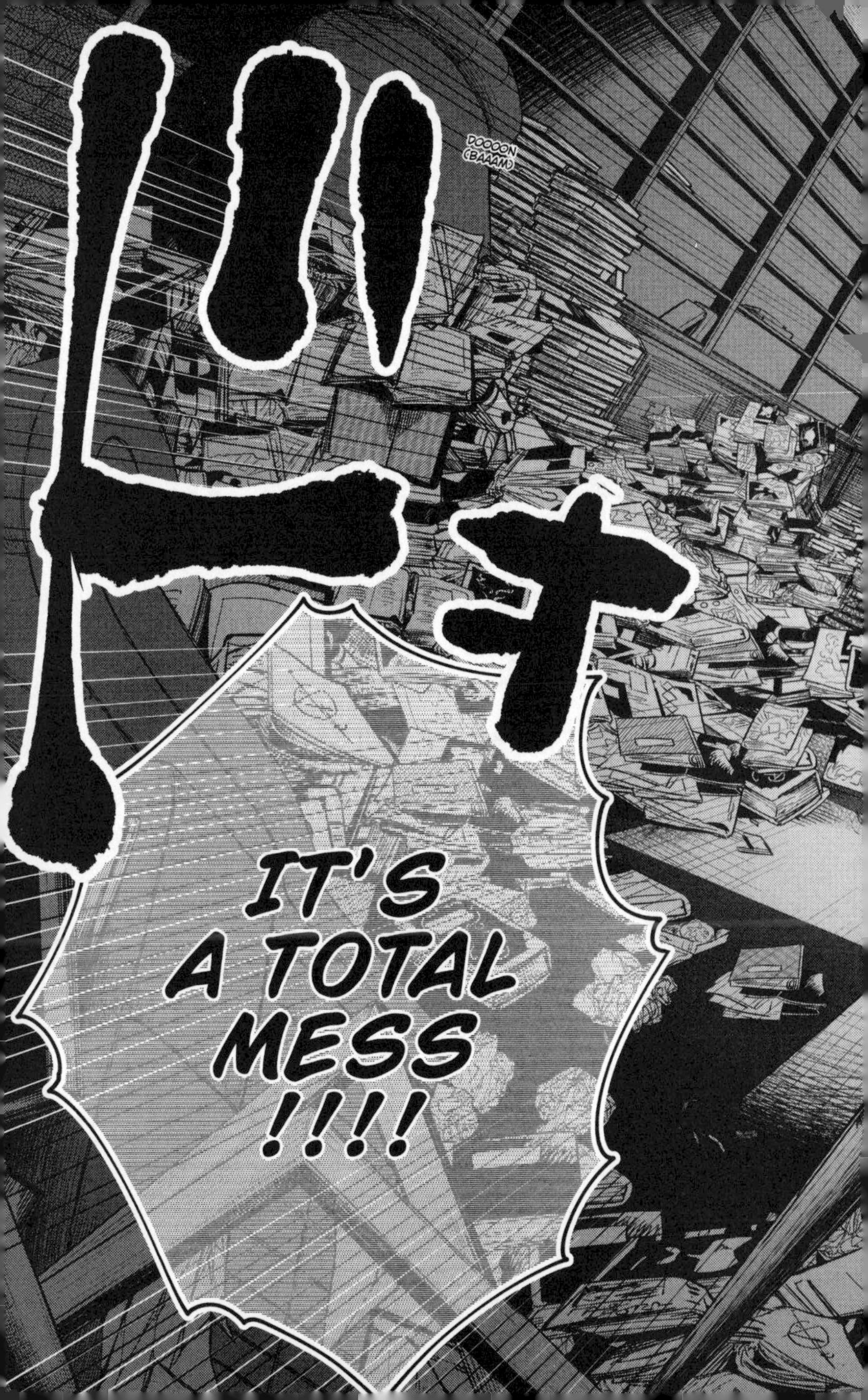
DOOOON (BAAAM)
IT'S A TOTAL MESS !!!!

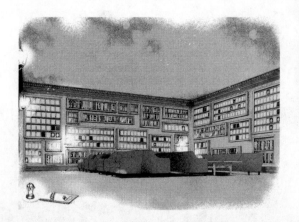

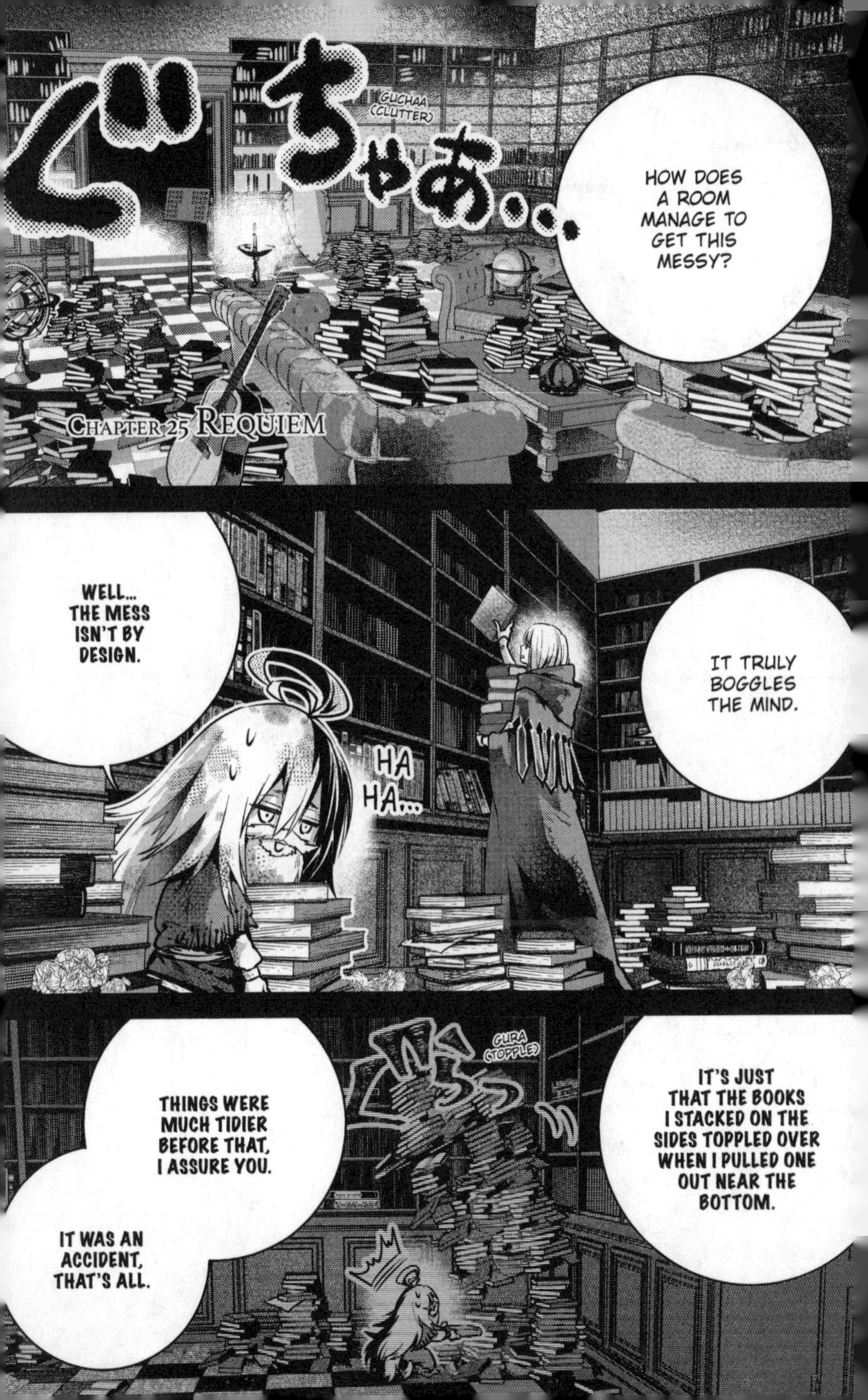
HOW DOES A ROOM MANAGE TO GET THIS MESSY?
GUCHAA (CLUTTER)
ぐっちゃあ...
CHAPTER 25 REQUIEM
IT TRULY BOGGLES THE MIND.
WELL... THE MESS ISN'T BY DESIGN.
HA HA...
IT'S JUST THAT THE BOOKS I STACKED ON THE SIDES TOPPLED OVER WHEN I PULLED ONE OUT NEAR THE BOTTOM.
GURA (TOPPLE)
THINGS WERE MUCH TIDIER BEFORE THAT, I ASSURE YOU.
IT WAS AN ACCIDENT, THAT'S ALL.

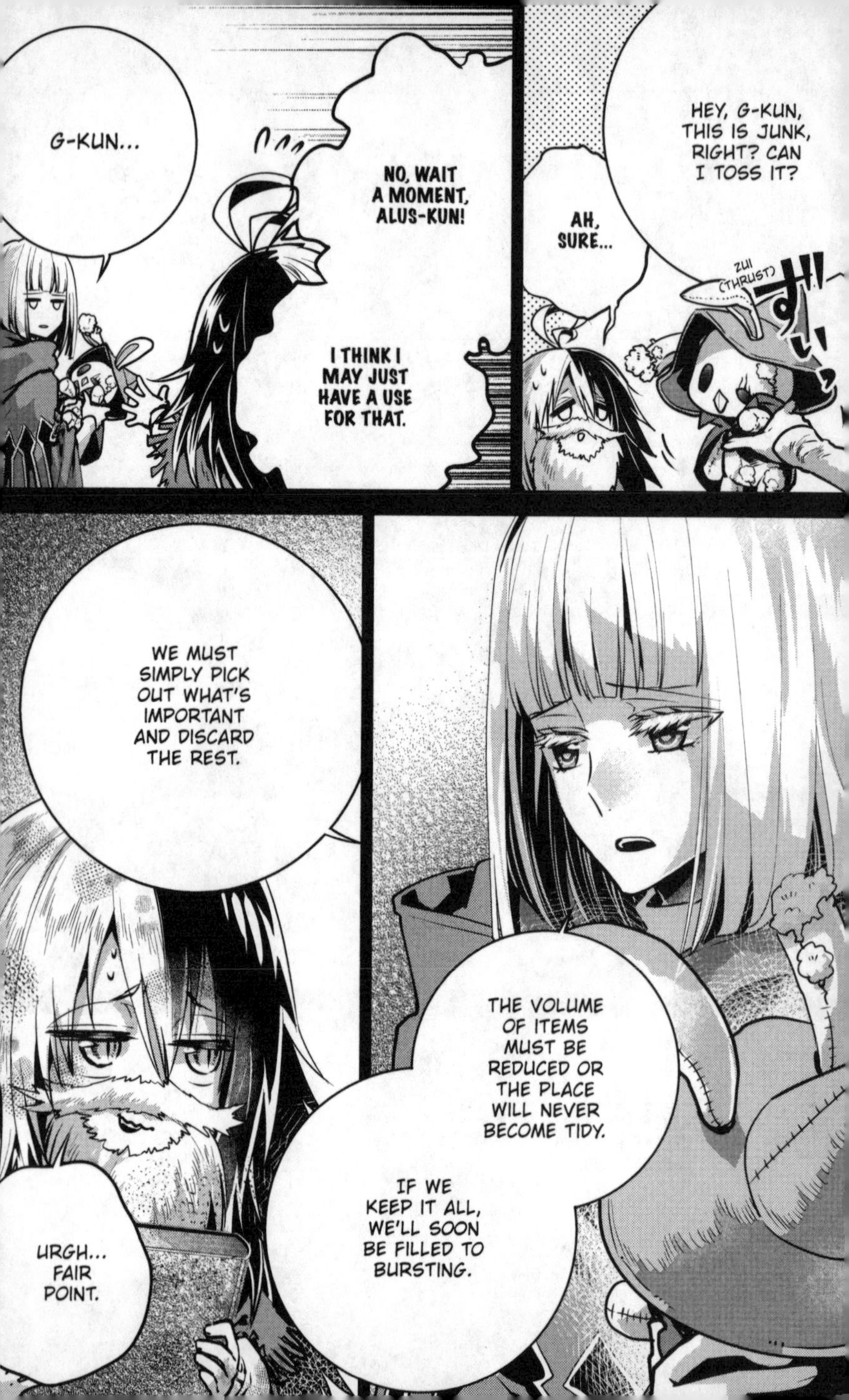
HEY, G-KUN, THIS IS JUNK, RIGHT? CAN I TOSS IT?
AH, SURE...
ZUI (THRUST)
G-KUN...
NO, WAIT A MOMENT, ALUS-KUN!
I THINK I MAY JUST HAVE A USE FOR THAT.
THE VOLUME OF ITEMS MUST BE REDUCED OR THE PLACE WILL NEVER BECOME TIDY.
IF WE KEEP IT ALL, WE'LL SOON BE FILLED TO BURSTING.
WE MUST SIMPLY PICK OUT WHAT'S IMPORTANT AND DISCARD THE REST.
URGH... FAIR POINT.

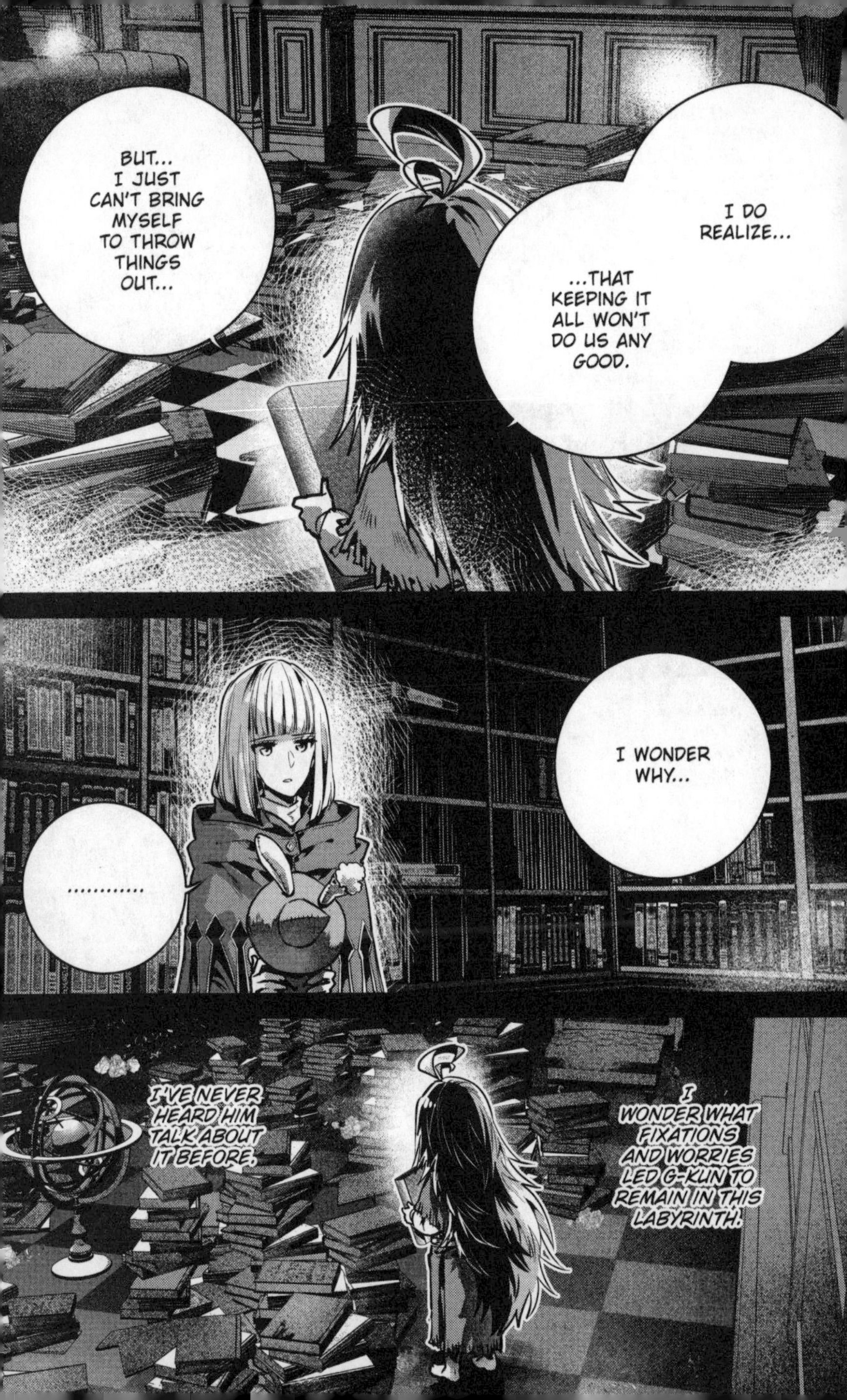
I DO REALIZE...
...THAT KEEPING IT ALL WON'T DO US ANY GOOD.
BUT... I JUST CAN'T BRING MYSELF TO THROW THINGS OUT...
I WONDER WHY...
...........
I WONDER WHAT FIXATIONS AND WORRIES LED G-KUN TO REMAIN IN THIS LABYRINTH.
I'VE NEVER HEARD HIM TALK ABOUT IT BEFORE.

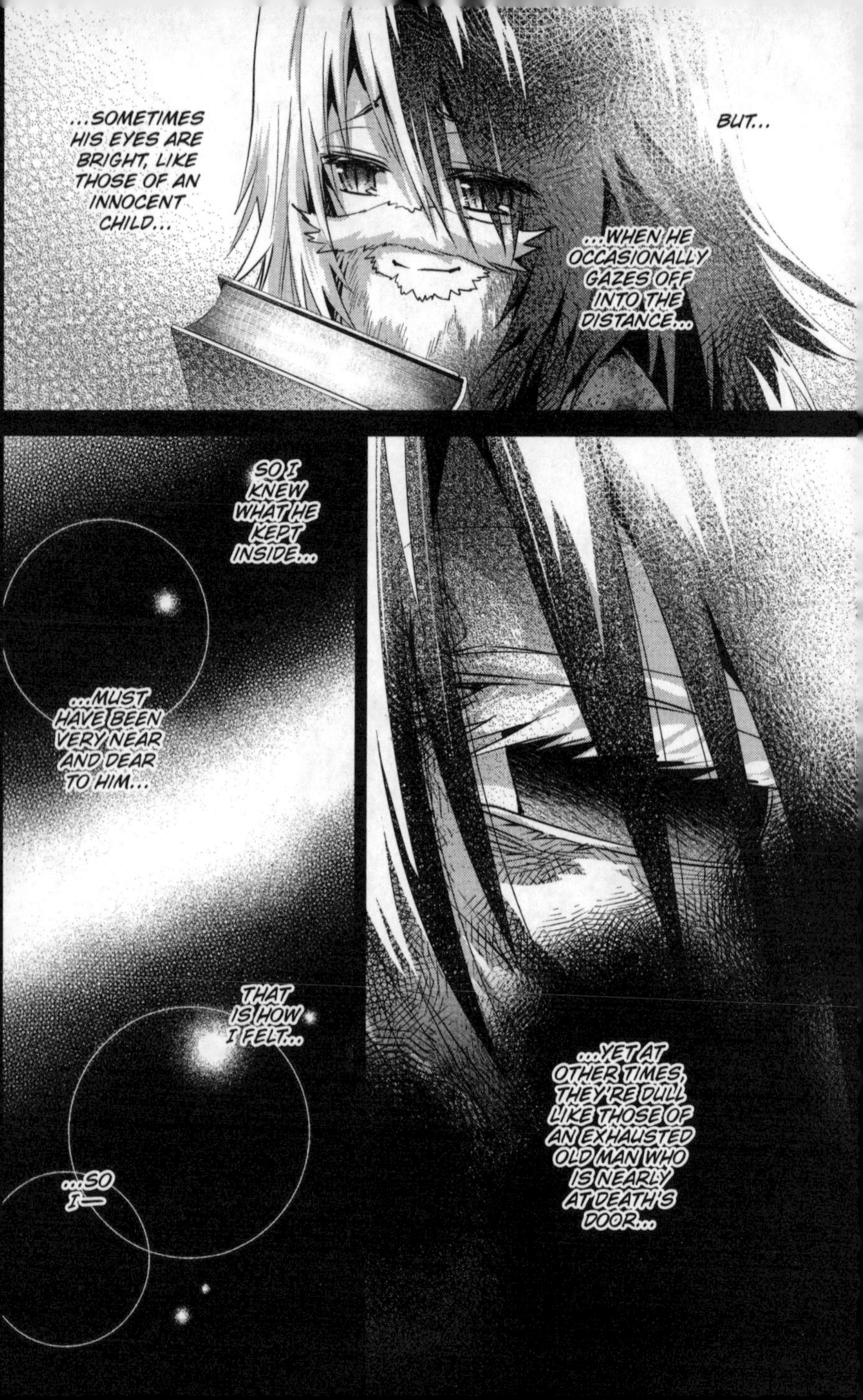
BUT...
...WHEN HE OCCASIONALLY GAZES OFF INTO THE DISTANCE...
...SOMETIMES HIS EYES ARE BRIGHT, LIKE THOSE OF AN INNOCENT CHILD...
...YET AT OTHER TIMES, THEY'RE DULL LIKE THOSE OF AN EXHAUSTED OLD MAN WHO IS NEARLY AT DEATH'S DOOR...
SO I KNEW WHAT HE KEPT INSIDE...
...MUST HAVE BEEN VERY NEAR AND DEAR TO HIM...
THAT IS HOW I FELT...
...SO I—

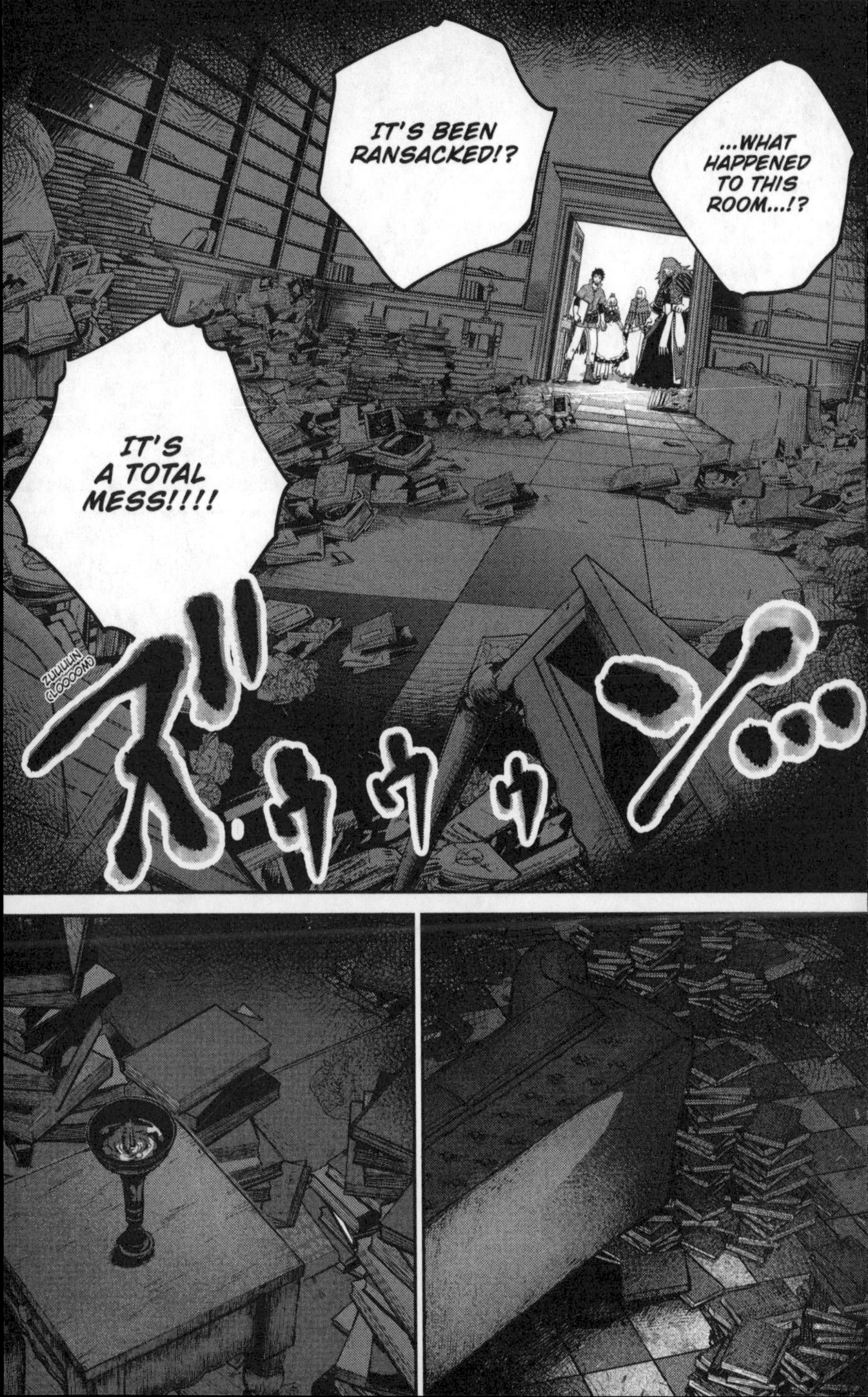
...WHAT HAPPENED TO THIS ROOM...!?
IT'S BEEN RANSACKED!?
IT'S A TOTAL MESS!!!!
ZUUUUN (GLOOOOM)

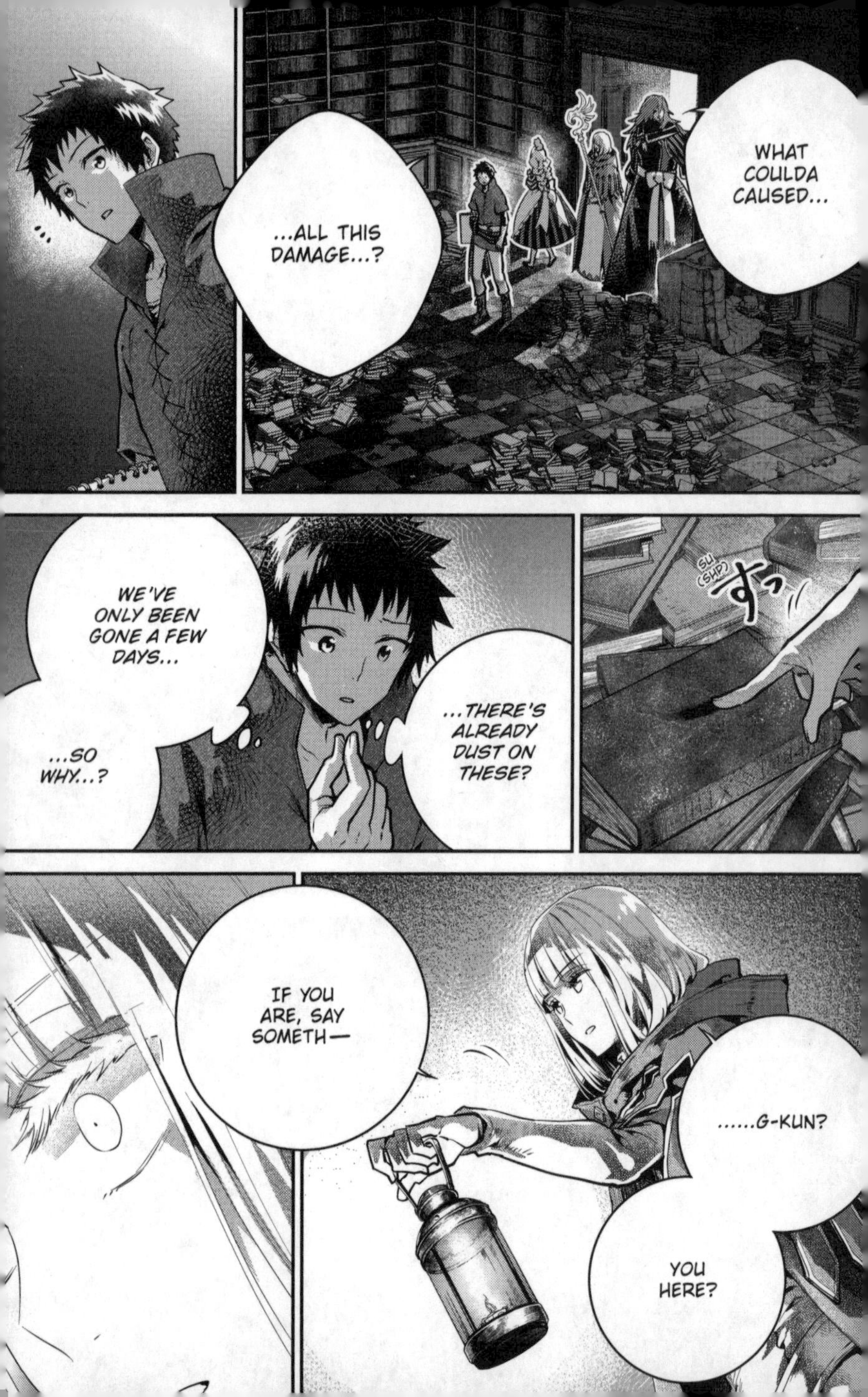
WHAT COULDA CAUSED...
...ALL THIS DAMAGE...?
SU (SHP)
WE'VE ONLY BEEN GONE A FEW DAYS...
...THERE'S ALREADY DUST ON THESE?
...SO WHY...?
......G-KUN?
YOU HERE?
IF YOU ARE, SAY SOMETH—

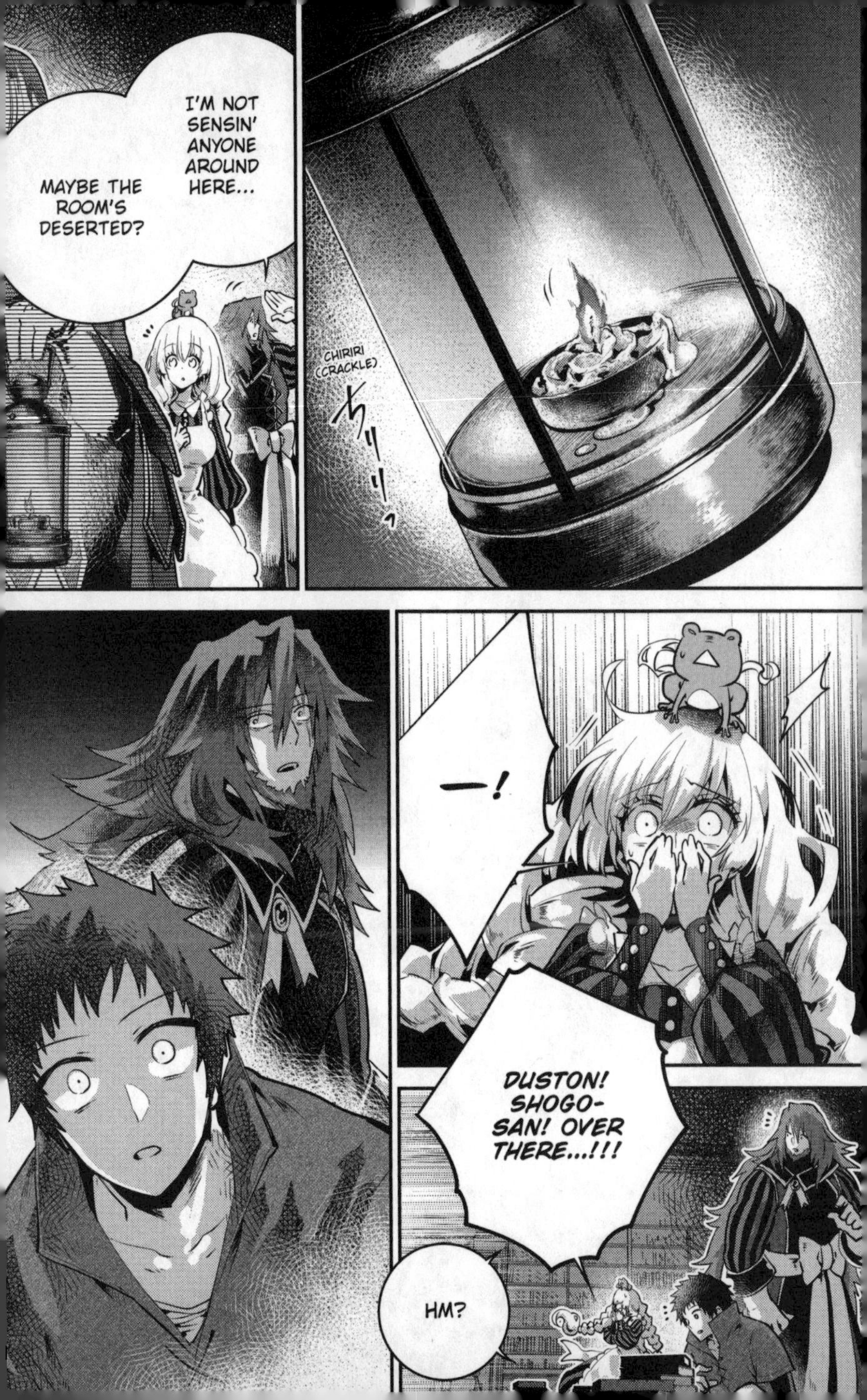
CHIRIRI (CRACKLE)
ちりりっ
I'M NOT SENSIN' ANYONE AROUND HERE...
MAYBE THE ROOM'S DESERTED?
—!
DUSTON! SHOGO-SAN! OVER THERE...!!!
HM?

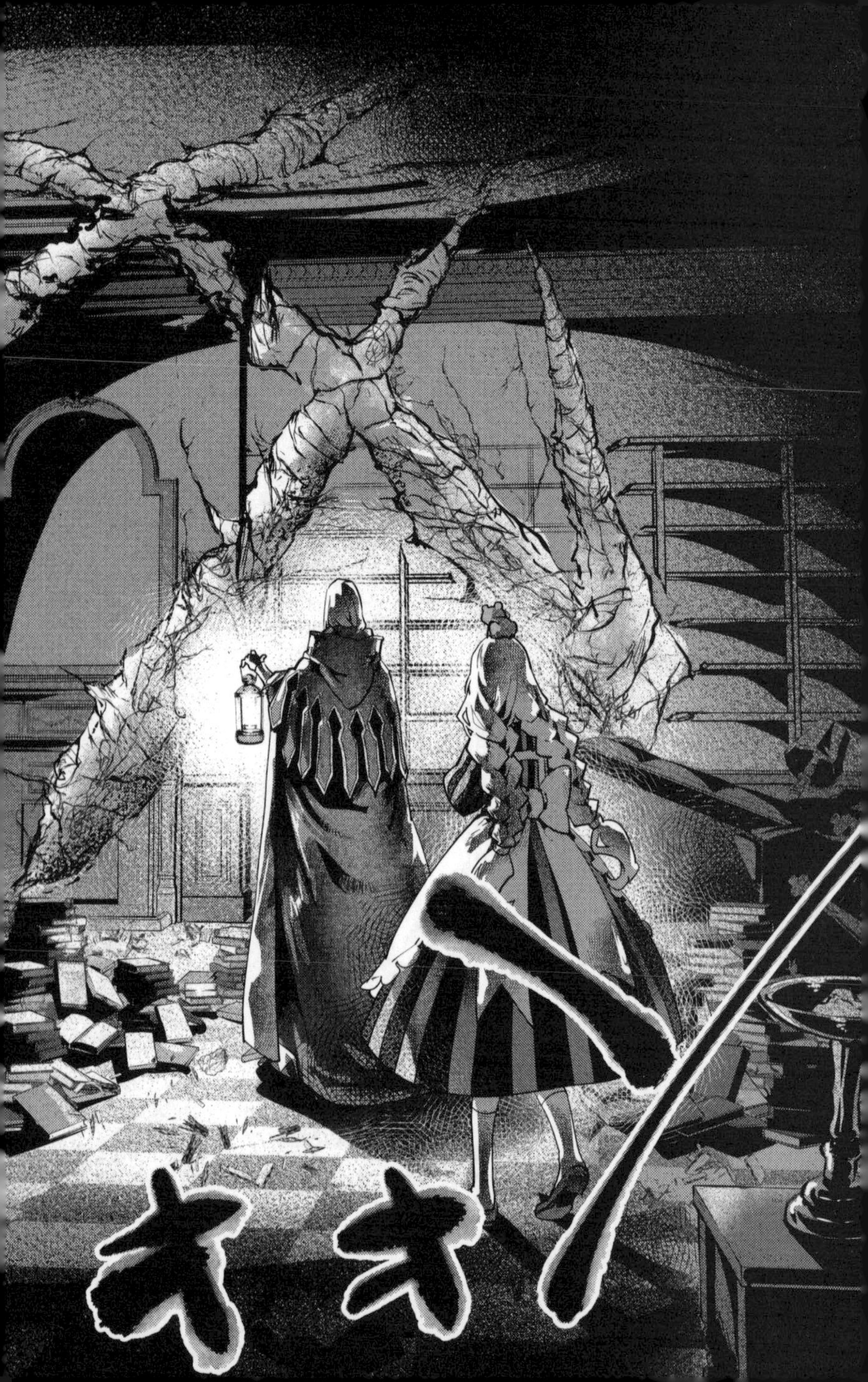
オオン

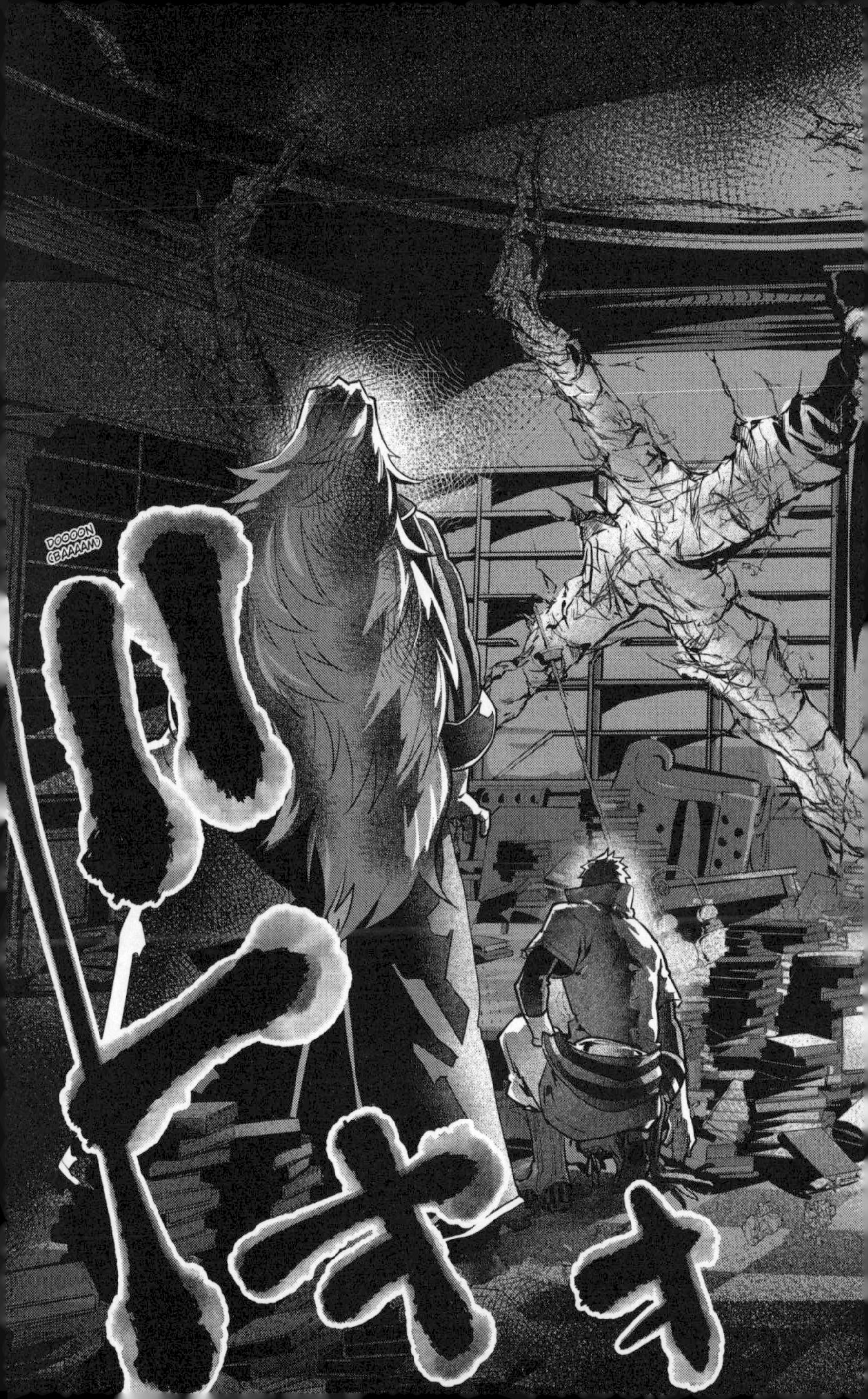
DOOOON
(BAAAAM)

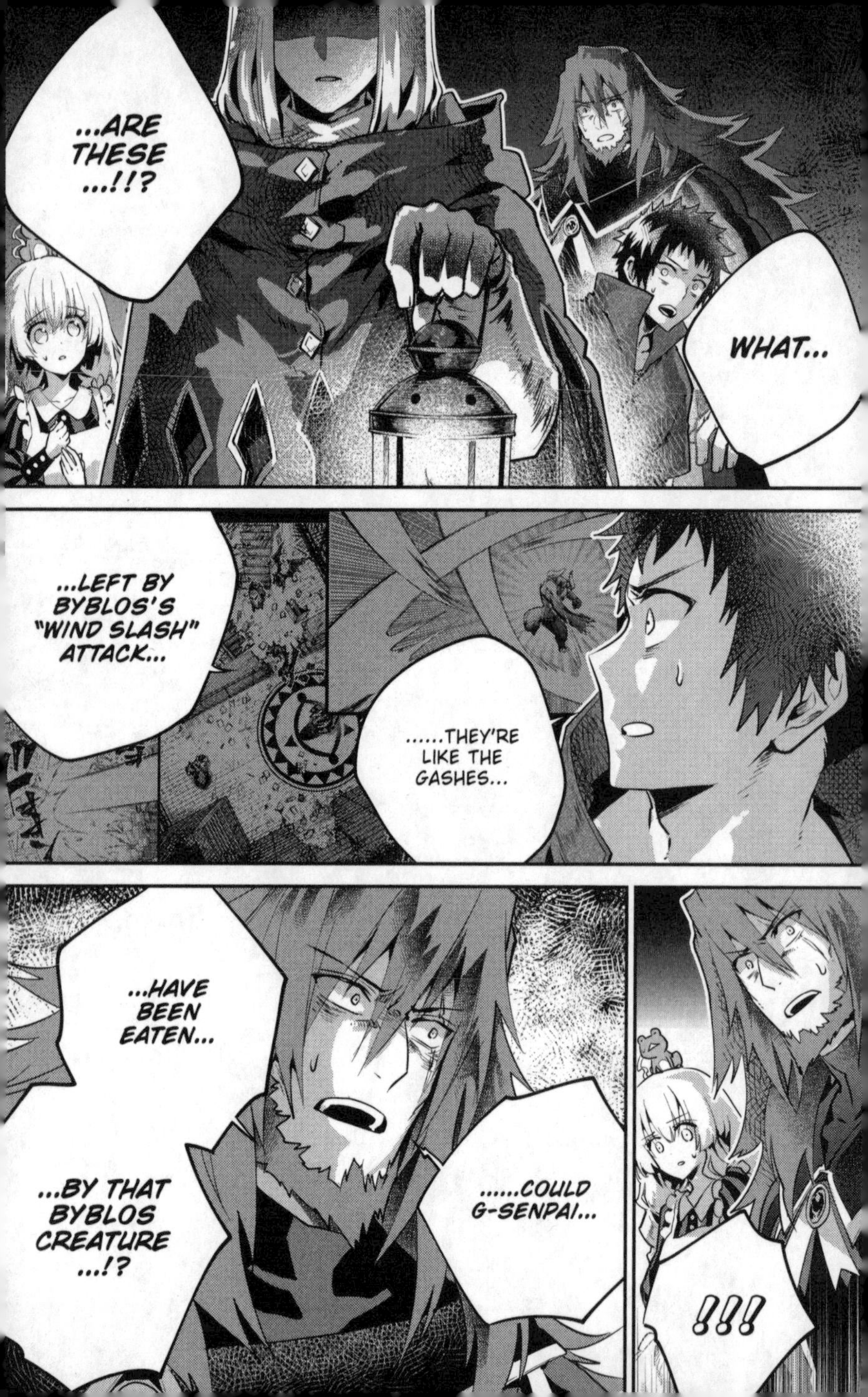
WHAT...
...ARE THESE ...!!?
......THEY'RE LIKE THE GASHES...
...LEFT BY BYBLOS'S "WIND SLASH" ATTACK...
!!!
......COULD G-SENPAI...
...HAVE BEEN EATEN...
...BY THAT BYBLOS CREATURE ...!?

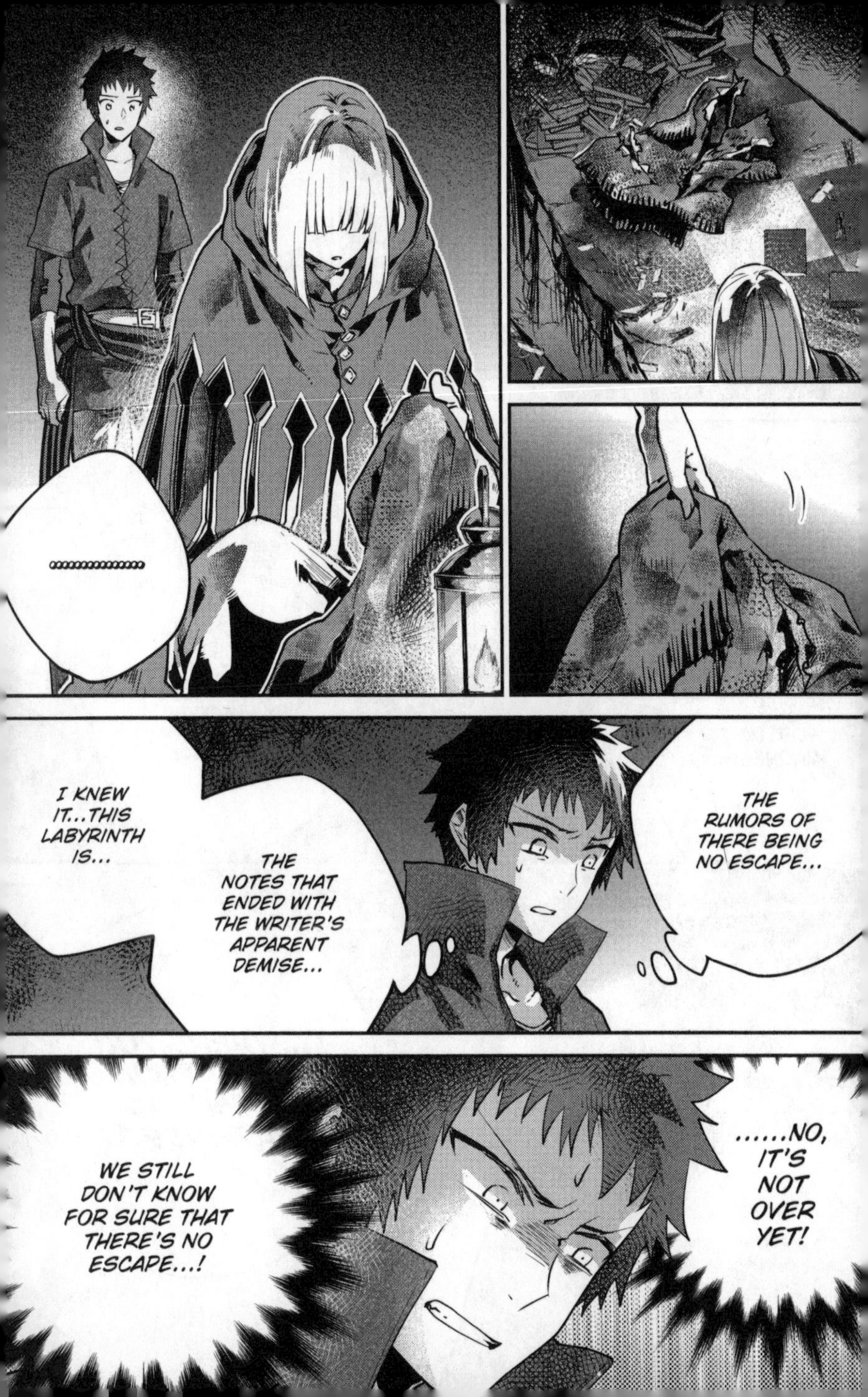
................
THE RUMORS OF THERE BEING NO ESCAPE...
THE NOTES THAT ENDED WITH THE WRITER'S APPARENT DEMISE...
I KNEW IT...THIS LABYRINTH IS...
......NO, IT'S NOT OVER YET!
WE STILL DON'T KNOW FOR SURE THAT THERE'S NO ESCAPE...!

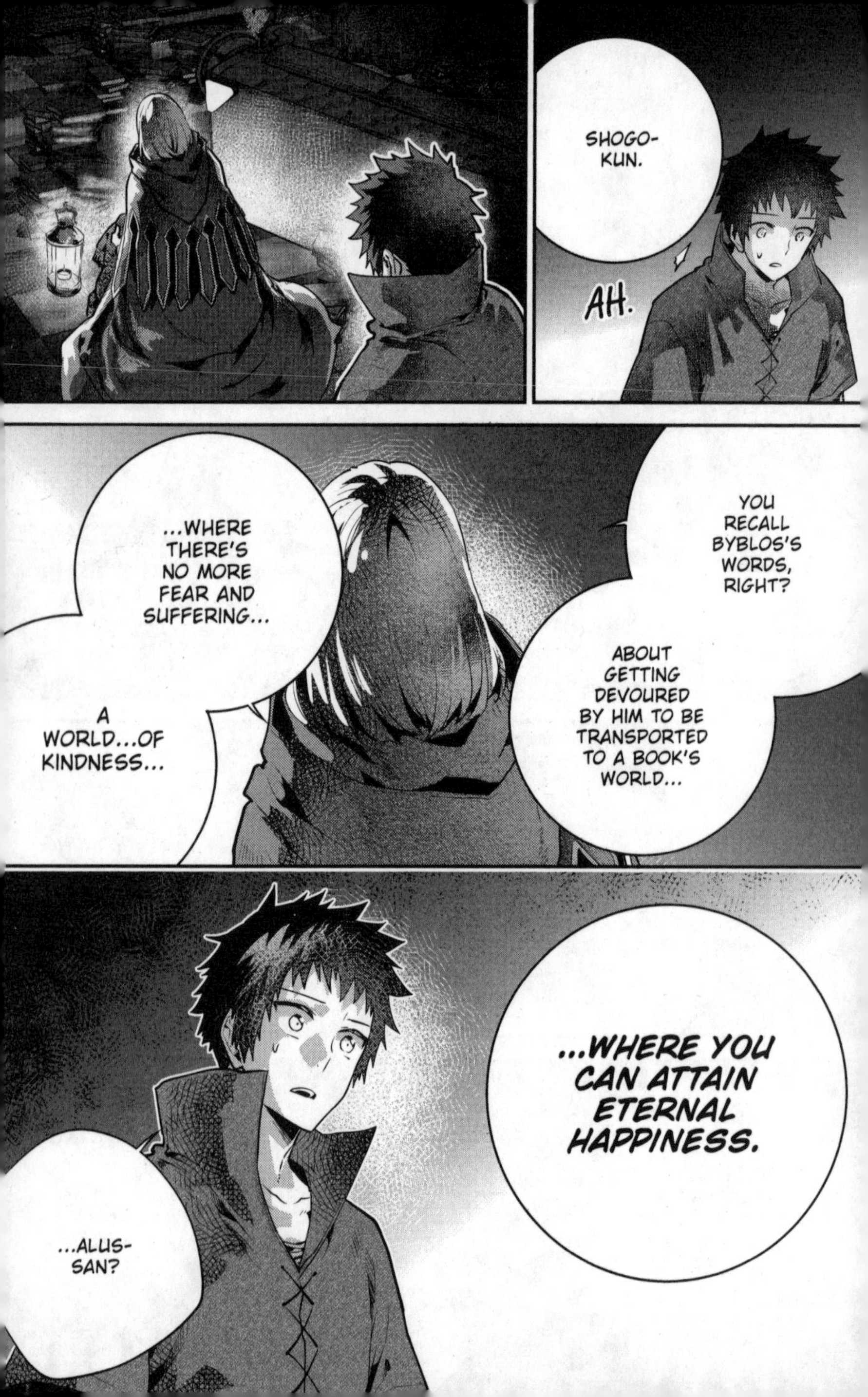
SHOGO-KUN.
AH.
YOU RECALL BYBLOS'S WORDS, RIGHT?
ABOUT GETTING DEVOURED BY HIM TO BE TRANSPORTED TO A BOOK'S WORLD...
...WHERE THERE'S NO MORE FEAR AND SUFFERING...
A WORLD...OF KINDNESS...
...WHERE YOU CAN ATTAIN ETERNAL HAPPINESS.
...ALUS-SAN?

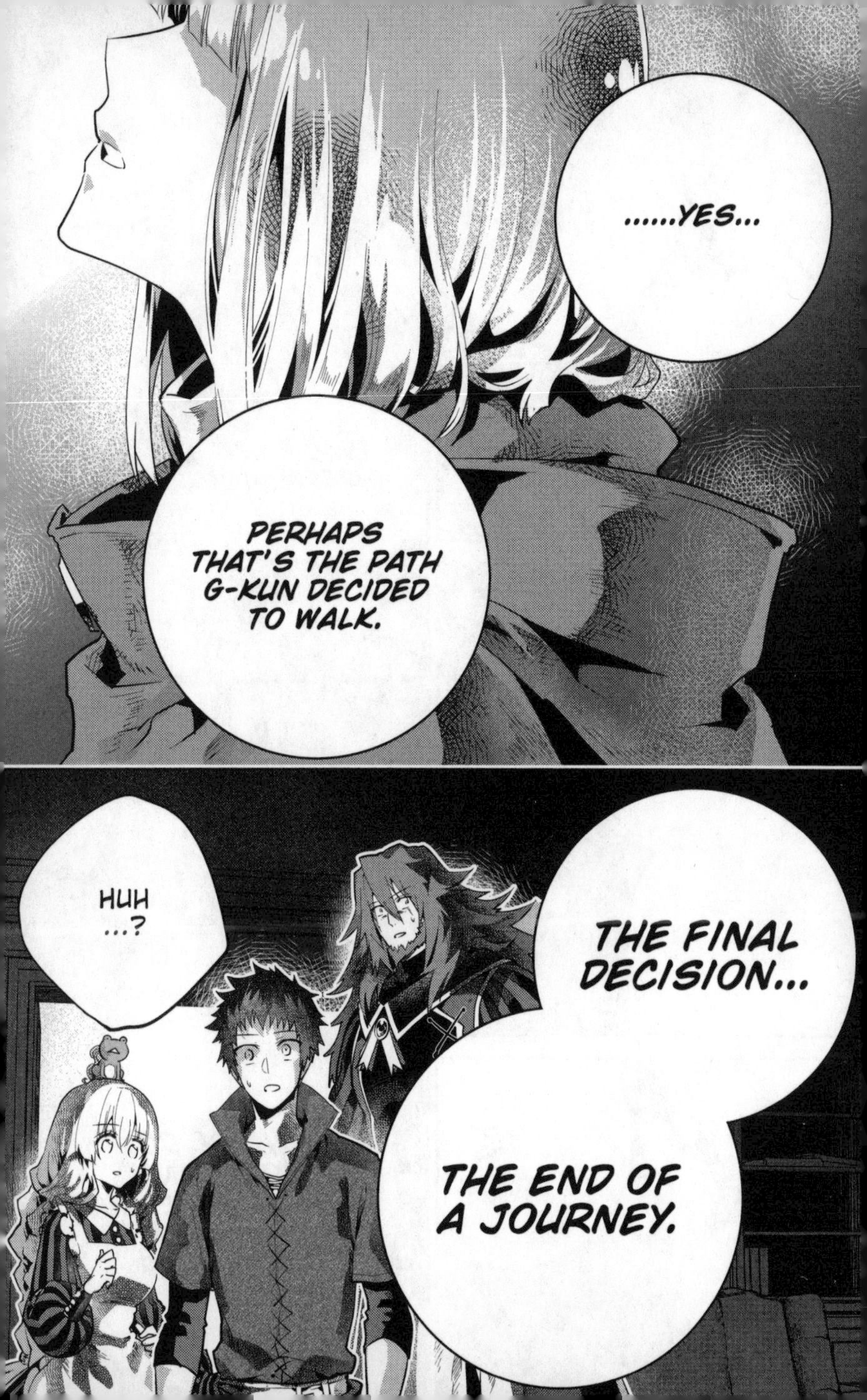
......YES...
PERHAPS THAT'S THE PATH G-KUN DECIDED TO WALK.
THE FINAL DECISION...
THE END OF A JOURNEY.
HUH ...?

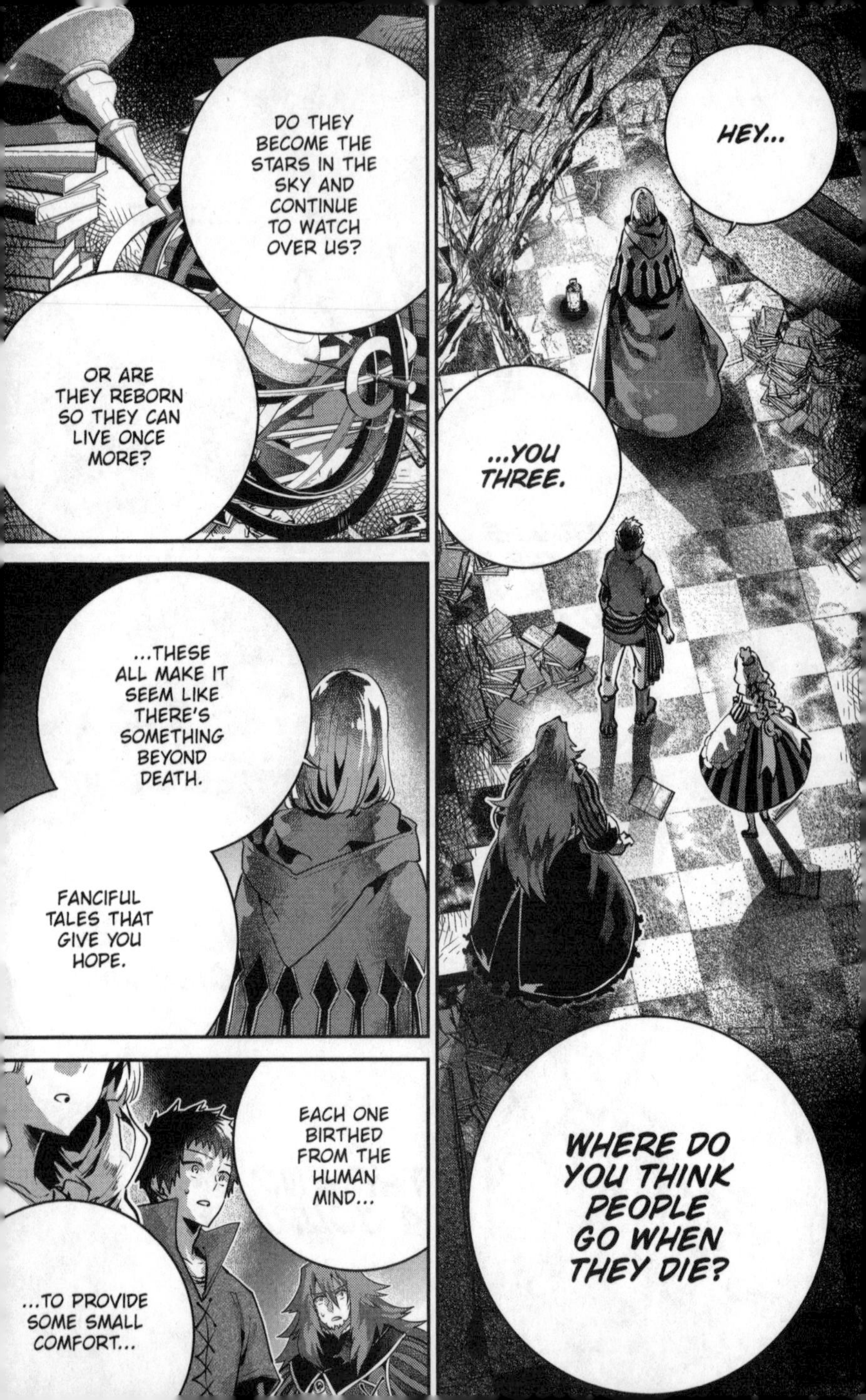
HEY...
...YOU THREE.
WHERE DO YOU THINK PEOPLE GO WHEN THEY DIE?
DO THEY BECOME THE STARS IN THE SKY AND CONTINUE TO WATCH OVER US?
OR ARE THEY REBORN SO THEY CAN LIVE ONCE MORE?
...THESE ALL MAKE IT SEEM LIKE THERE'S SOMETHING BEYOND DEATH.
FANCIFUL TALES THAT GIVE YOU HOPE.
EACH ONE BIRTHED FROM THE HUMAN MIND...
...TO PROVIDE SOME SMALL COMFORT...

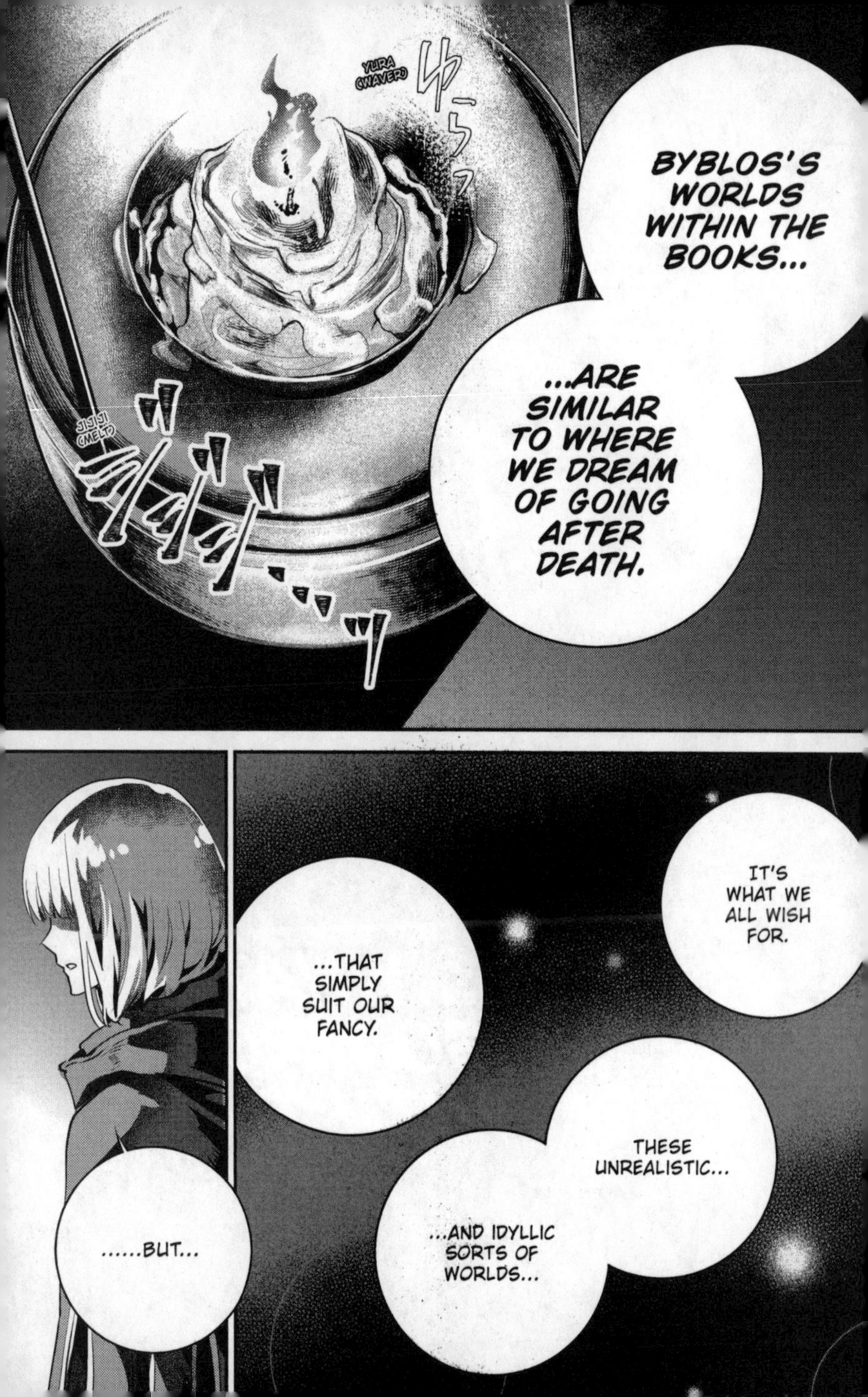
YURA (WAVER)
BYBLOS'S WORLDS WITHIN THE BOOKS...
...ARE SIMILAR TO WHERE WE DREAM OF GOING AFTER DEATH.
JIJIJI (MELT)
IT'S WHAT WE ALL WISH FOR.
THESE UNREALISTIC...
...AND IDYLLIC SORTS OF WORLDS...
...THAT SIMPLY SUIT OUR FANCY.
......BUT...

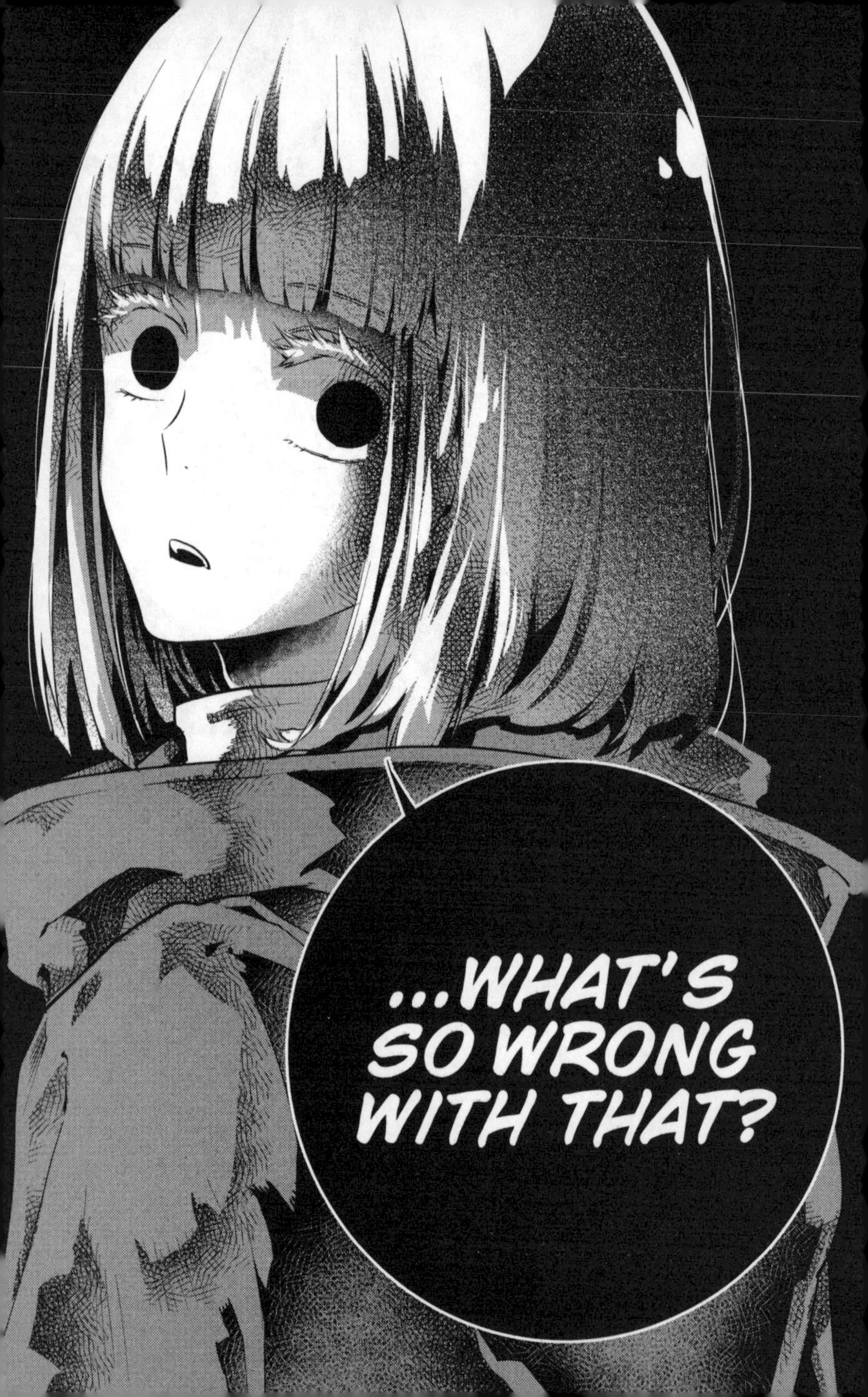
...WHAT'S SO WRONG WITH THAT?

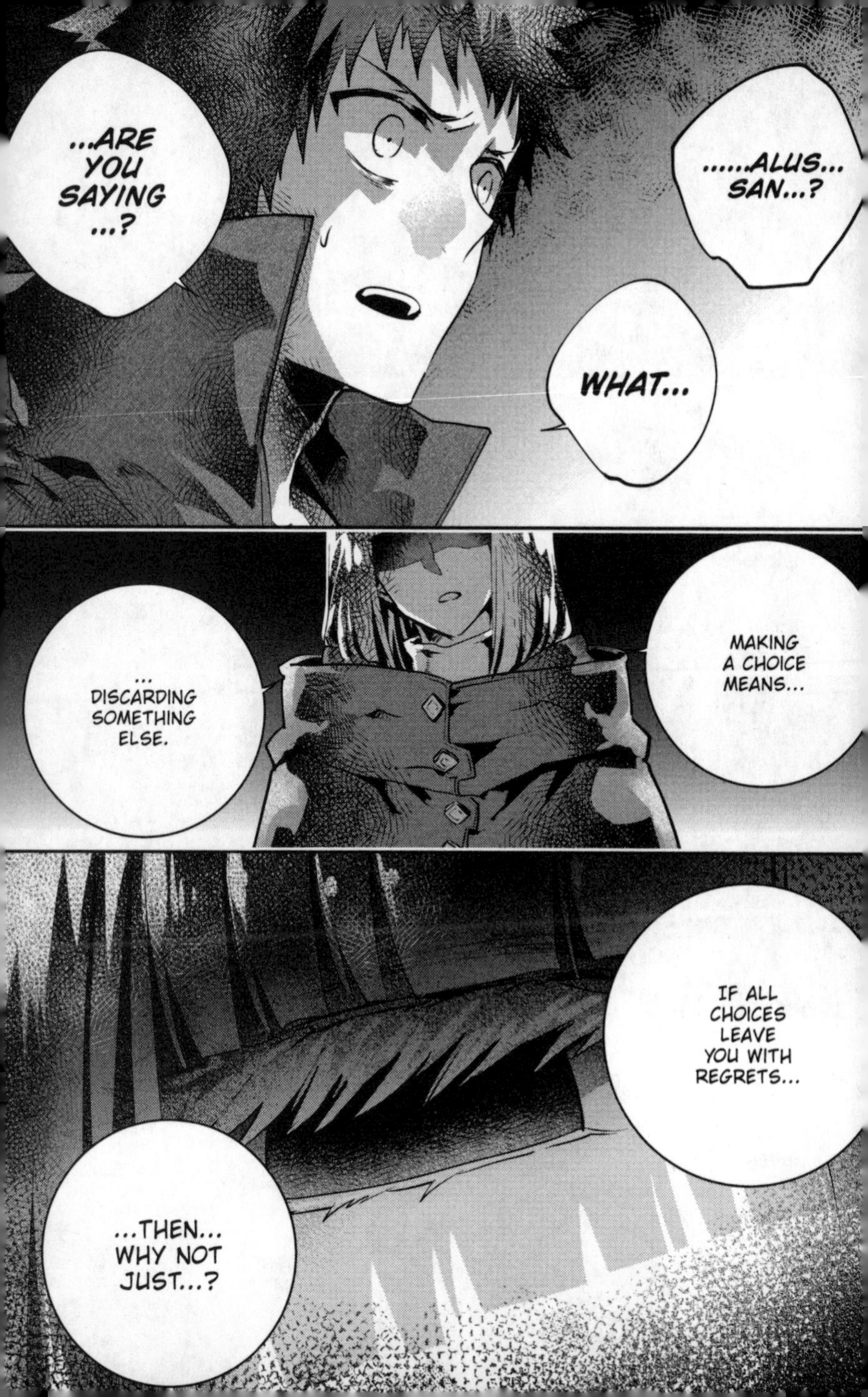
......ALUS... SAN...?
WHAT...
...ARE YOU SAYING ...?
MAKING A CHOICE MEANS...
... DISCARDING SOMETHING ELSE.
IF ALL CHOICES LEAVE YOU WITH REGRETS...
...THEN... WHY NOT JUST...?

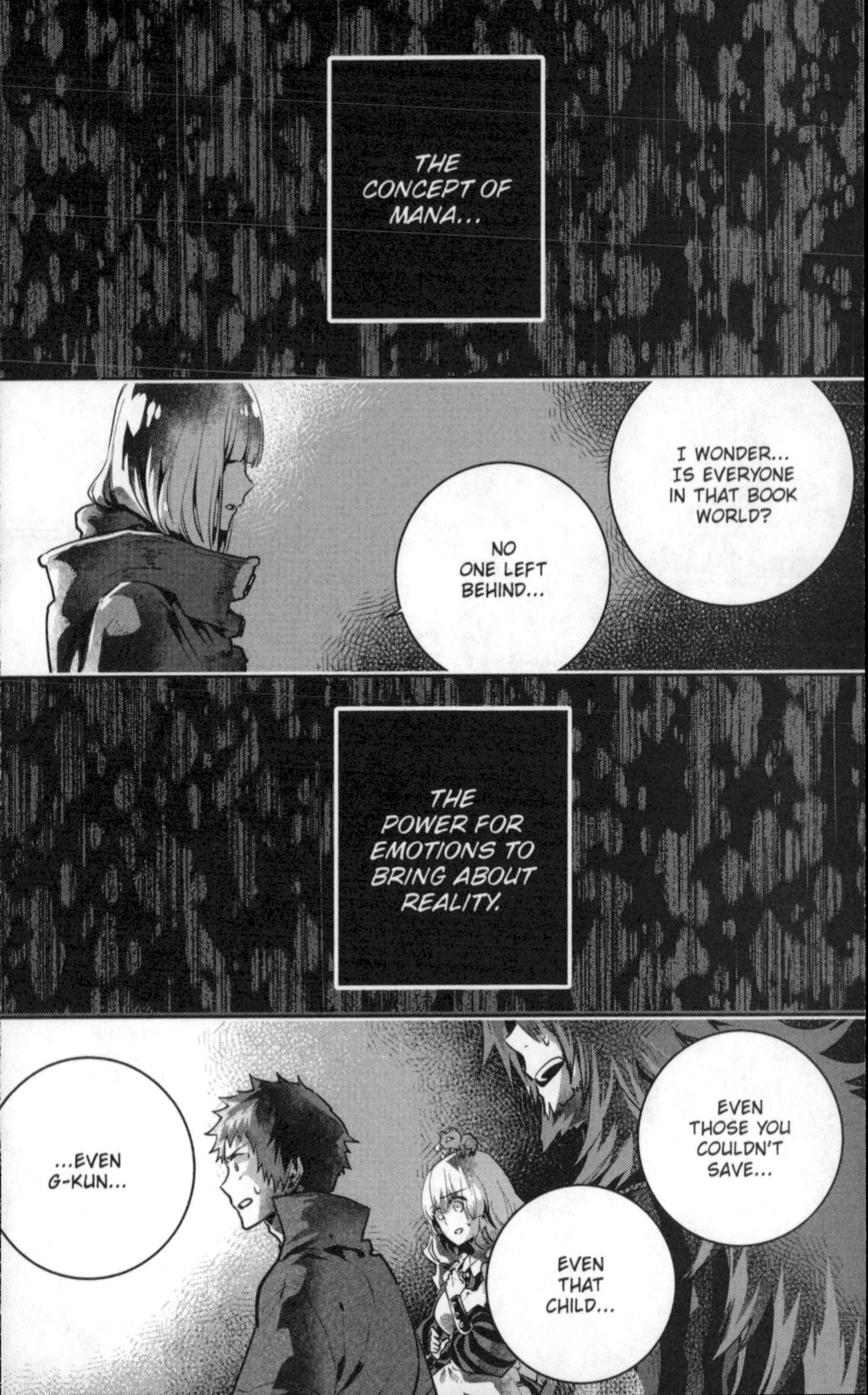
THE CONCEPT OF MANA...
I WONDER... IS EVERYONE IN THAT BOOK WORLD?
NO ONE LEFT BEHIND...
THE POWER FOR EMOTIONS TO BRING ABOUT REALITY.
EVEN THOSE YOU COULDN'T SAVE...
EVEN THAT CHILD...
...EVEN G-KUN...

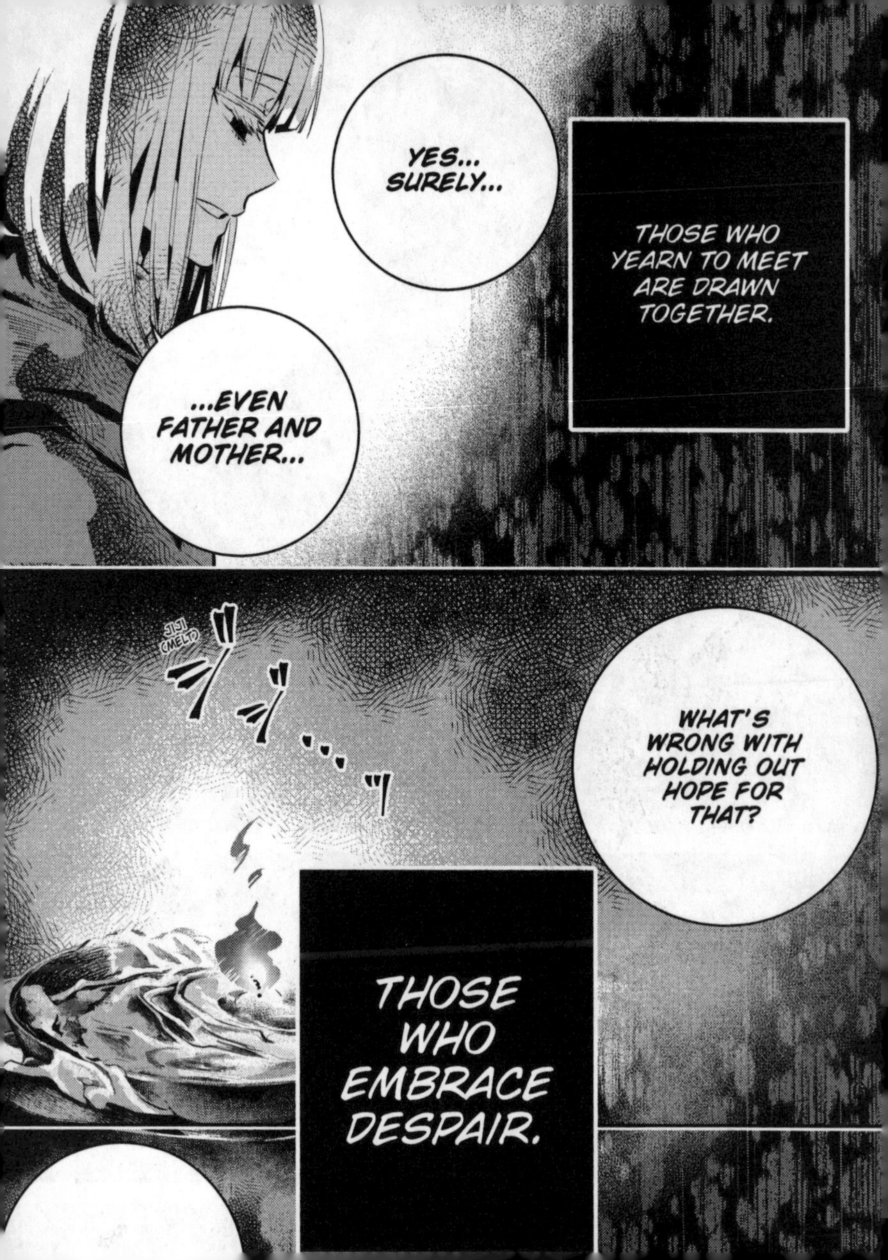
THOSE WHO YEARN TO MEET ARE DRAWN TOGETHER.
YES... SURELY...
...EVEN FATHER AND MOTHER...
WHAT'S WRONG WITH HOLDING OUT HOPE FOR THAT?
JIJI (MELT)
THOSE WHO EMBRACE DESPAIR.

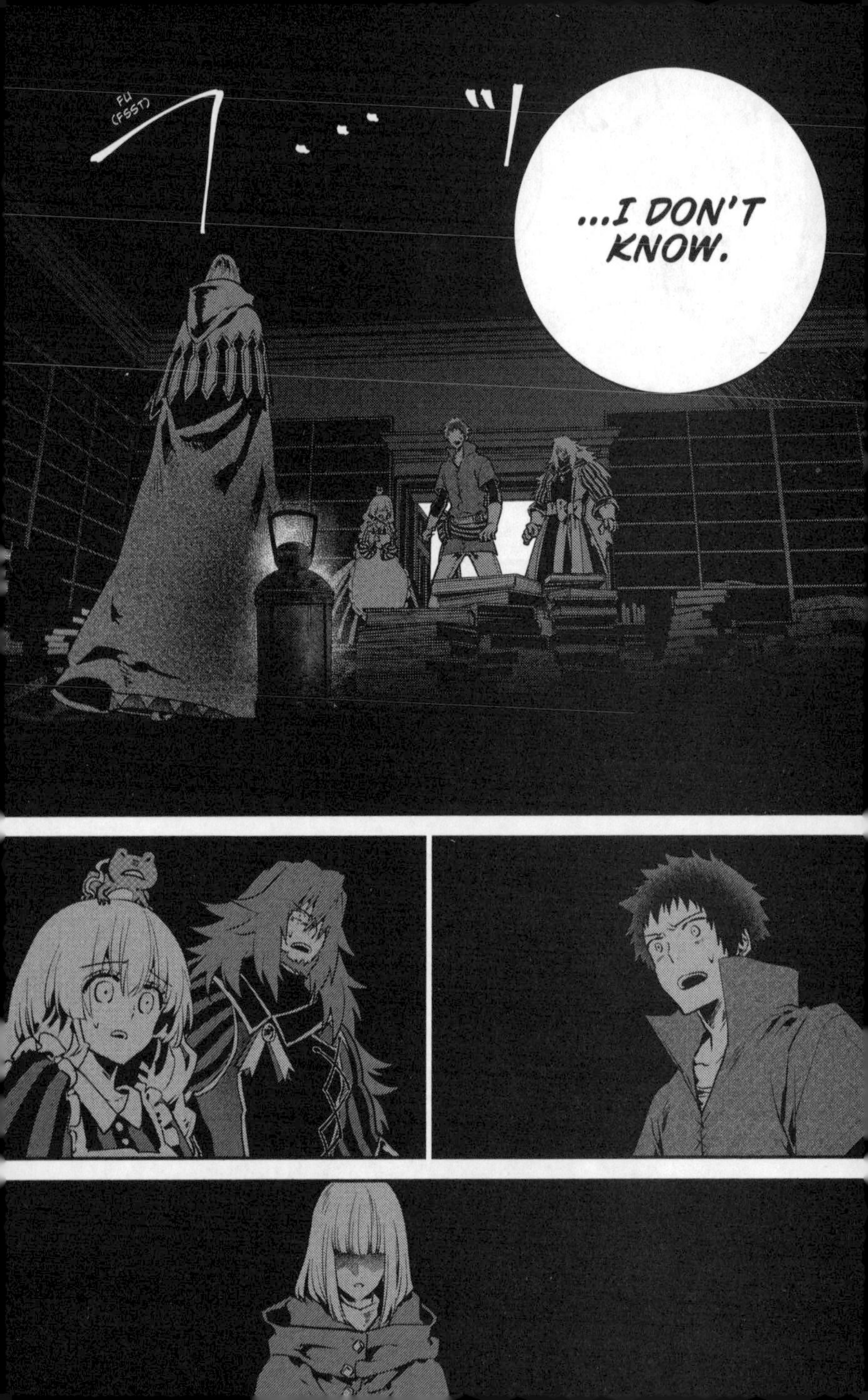
...I DON'T KNOW.
FU (FSST)

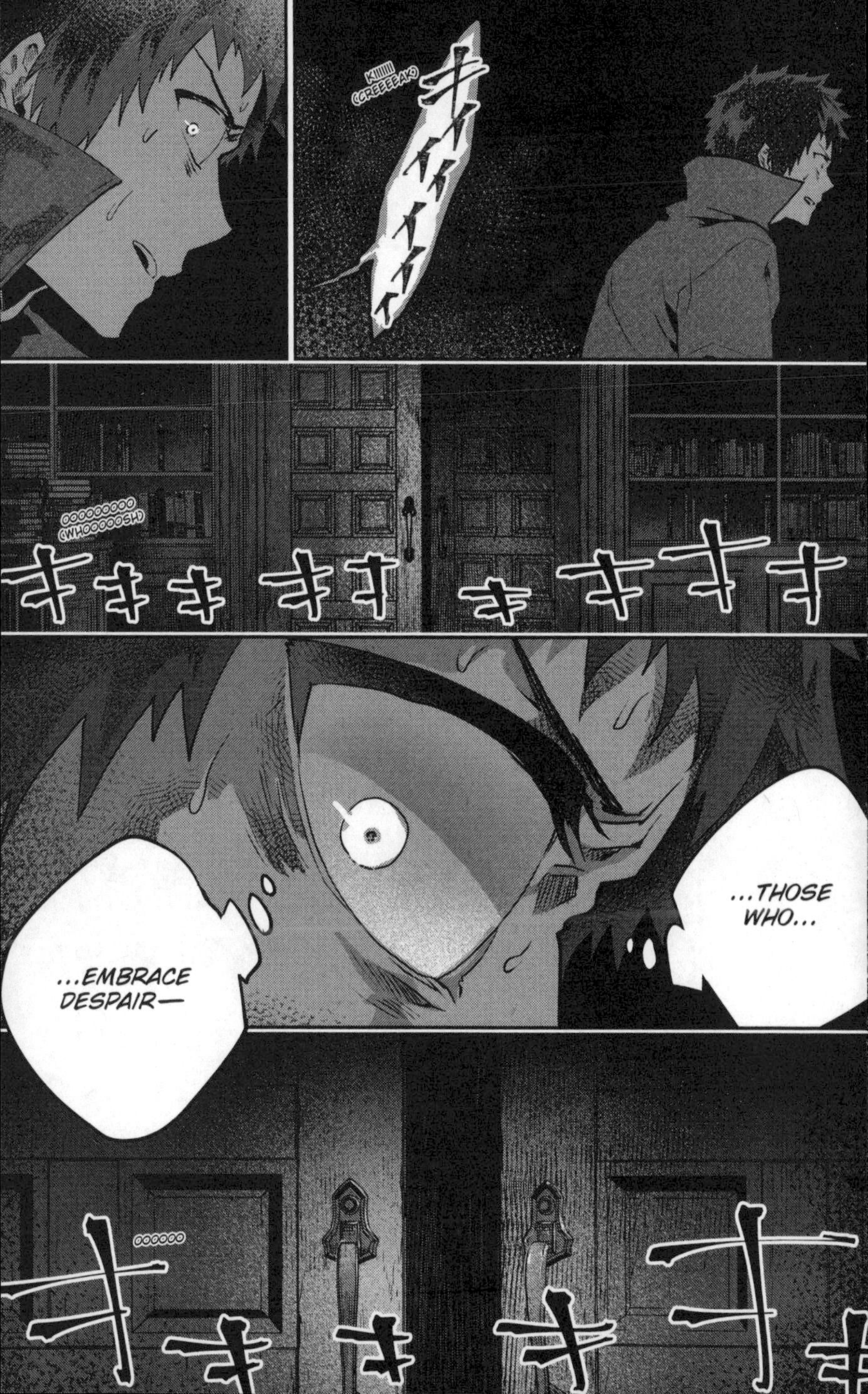
KIIIIIII
(CREEEEAK)
OOOOOOOOO
(WHOOOOOSH)
...THOSE WHO...
...EMBRACE DESPAIR—
OOOOOO

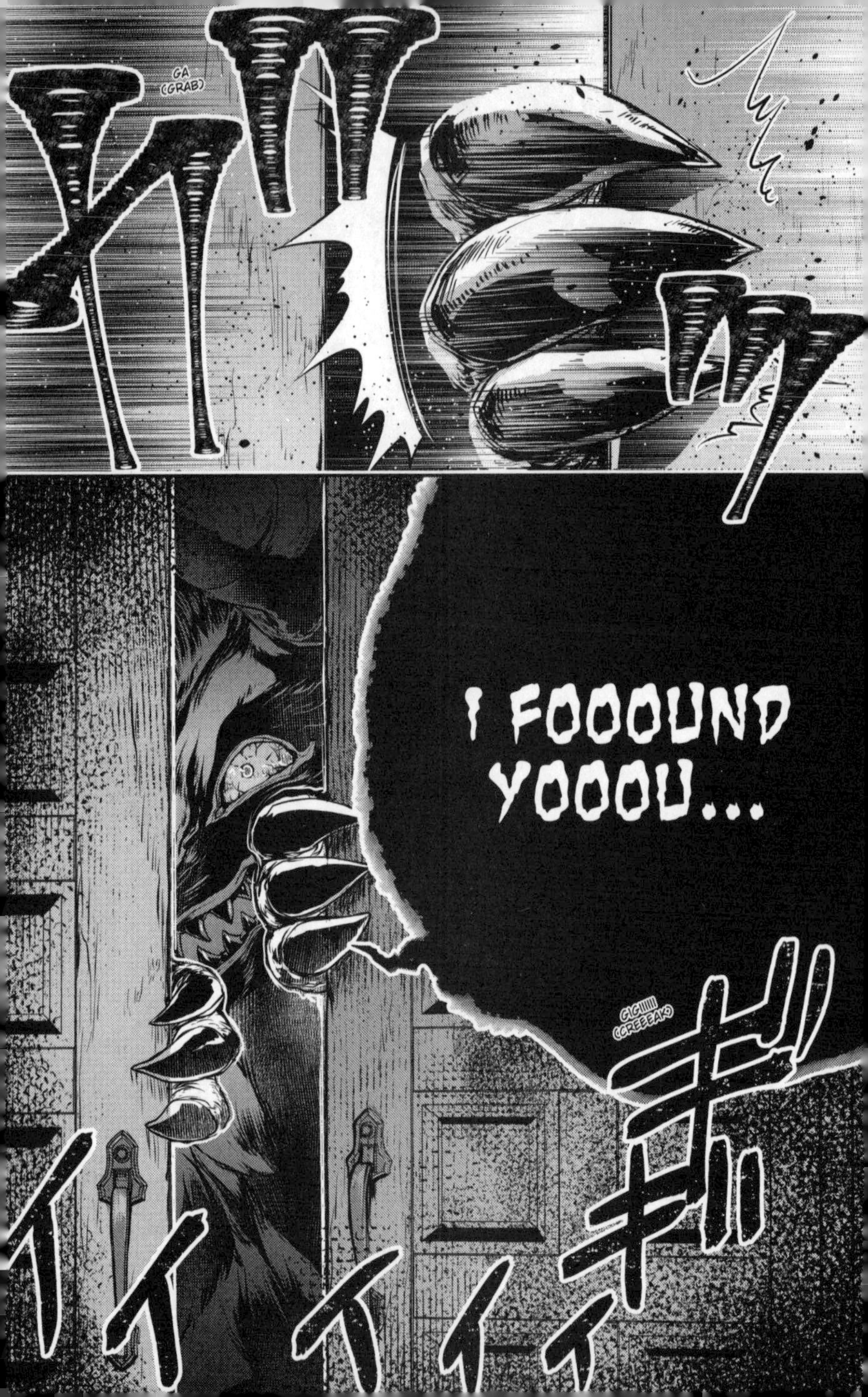
GA (GRAB)
I FOOOUND YOOOU...
GIGIIIIII (CREEEAK)

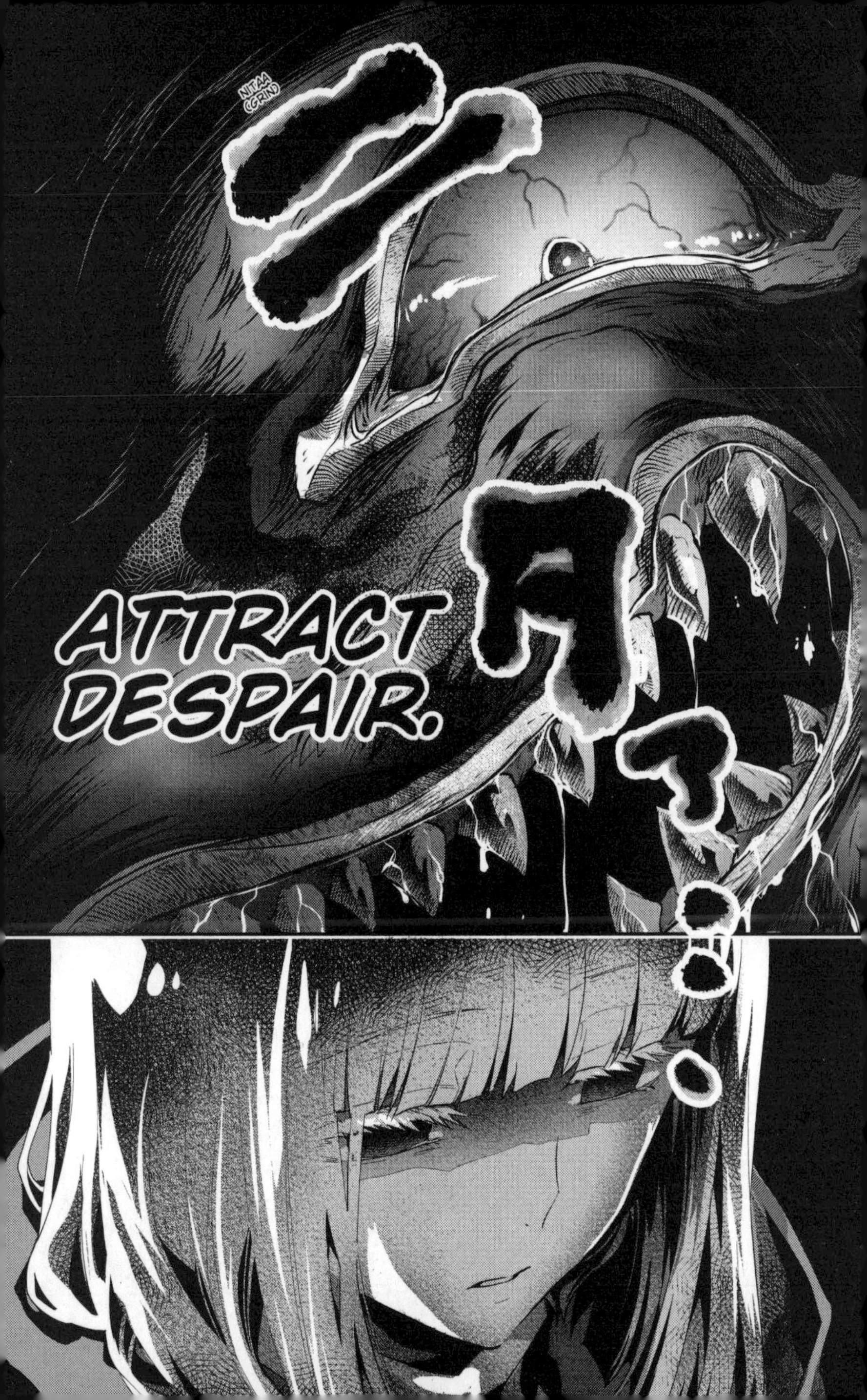
NITAA (GRIN)
ATTRACT DESPAIR.

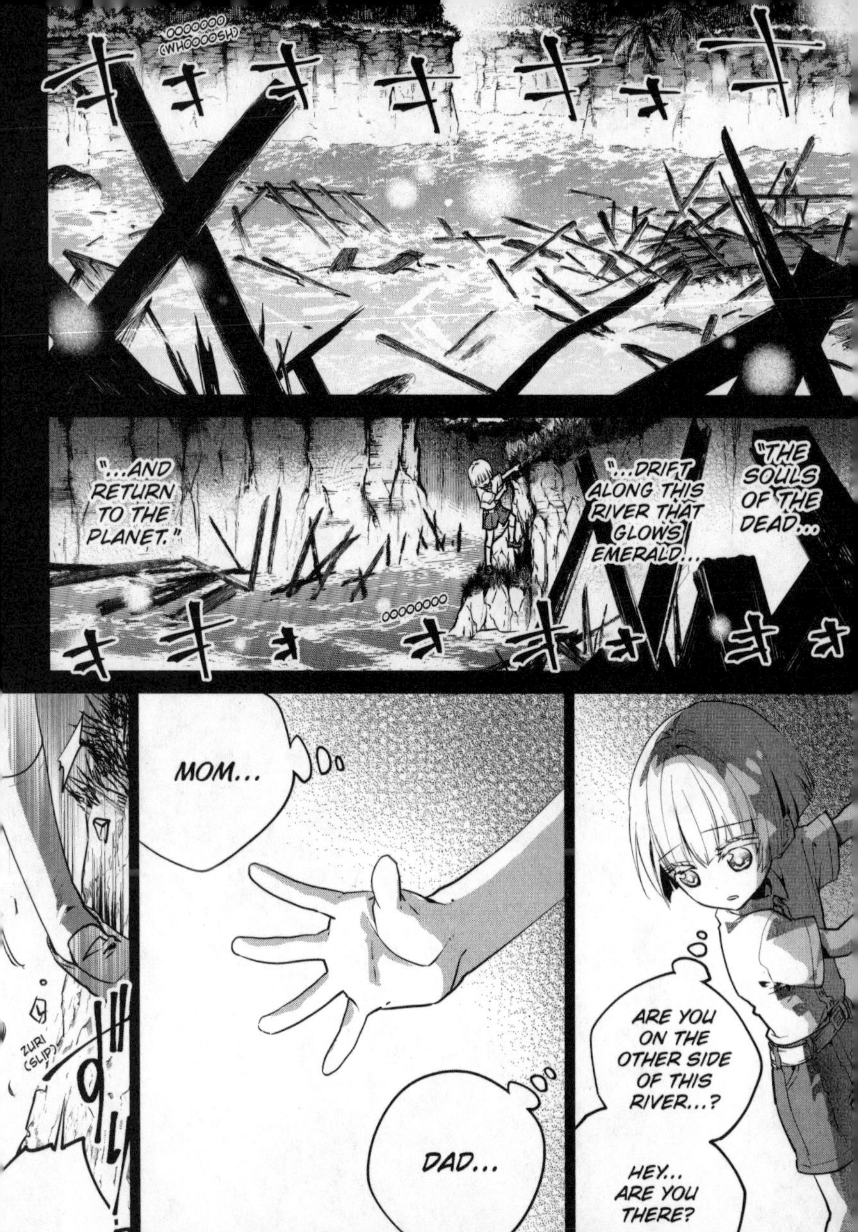
OOOOOOO
(WHOOOOSH)
"THE SOULS OF THE DEAD...
"...DRIFT ALONG THIS RIVER THAT GLOWS EMERALD...
"...AND RETURN TO THE PLANET."
OOOOOOOO
ARE YOU ON THE OTHER SIDE OF THIS RIVER...?
HEY... ARE YOU THERE?
MOM...
DAD...
ZURI (SLIP)
AH!

## Chapter 26 Lifestream

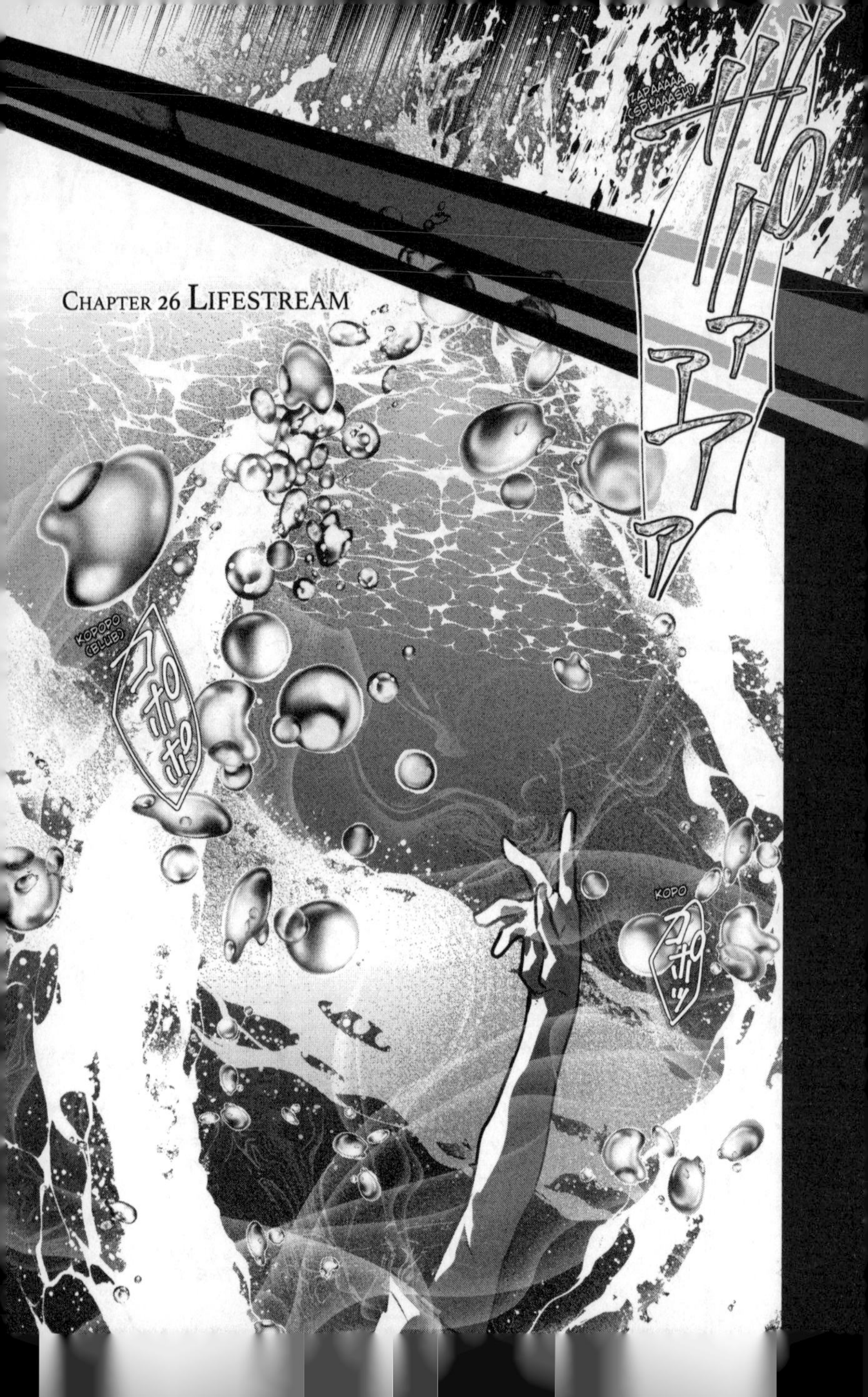
ザパアアアア
ZAPAAAAA (SPLAAASH)
コポポ
KOPOPO (BLUB)
コポッ
KOPO

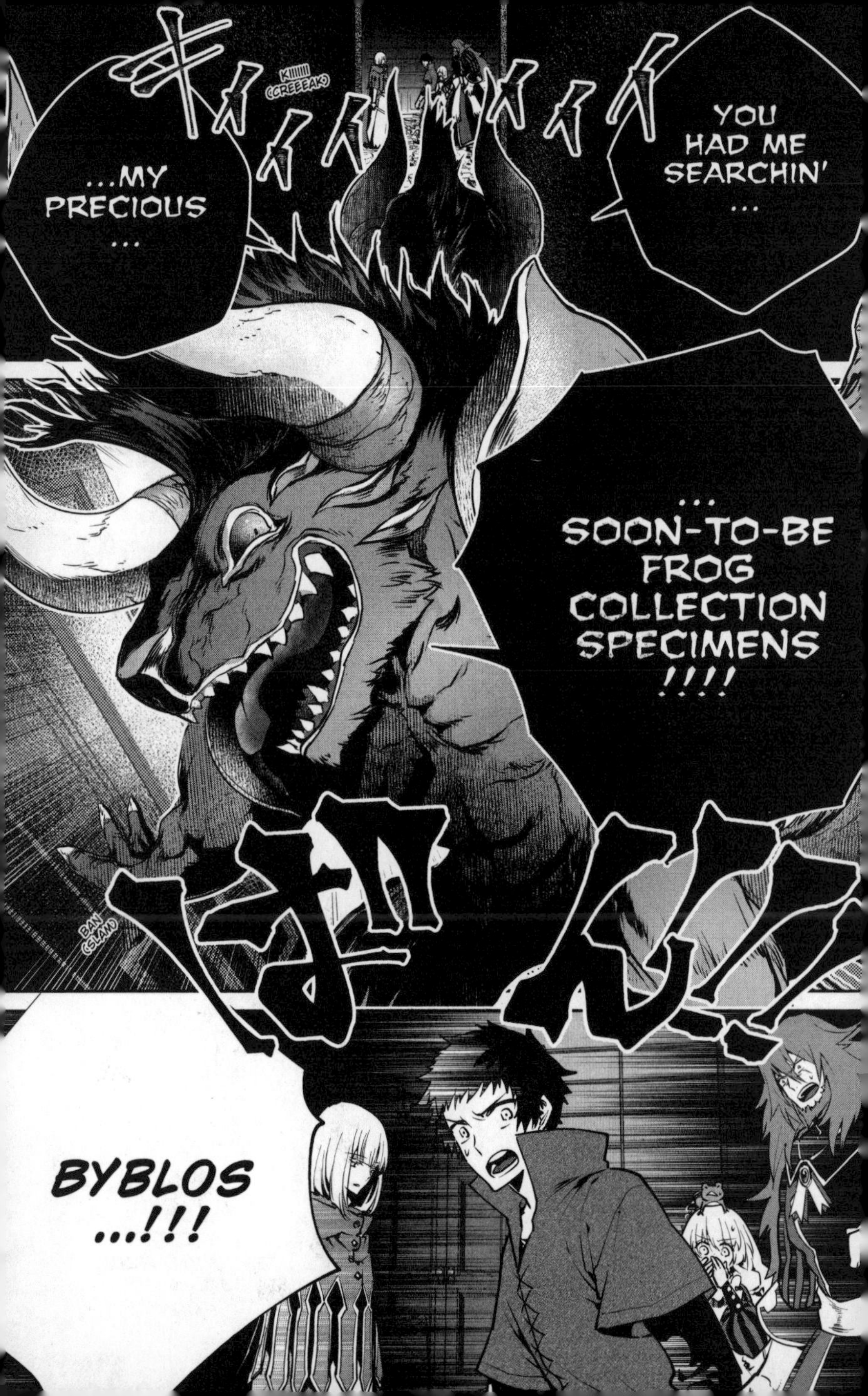
KIIIIIII (CREEEAK)
YOU HAD ME SEARCHIN' ...
...MY PRECIOUS ...
... SOON-TO-BE FROG COLLECTION SPECIMENS !!!!
BAN (SLAM)
BYBLOS ...!!!

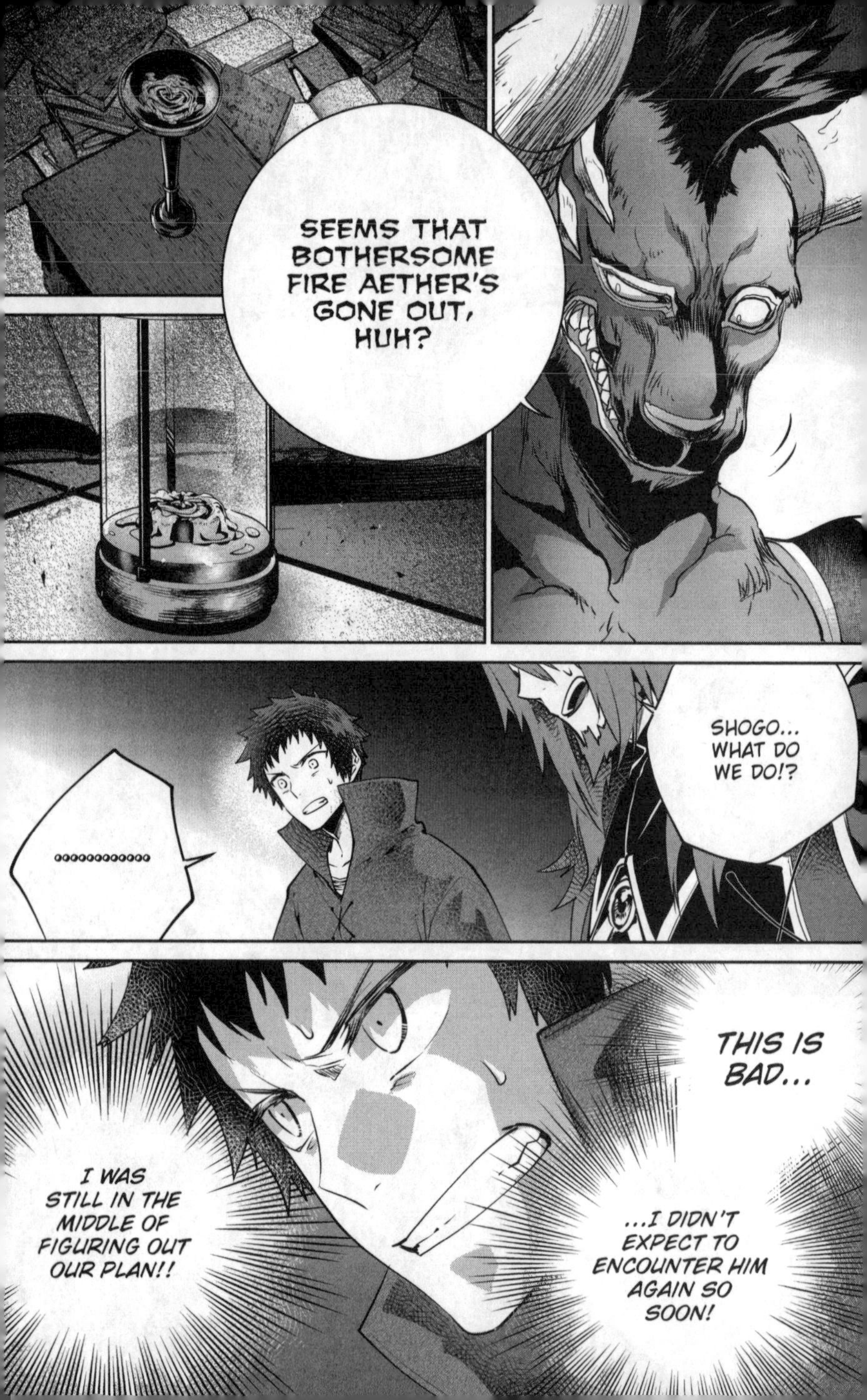
SEEMS THAT BOTHERSOME FIRE AETHER'S GONE OUT, HUH?
SHOGO... WHAT DO WE DO!?
............
THIS IS BAD...
...I DIDN'T EXPECT TO ENCOUNTER HIM AGAIN SO SOON!
I WAS STILL IN THE MIDDLE OF FIGURING OUT OUR PLAN!!

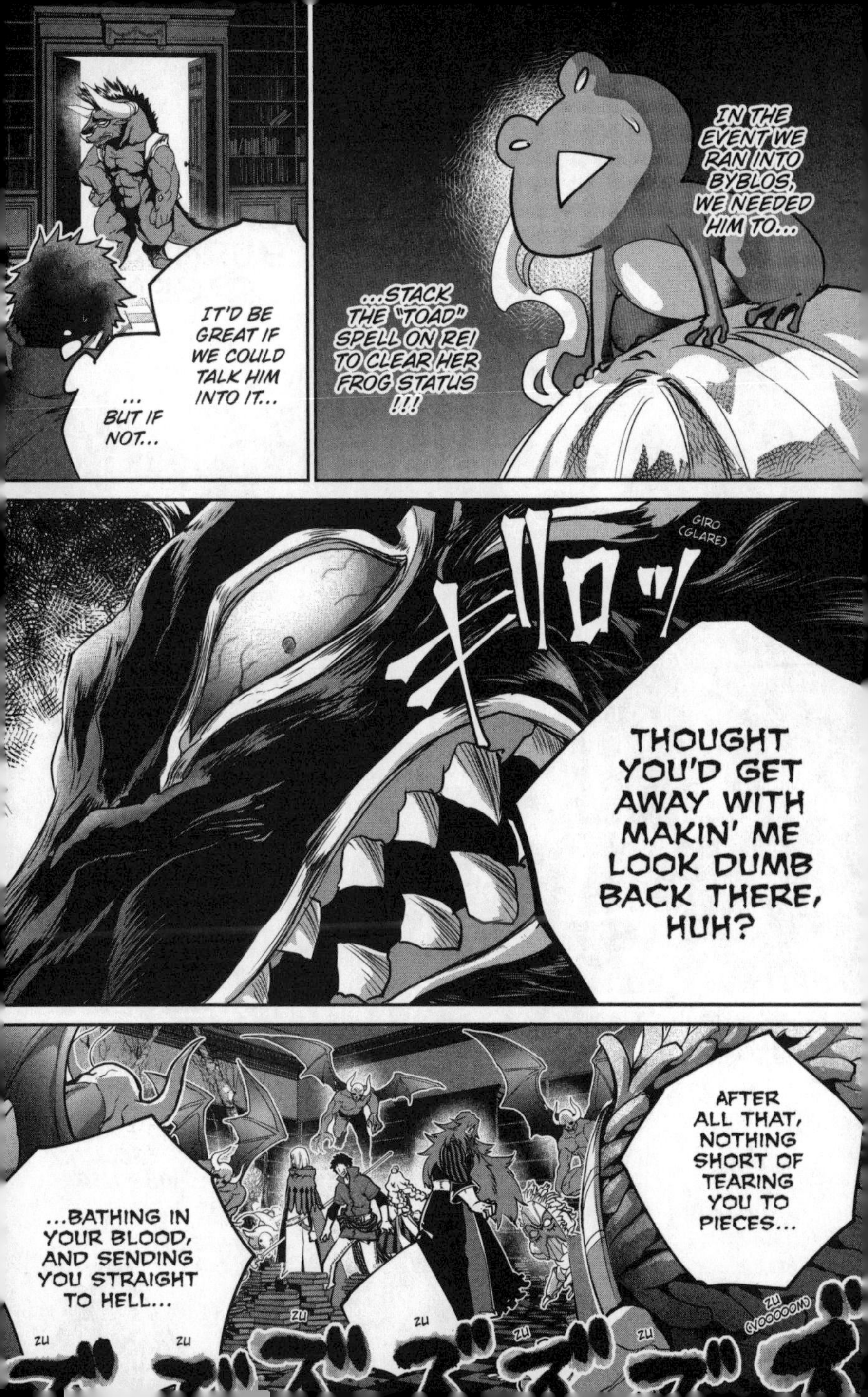
IN THE EVENT WE RAN INTO BYBLOS, WE NEEDED HIM TO...
...STACK THE "TOAD" SPELL ON REI TO CLEAR HER FROG STATUS !!!
IT'D BE GREAT IF WE COULD TALK HIM INTO IT...
... BUT IF NOT...
GIRO (GLARE)
THOUGHT YOU'D GET AWAY WITH MAKIN' ME LOOK DUMB BACK THERE, HUH?
AFTER ALL THAT, NOTHING SHORT OF TEARING YOU TO PIECES...
...BATHING IN YOUR BLOOD, AND SENDING YOU STRAIGHT TO HELL...
ZU (VOOOOOM)
ZU
ZU
ZU
ZU
ZU
ZU
ZU

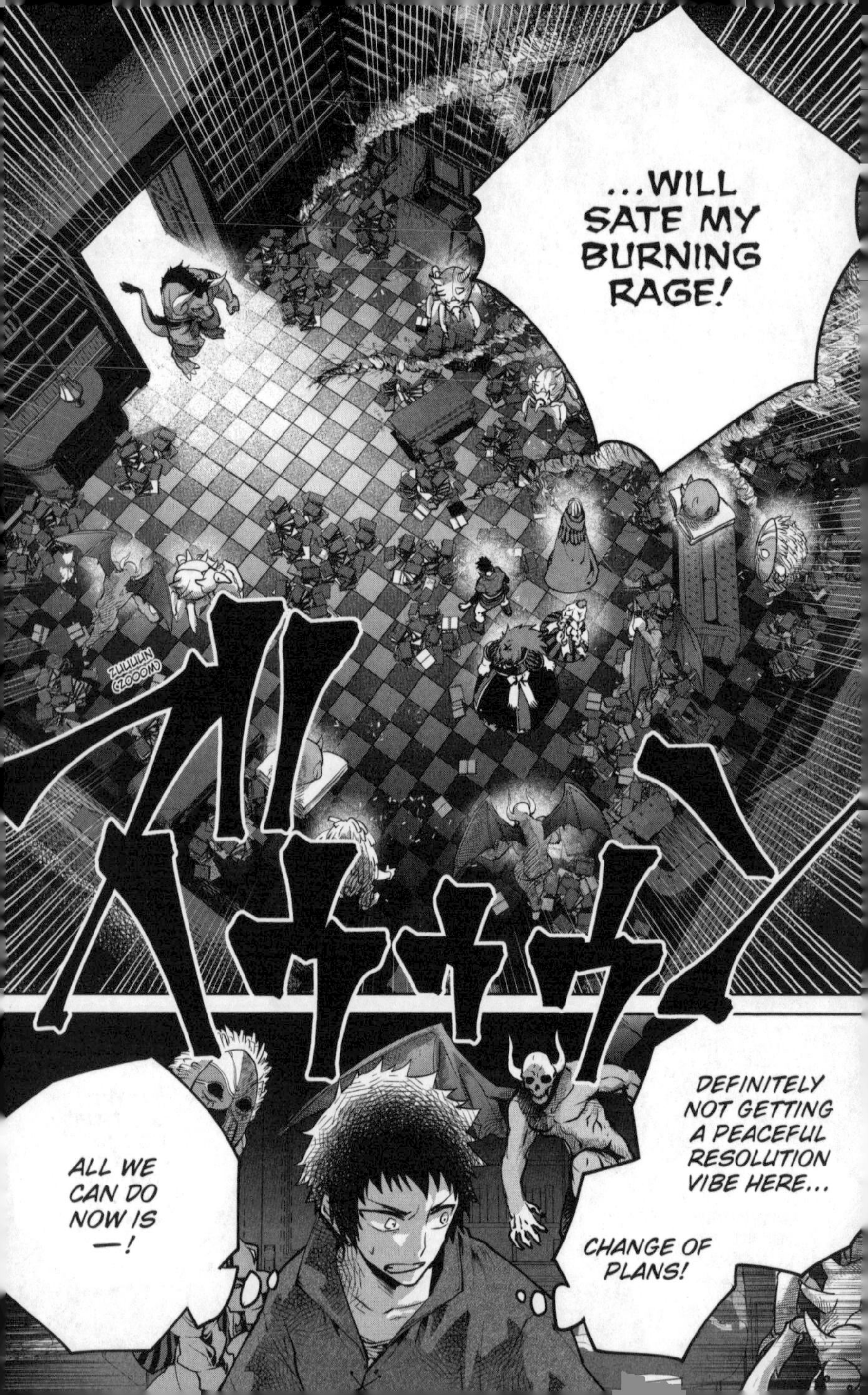
...WILL SATE MY BURNING RAGE!
ZUUUUN (ZOOOM)
DEFINITELY NOT GETTING A PEACEFUL RESOLUTION VIBE HERE...
CHANGE OF PLANS!
ALL WE CAN DO NOW IS —!

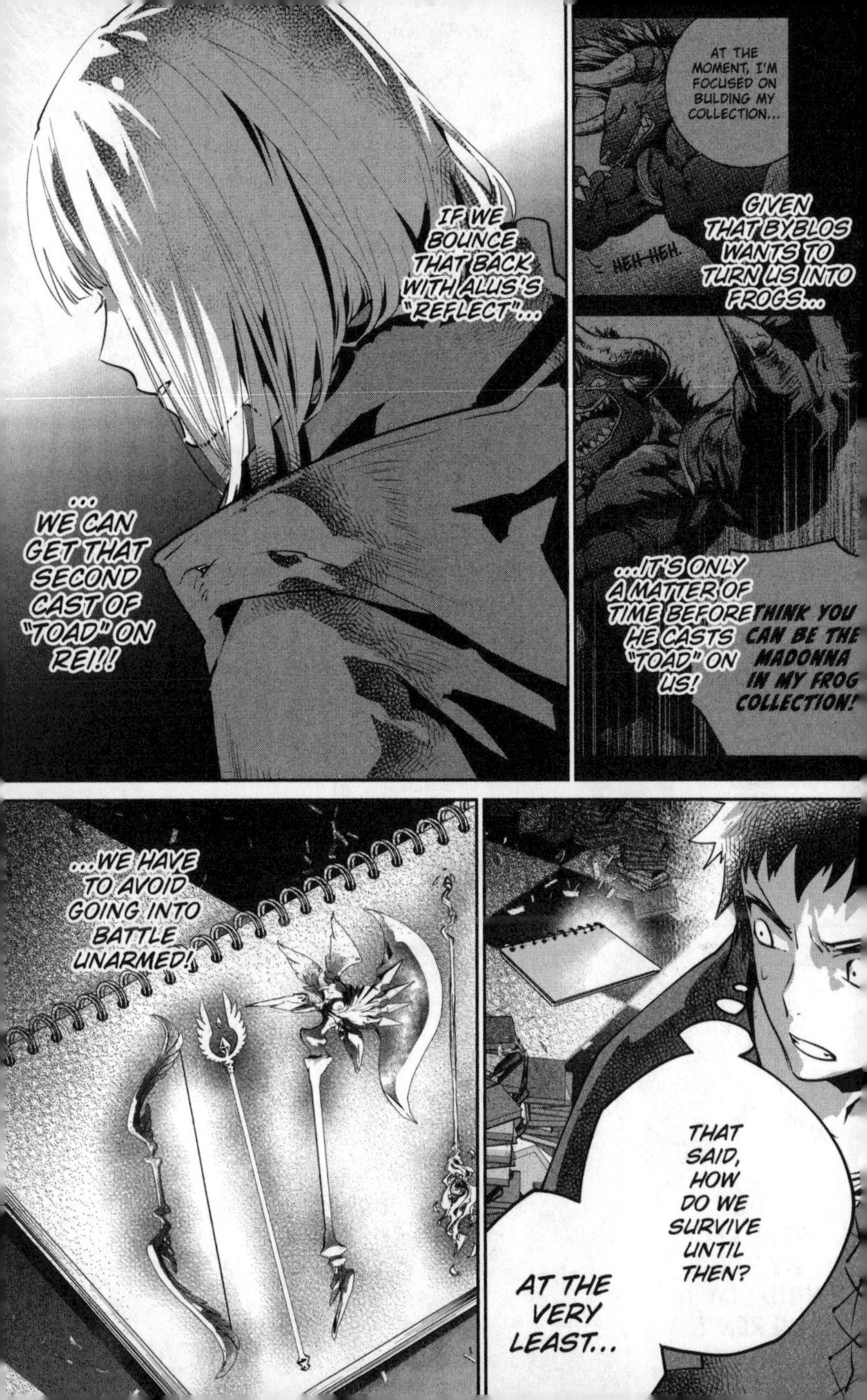
AT THE MOMENT, I'M FOCUSED ON BULDING MY COLLECTION...
HEH HEH.
GIVEN THAT BYBLOS WANTS TO TURN US INTO FROGS...
THINK YOU CAN BE THE MADONNA IN MY FROG COLLECTION!
...IT'S ONLY A MATTER OF TIME BEFORE HE CASTS "TOAD" ON US!
IF WE BOUNCE THAT BACK WITH ALUS'S "REFLECT"...
...WE CAN GET THAT SECOND CAST OF "TOAD" ON REI!!
THAT SAID, HOW DO WE SURVIVE UNTIL THEN?
AT THE VERY LEAST...
...WE HAVE TO AVOID GOING INTO BATTLE UNARMED!

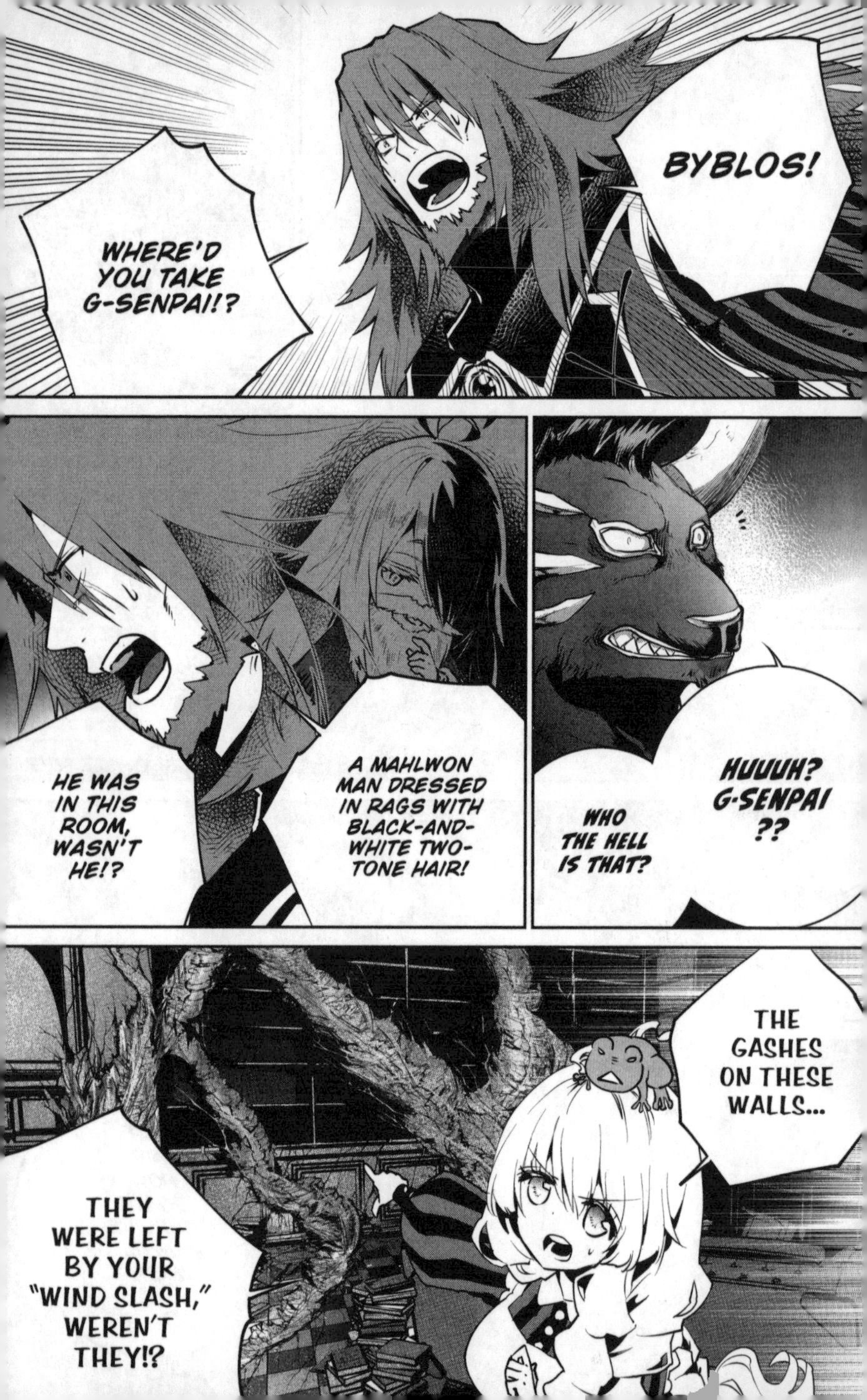
BYBLOS!
WHERE'D YOU TAKE G-SENPAI!?
HUUUH? G-SENPAI ??
WHO THE HELL IS THAT?
A MAHLWON MAN DRESSED IN RAGS WITH BLACK-AND-WHITE TWO-TONE HAIR!
HE WAS IN THIS ROOM, WASN'T HE!?
THE GASHES ON THESE WALLS...
THEY WERE LEFT BY YOUR "WIND SLASH," WEREN'T THEY!?

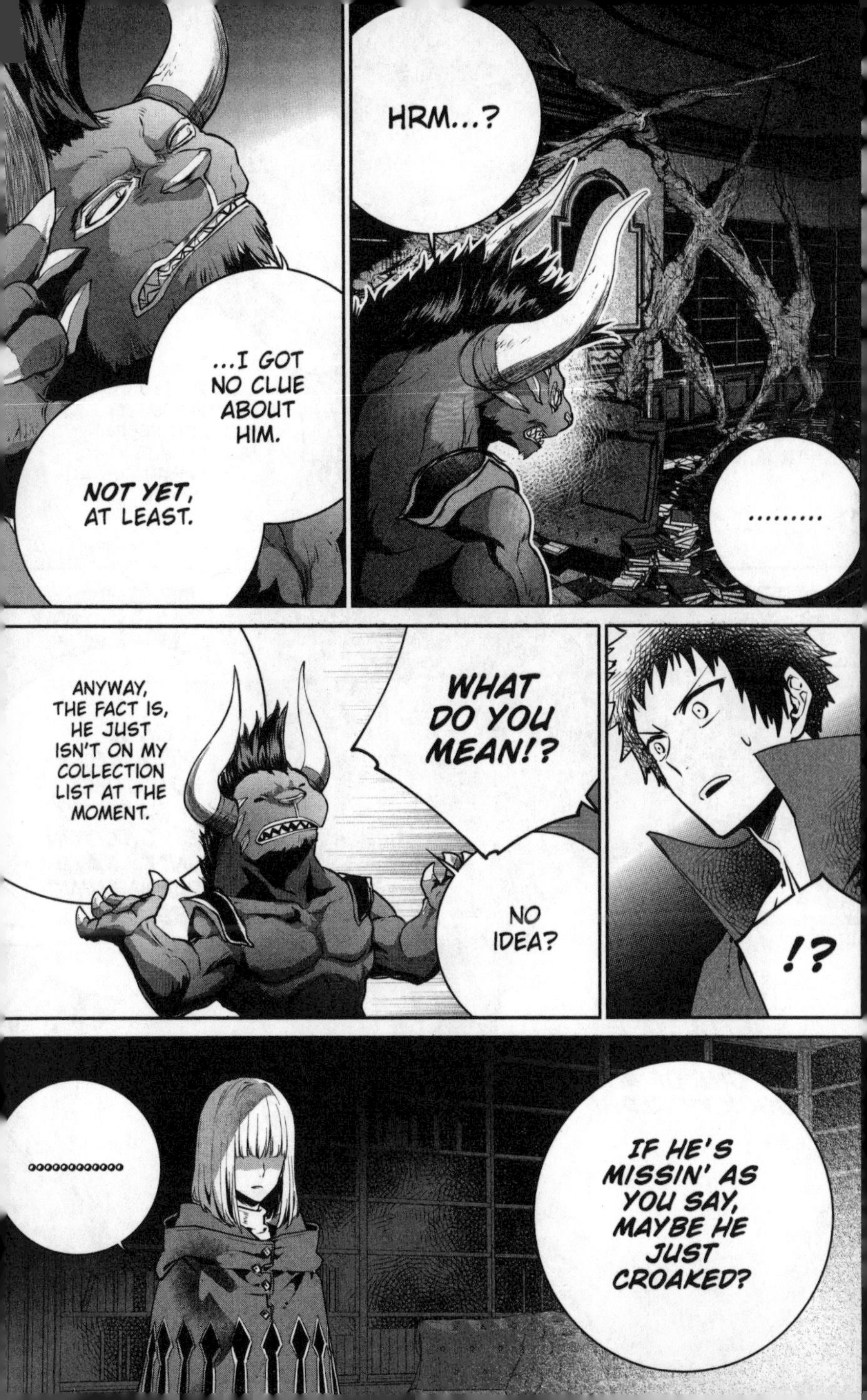

HRM...?
.........
...I GOT NO CLUE ABOUT HIM.
NOT YET, AT LEAST.
!?
WHAT DO YOU MEAN!?
NO IDEA?
ANYWAY, THE FACT IS, HE JUST ISN'T ON MY COLLECTION LIST AT THE MOMENT.
IF HE'S MISSIN' AS YOU SAY, MAYBE HE JUST CROAKED?
.............

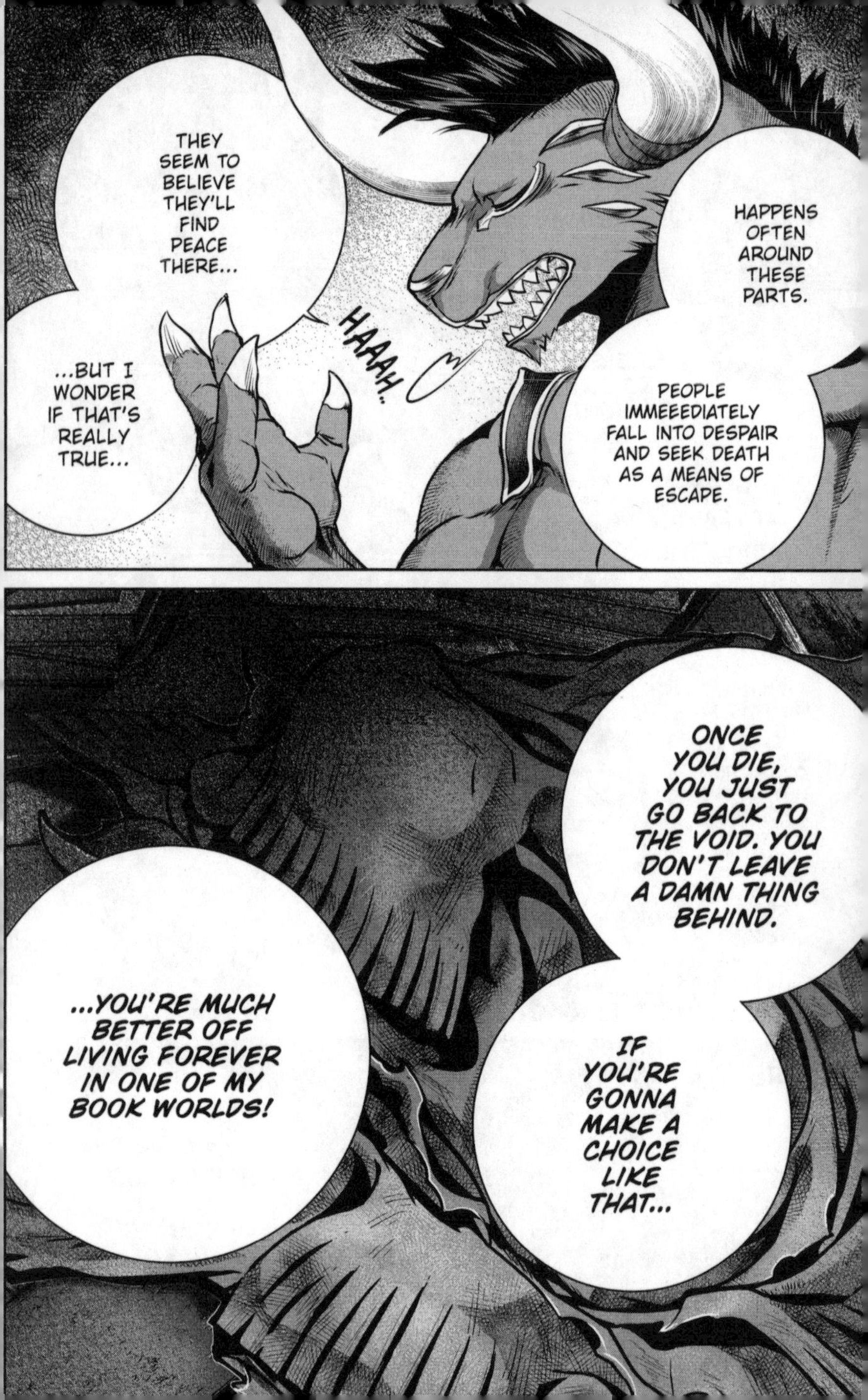
HAPPENS OFTEN AROUND THESE PARTS.
PEOPLE IMMEEEDIATELY FALL INTO DESPAIR AND SEEK DEATH AS A MEANS OF ESCAPE.
THEY SEEM TO BELIEVE THEY'LL FIND PEACE THERE...
HAAAH..
...BUT I WONDER IF THAT'S REALLY TRUE...
ONCE YOU DIE, YOU JUST GO BACK TO THE VOID. YOU DON'T LEAVE A DAMN THING BEHIND.
IF YOU'RE GONNA MAKE A CHOICE LIKE THAT...
...YOU'RE MUCH BETTER OFF LIVING FOREVER IN ONE OF MY BOOK WORLDS!

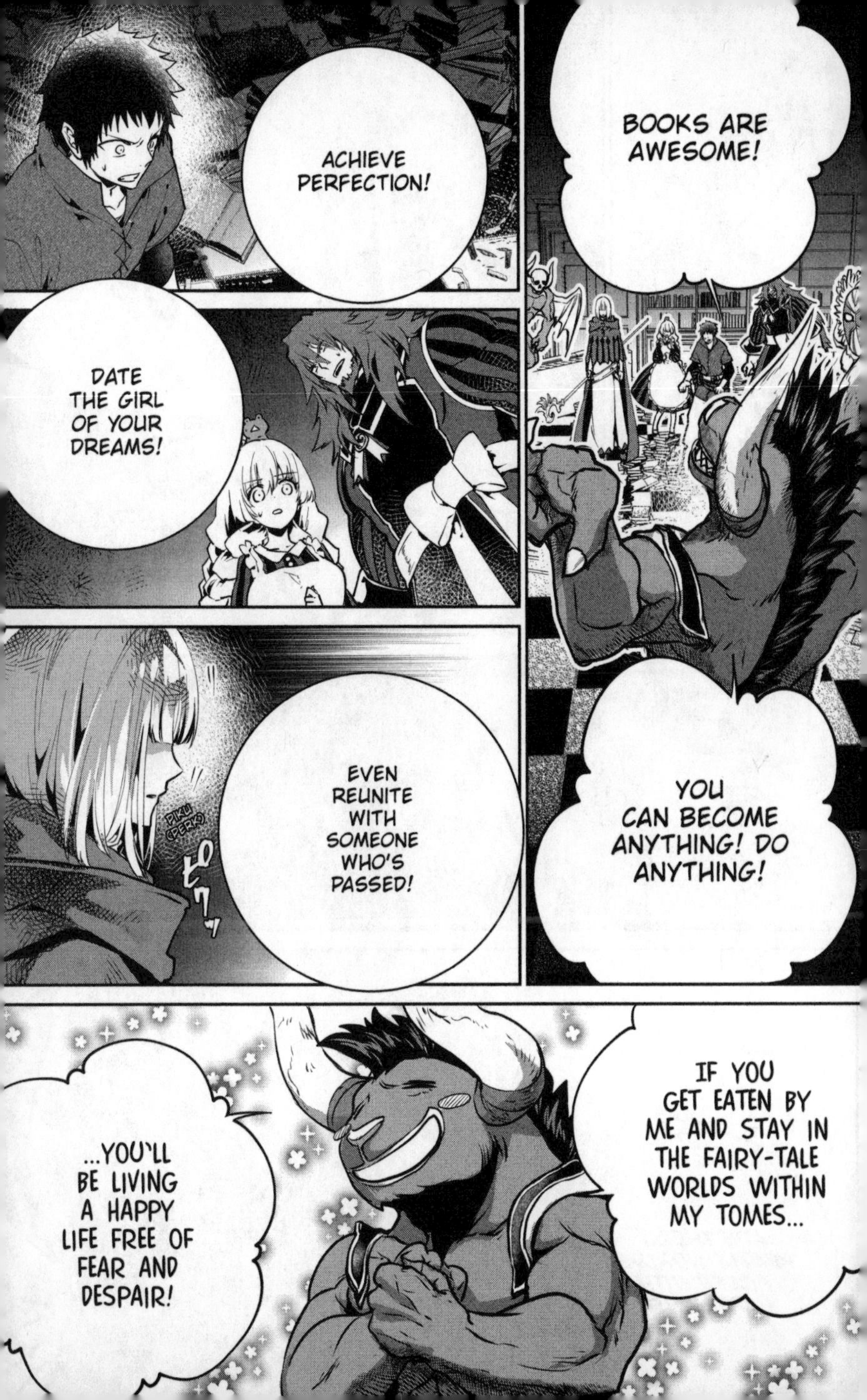
BOOKS ARE AWESOME!
YOU CAN BECOME ANYTHING! DO ANYTHING!
ACHIEVE PERFECTION!
DATE THE GIRL OF YOUR DREAMS!
EVEN REUNITE WITH SOMEONE WHO'S PASSED!
PIKU (PERK)
IF YOU GET EATEN BY ME AND STAY IN THE FAIRY-TALE WORLDS WITHIN MY TOMES...
...YOU'LL BE LIVING A HAPPY LIFE FREE OF FEAR AND DESPAIR!

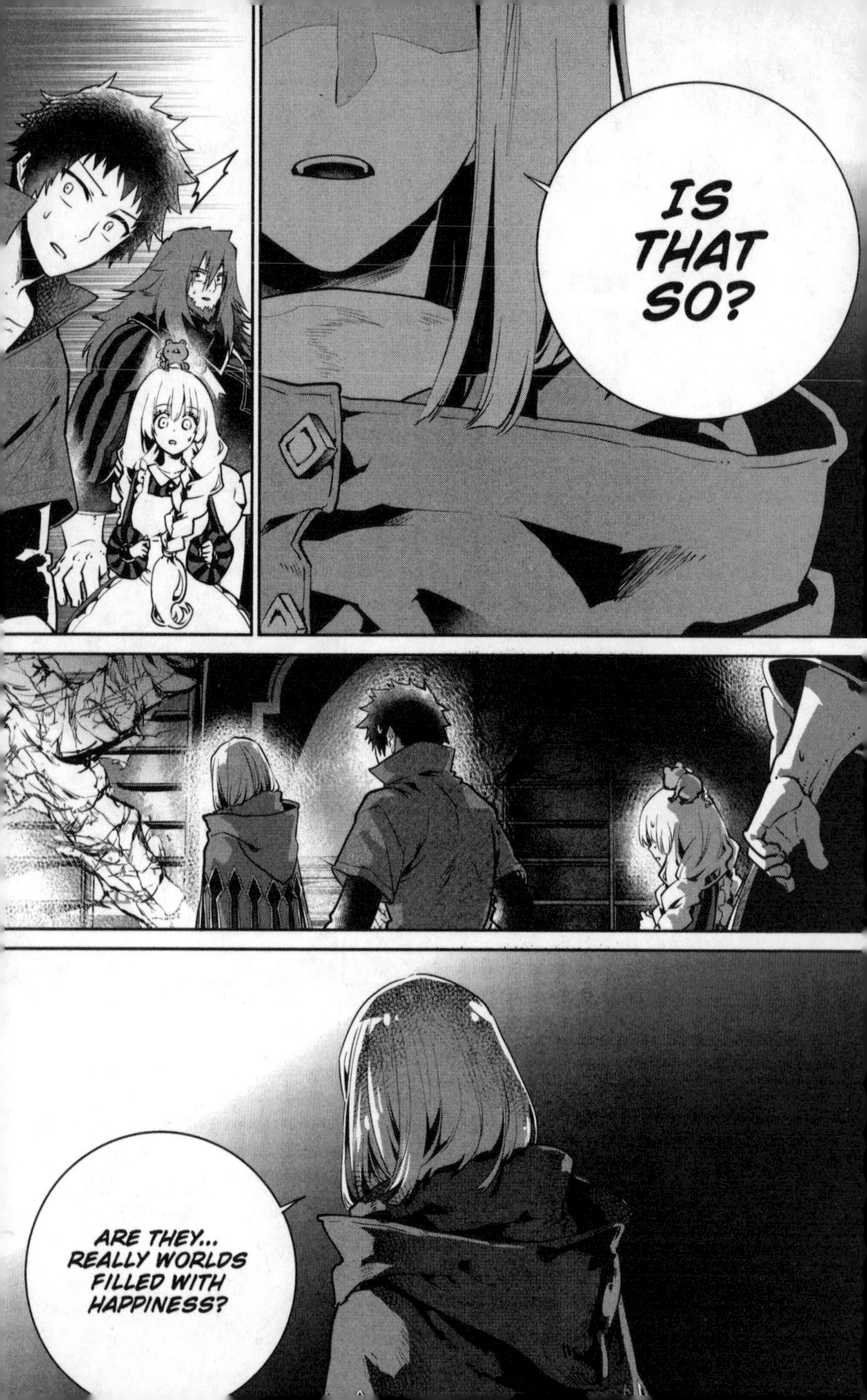
IS THAT SO?
ARE THEY... REALLY WORLDS FILLED WITH HAPPINESS?

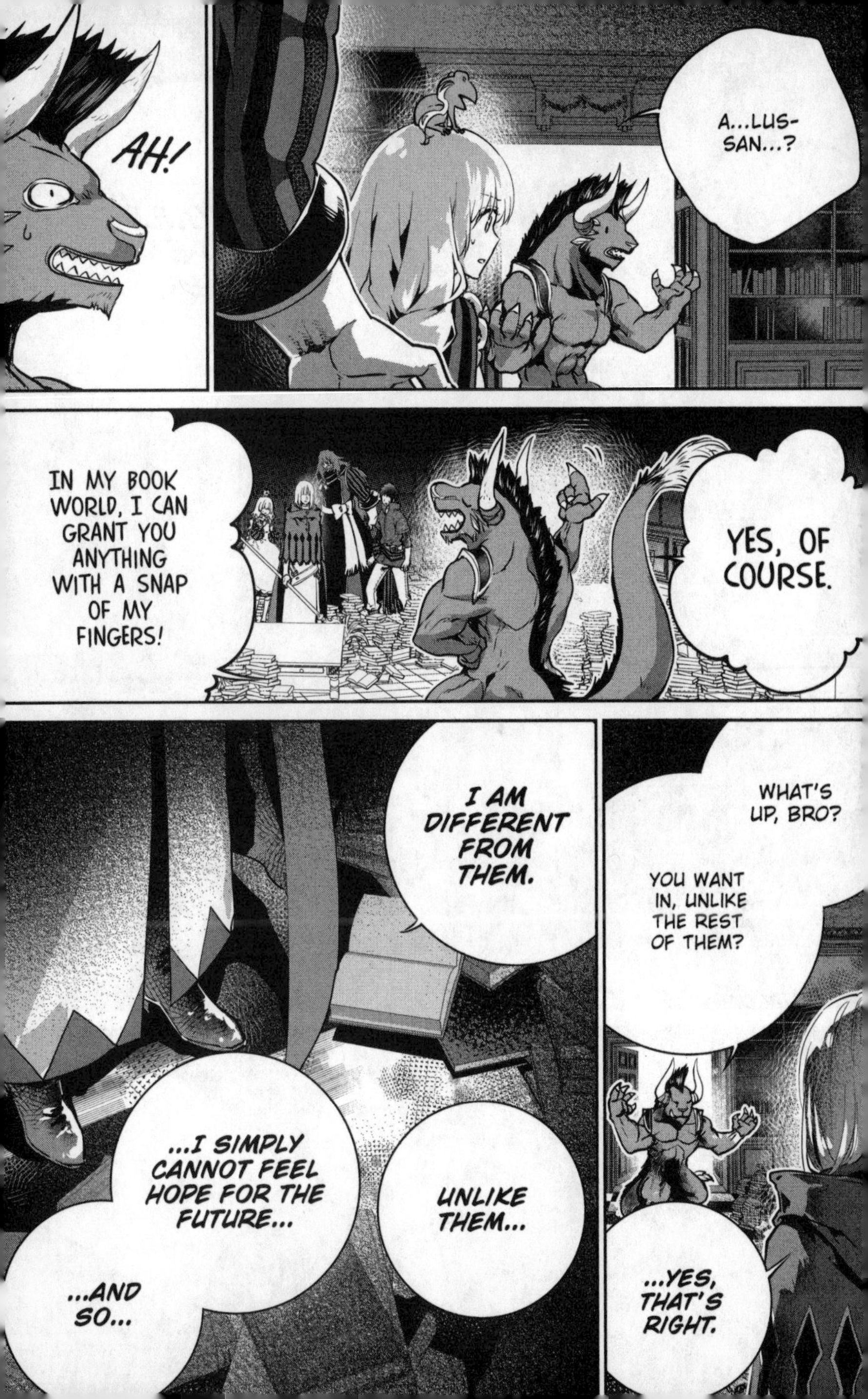
A...LUS-SAN...?
AH!
YES, OF COURSE.
IN MY BOOK WORLD, I CAN GRANT YOU ANYTHING WITH A SNAP OF MY FINGERS!
WHAT'S UP, BRO?
YOU WANT IN, UNLIKE THE REST OF THEM?
...YES, THAT'S RIGHT.
I AM DIFFERENT FROM THEM.
UNLIKE THEM...
...I SIMPLY CANNOT FEEL HOPE FOR THE FUTURE...
...AND SO...

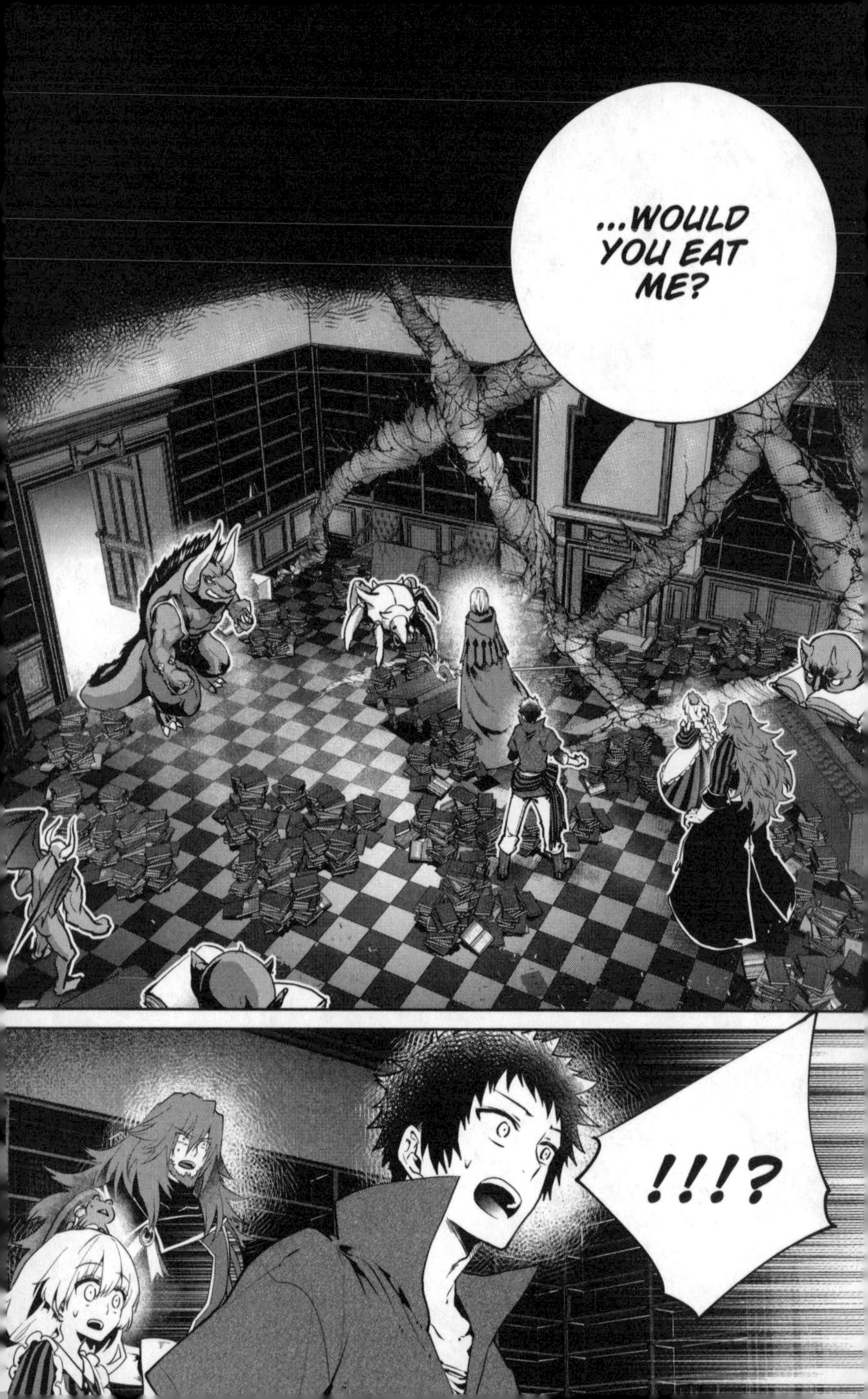
...WOULD YOU EAT ME?
!!!?

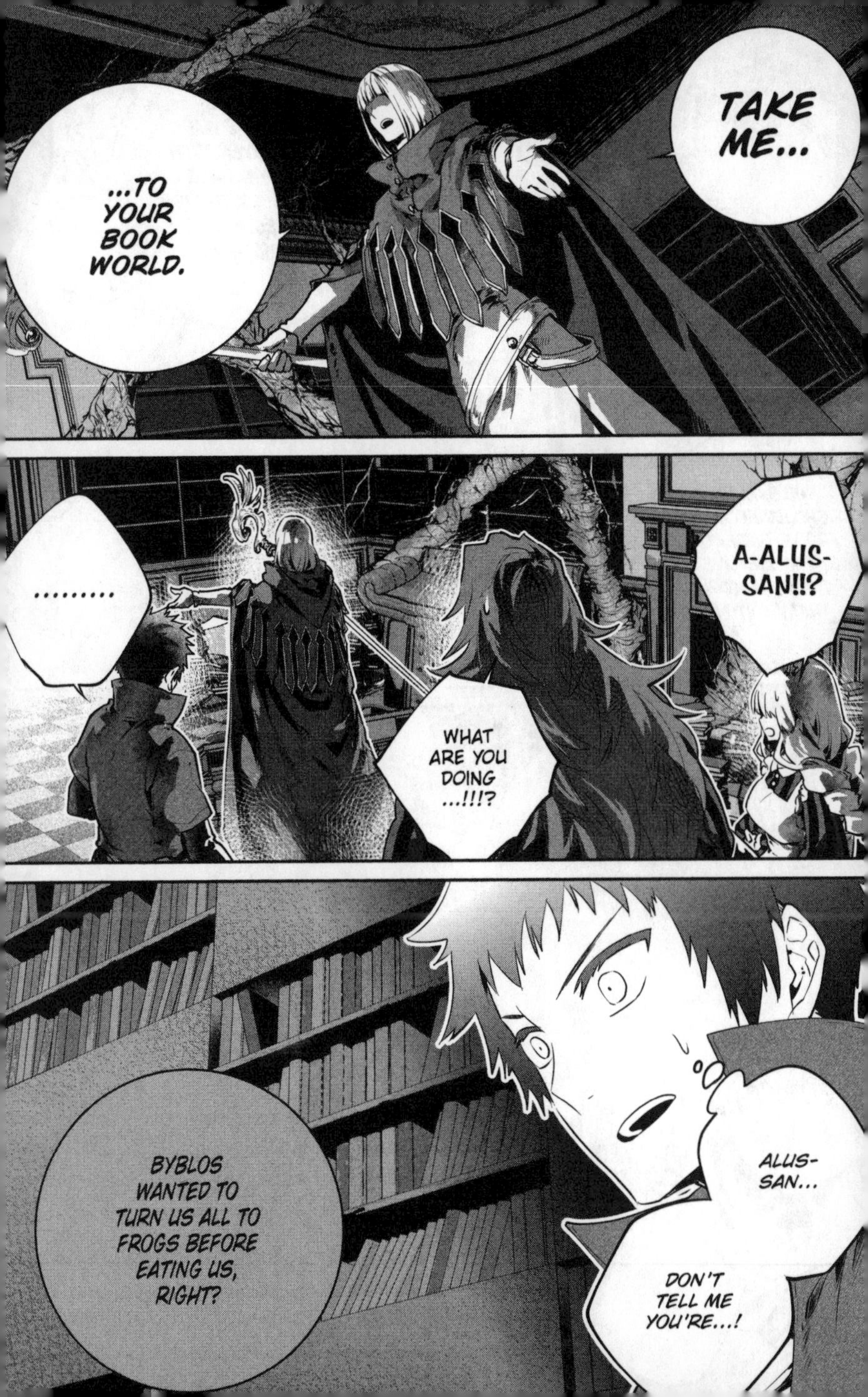
TAKE ME...
...TO YOUR BOOK WORLD.
A-ALUS-SAN!!?
WHAT ARE YOU DOING ...!!!?
.........
ALUS-SAN...
DON'T TELL ME YOU'RE...!
BYBLOS WANTED TO TURN US ALL TO FROGS BEFORE EATING US, RIGHT?

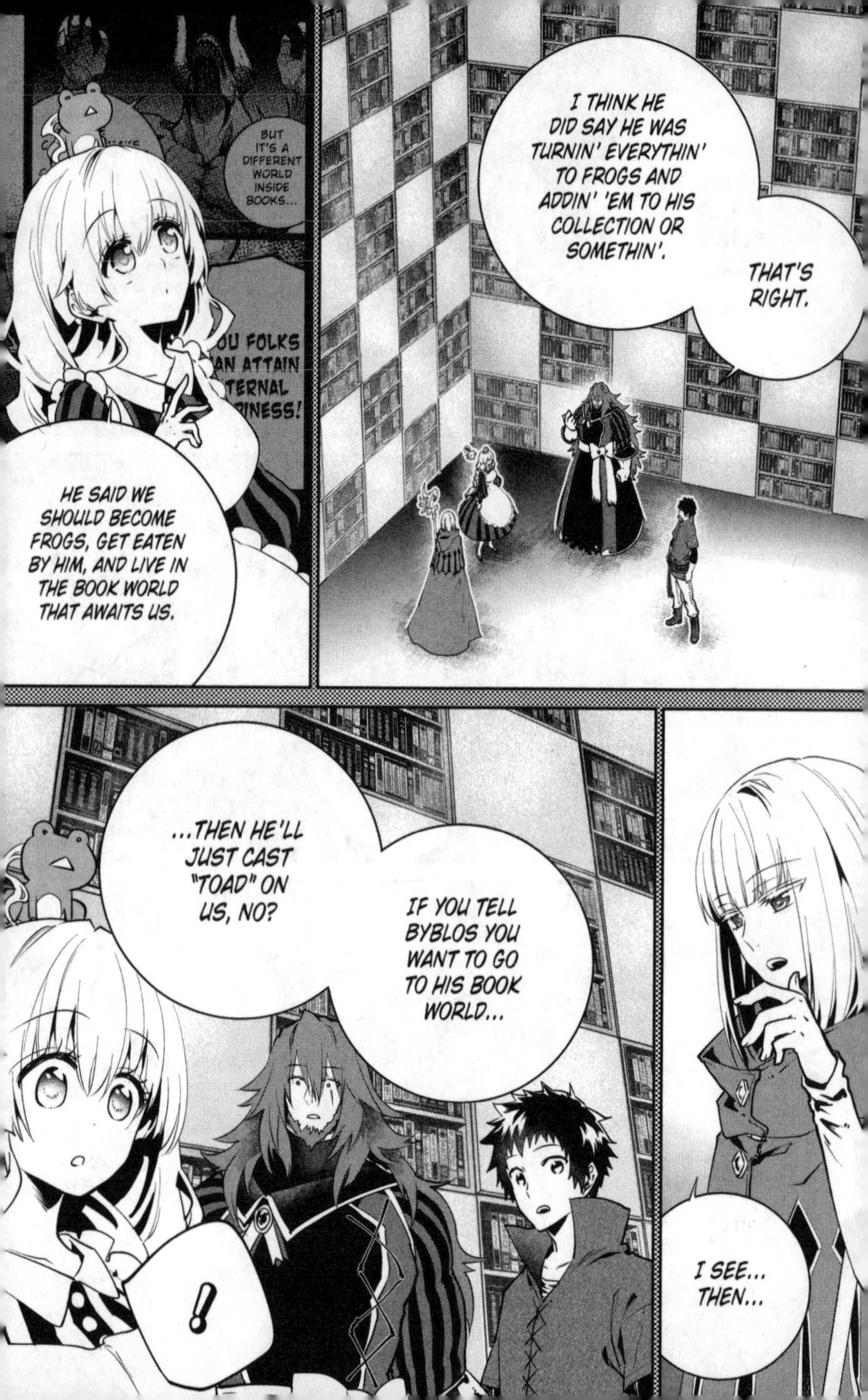
I THINK HE DID SAY HE WAS TURNIN' EVERYTHIN' TO FROGS AND ADDIN' 'EM TO HIS COLLECTION OR SOMETHIN'.
THAT'S RIGHT.
BUT IT'S A DIFFERENT WORLD INSIDE BOOKS...
HE SAID WE SHOULD BECOME FROGS, GET EATEN BY HIM, AND LIVE IN THE BOOK WORLD THAT AWAITS US.
I SEE... THEN...
IF YOU TELL BYBLOS YOU WANT TO GO TO HIS BOOK WORLD...
...THEN HE'LL JUST CAST "TOAD" ON US, NO?
!

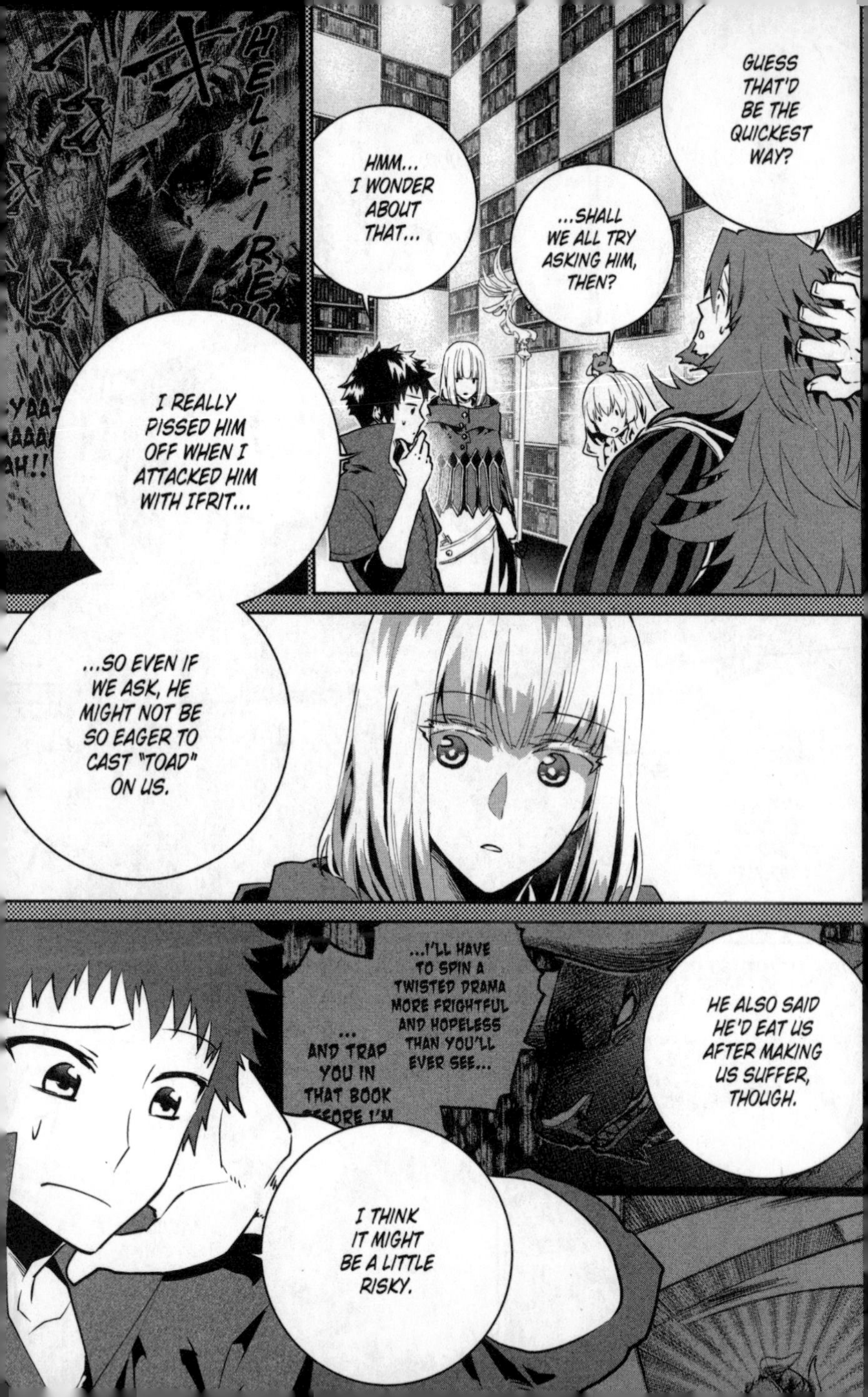
GUESS THAT'D BE THE QUICKEST WAY?
...SHALL WE ALL TRY ASKING HIM, THEN?
HMM... I WONDER ABOUT THAT...
I REALLY PISSED HIM OFF WHEN I ATTACKED HIM WITH IFRIT...
HELLFIRE!!
...SO EVEN IF WE ASK, HE MIGHT NOT BE SO EAGER TO CAST "TOAD" ON US.
HE ALSO SAID HE'D EAT US AFTER MAKING US SUFFER, THOUGH.
...I'LL HAVE TO SPIN A TWISTED DRAMA MORE FRIGHTFUL AND HOPELESS THAN YOU'LL EVER SEE...
...AND TRAP YOU IN THAT BOOK
I THINK IT MIGHT BE A LITTLE RISKY.

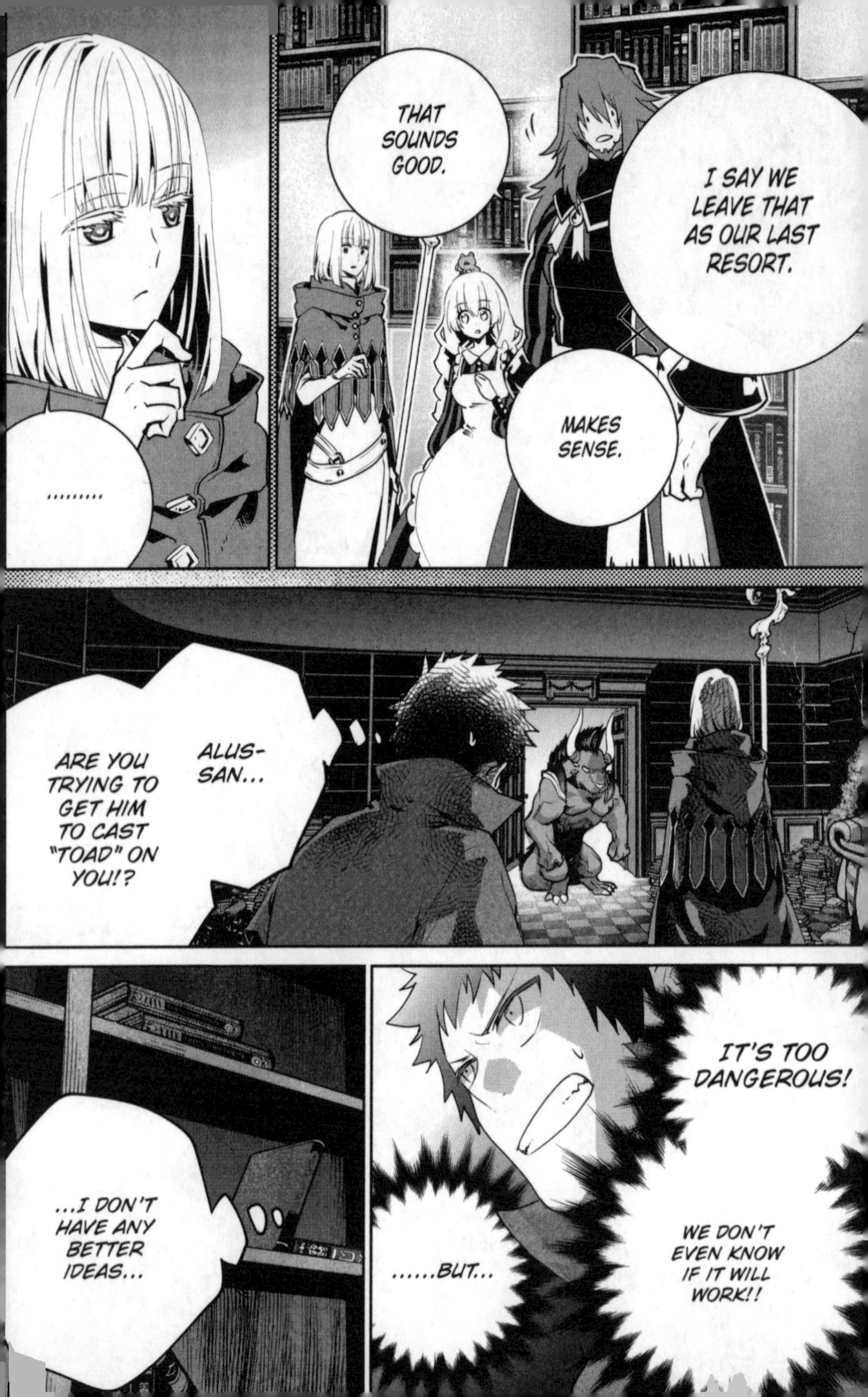
I SAY WE LEAVE THAT AS OUR LAST RESORT.
THAT SOUNDS GOOD.
MAKES SENSE.
.........
ALUS-SAN...
ARE YOU TRYING TO GET HIM TO CAST "TOAD" ON YOU!?
IT'S TOO DANGEROUS!
WE DON'T EVEN KNOW IF IT WILL WORK!!
......BUT...
...I DON'T HAVE ANY BETTER IDEAS...

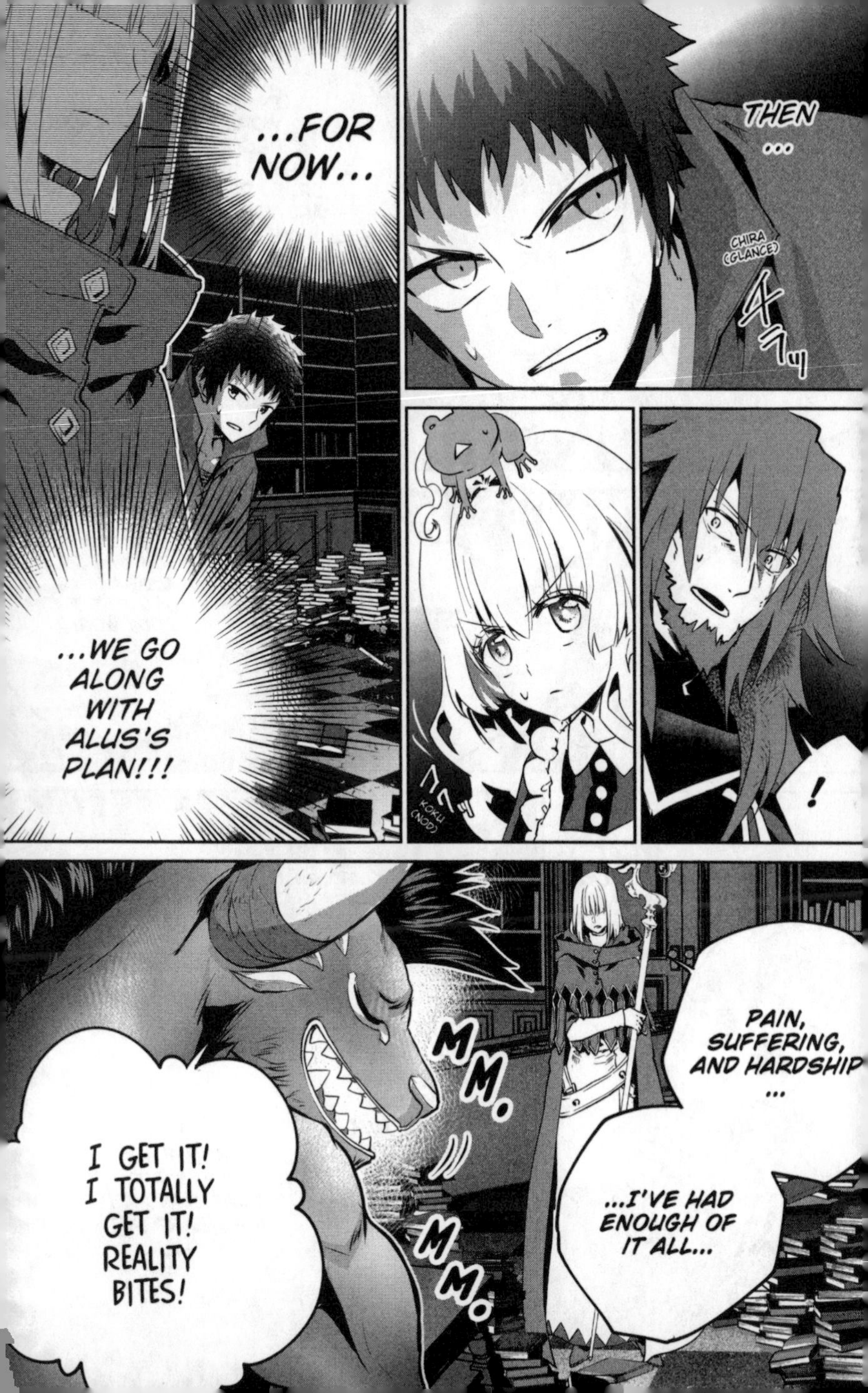
THEN...
CHIRA (GLANCE)
チラッ
!
KOKU (NOD)
...FOR NOW...
...WE GO ALONG WITH ALUS'S PLAN!!!
PAIN, SUFFERING, AND HARDSHIP...
...I'VE HAD ENOUGH OF IT ALL...
MM.
MM.
I GET IT! I TOTALLY GET IT! REALITY BITES!

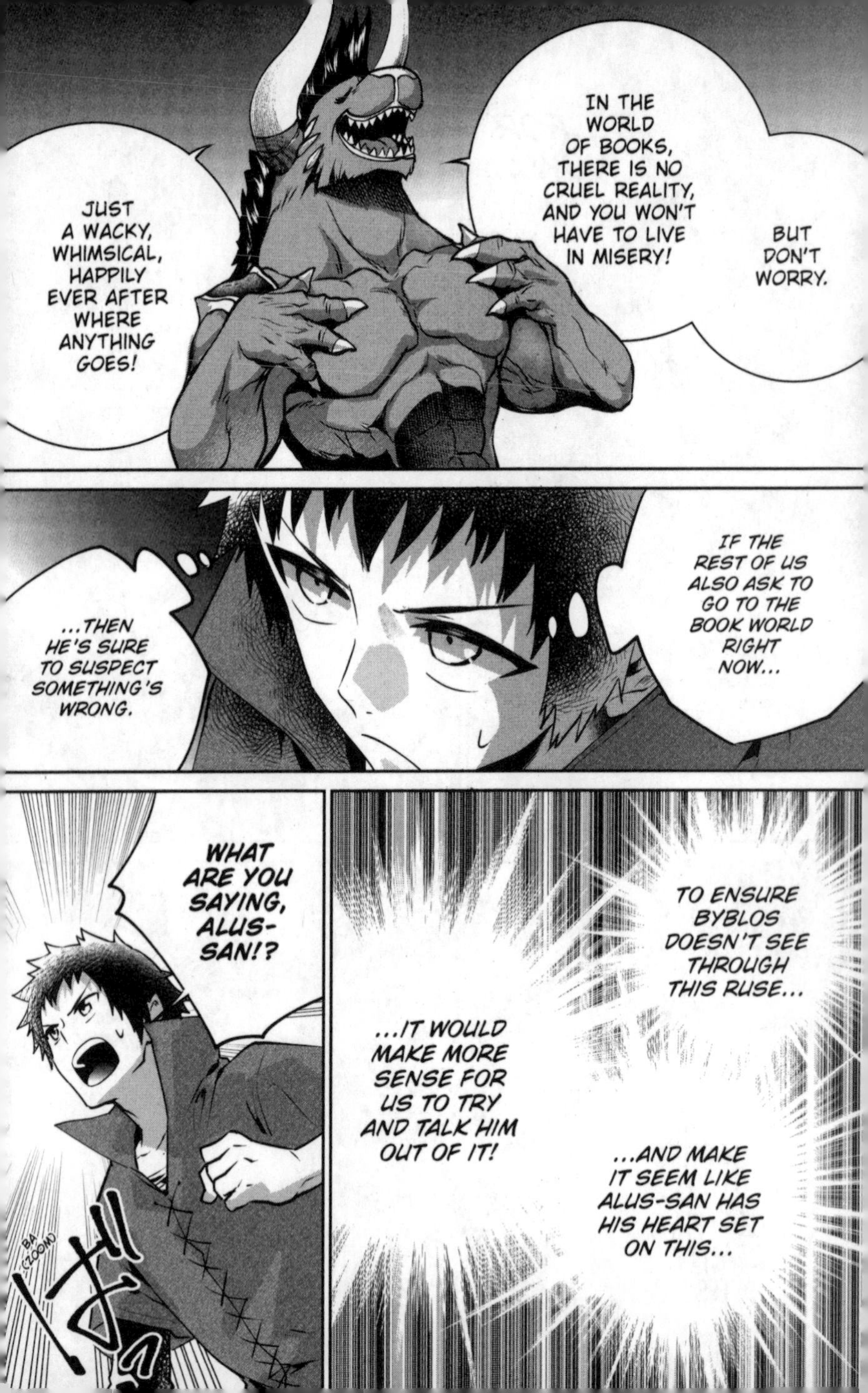
BUT DON'T WORRY.
IN THE WORLD OF BOOKS, THERE IS NO CRUEL REALITY, AND YOU WON'T HAVE TO LIVE IN MISERY!
JUST A WACKY, WHIMSICAL, HAPPILY EVER AFTER WHERE ANYTHING GOES!
IF THE REST OF US ALSO ASK TO GO TO THE BOOK WORLD RIGHT NOW...
...THEN HE'S SURE TO SUSPECT SOMETHING'S WRONG.
TO ENSURE BYBLOS DOESN'T SEE THROUGH THIS RUSE...
...AND MAKE IT SEEM LIKE ALUS-SAN HAS HIS HEART SET ON THIS...
...IT WOULD MAKE MORE SENSE FOR US TO TRY AND TALK HIM OUT OF IT!
WHAT ARE YOU SAYING, ALUS-SAN!?
BA (ZOOM)

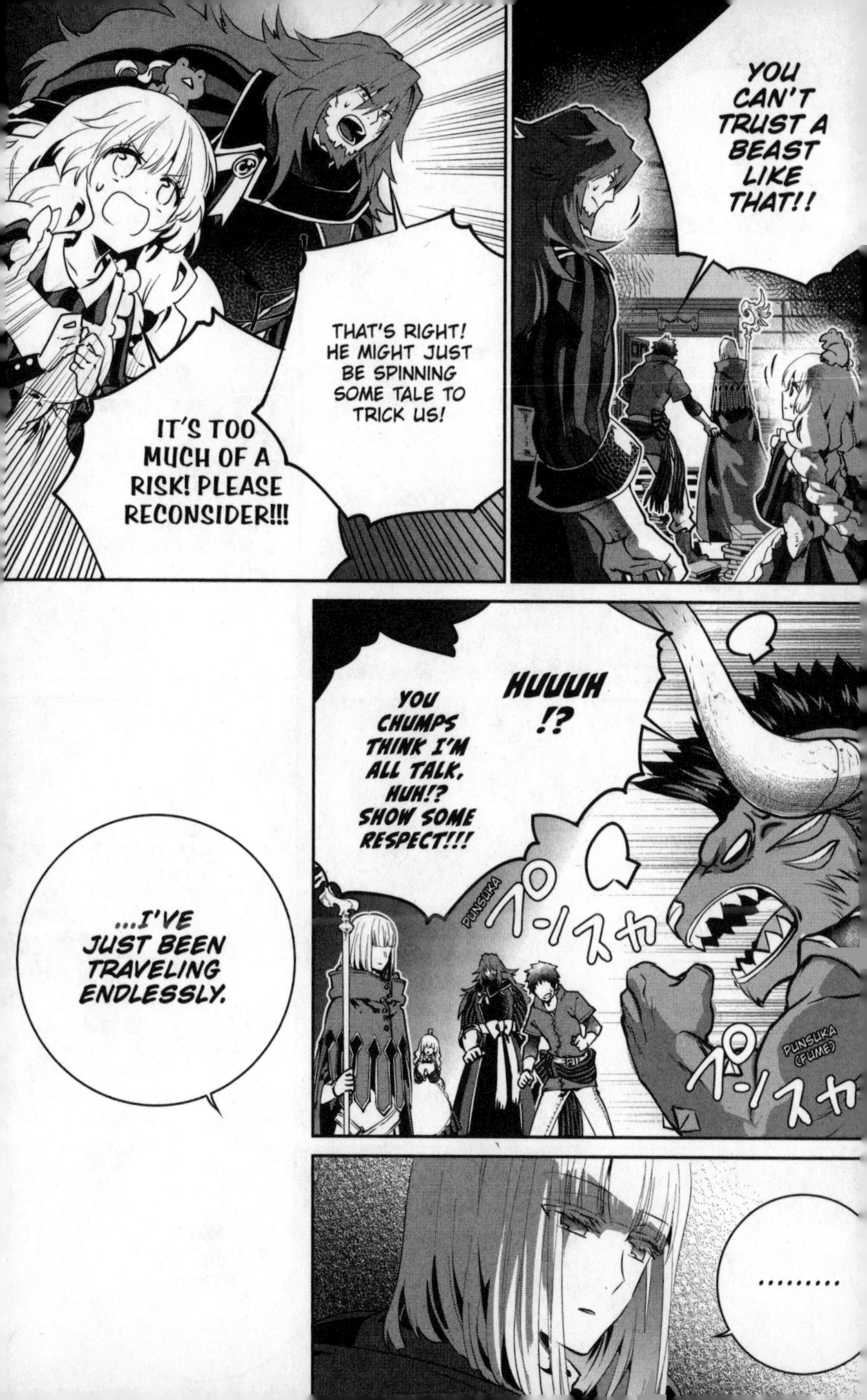
YOU CAN'T TRUST A BEAST LIKE THAT!!
THAT'S RIGHT! HE MIGHT JUST BE SPINNING SOME TALE TO TRICK US!
IT'S TOO MUCH OF A RISK! PLEASE RECONSIDER!!!
HUUUH !?
YOU CHUMPS THINK I'M ALL TALK, HUH!? SHOW SOME RESPECT!!!
プーンスカ
PUNSUKA
プーンスカ
PUNSUKA (FUME)
.........
...I'VE JUST BEEN TRAVELING ENDLESSLY.

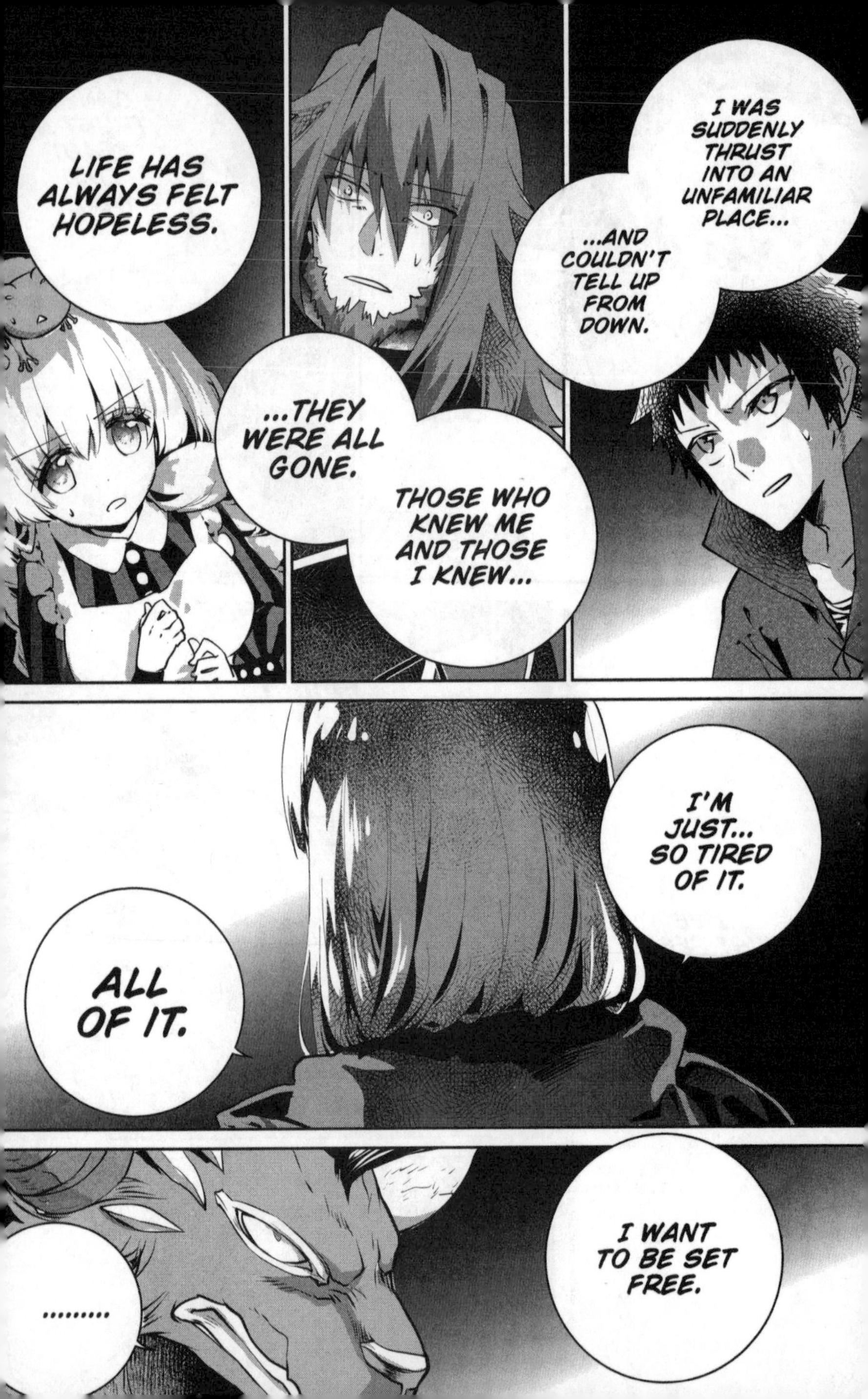
I WAS SUDDENLY THRUST INTO AN UNFAMILIAR PLACE...
...AND COULDN'T TELL UP FROM DOWN.
THOSE WHO KNEW ME AND THOSE I KNEW...
...THEY WERE ALL GONE.
LIFE HAS ALWAYS FELT HOPELESS.
I'M JUST... SO TIRED OF IT.
ALL OF IT.
I WANT TO BE SET FREE.
.........

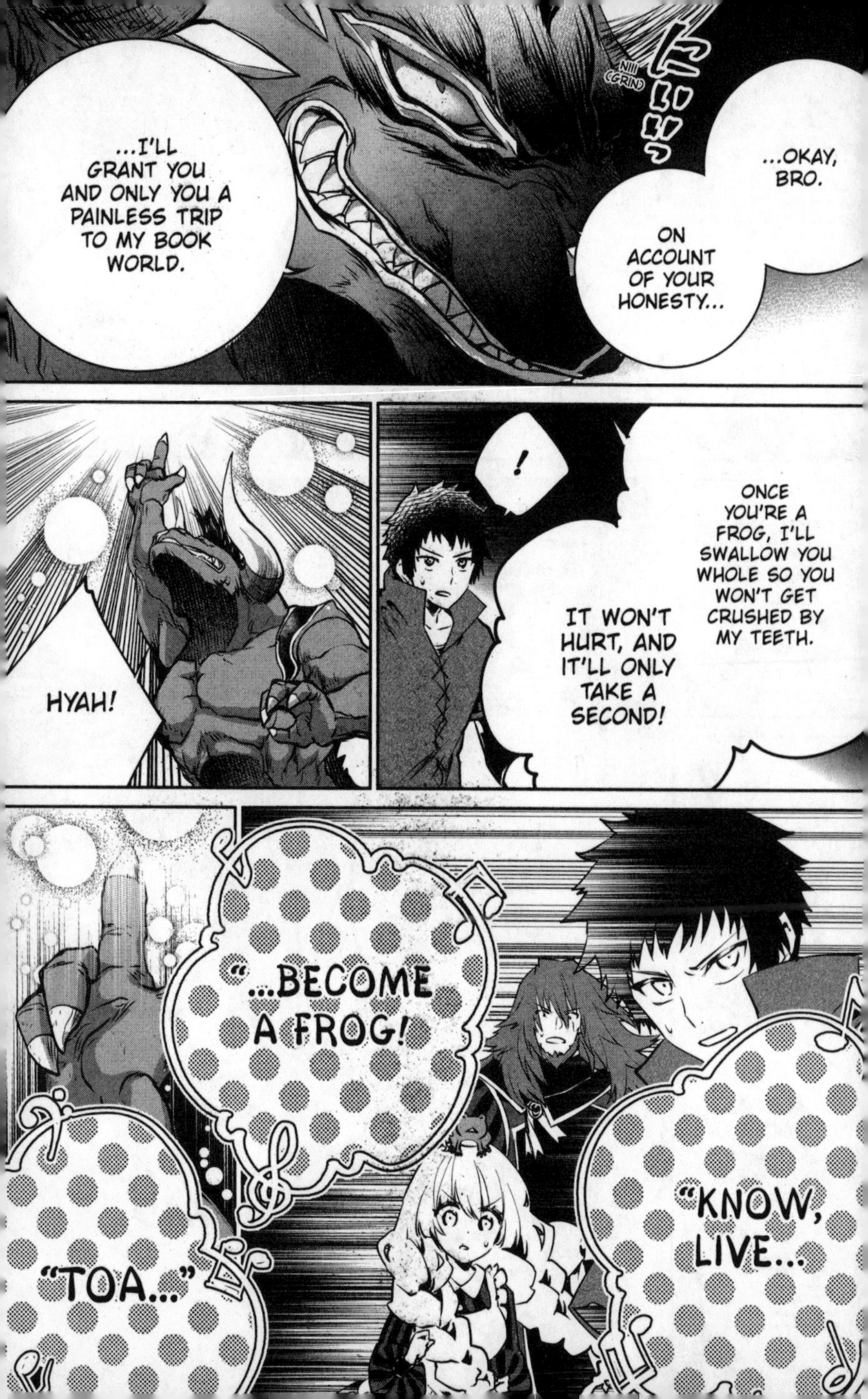
NIII (GRIN)
...OKAY, BRO.
ON ACCOUNT OF YOUR HONESTY...
...I'LL GRANT YOU AND ONLY YOU A PAINLESS TRIP TO MY BOOK WORLD.
!
ONCE YOU'RE A FROG, I'LL SWALLOW YOU WHOLE SO YOU WON'T GET CRUSHED BY MY TEETH.
IT WON'T HURT, AND IT'LL ONLY TAKE A SECOND!
HYAH!
"KNOW, LIVE...
"...BECOME A FROG!
"TOA..."

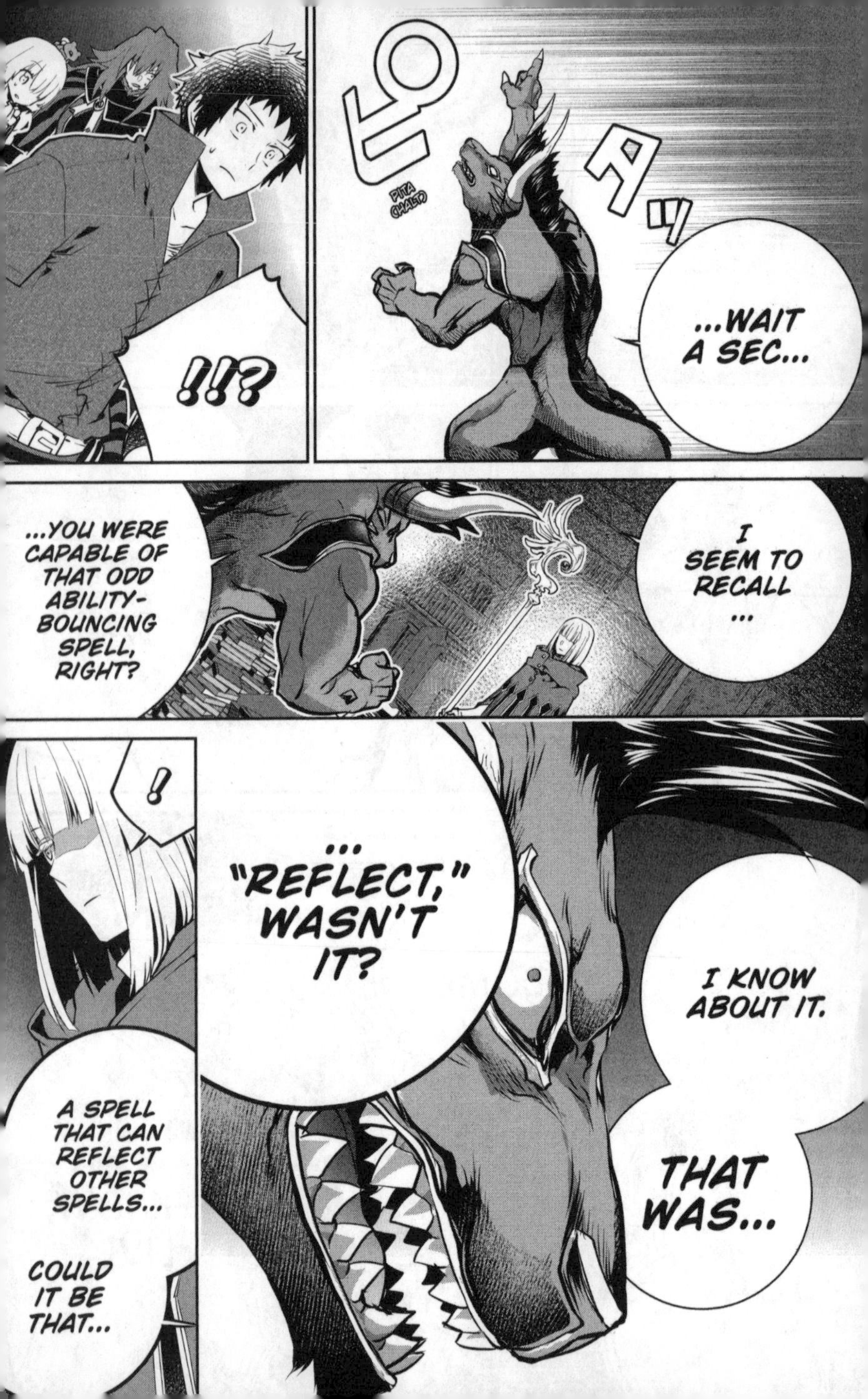

ピタッ
PITA (HALT)
...WAIT A SEC...
!!?
I SEEM TO RECALL ...
...YOU WERE CAPABLE OF THAT ODD ABILITY-BOUNCING SPELL, RIGHT?
I KNOW ABOUT IT.
A SPELL THAT CAN REFLECT OTHER SPELLS...
COULD IT BE THAT...
THAT WAS...
... "REFLECT," WASN'T IT?
!

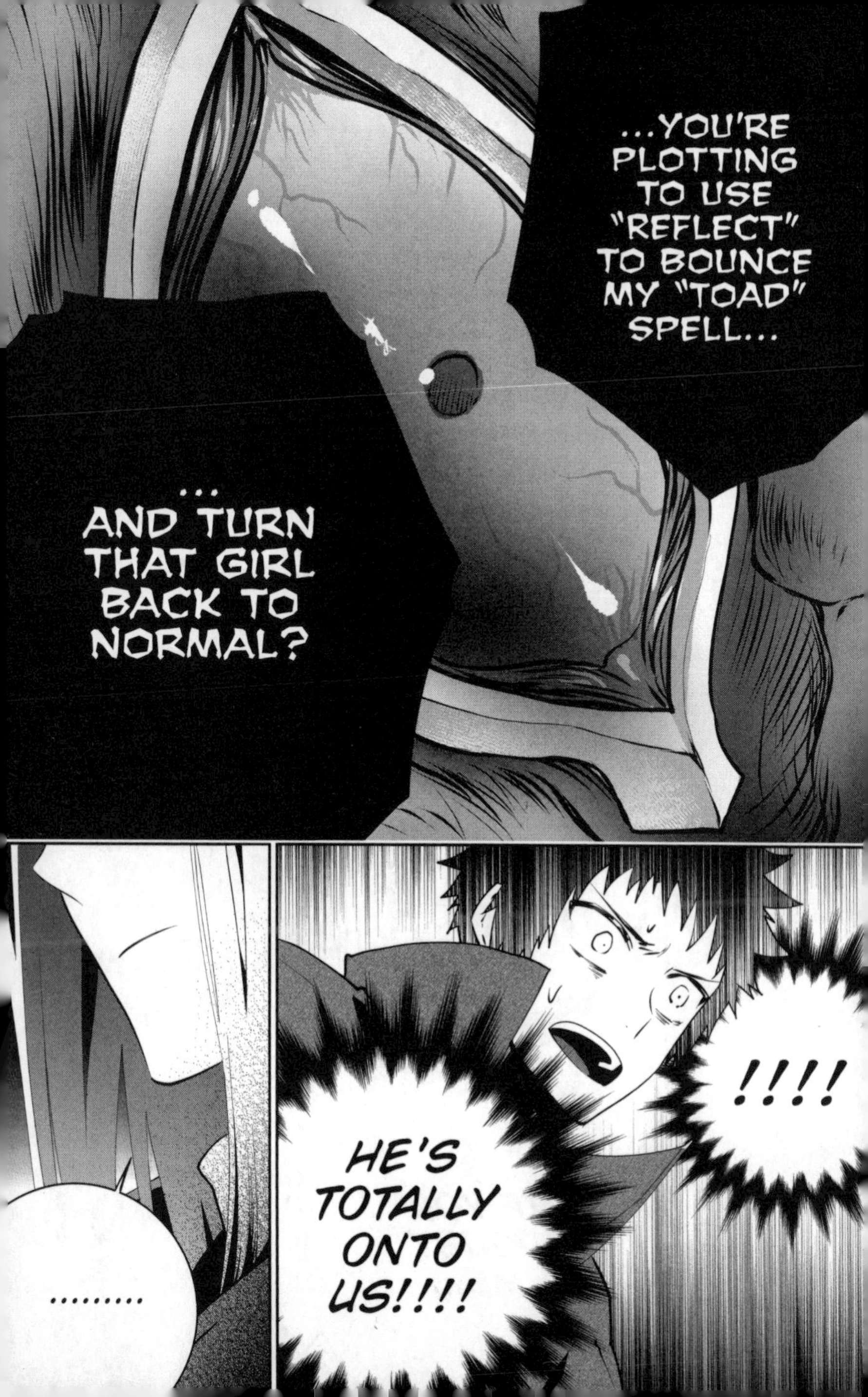
...YOU'RE PLOTTING TO USE "REFLECT" TO BOUNCE MY "TOAD" SPELL...
... AND TURN THAT GIRL BACK TO NORMAL?
!!!!
HE'S TOTALLY ONTO US!!!!
.........

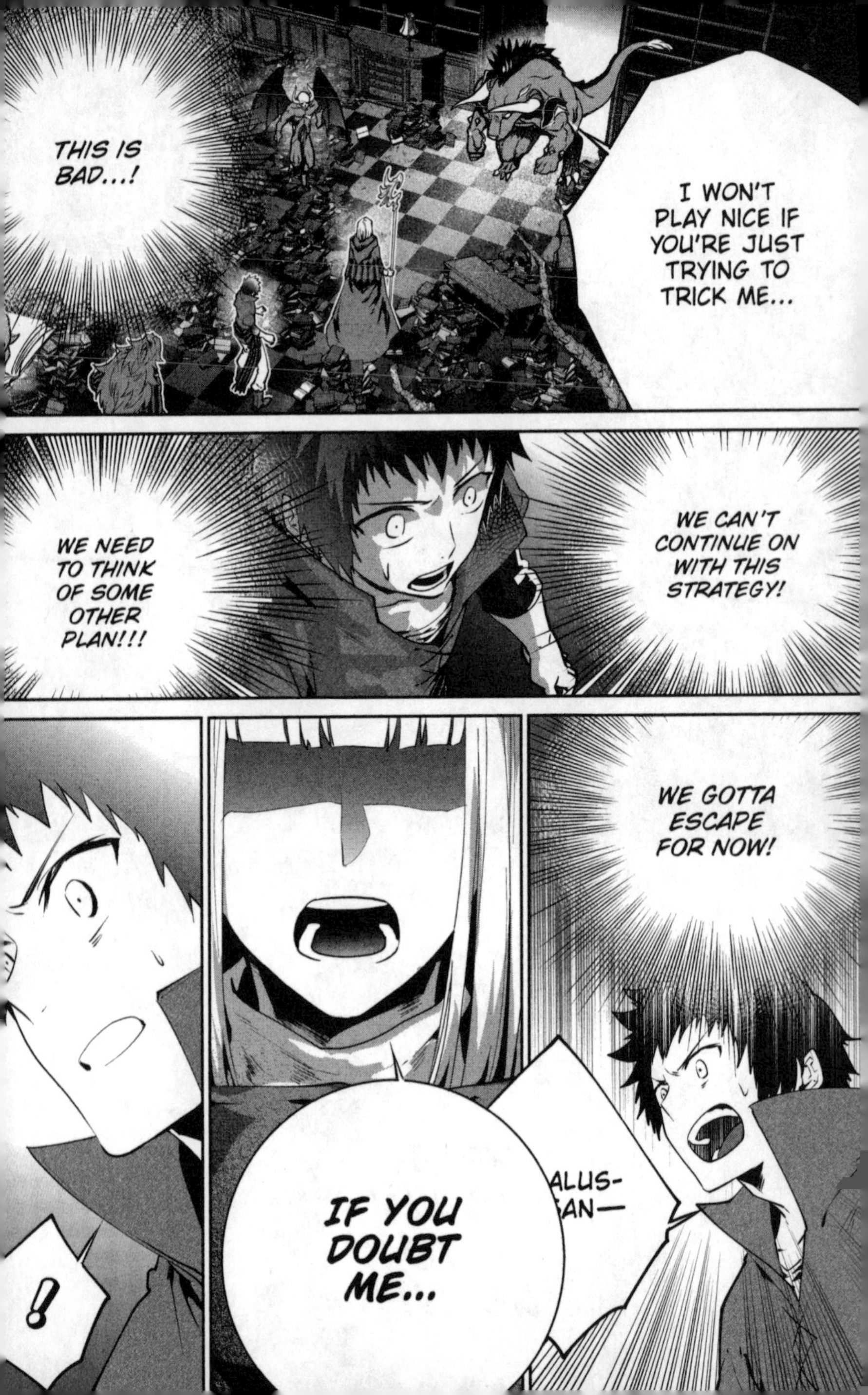
I WON'T PLAY NICE IF YOU'RE JUST TRYING TO TRICK ME...
THIS IS BAD...!
WE CAN'T CONTINUE ON WITH THIS STRATEGY!
WE NEED TO THINK OF SOME OTHER PLAN!!!
WE GOTTA ESCAPE FOR NOW!
ALUS-SAN—
IF YOU DOUBT ME...
!

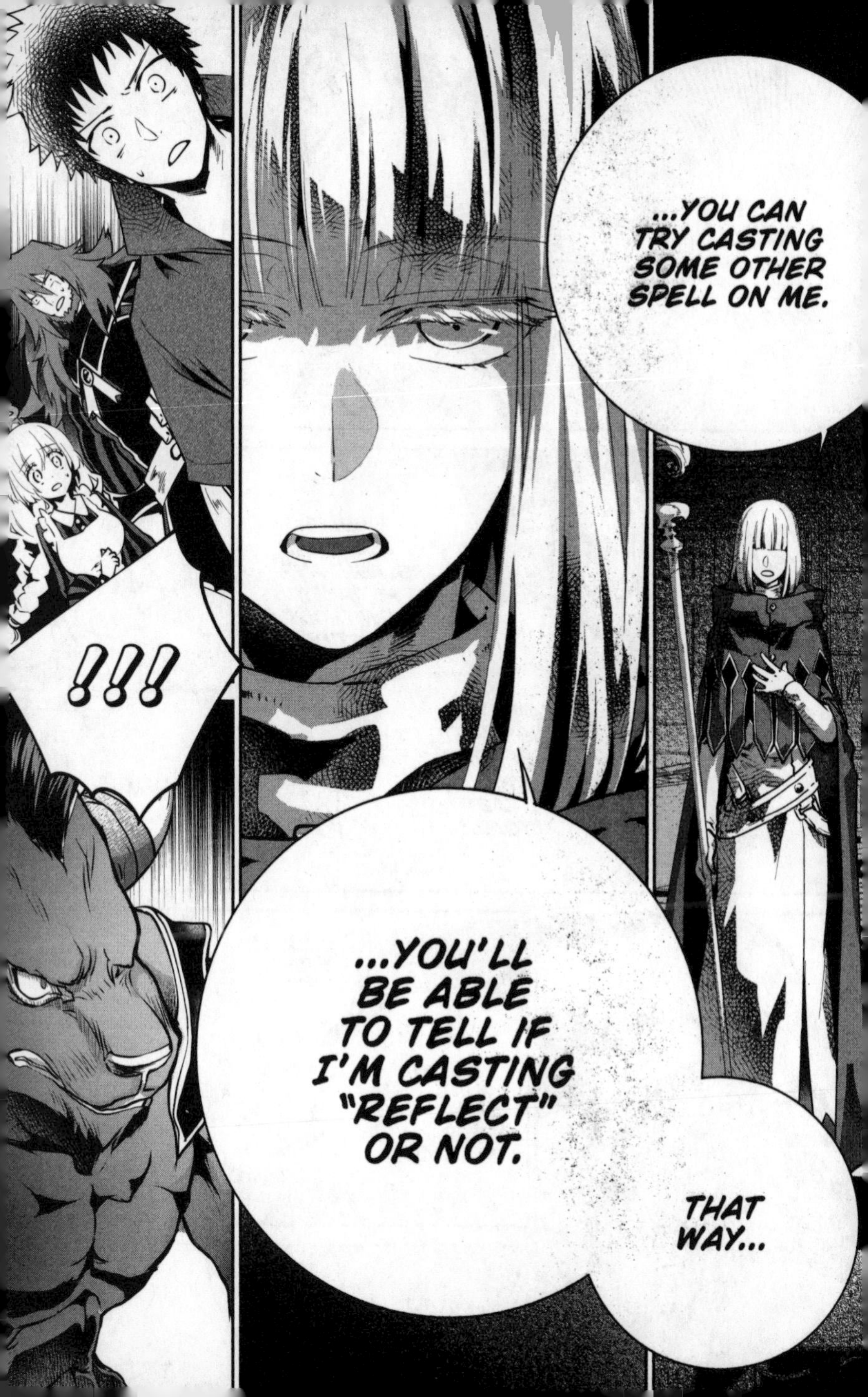
...YOU CAN TRY CASTING SOME OTHER SPELL ON ME.
THAT WAY...
...YOU'LL BE ABLE TO TELL IF I'M CASTING "REFLECT" OR NOT.
!!!

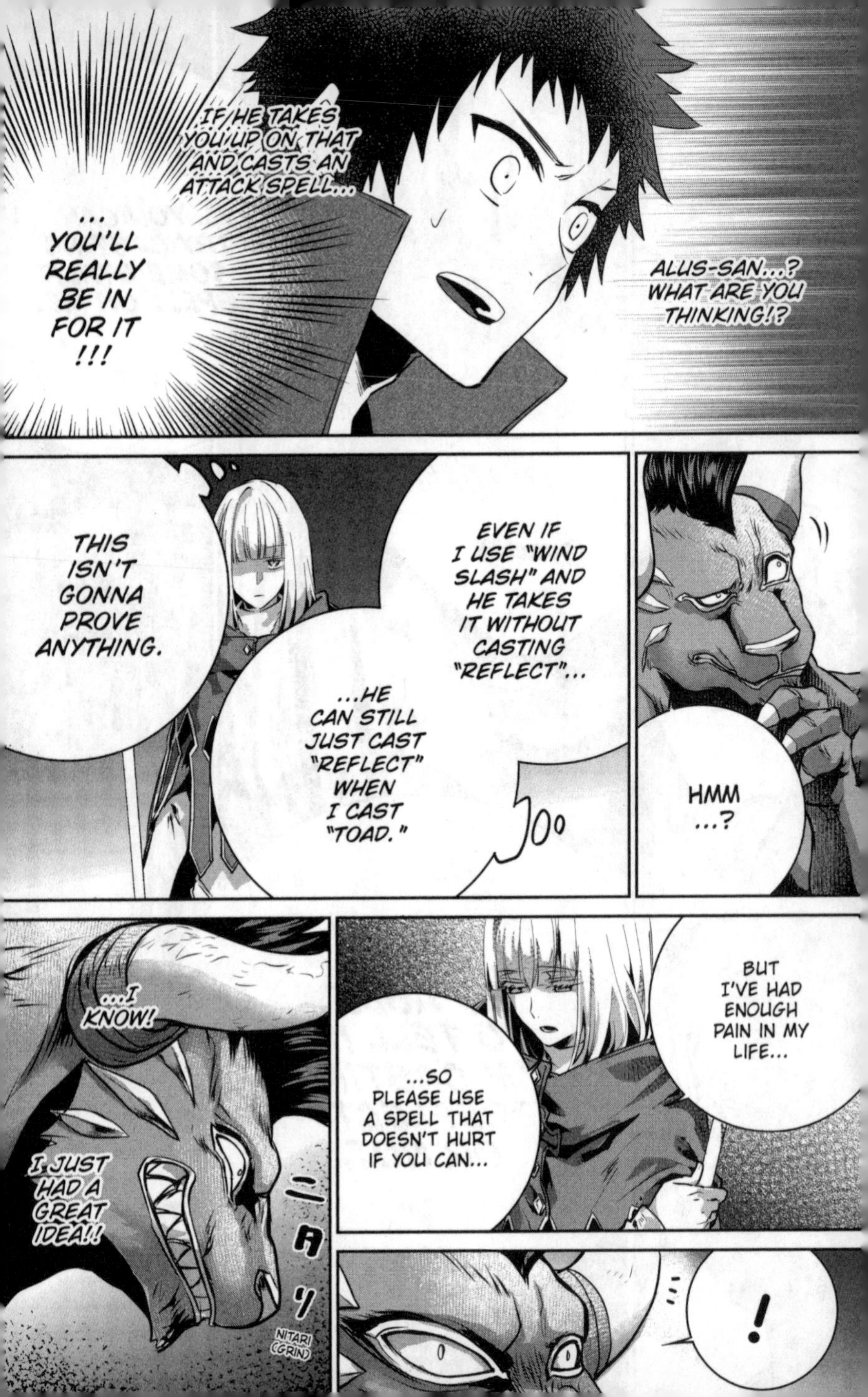
ALUS-SAN...? WHAT ARE YOU THINKING!?
IF HE TAKES YOU UP ON THAT AND CASTS AN ATTACK SPELL...
...YOU'LL REALLY BE IN FOR IT!!!
HMM ...?
EVEN IF I USE "WIND SLASH" AND HE TAKES IT WITHOUT CASTING "REFLECT"...
...HE CAN STILL JUST CAST "REFLECT" WHEN I CAST "TOAD."
THIS ISN'T GONNA PROVE ANYTHING.
BUT I'VE HAD ENOUGH PAIN IN MY LIFE...
...SO PLEASE USE A SPELL THAT DOESN'T HURT IF YOU CAN...
!
...I KNOW!
I JUST HAD A GREAT IDEA!!
NITARI (GRIN)

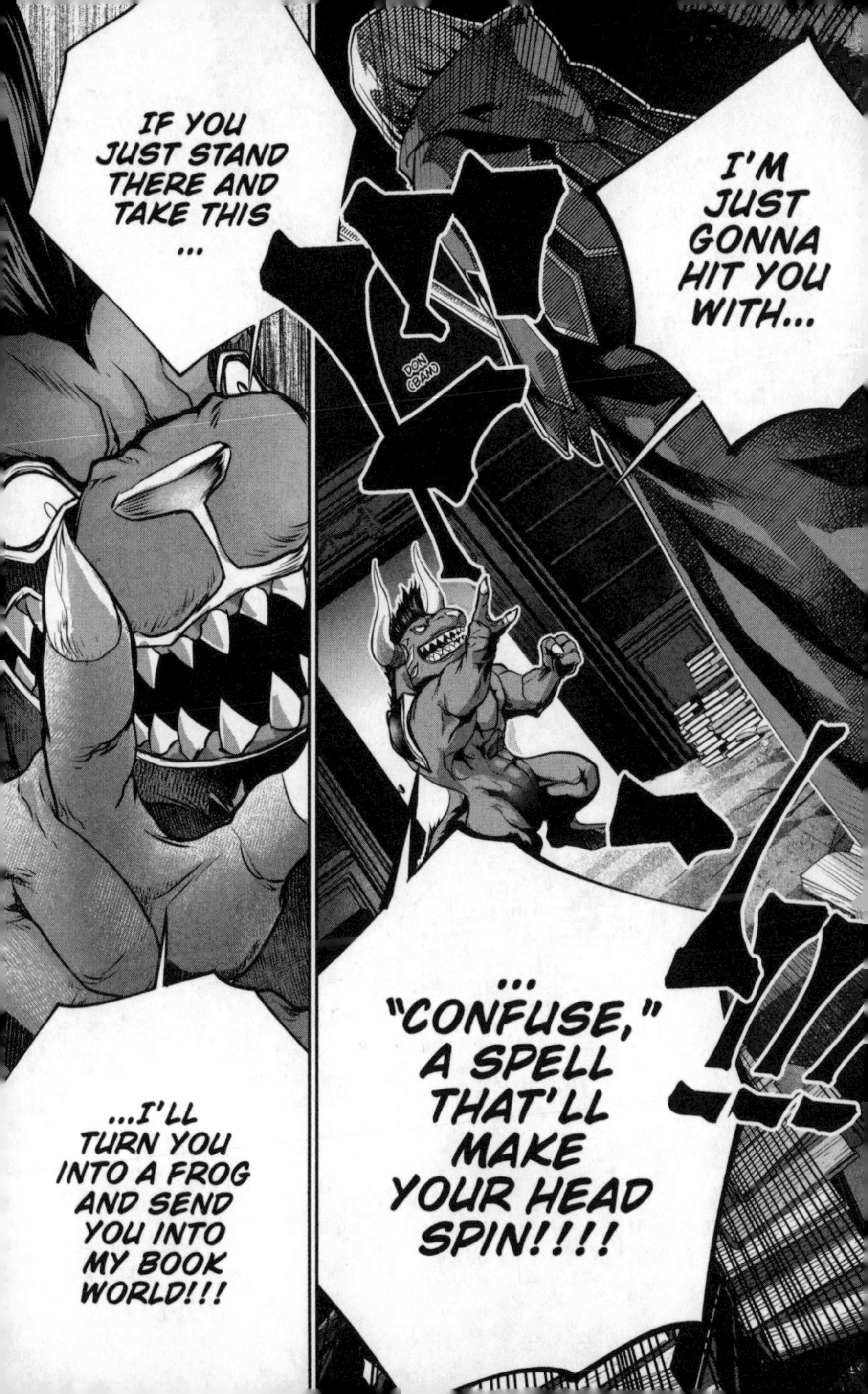
I'M JUST GONNA HIT YOU WITH...
DON (BAM)
..."CONFUSE," A SPELL THAT'LL MAKE YOUR HEAD SPIN!!!!
IF YOU JUST STAND THERE AND TAKE THIS ...
...I'LL TURN YOU INTO A FROG AND SEND YOU INTO MY BOOK WORLD!!!

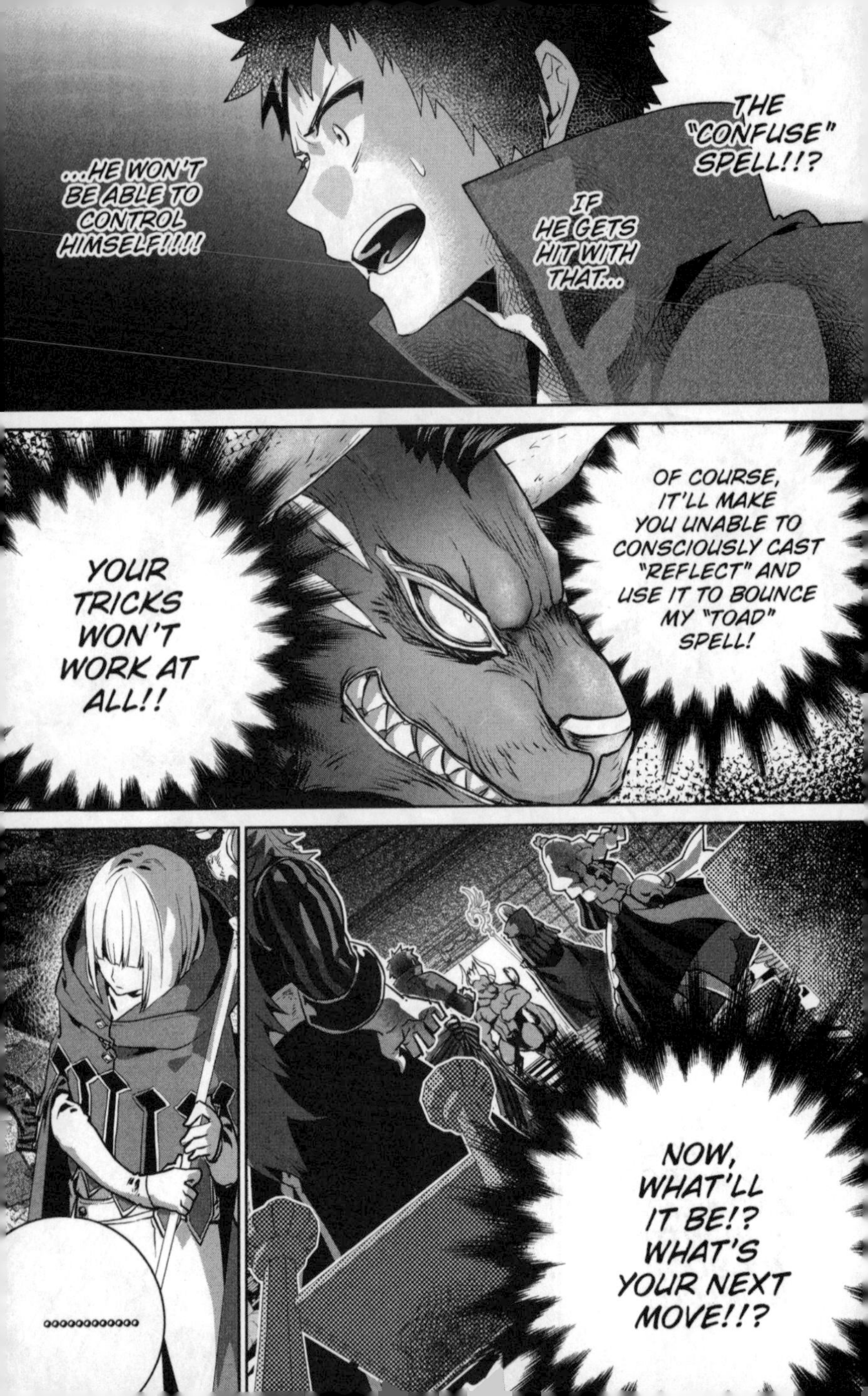
THE "CONFUSE" SPELL!!?
IF HE GETS HIT WITH THAT...
...HE WON'T BE ABLE TO CONTROL HIMSELF!!!!
OF COURSE, IT'LL MAKE YOU UNABLE TO CONSCIOUSLY CAST "REFLECT" AND USE IT TO BOUNCE MY "TOAD" SPELL!
YOUR TRICKS WON'T WORK AT ALL!!
NOW, WHAT'LL IT BE!? WHAT'S YOUR NEXT MOVE!!?
............

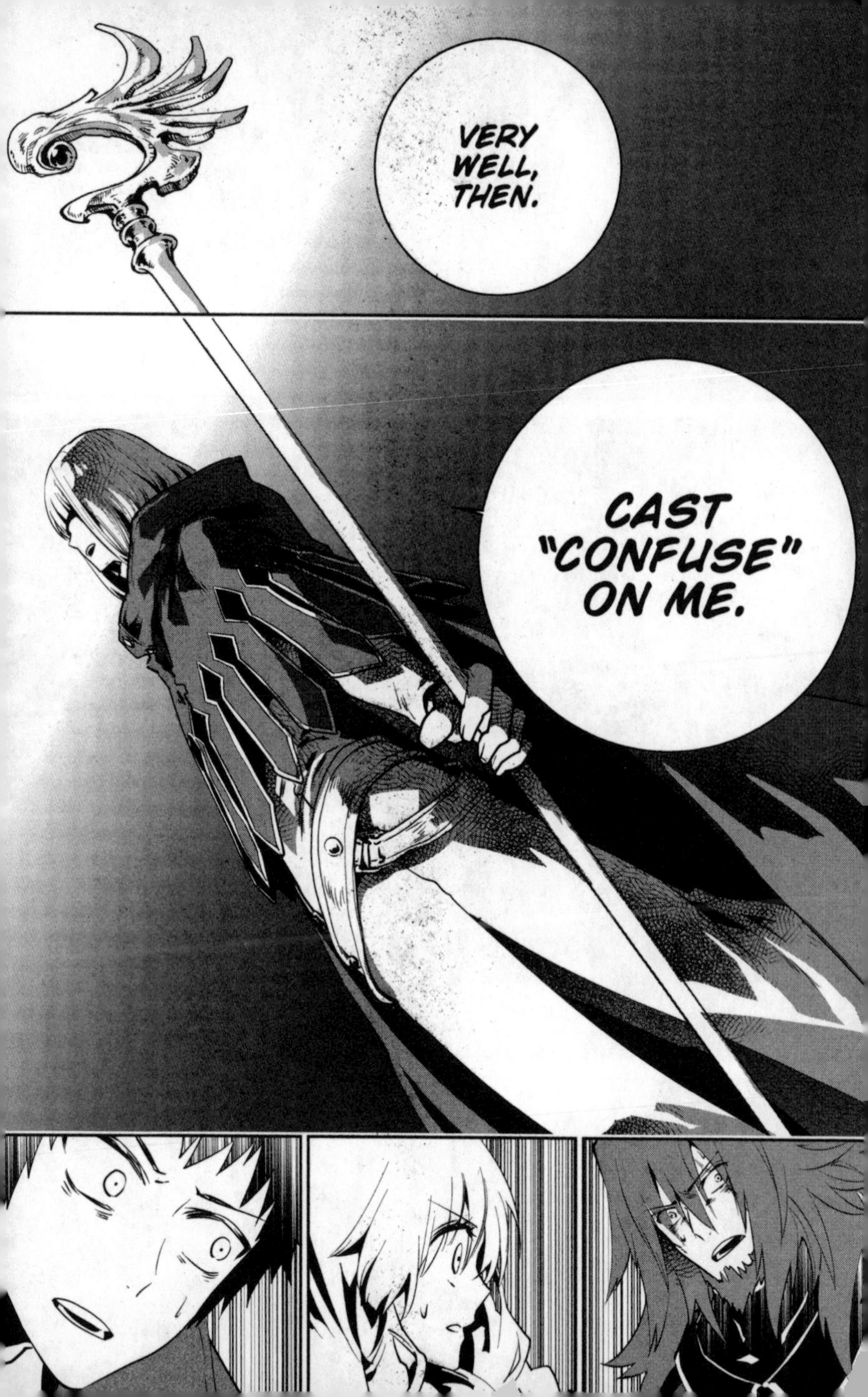
VERY WELL, THEN.
CAST "CONFUSE" ON ME.

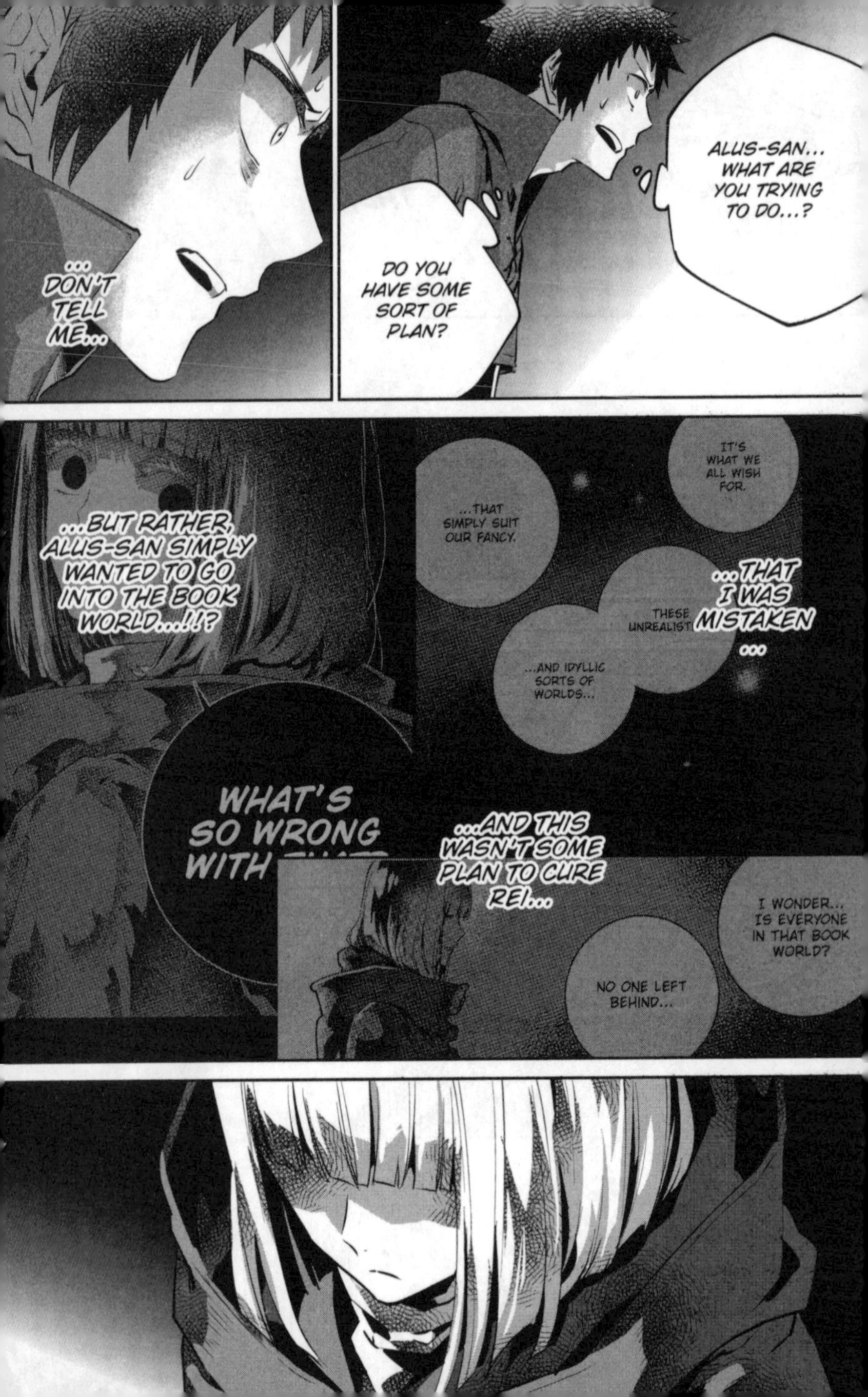
ALUS-SAN... WHAT ARE YOU TRYING TO DO...?
DO YOU HAVE SOME SORT OF PLAN?
...DON'T TELL ME...
IT'S WHAT WE ALL WISH FOR.
...THAT I WAS MISTAKEN...
...THAT SIMPLY SUIT OUR FANCY.
THESE UNREALIST
...AND IDYLLIC SORTS OF WORLDS...
...BUT RATHER, ALUS-SAN SIMPLY WANTED TO GO INTO THE BOOK WORLD...!!?
WHAT'S SO WRONG WITH
...AND THIS WASN'T SOME PLAN TO CURE REI...
I WONDER... IS EVERYONE IN THAT BOOK WORLD?
NO ONE LEFT BEHIND...

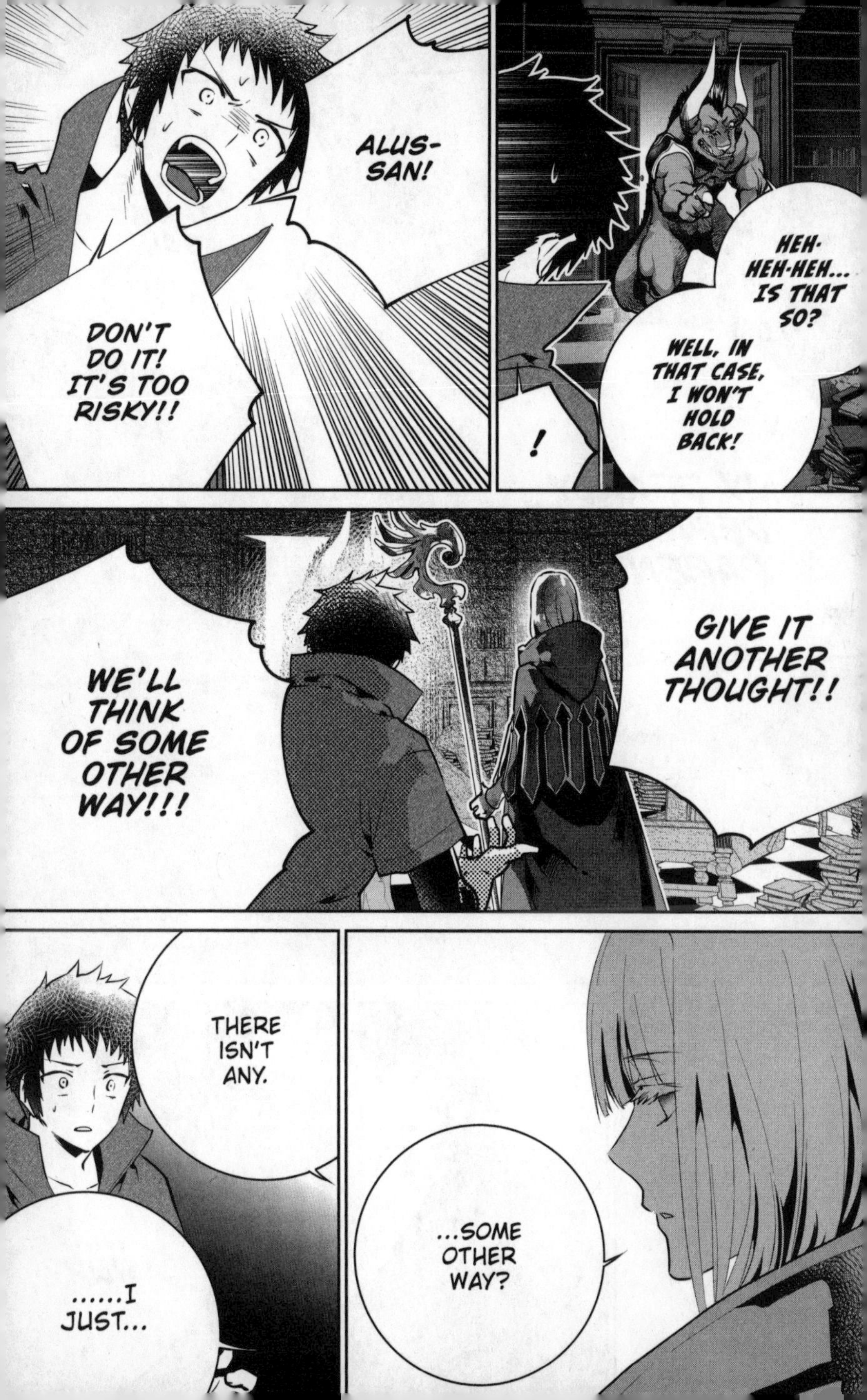
HEH-HEH-HEH... IS THAT SO?
WELL, IN THAT CASE, I WON'T HOLD BACK!
!
ALUS-SAN!
DON'T DO IT! IT'S TOO RISKY!!
GIVE IT ANOTHER THOUGHT!!
WE'LL THINK OF SOME OTHER WAY!!!
...SOME OTHER WAY?
THERE ISN'T ANY.
......I JUST...

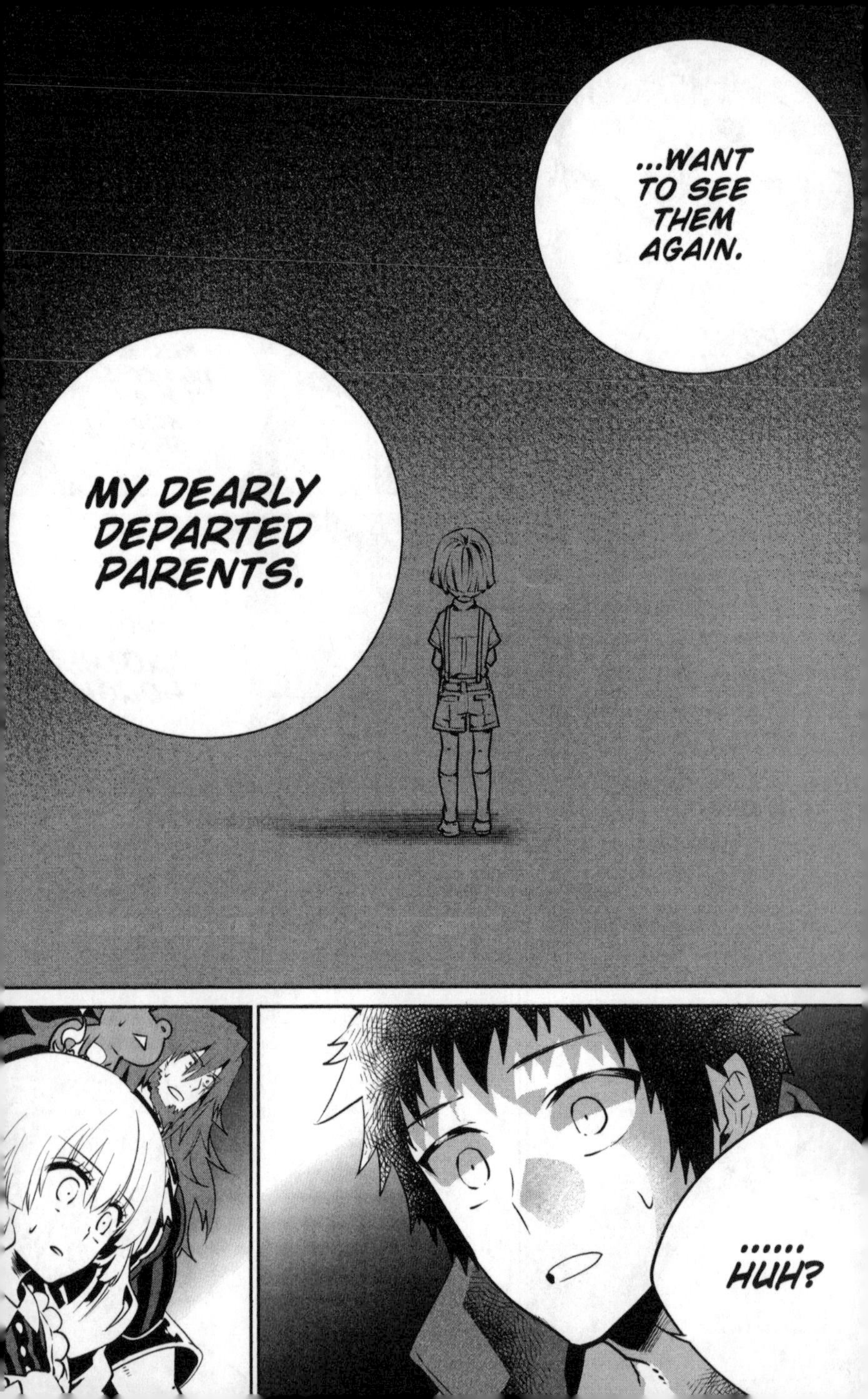
...WANT TO SEE THEM AGAIN.
MY DEARLY DEPARTED PARENTS.
......HUH?

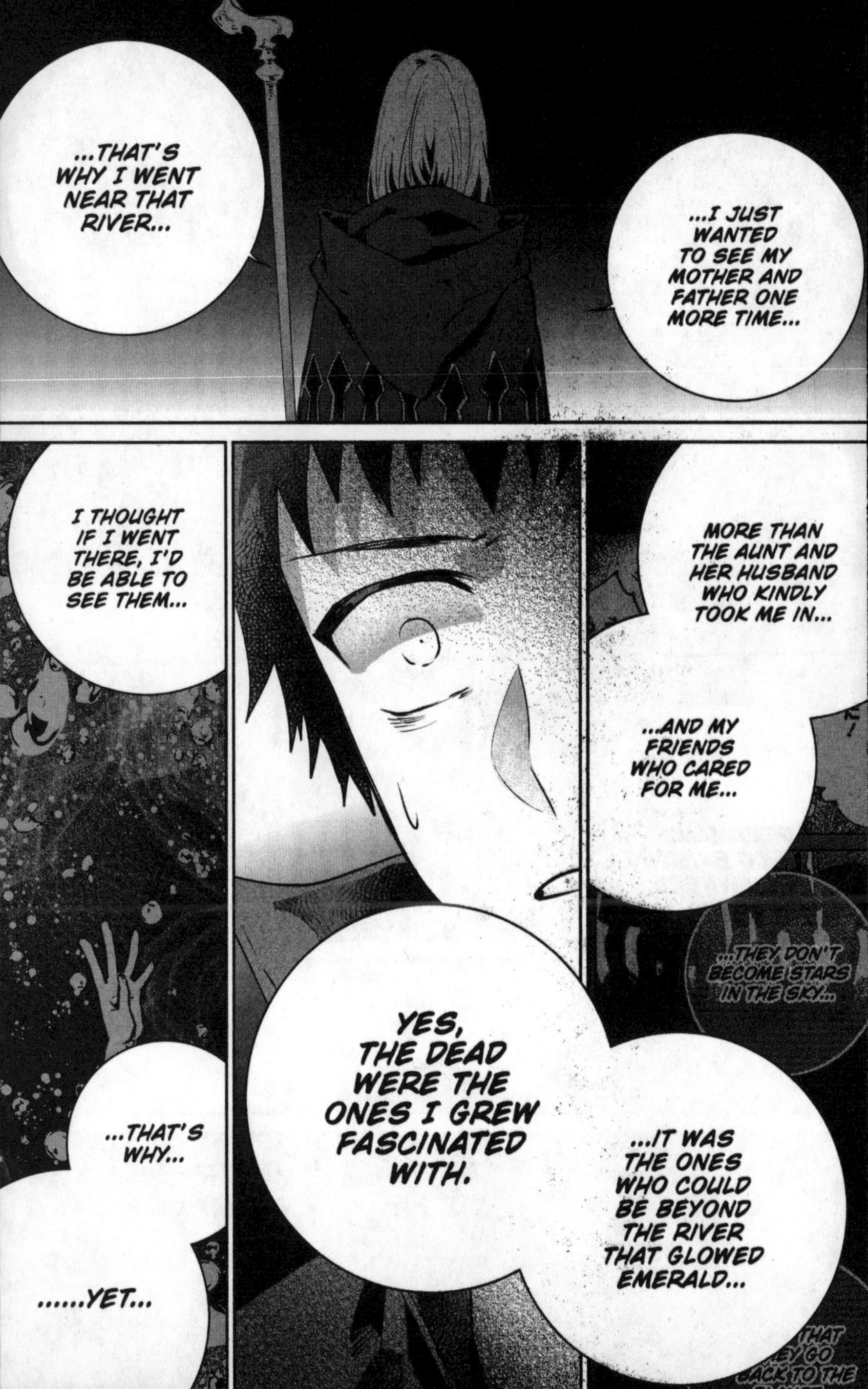
...I JUST WANTED TO SEE MY MOTHER AND FATHER ONE MORE TIME...
...THAT'S WHY I WENT NEAR THAT RIVER...
MORE THAN THE AUNT AND HER HUSBAND WHO KINDLY TOOK ME IN...
...AND MY FRIENDS WHO CARED FOR ME...
...THEY DON'T BECOME STARS IN THE SKY...
...IT WAS THE ONES WHO COULD BE BEYOND THE RIVER THAT GLOWED EMERALD...
YES, THE DEAD WERE THE ONES I GREW FASCINATED WITH.
I THOUGHT IF I WENT THERE, I'D BE ABLE TO SEE THEM...
...THAT'S WHY...
......YET...

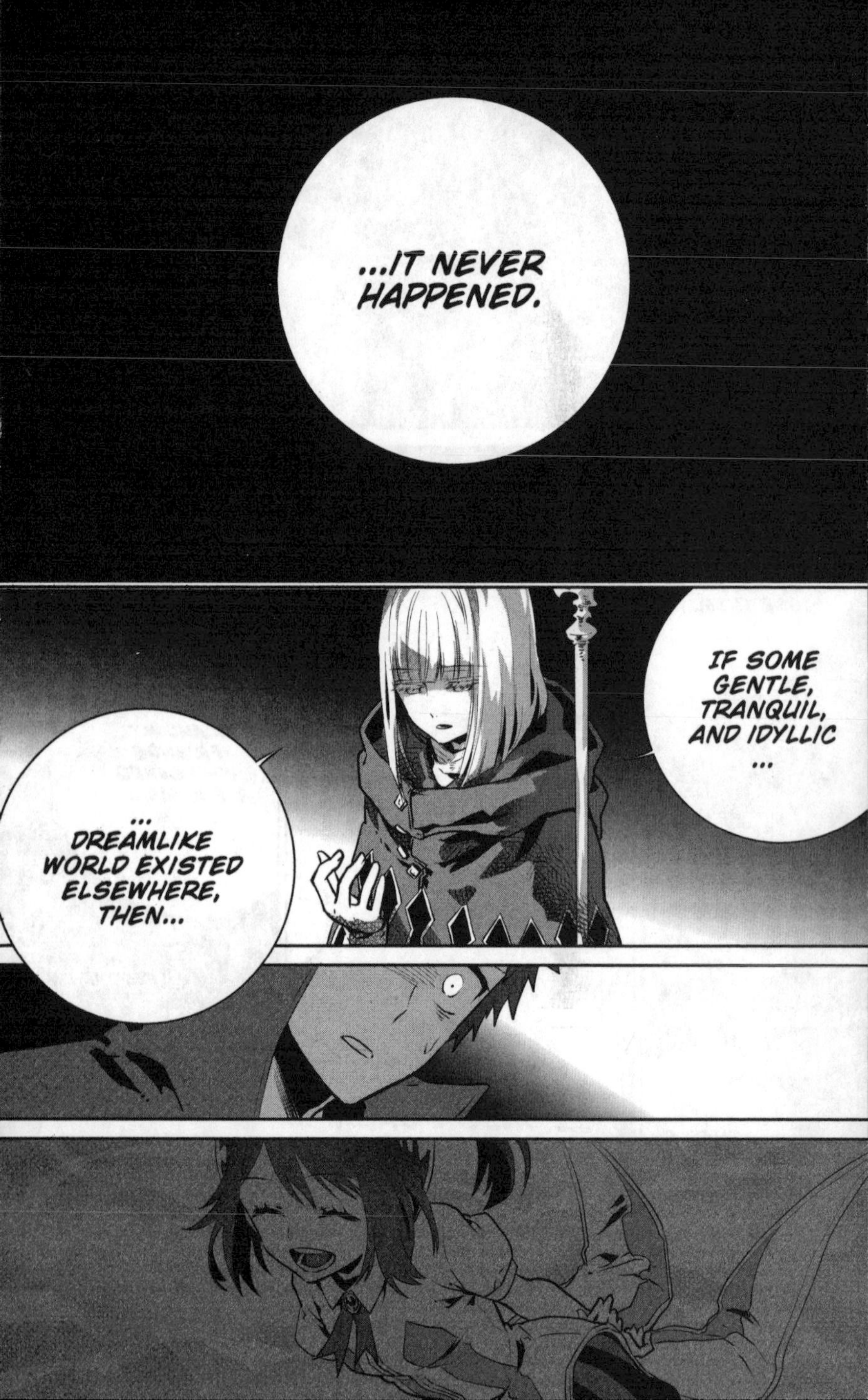
...IT NEVER HAPPENED.
IF SOME GENTLE, TRANQUIL, AND IDYLLIC ...
... DREAMLIKE WORLD EXISTED ELSEWHERE, THEN...

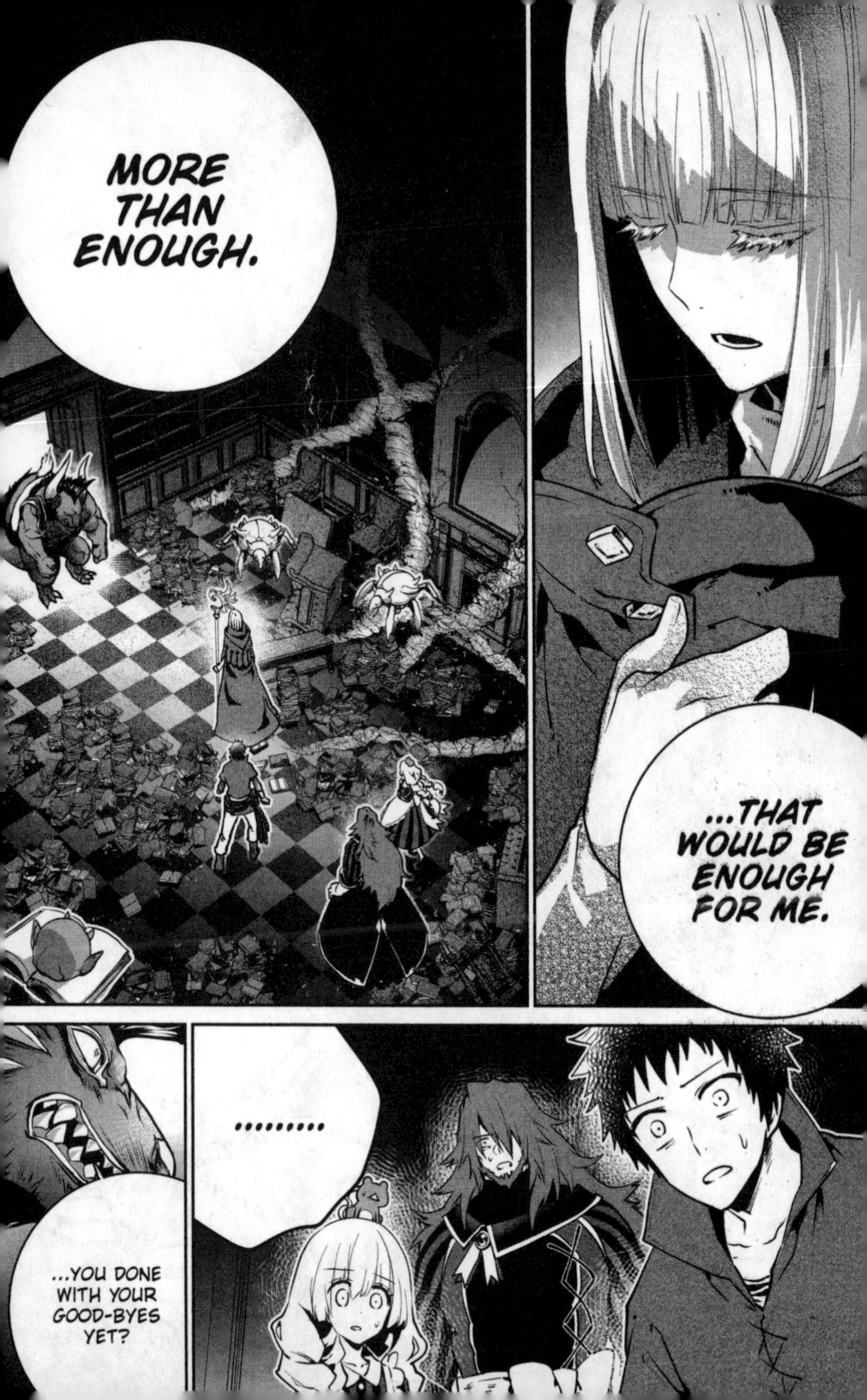
...THAT WOULD BE ENOUGH FOR ME.
MORE THAN ENOUGH.
.........
...YOU DONE WITH YOUR GOOD-BYES YET?

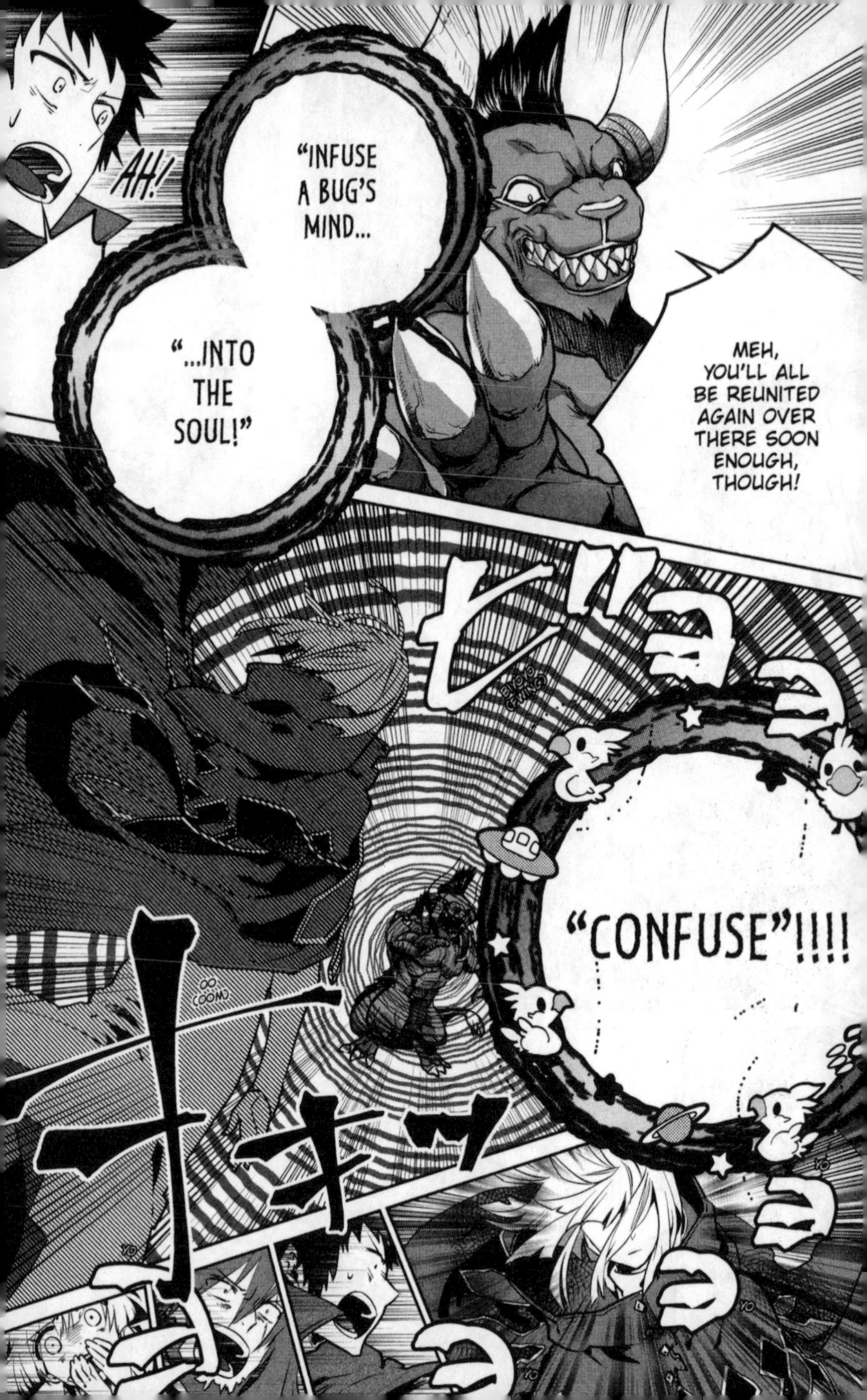
MEH, YOU'LL ALL BE REUNITED AGAIN OVER THERE SOON ENOUGH, THOUGH!
"INFUSE A BUG'S MIND...
"...INTO THE SOUL!"
AH!
BIYOYO (FWING)
"CONFUSE"!!!!
YO
YO
OO (OOM)
YO

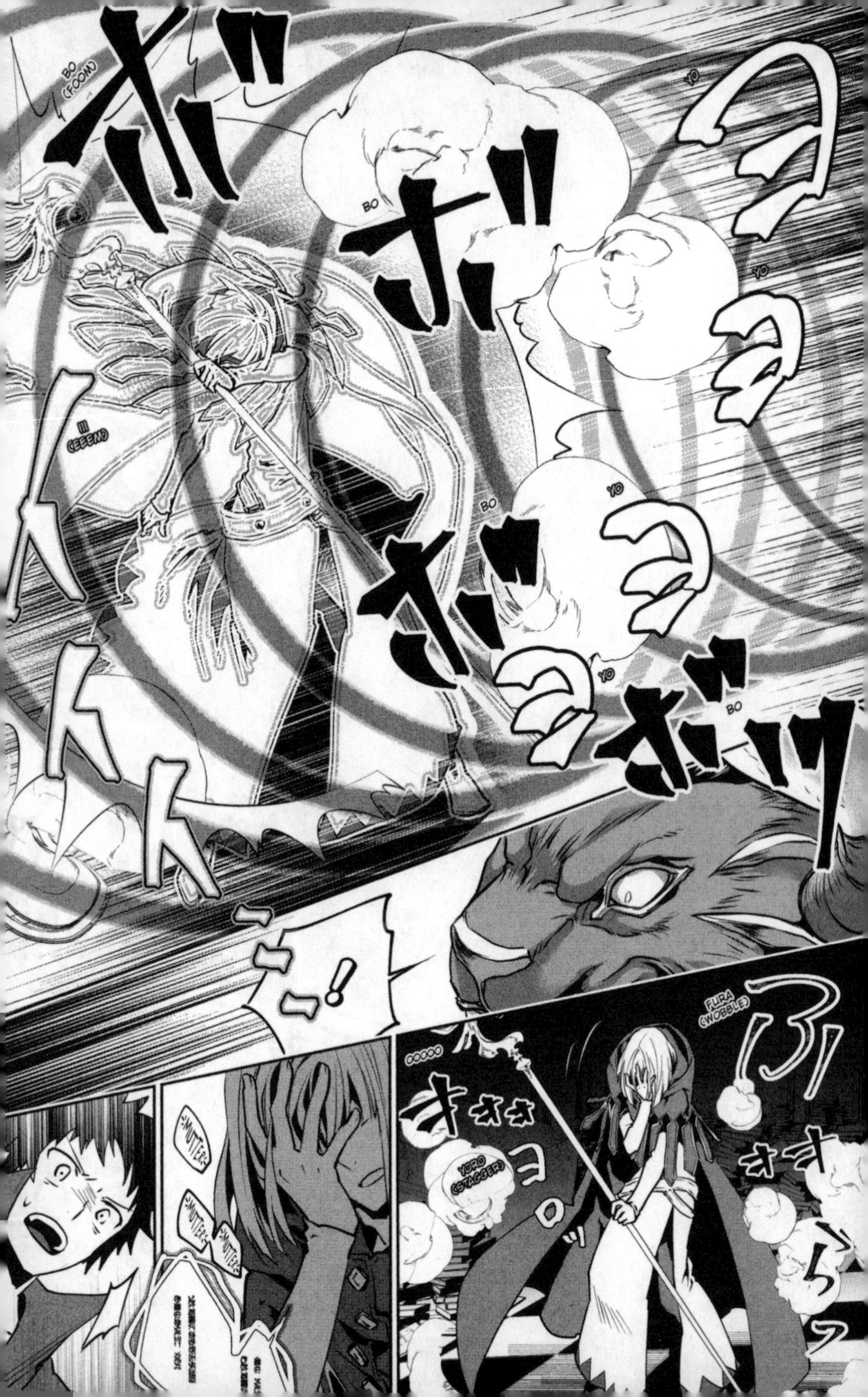
YO
YO
BO (FOOM)
BO
YO
BO
YO
BO
III (EEEEM)
FURA (WOBBLE)
OOOOO
YORO (STAGGER)
MUTTER
MUTTER
MUTTER

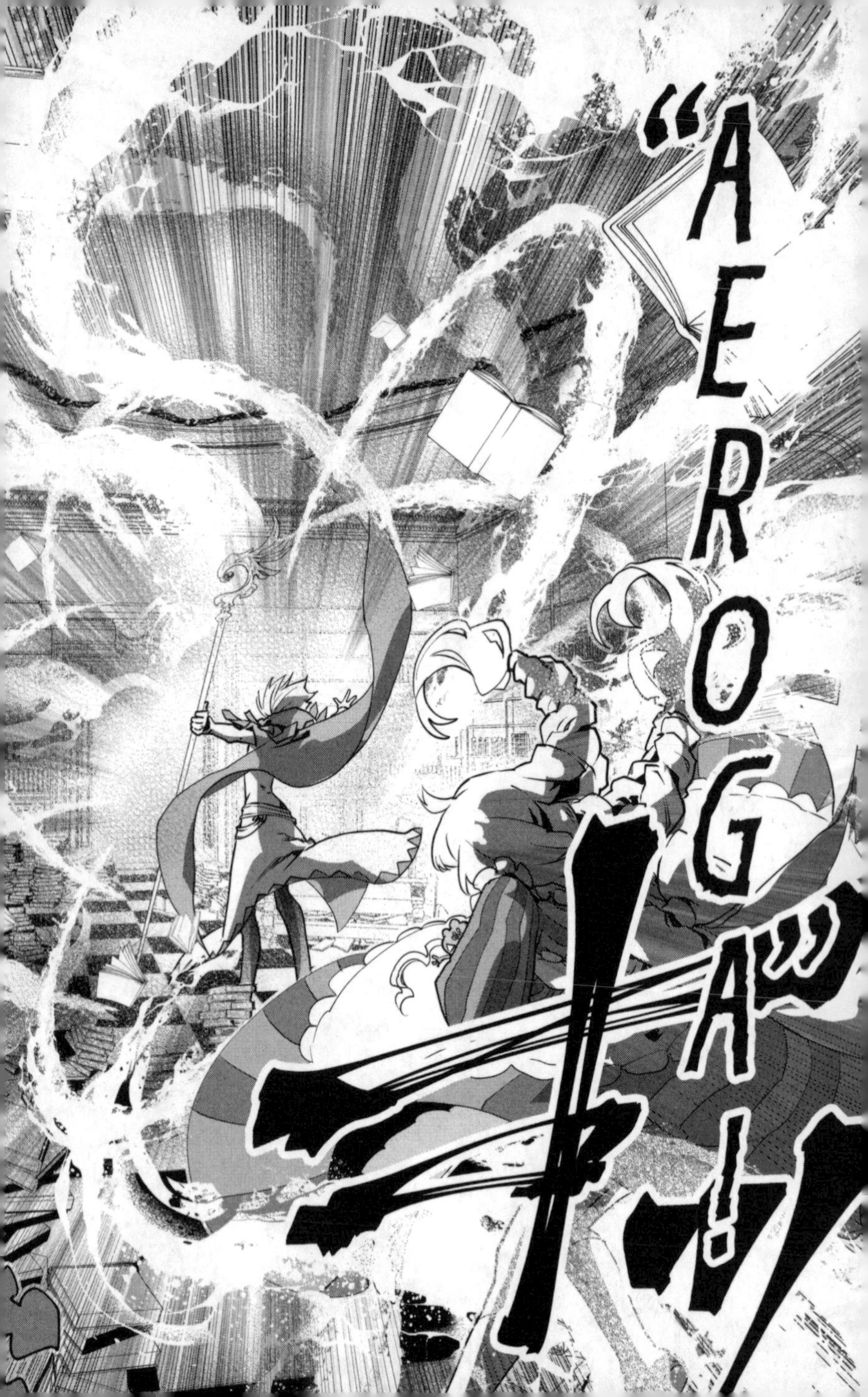
“AEROGA!”

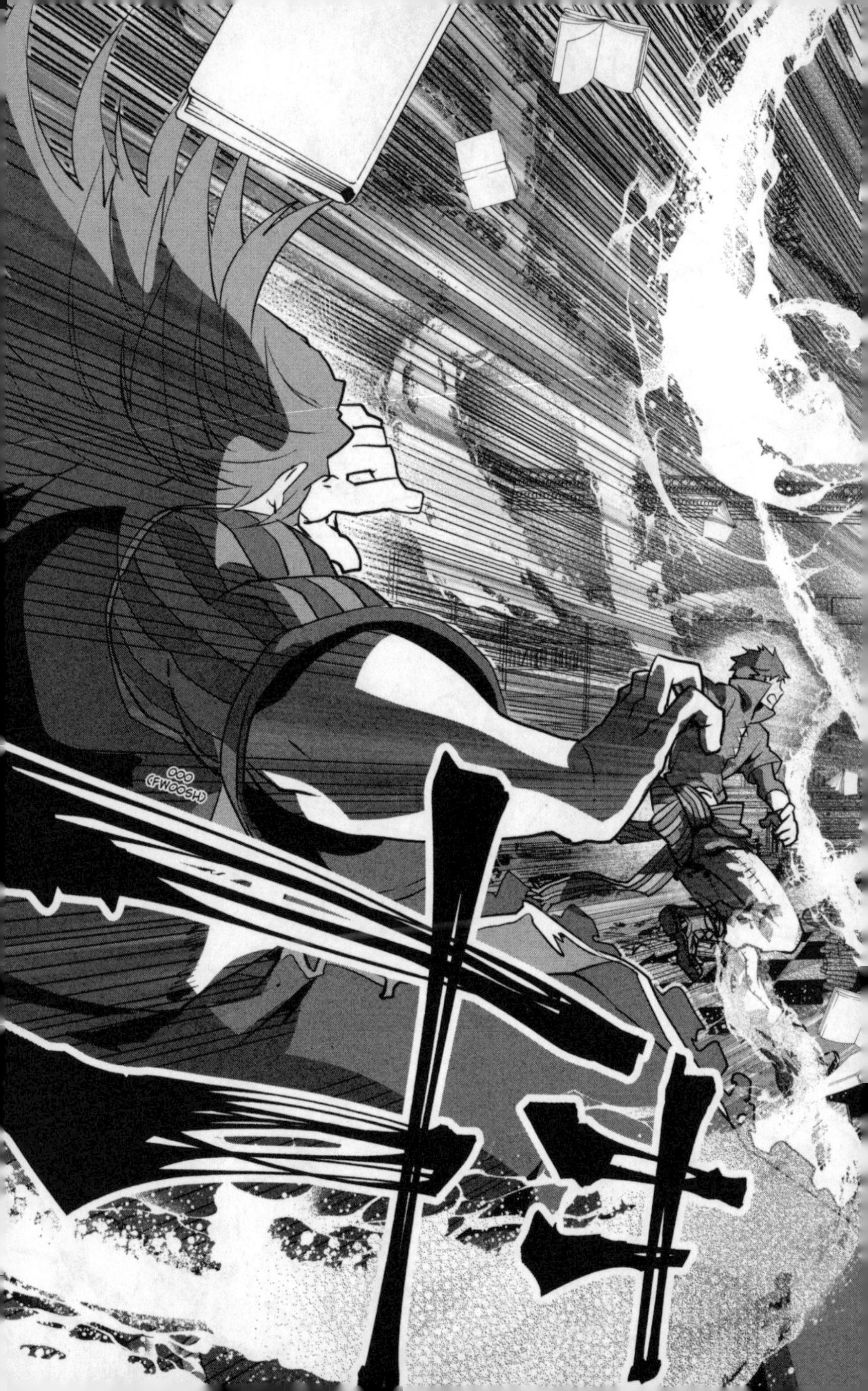
OOO
(FWOOSH)

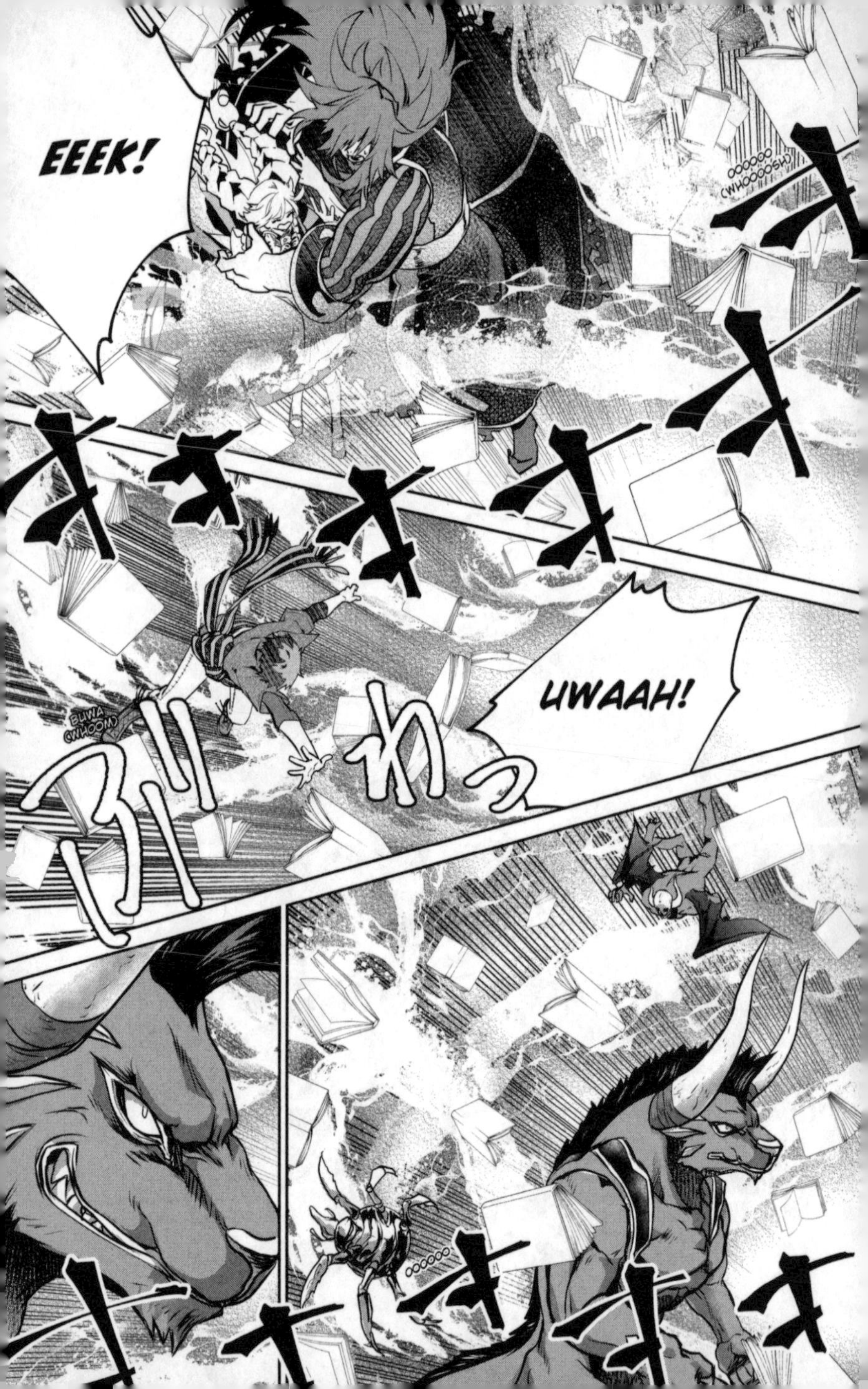
EEEK!
OOOOOO
(WHOOOOOSH)
BUWA
(WHOOM)
UWAAH!
OOOOOO

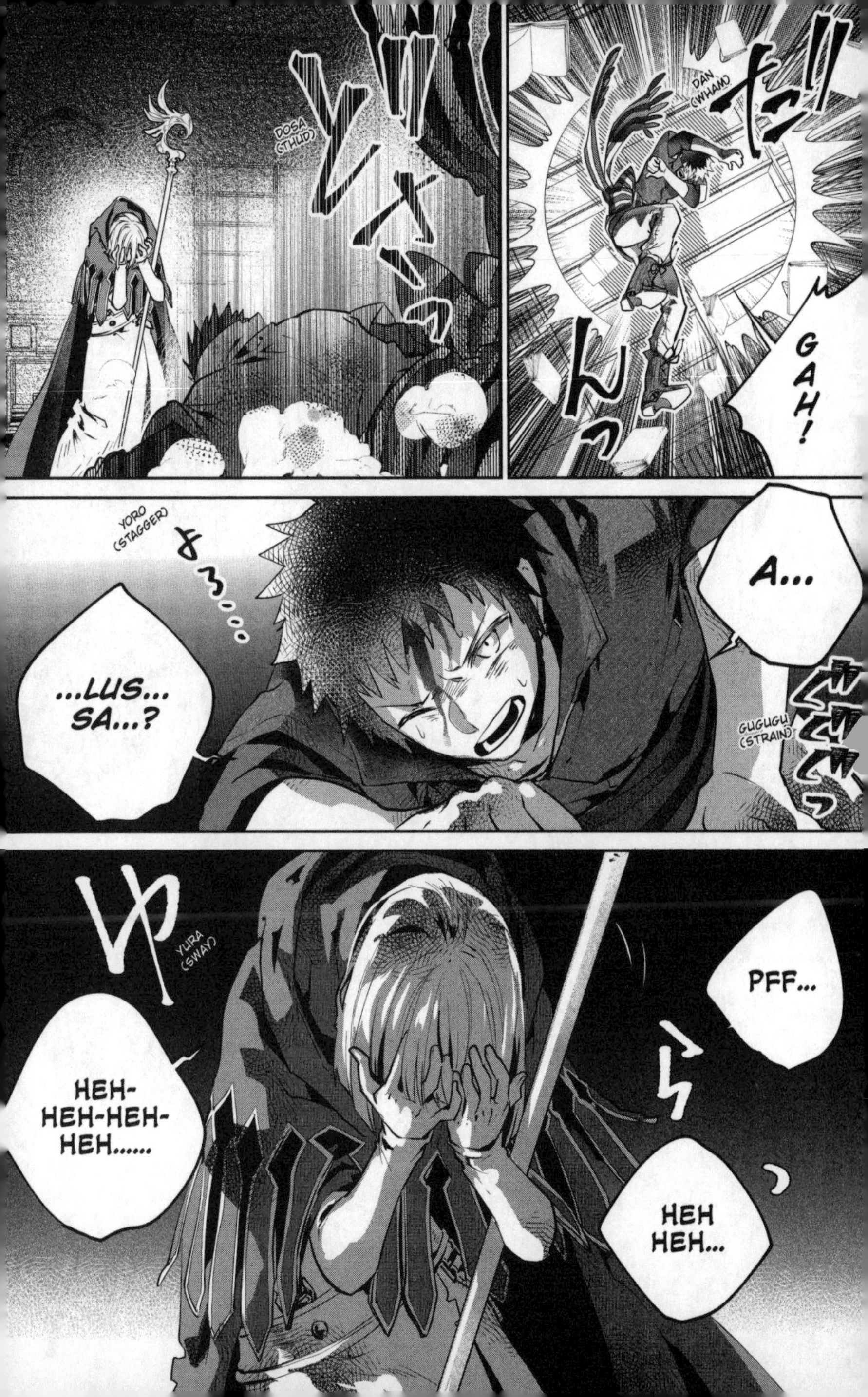
DAN (WHAM)
GAH!
DOSA (THUD)
A...
GUGUGU (STRAIN)
YORO (STAGGER)
...LUS... SA...?
PFF...
HEH HEH...
YURA (SWAY)
HEH-HEH-HEH-HEH......

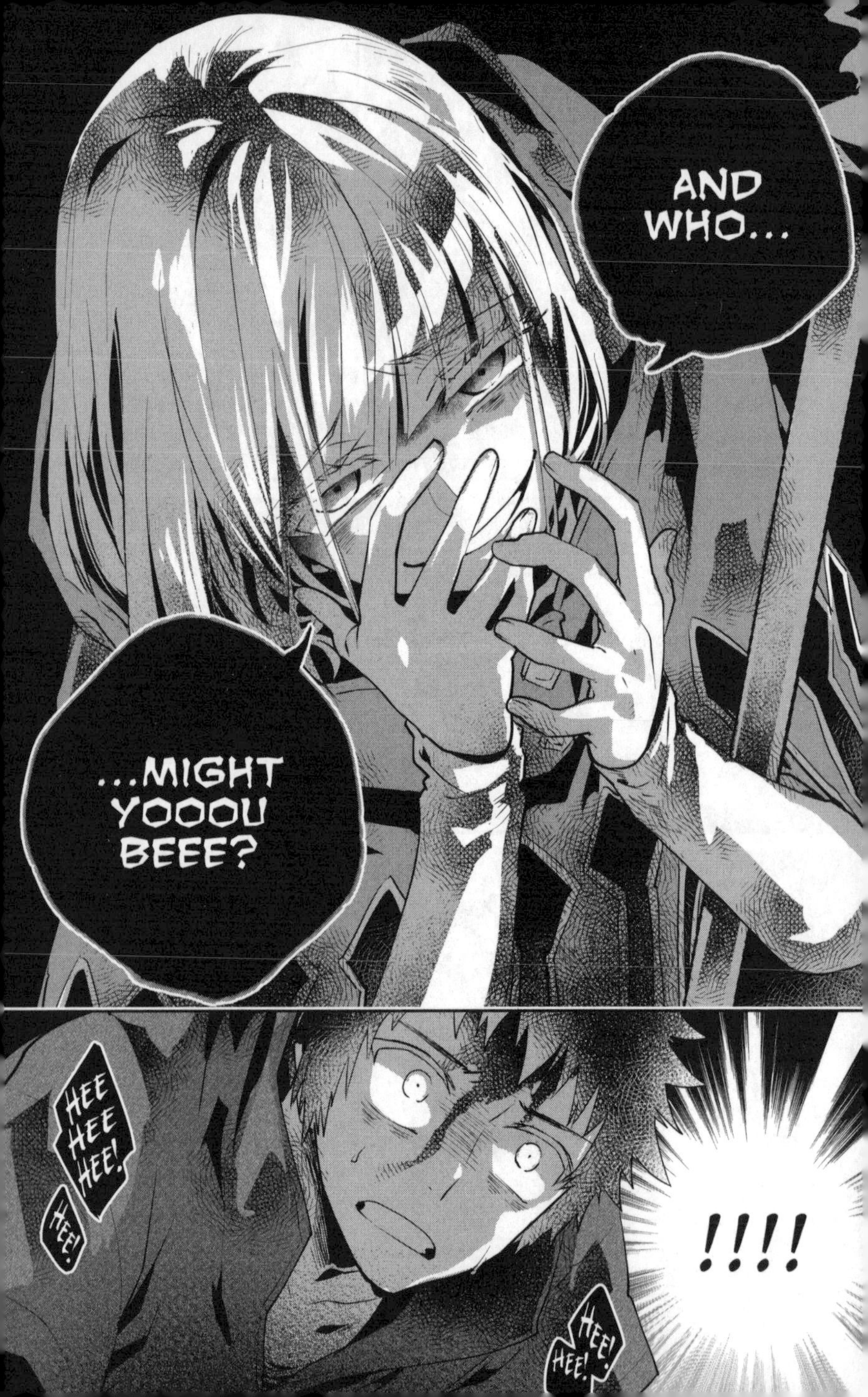
AND WHO...
...MIGHT YOOOU BEEE?
!!!!
HEE HEE HEE!
HEE!
HEE! HEE!

FINAL FANTASY®

ファイナルファンタジー　ロスト・ストレンジャー

LOST STRANGER

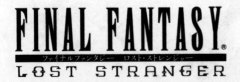

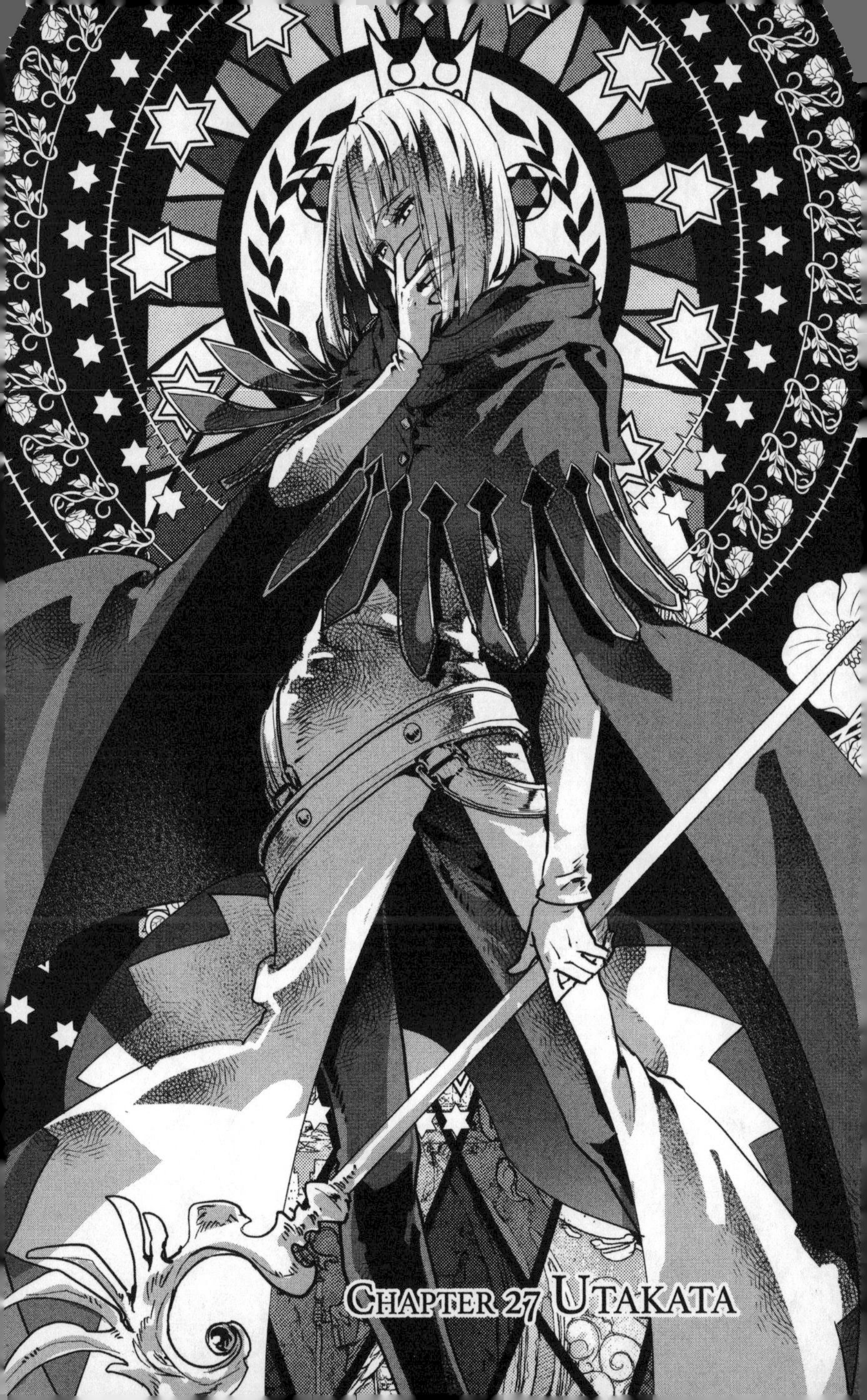
Chapter 27 Utakata

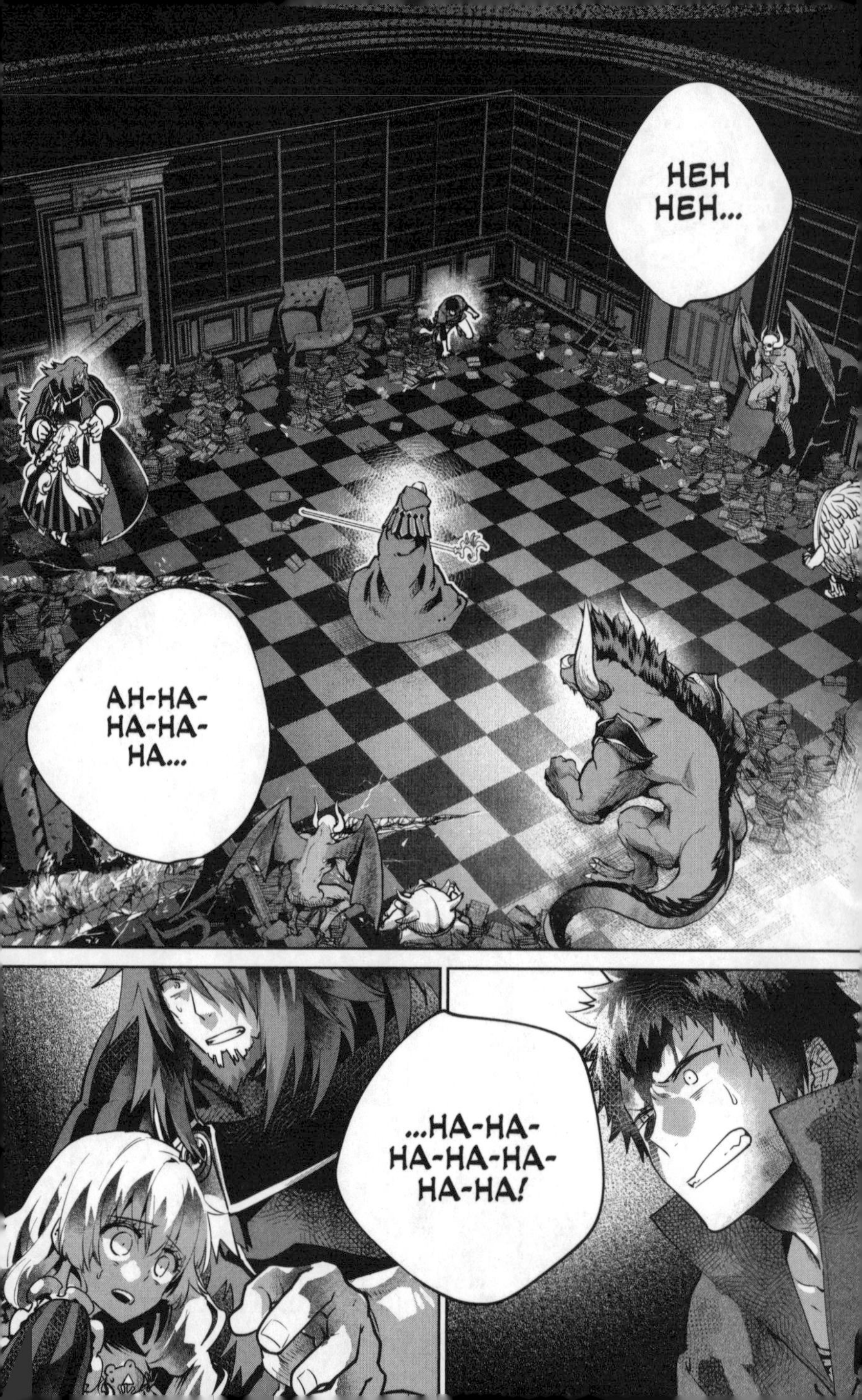
HEH HEH...
AH-HA-HA-HA-HA...
...HA-HA-HA-HA-HA-HA-HA!

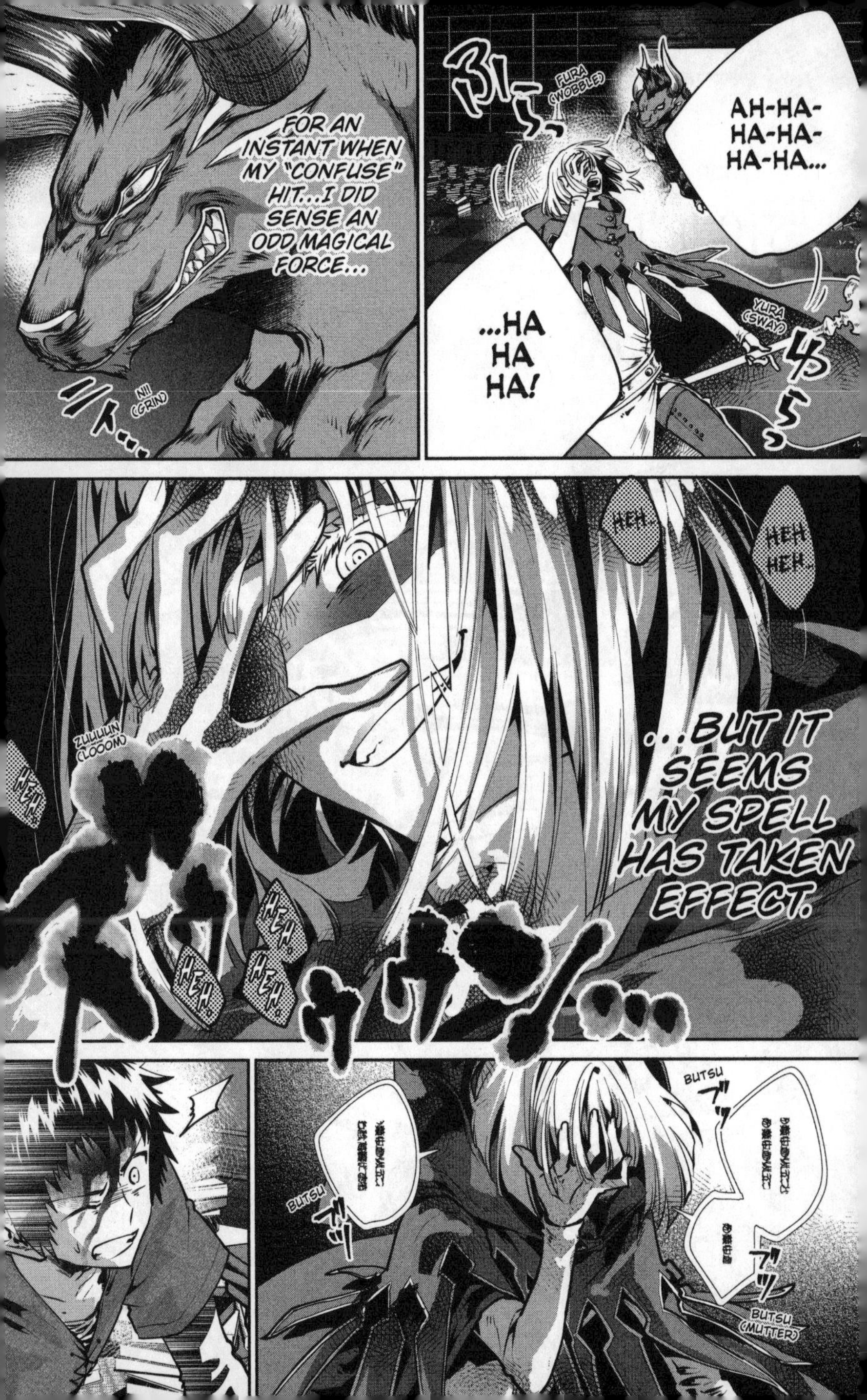

AH-HA-HA-HA-HA-HA...
FURA (WOBBLE)
YURA (SWAY)
...HA HA HA!
FOR AN INSTANT WHEN MY "CONFUSE" HIT...I DID SENSE AN ODD MAGICAL FORCE...
NII (GRIN)
HEH HEH...
HEH...
...BUT IT SEEMS MY SPELL HAS TAKEN EFFECT.
ZUUUUN (LOOOM)
HEH...
HEH, HEH.
HEH
HEH
BUTSU
BUTSU (MUTTER)
BUTSU

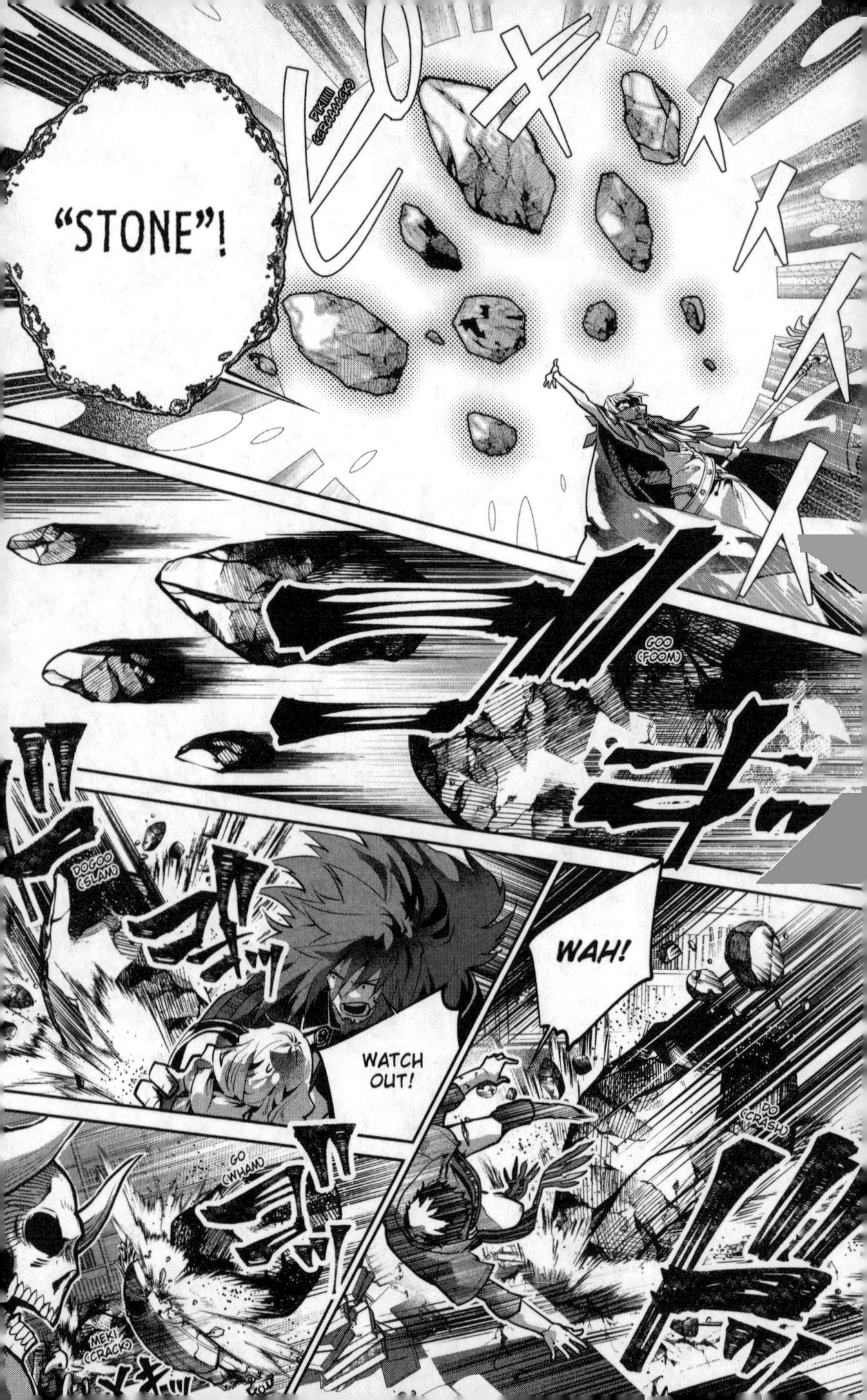
"STONE"!
PIKIIII (CRAAAACK)
GOO (FOOM)
DOGOO (SLAM)
WAH!
DO (CRASH)
WATCH OUT!
GO (WHAM)
MEKI (CRACK)

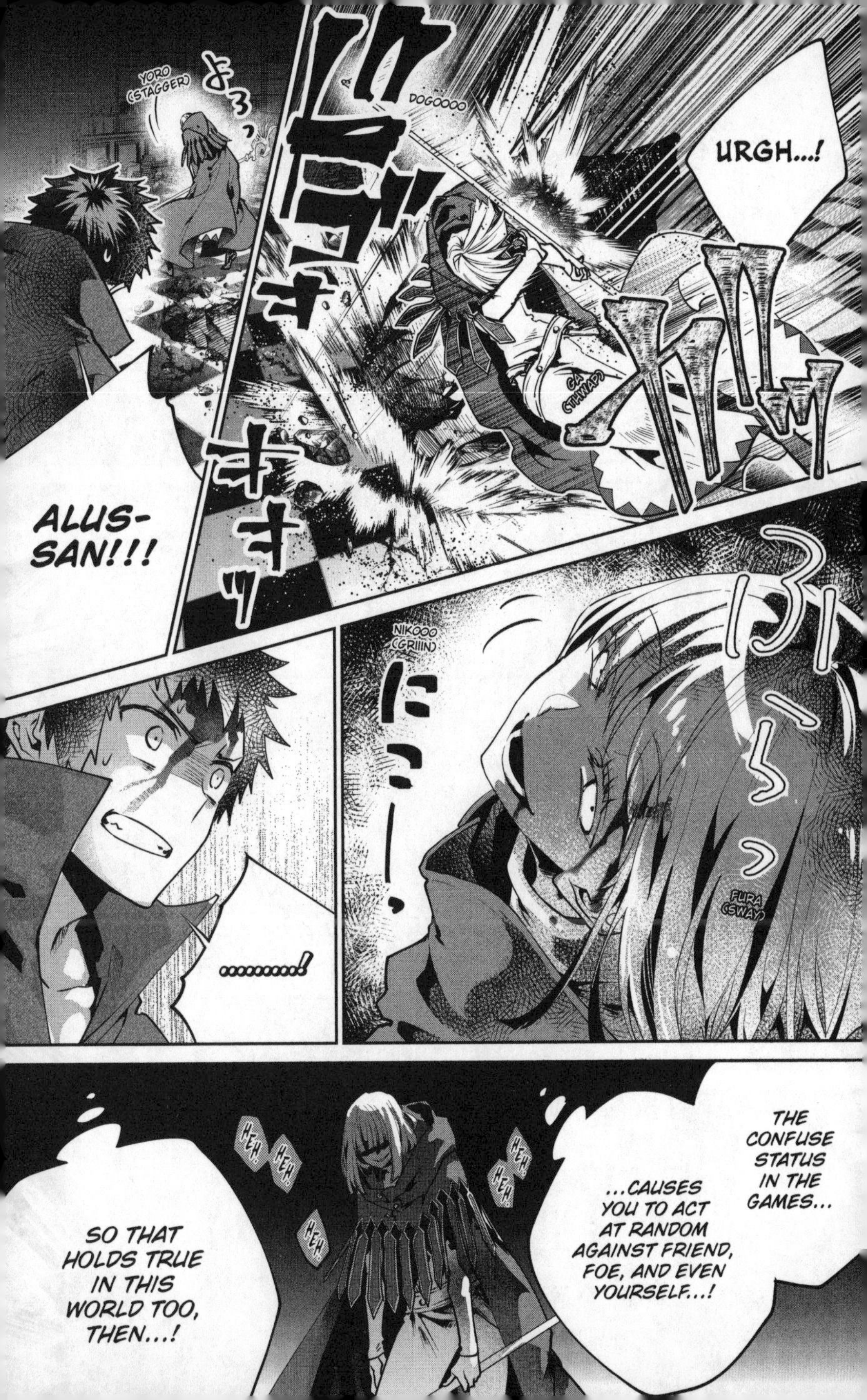
DOGOOOO
URGH...!
GA (THWAP)
YORO (STAGGER)
ALUS-SAN!!!
NIKOOO (GRIIIN)
FURA (SWAY)
..........!
THE CONFUSE STATUS IN THE GAMES...
...CAUSES YOU TO ACT AT RANDOM AGAINST FRIEND, FOE, AND EVEN YOURSELF...!
HEH HEH HEH HEH HEH
SO THAT HOLDS TRUE IN THIS WORLD TOO, THEN...!

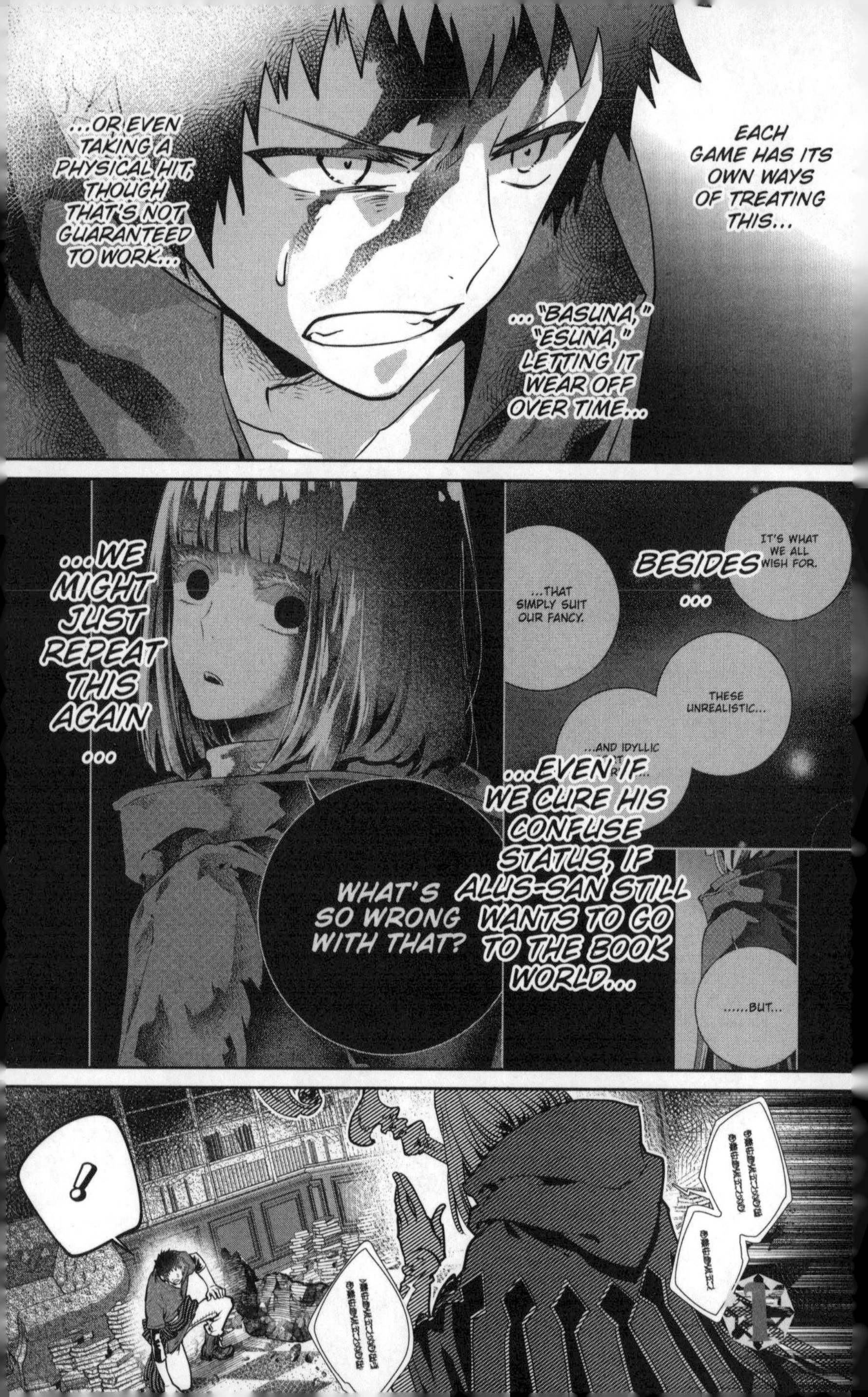
EACH GAME HAS ITS OWN WAYS OF TREATING THIS...
..."BASUNA," "ESUNA," LETTING IT WEAR OFF OVER TIME...
...OR EVEN TAKING A PHYSICAL HIT, THOUGH THAT'S NOT GUARANTEED TO WORK...
IT'S WHAT WE ALL WISH FOR.
BESIDES...
...THAT SIMPLY SUIT OUR FANCY.
THESE UNREALISTIC...
...AND IDYLLIC
...EVEN IF WE CURE HIS CONFUSE STATUS, IF ALUS-SAN STILL WANTS TO GO TO THE BOOK WORLD...
......BUT...
...WE MIGHT JUST REPEAT THIS AGAIN...
WHAT'S SO WRONG WITH THAT?
!

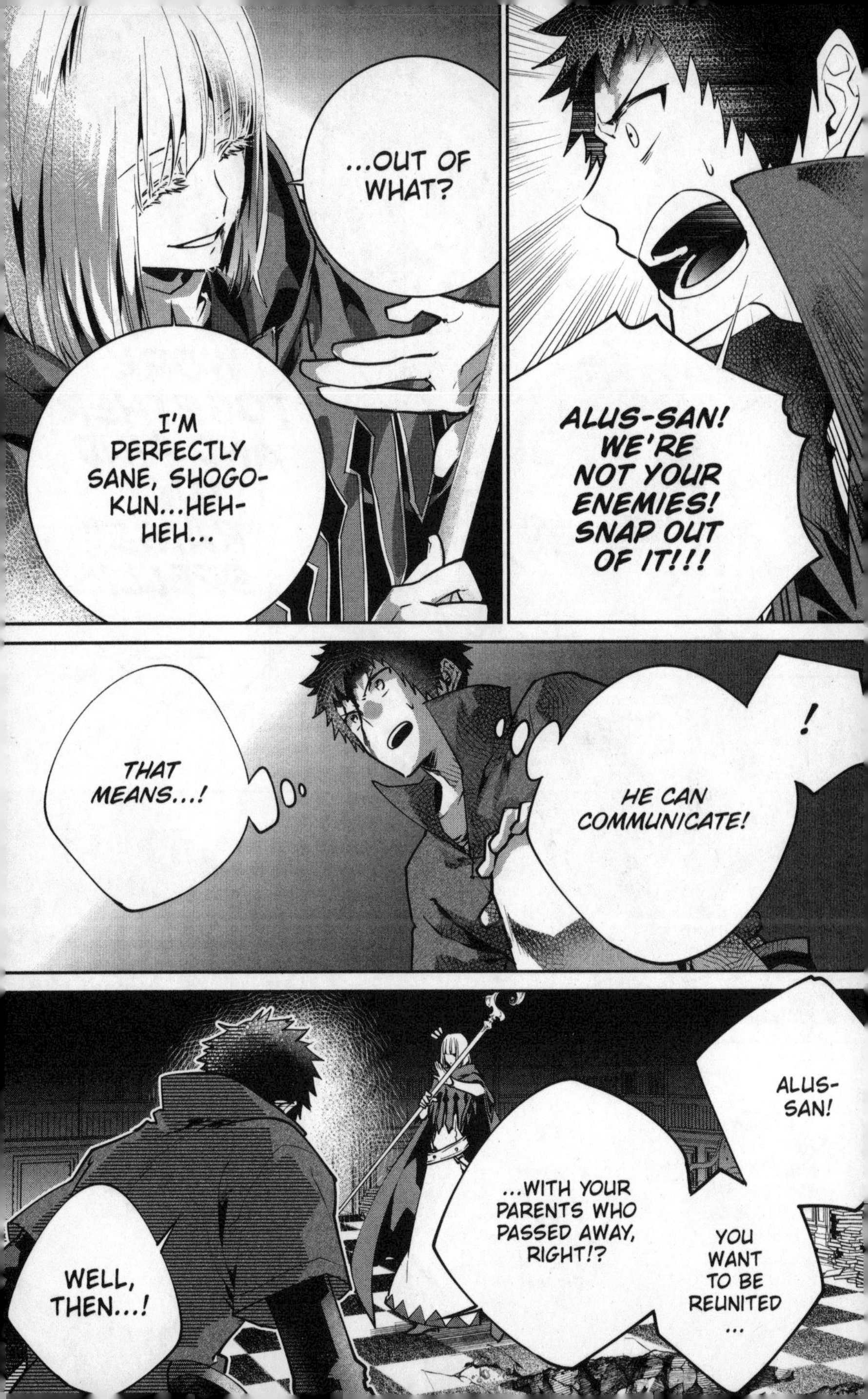
ALUS-SAN! WE'RE NOT YOUR ENEMIES! SNAP OUT OF IT!!!
...OUT OF WHAT?
I'M PERFECTLY SANE, SHOGO-KUN...HEH-HEH...
!
HE CAN COMMUNICATE!
THAT MEANS...!
ALUS-SAN!
YOU WANT TO BE REUNITED ...
...WITH YOUR PARENTS WHO PASSED AWAY, RIGHT!?
WELL, THEN...!

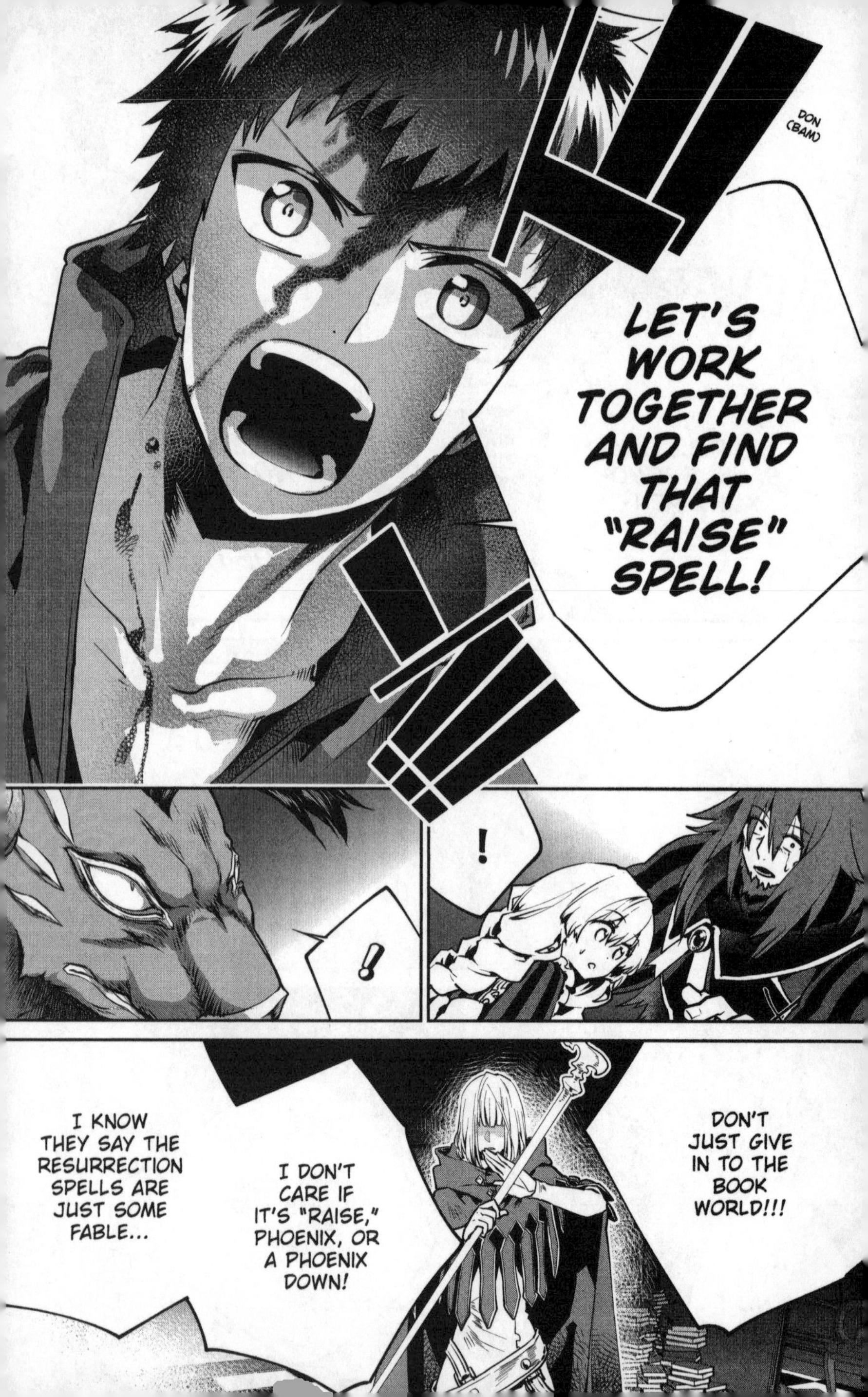
DON (BAM)
LET'S WORK TOGETHER AND FIND THAT "RAISE" SPELL!
!
!
DON'T JUST GIVE IN TO THE BOOK WORLD!!!
I DON'T CARE IF IT'S "RAISE," PHOENIX, OR A PHOENIX DOWN!
I KNOW THEY SAY THE RESURRECTION SPELLS ARE JUST SOME FABLE...

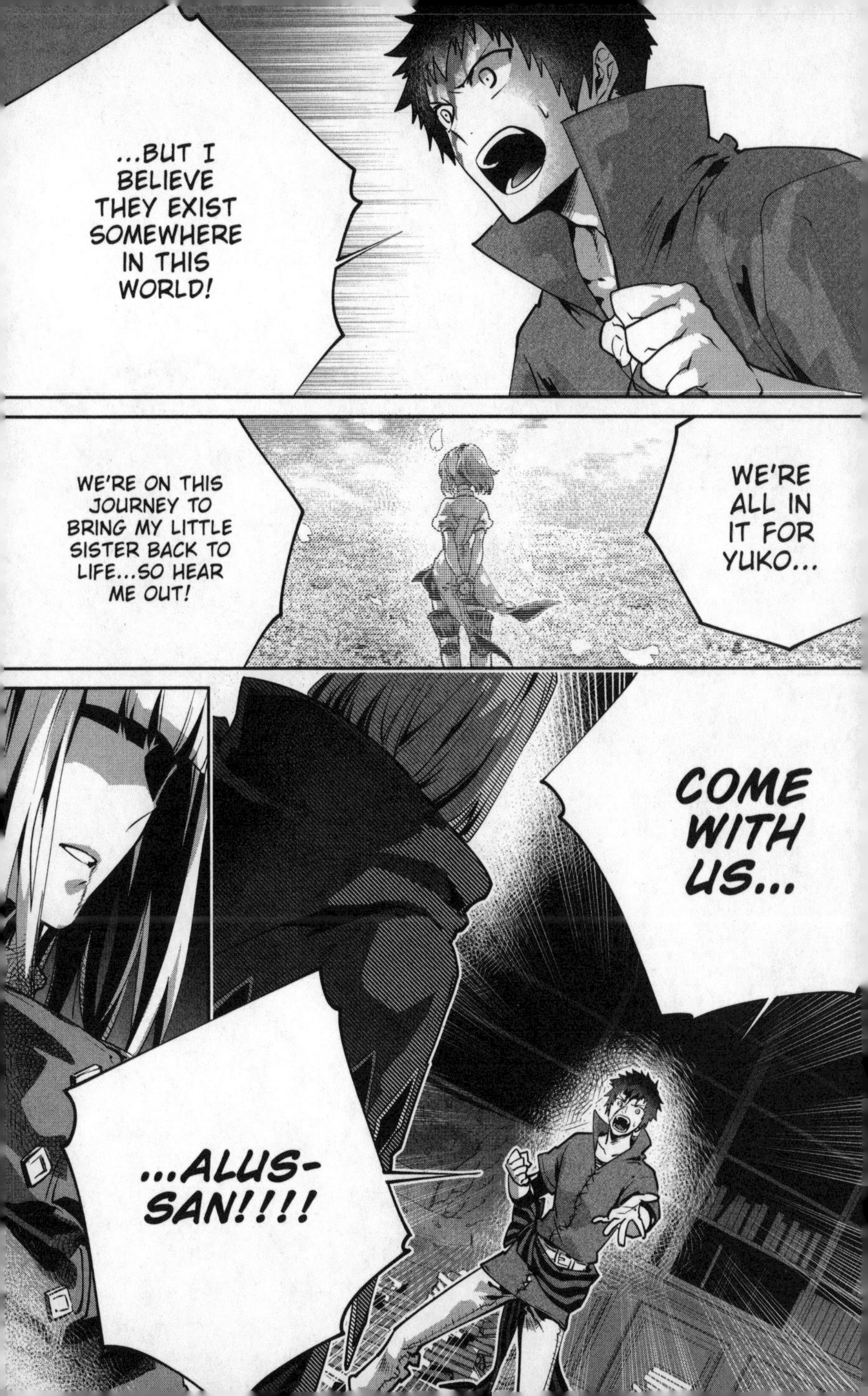
...BUT I BELIEVE THEY EXIST SOMEWHERE IN THIS WORLD!
WE'RE ALL IN IT FOR YUKO...
WE'RE ON THIS JOURNEY TO BRING MY LITTLE SISTER BACK TO LIFE...SO HEAR ME OUT!
COME WITH US...
...ALUS-SAN!!!!

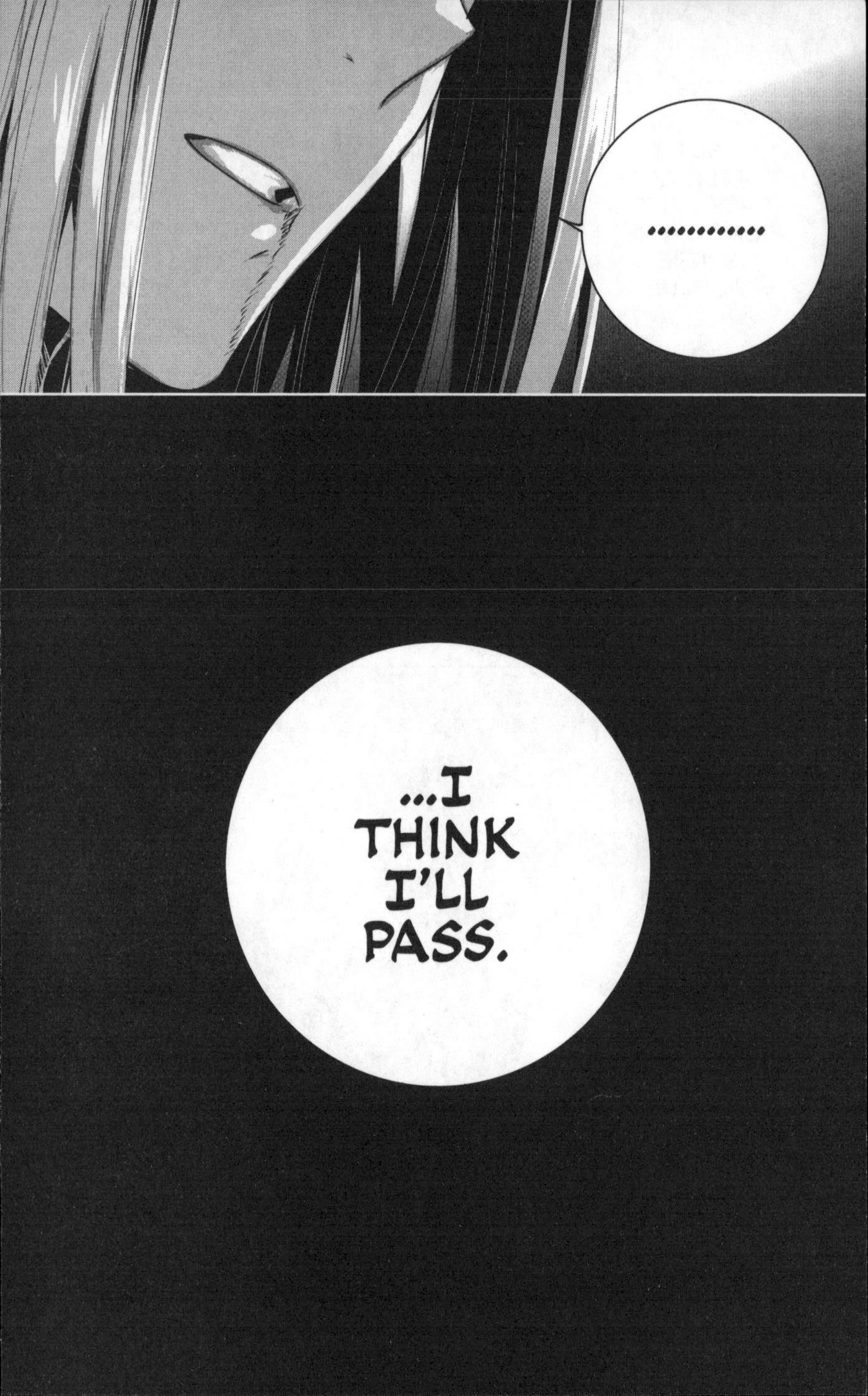
............
...I THINK I'LL PASS.

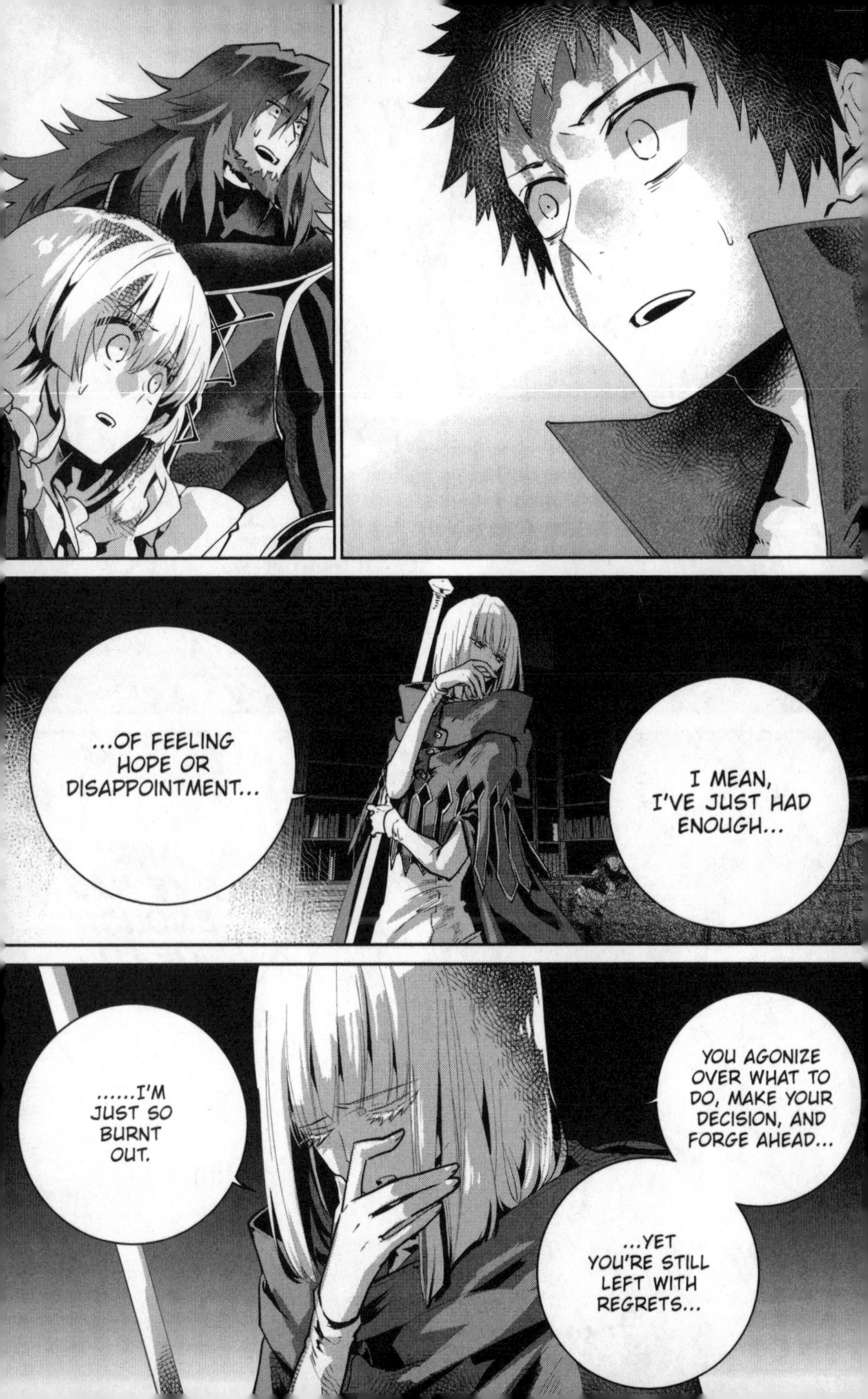
I MEAN, I'VE JUST HAD ENOUGH...
...OF FEELING HOPE OR DISAPPOINTMENT...
YOU AGONIZE OVER WHAT TO DO, MAKE YOUR DECISION, AND FORGE AHEAD...
...YET YOU'RE STILL LEFT WITH REGRETS...
......I'M JUST SO BURNT OUT.

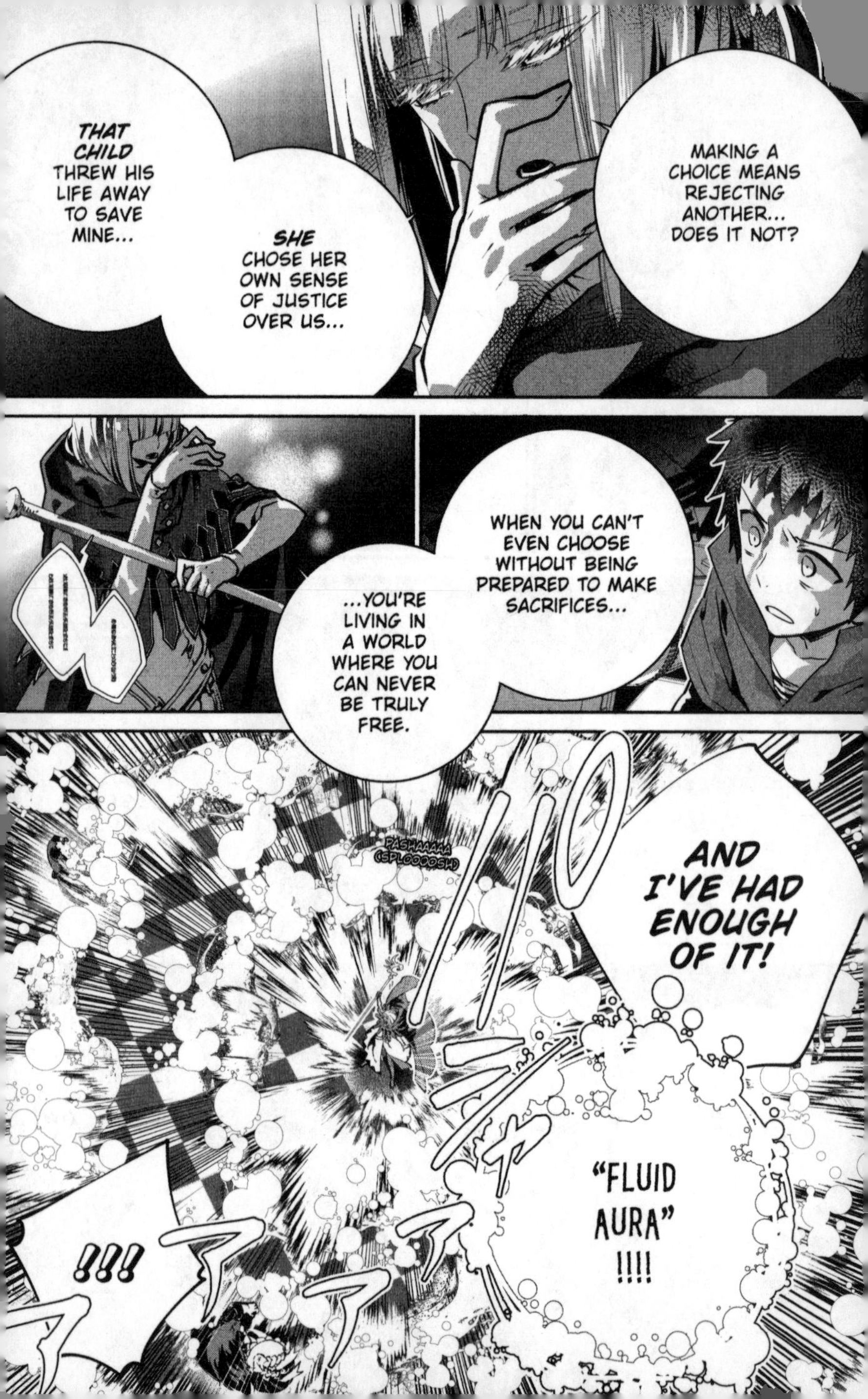

MAKING A CHOICE MEANS REJECTING ANOTHER... DOES IT NOT?
*SHE* CHOSE HER OWN SENSE OF JUSTICE OVER US...
*THAT CHILD* THREW HIS LIFE AWAY TO SAVE MINE...
WHEN YOU CAN'T EVEN CHOOSE WITHOUT BEING PREPARED TO MAKE SACRIFICES...
...YOU'RE LIVING IN A WORLD WHERE YOU CAN NEVER BE TRULY FREE.
AND I'VE HAD ENOUGH OF IT!
PASHAAAAA (SPLOOOOSH)
"FLUID AURA" !!!!
!!!

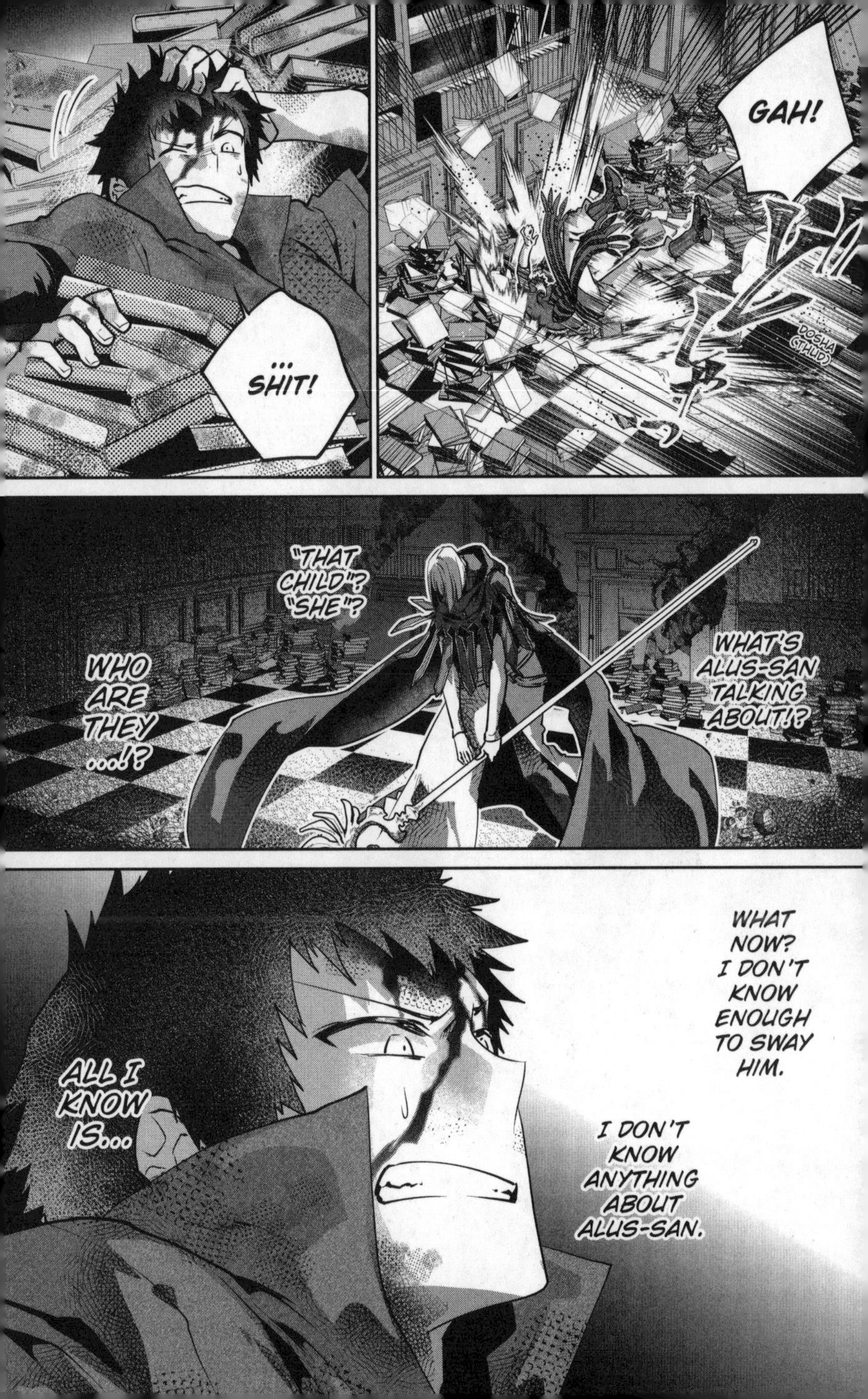
GAH!
DOSHA (THUD)
...SHIT!
"THAT CHILD"? "SHE"?
WHAT'S ALUS-SAN TALKING ABOUT!?
WHO ARE THEY...!?
WHAT NOW? I DON'T KNOW ENOUGH TO SWAY HIM.
I DON'T KNOW ANYTHING ABOUT ALUS-SAN.
ALL I KNOW IS...

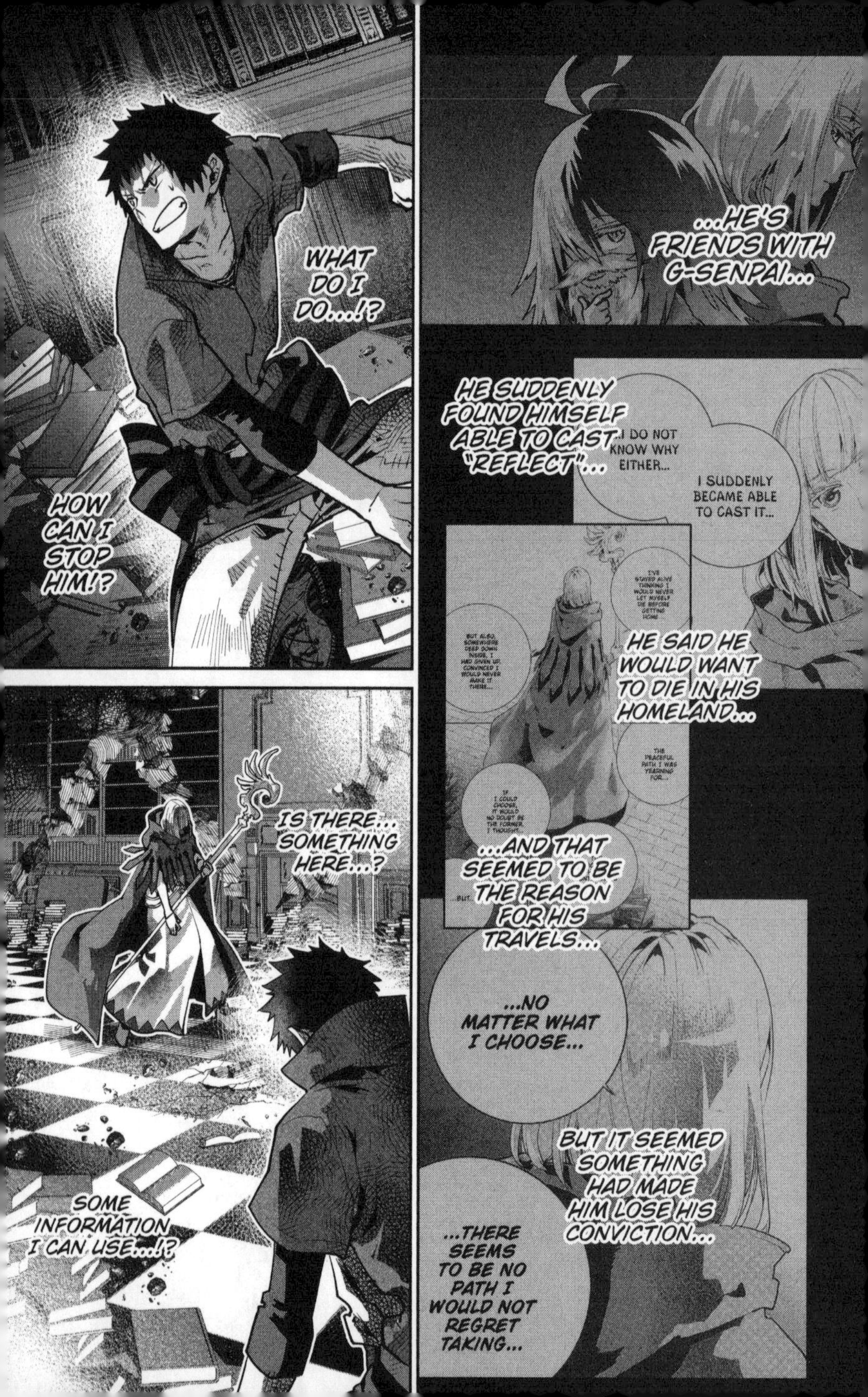
...HE'S FRIENDS WITH G-SENPAI...
HE SUDDENLY FOUND HIMSELF ABLE TO CAST "REFLECT"...
I DO NOT KNOW WHY EITHER...
I SUDDENLY BECAME ABLE TO CAST IT...
I'VE STAYED ALIVE THINKING I WOULD NEVER LET MYSELF DIE BEFORE GETTING HOME...
BUT ALSO, SOMEWHERE DEEP DOWN INSIDE, I HAD GIVEN UP, CONVINCED I WOULD NEVER MAKE IT THERE...
HE SAID HE WOULD WANT TO DIE IN HIS HOMELAND...
THE PEACEFUL PATH I WAS YEARNING FOR...
IF I COULD CHOOSE, IT WOULD NO DOUBT BE THE FORMER, I THOUGHT...
...BUT.
...AND THAT SEEMED TO BE THE REASON FOR HIS TRAVELS...
...NO MATTER WHAT I CHOOSE...
BUT IT SEEMED SOMETHING HAD MADE HIM LOSE HIS CONVICTION...
...THERE SEEMS TO BE NO PATH I WOULD NOT REGRET TAKING...
WHAT DO I DO...!?
HOW CAN I STOP HIM!?
IS THERE... SOMETHING HERE...?
SOME INFORMATION I CAN USE...!?

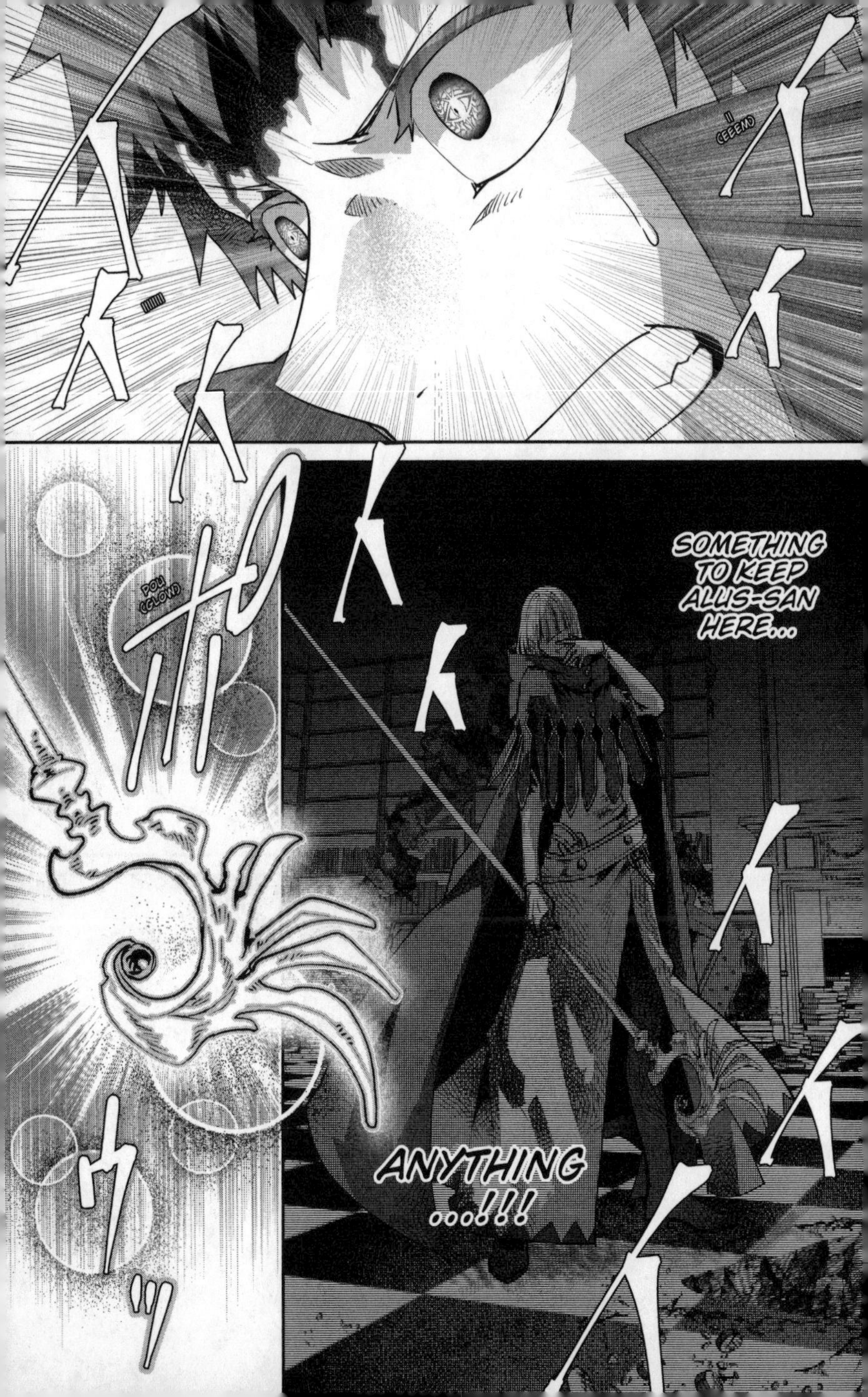
II (EEEM)
SOMETHING TO KEEP ALUS-SAN HERE...
ANYTHING ...!!!
POU (GLOW)

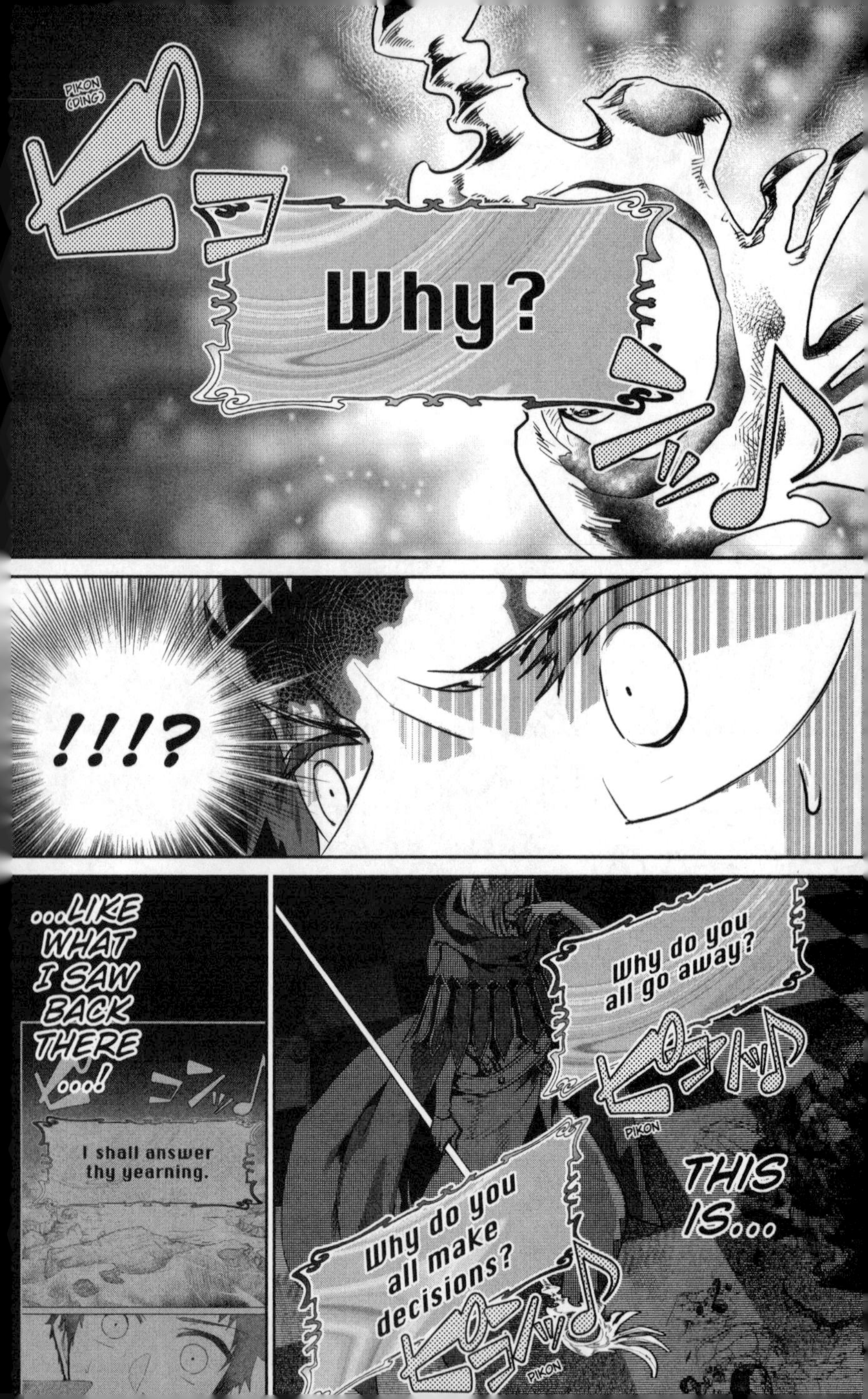

PIKON (DING)
Why?
!!!?
Why do you all go away?
PIKON
THIS IS...
Why do you all make decisions?
PIKON
...LIKE WHAT I SAW BACK THERE...!
I shall answer thy yearning.

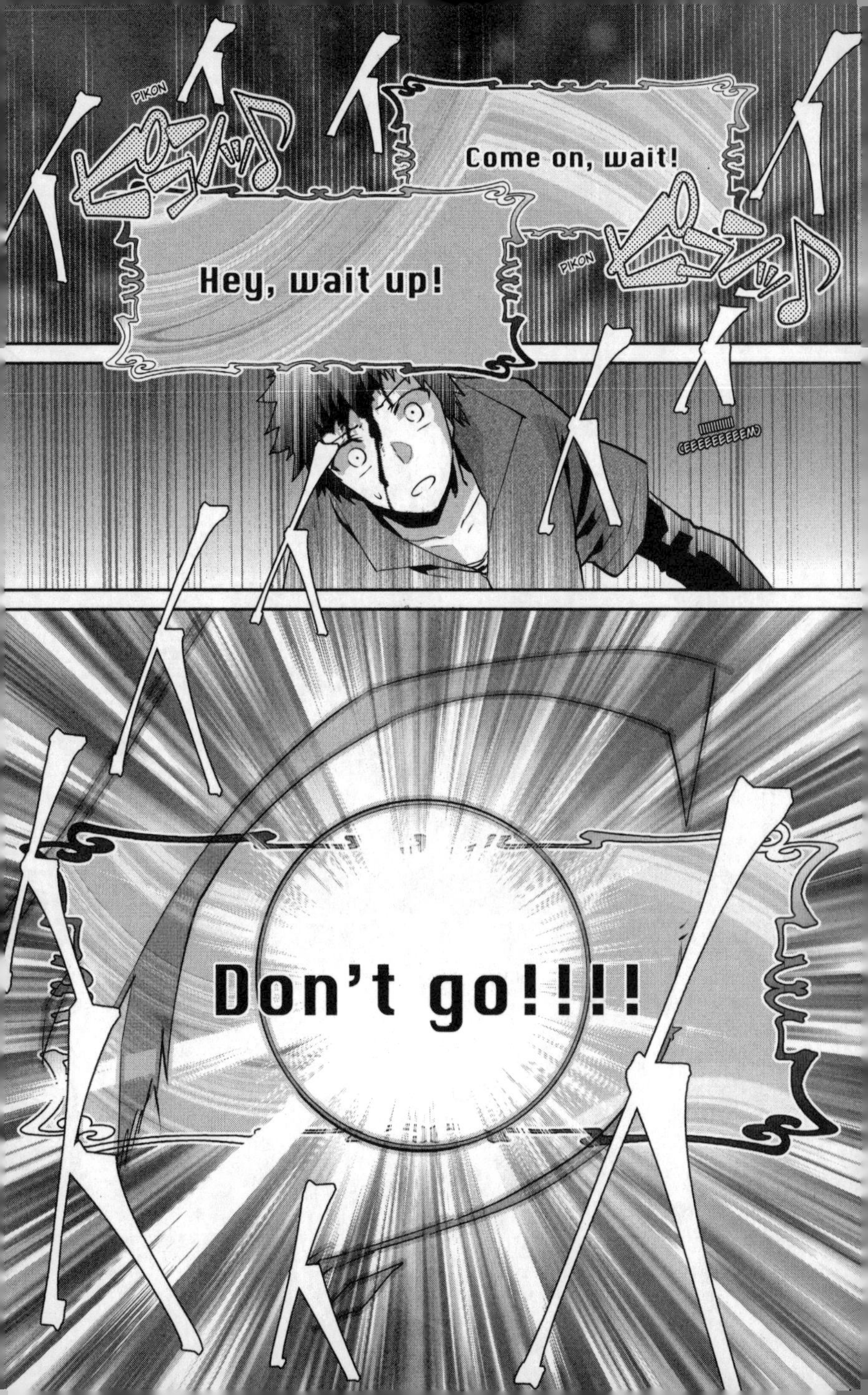
PIKON
Come on, wait!
Hey, wait up!
PIKON
(EEEEEEEEEM)
Don't go!!!!

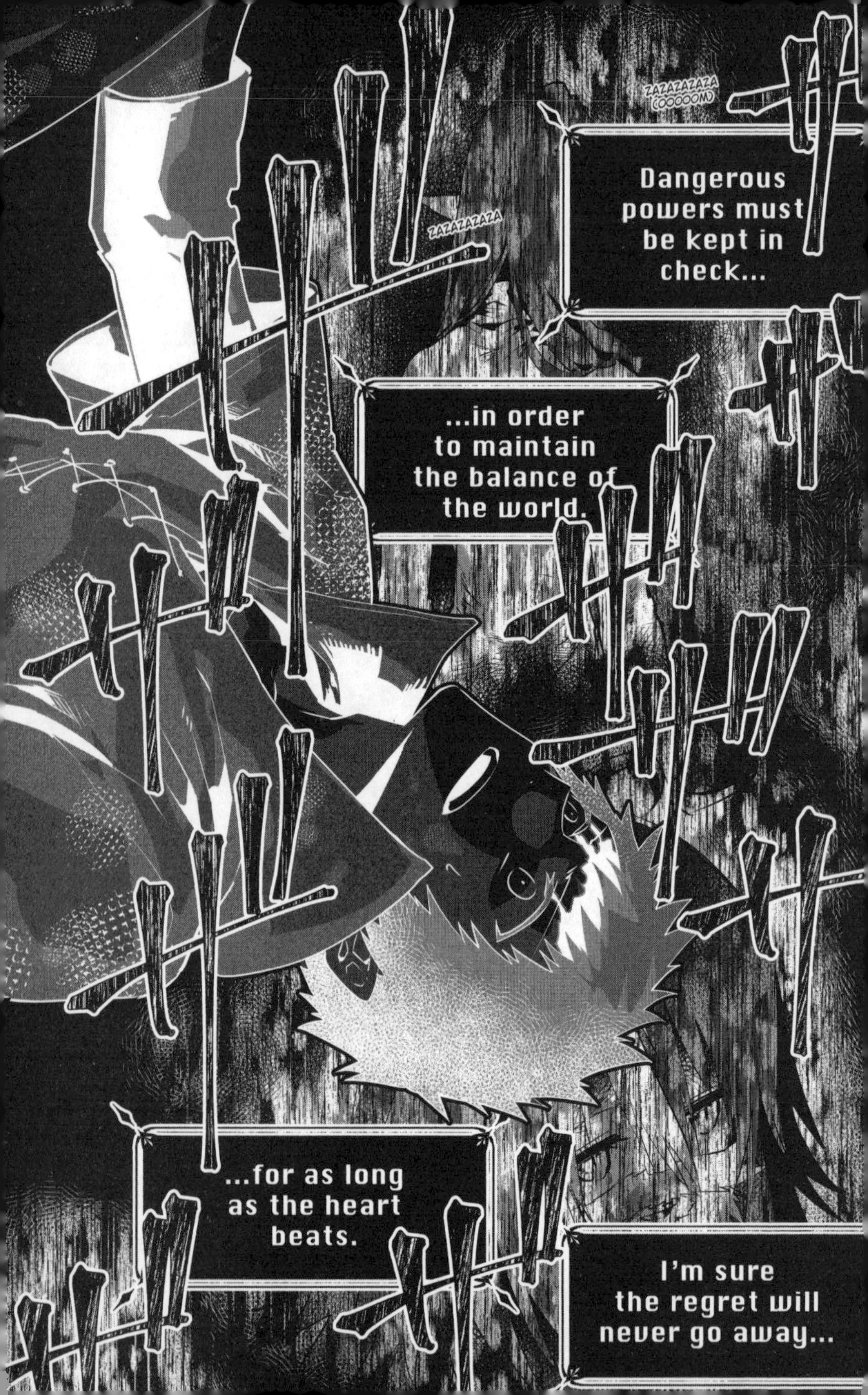
ZAZAZAZAZA (OOOOOM)
Dangerous powers must be kept in check...
ZAZAZAZAZA
...in order to maintain the balance of the world.
I'm sure the regret will never go away...
...for as long as the heart beats.

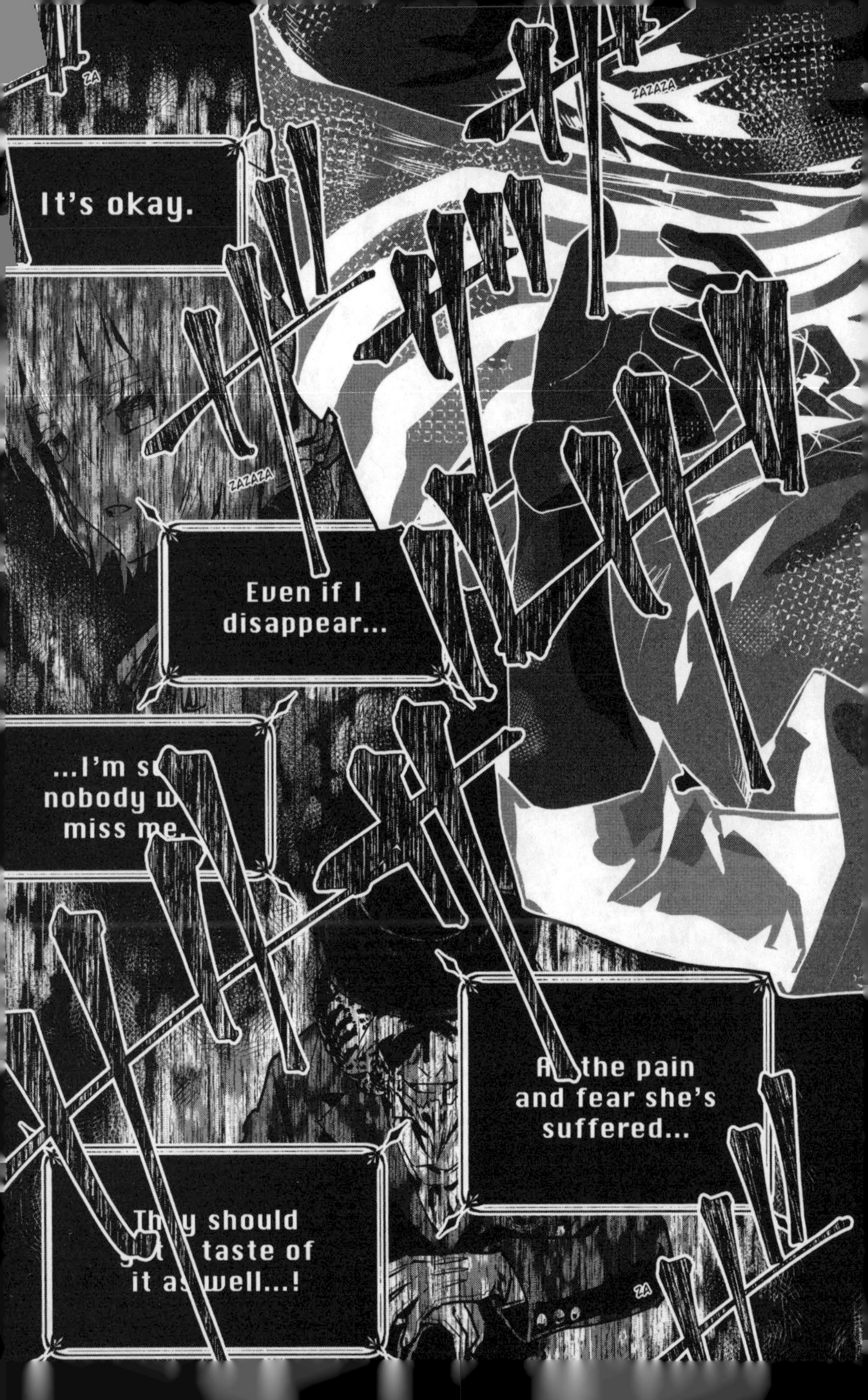
ZAZAZA
ZA
It's okay.
ZAZAZA
Even if I disappear...
...I'm s
nobody w
miss me.
A the pain and fear she's suffered...
Th y should
taste of
it as well...!
ZA

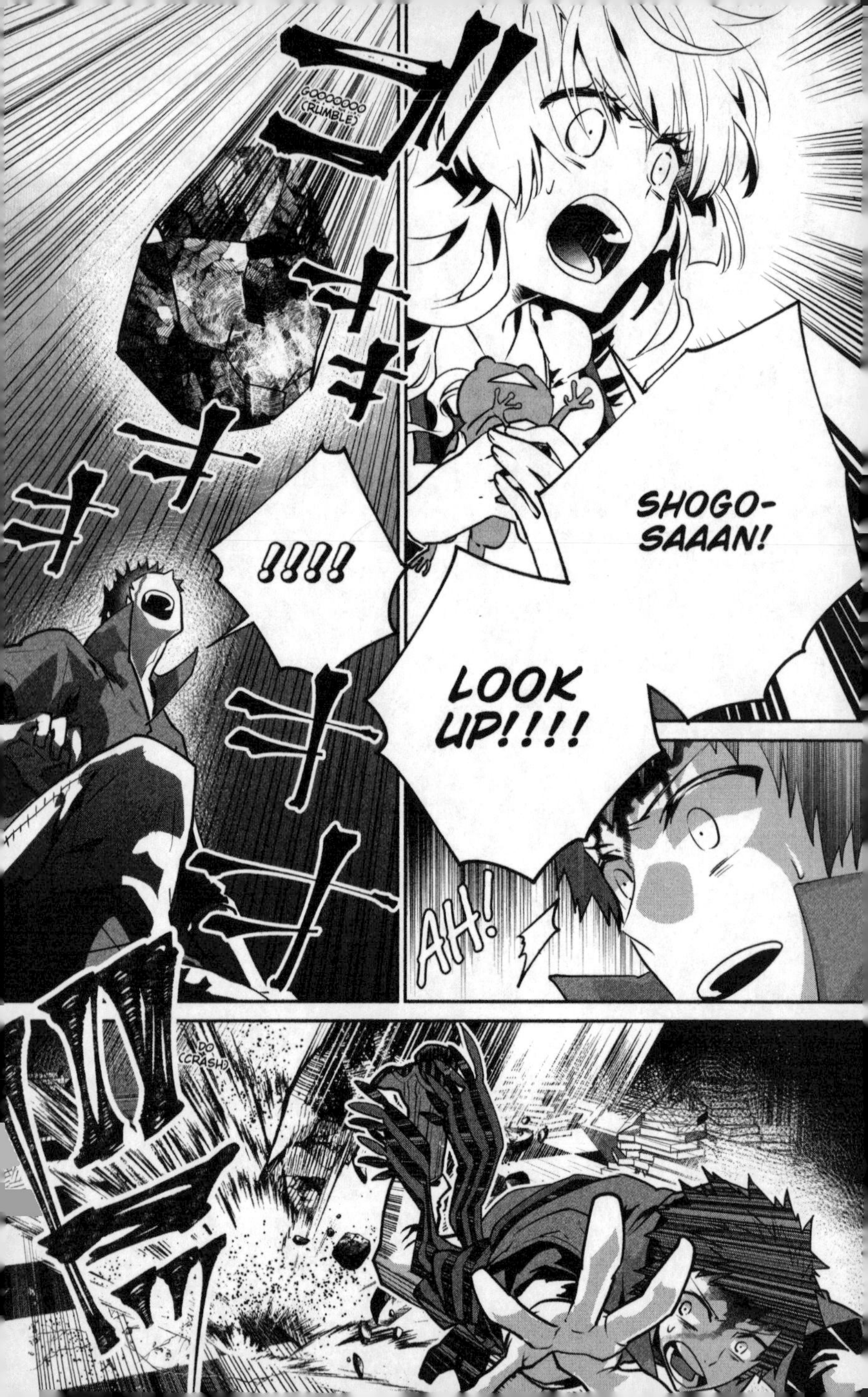
SHOGO-SAAAN!
LOOK UP!!!!
GOOOOOOO (RUMBLE)
!!!!
AH!
DO (CRASH)

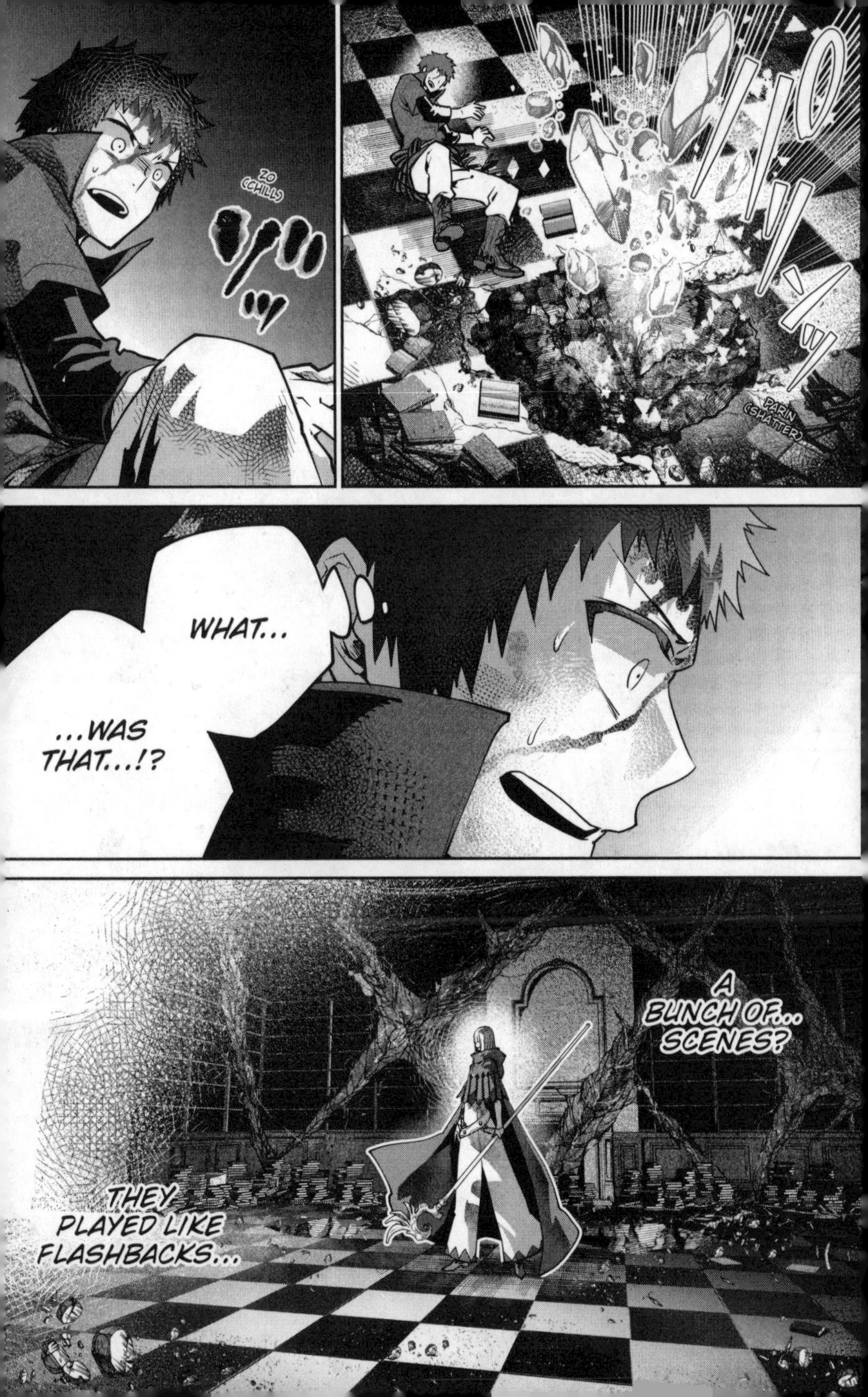
PARIN (SHATTER)
ZO (CHILL)
WHAT...
...WAS THAT...!?
A BUNCH OF... SCENES?
THEY PLAYED LIKE FLASHBACKS...

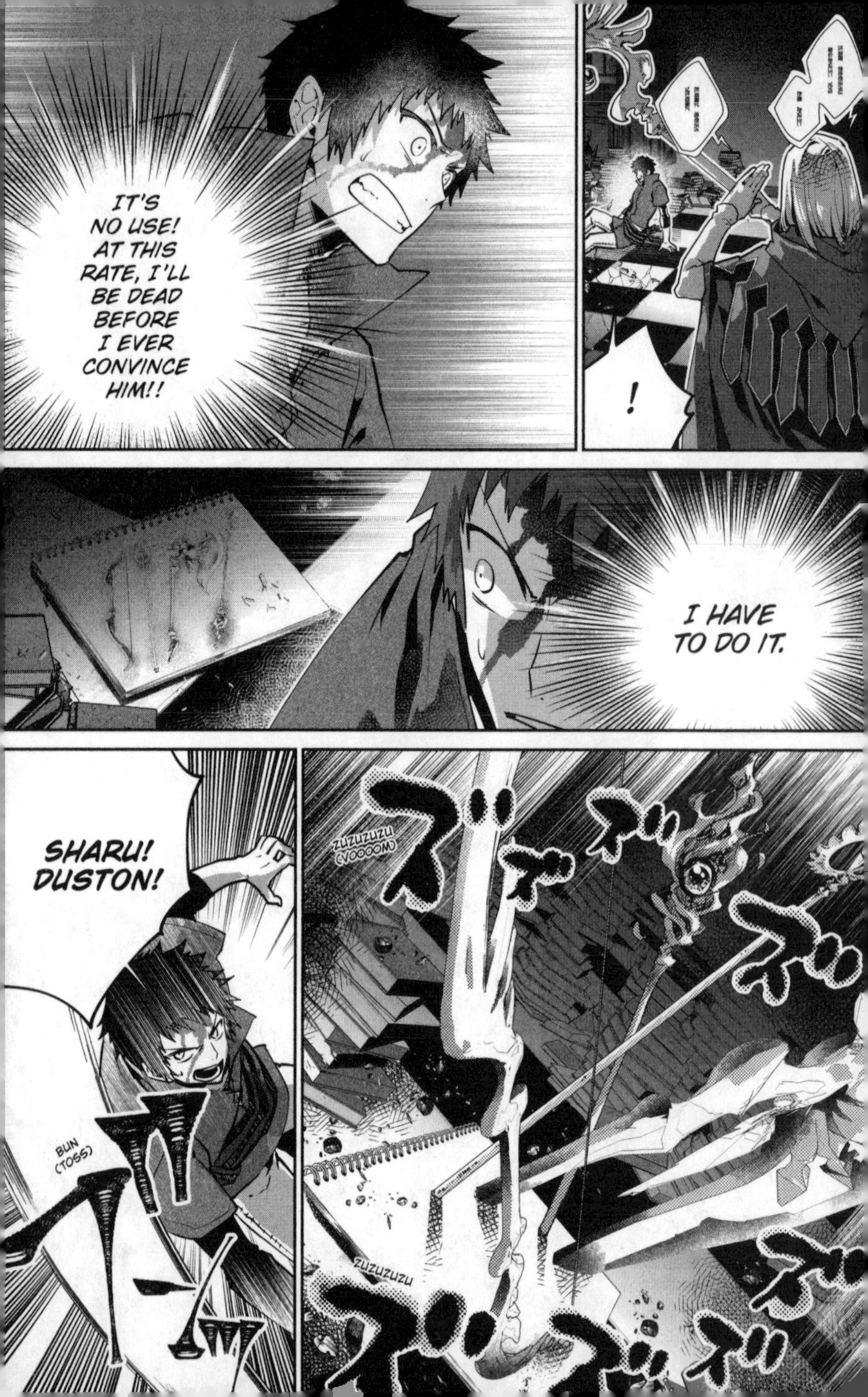
!
IT'S NO USE! AT THIS RATE, I'LL BE DEAD BEFORE I EVER CONVINCE HIM!!
I HAVE TO DO IT.
ZUZUZUZU (VOOOOM)
ZUZUZUZU
SHARU! DUSTON!
BUN (TOSS)

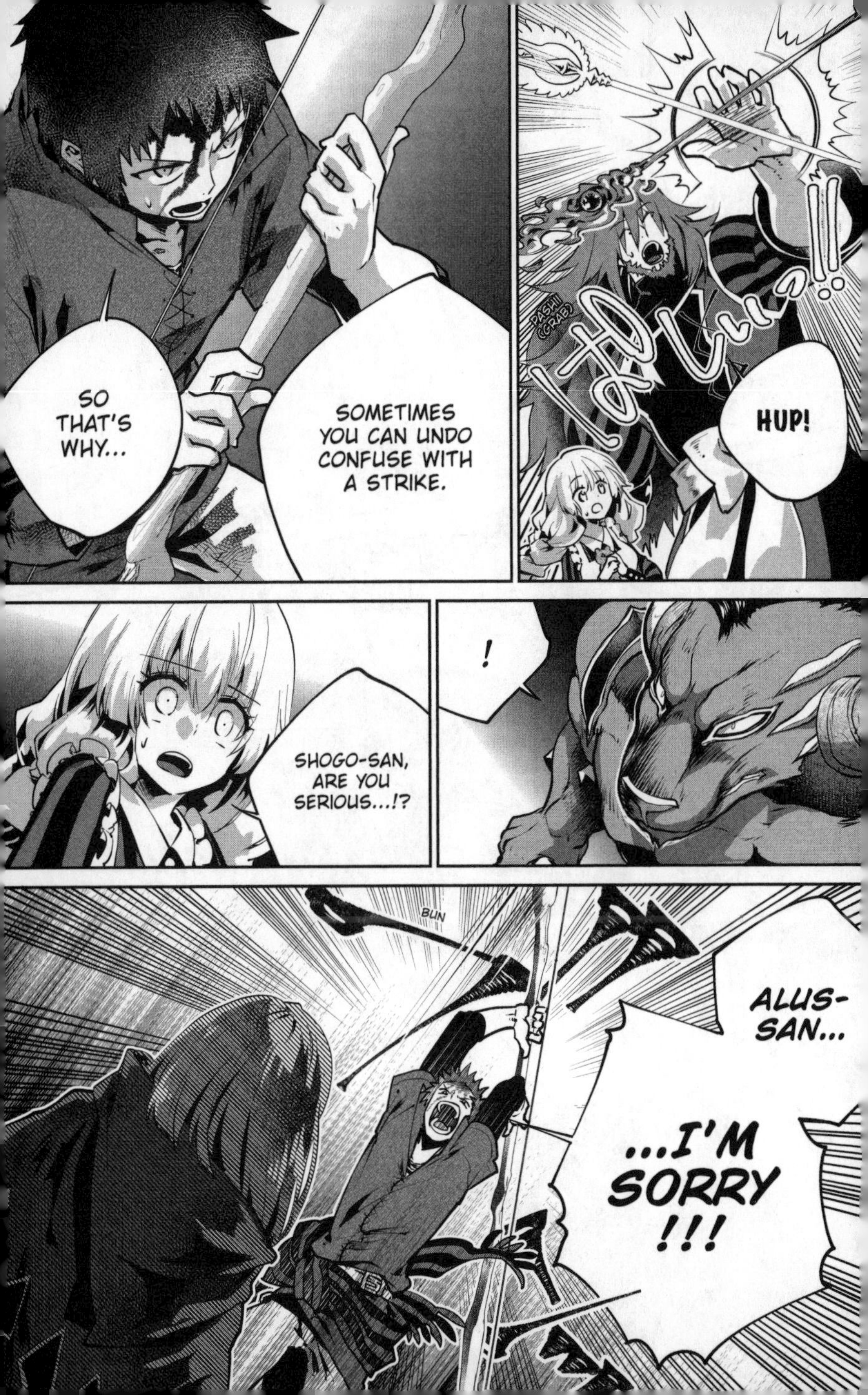
PASHI (GRAB)
HUP!
SOMETIMES YOU CAN UNDO CONFUSE WITH A STRIKE.
SO THAT'S WHY...
!
SHOGO-SAN, ARE YOU SERIOUS...!?
BUN
ALUS-SAN...
...I'M SORRY!!!

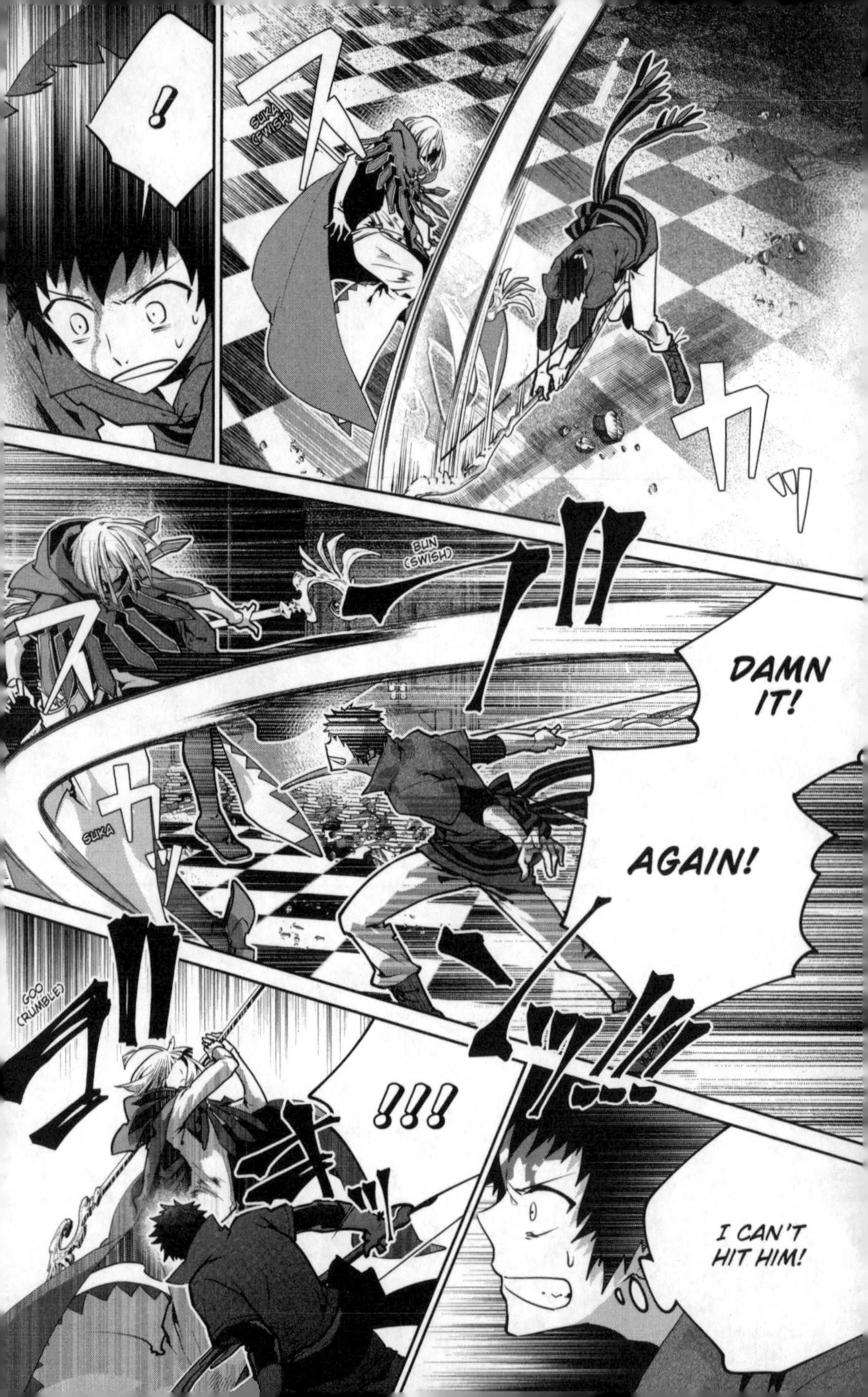
SUKA (SWISH)
!
DAMN IT!
BUN (SWISH)
AGAIN!
SUKA
I CAN'T HIT HIM!
!!!
GOO (RUMBLE)

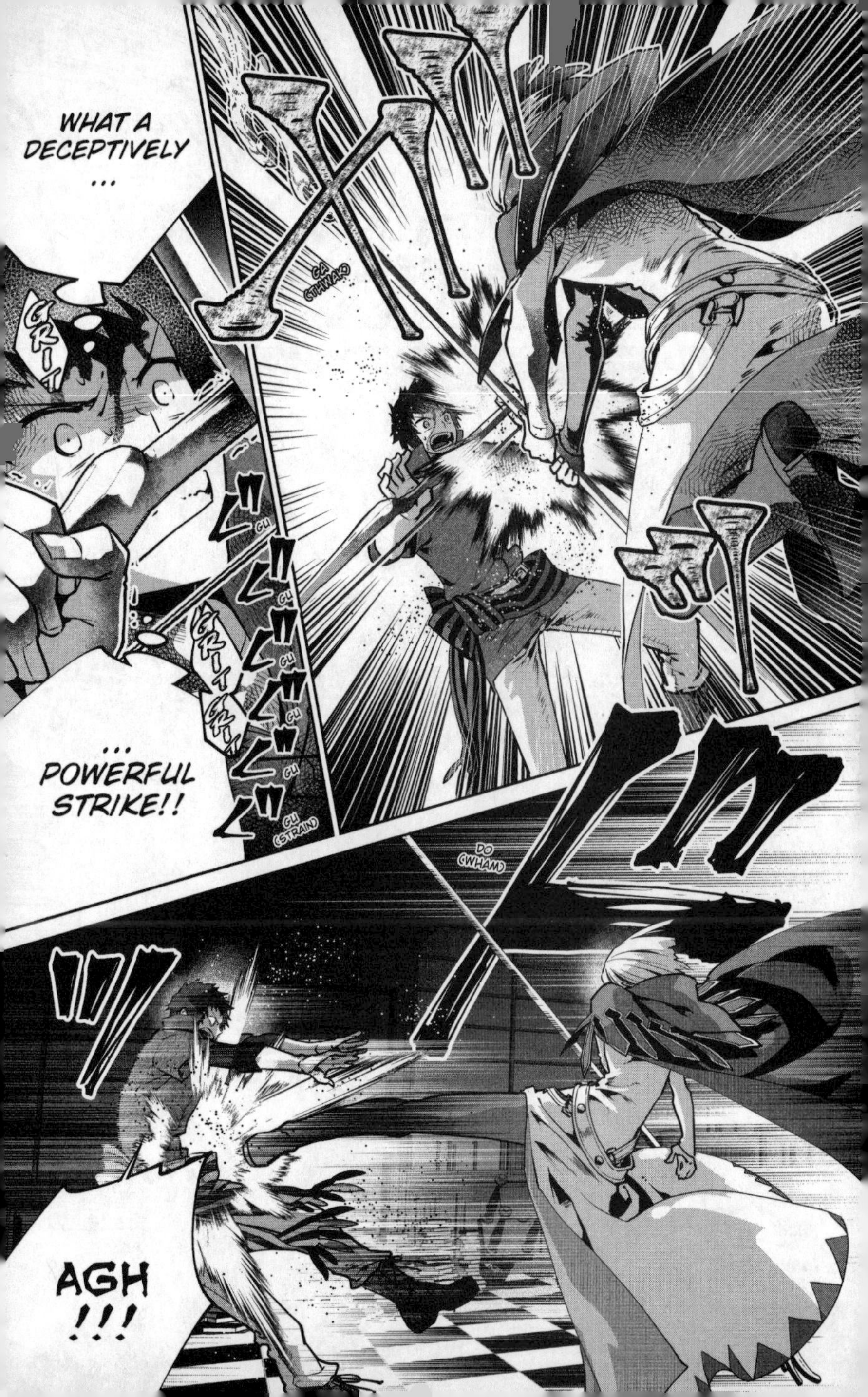
GA (THWAK)
WHAT A DECEPTIVELY ...
GRIT
GU GU GU GU GU GU (STRAIN)
GRIT GRIT
... POWERFUL STRIKE!!
DO (WHAM)
AGH !!!

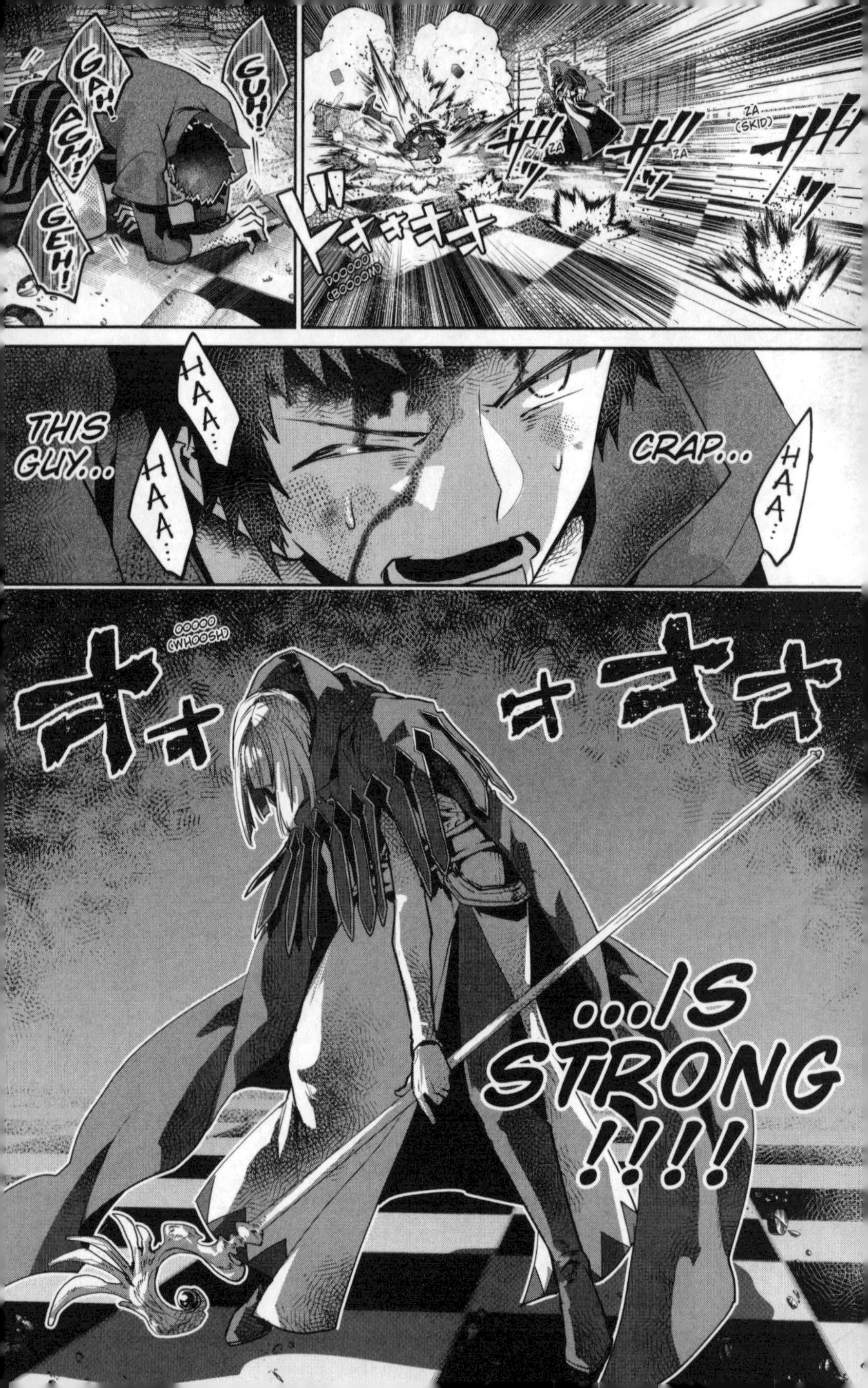
ZA (SKID)
ZA
ZA
DOOOOO (BOOOOM)
GUH!
GAH!
ACH!
GEH!
HAA...
CRAP...
HAA...
HAA...
THIS GUY...
OOOOO (WHOOSH)
...IS STRONG !!!!

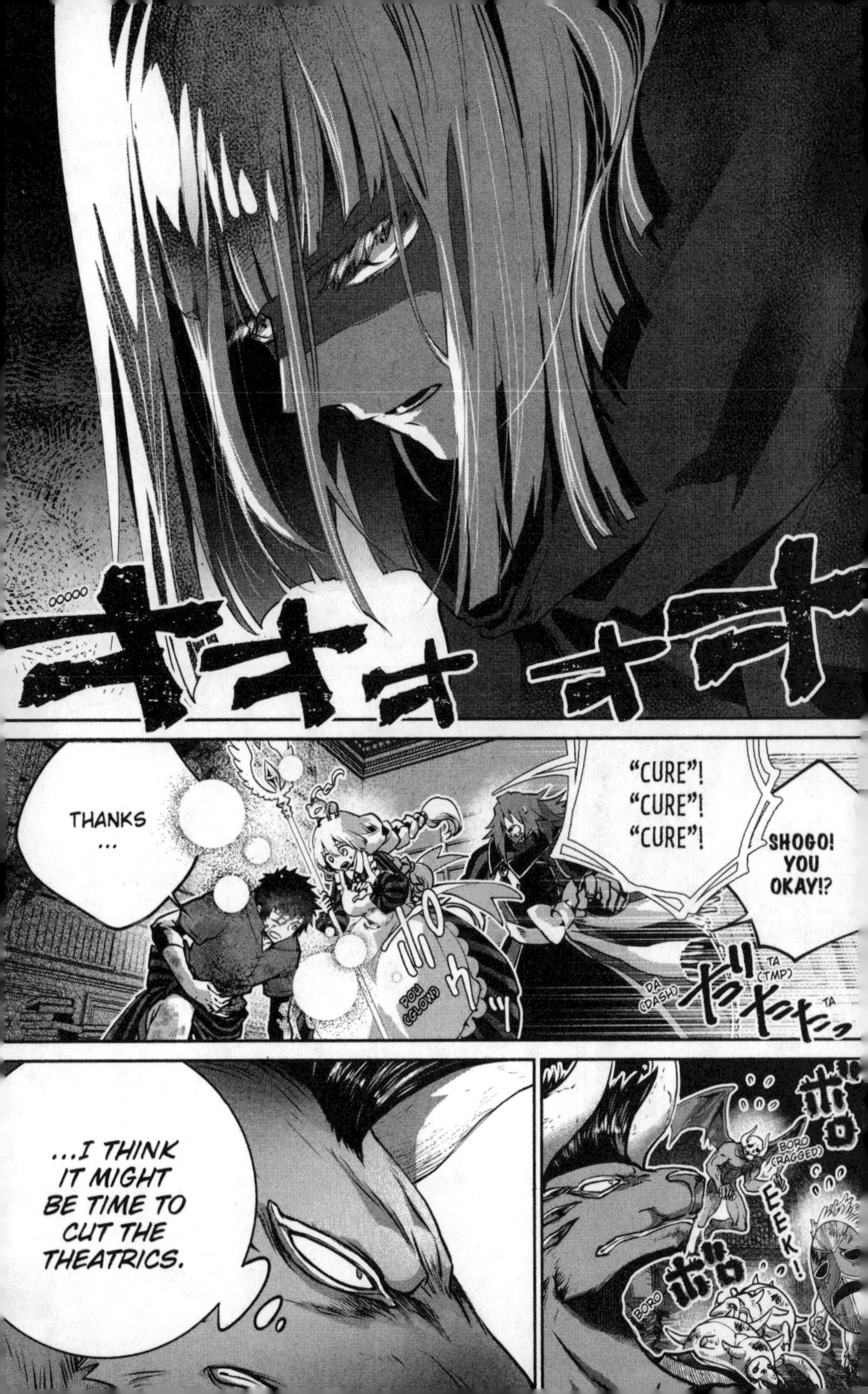
OOOOO
SHOGO! YOU OKAY!?
TA (TMP)
DA (DASH)
TA
"CURE"! "CURE"! "CURE"!
POU (GLOW)
THANKS ...
BORO (RAGGED)
EEEK!
BORO
...I THINK IT MIGHT BE TIME TO CUT THE THEATRICS.

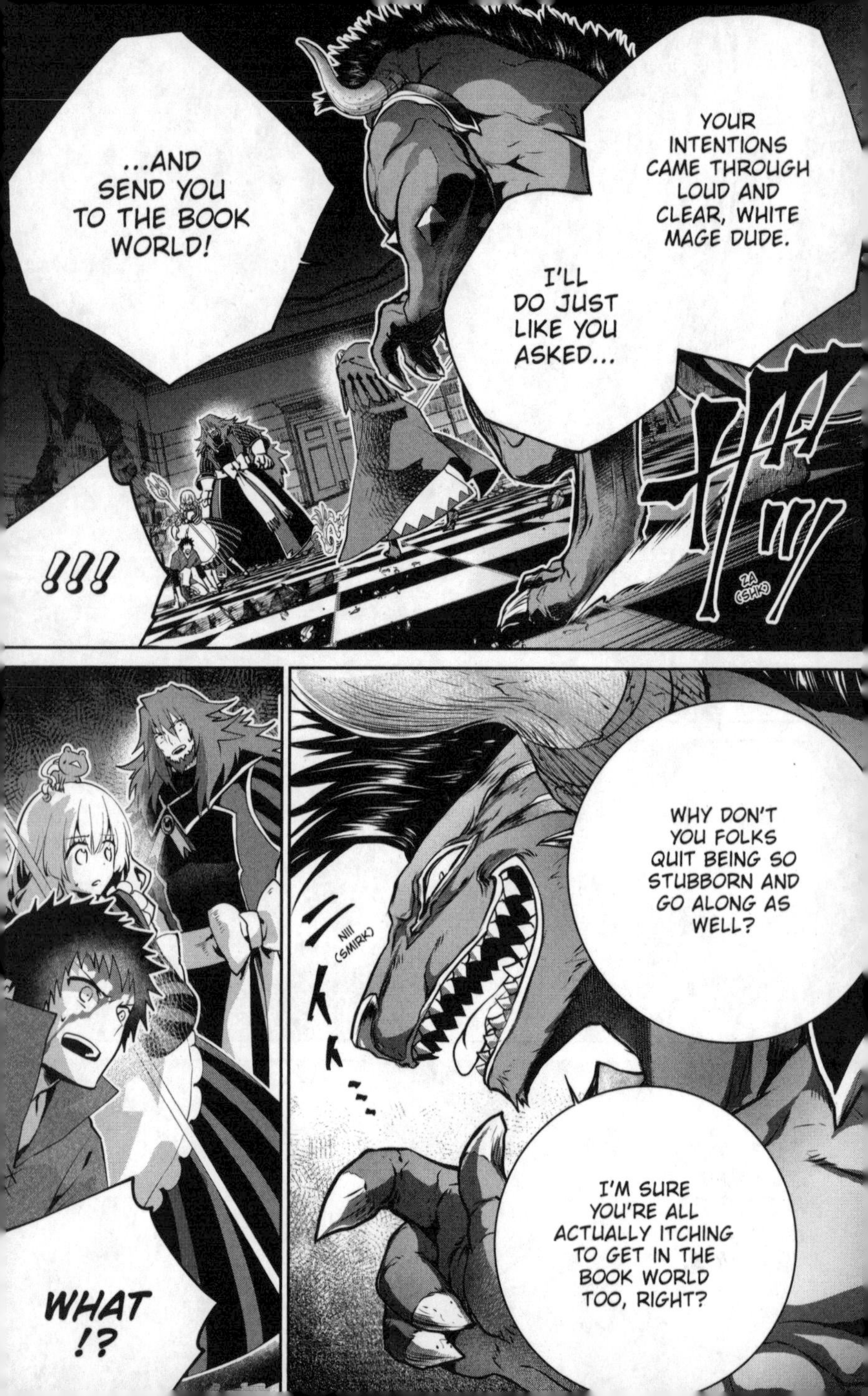
YOUR INTENTIONS CAME THROUGH LOUD AND CLEAR, WHITE MAGE DUDE.
I'LL DO JUST LIKE YOU ASKED...
...AND SEND YOU TO THE BOOK WORLD!
ZA (SHK)
!!!
WHY DON'T YOU FOLKS QUIT BEING SO STUBBORN AND GO ALONG AS WELL?
I'M SURE YOU'RE ALL ACTUALLY ITCHING TO GET IN THE BOOK WORLD TOO, RIGHT?
NIII (SMIRK)
WHAT!?

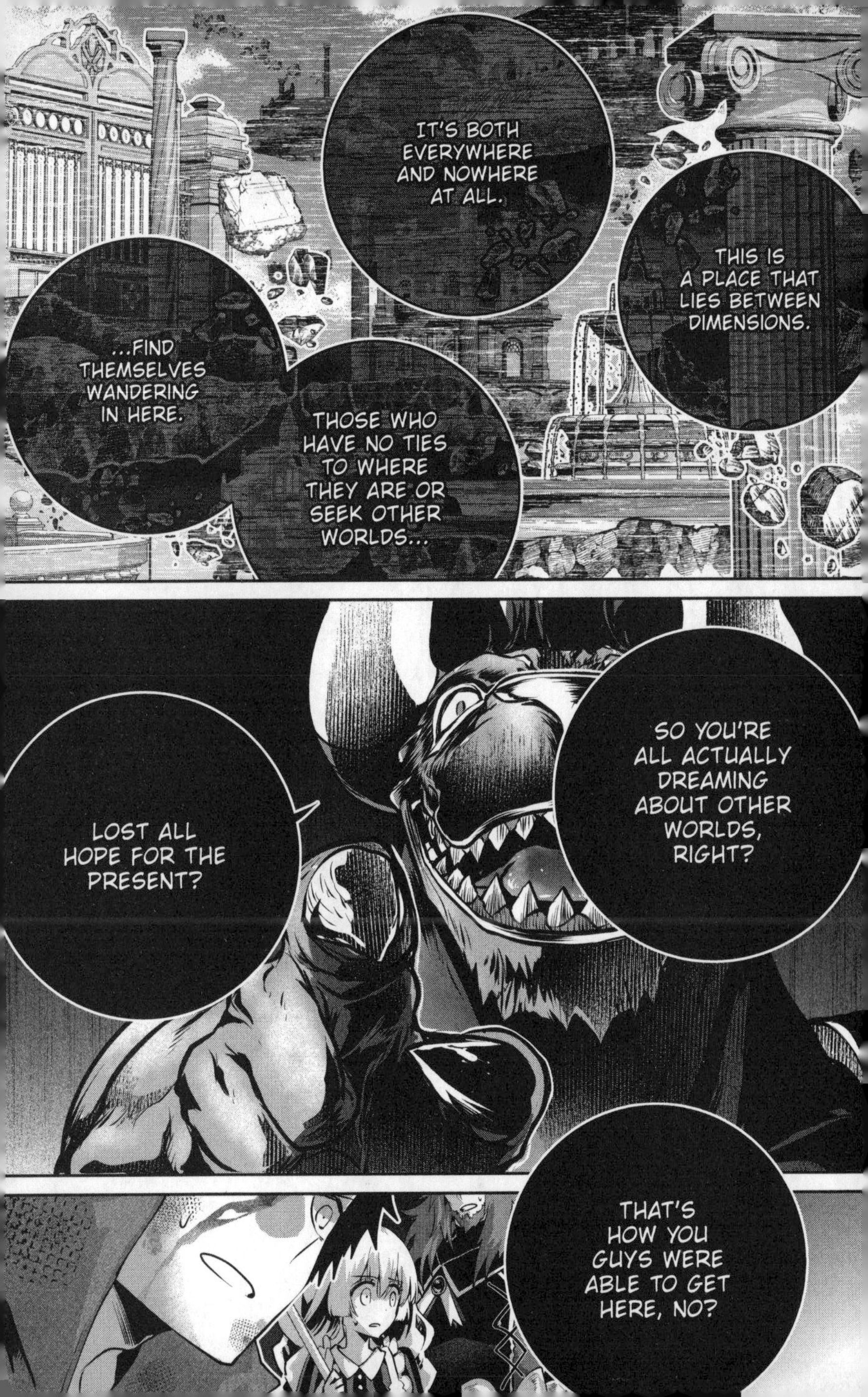
THIS IS A PLACE THAT LIES BETWEEN DIMENSIONS.
IT'S BOTH EVERYWHERE AND NOWHERE AT ALL.
THOSE WHO HAVE NO TIES TO WHERE THEY ARE OR SEEK OTHER WORLDS...
...FIND THEMSELVES WANDERING IN HERE.
SO YOU'RE ALL ACTUALLY DREAMING ABOUT OTHER WORLDS, RIGHT?
LOST ALL HOPE FOR THE PRESENT?
THAT'S HOW YOU GUYS WERE ABLE TO GET HERE, NO?

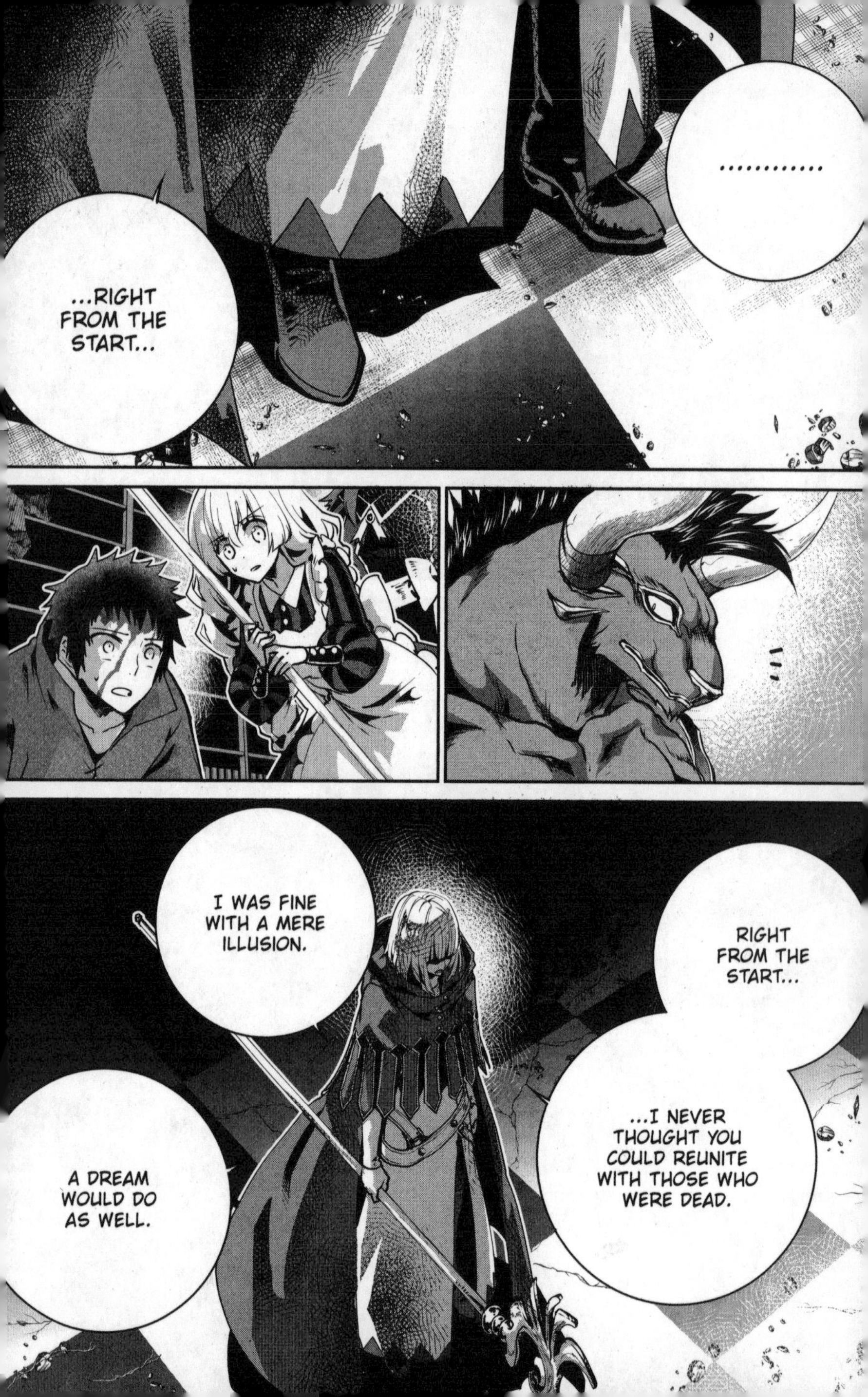
............
...RIGHT FROM THE START...
RIGHT FROM THE START...
...I NEVER THOUGHT YOU COULD REUNITE WITH THOSE WHO WERE DEAD.
I WAS FINE WITH A MERE ILLUSION.
A DREAM WOULD DO AS WELL.

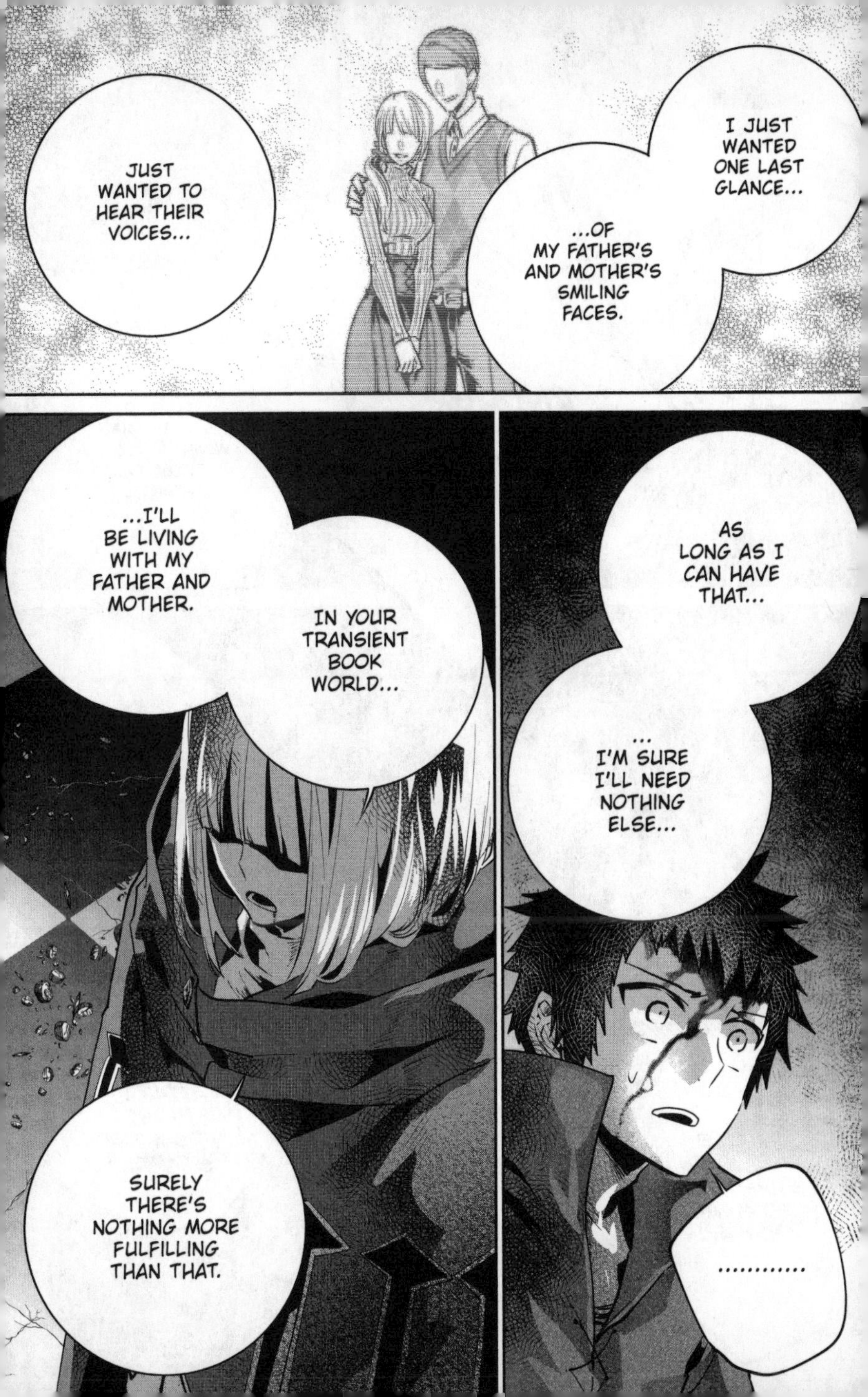
I JUST WANTED ONE LAST GLANCE...
...OF MY FATHER'S AND MOTHER'S SMILING FACES.
JUST WANTED TO HEAR THEIR VOICES...
AS LONG AS I CAN HAVE THAT...
... I'M SURE I'LL NEED NOTHING ELSE...
............
...I'LL BE LIVING WITH MY FATHER AND MOTHER.
IN YOUR TRANSIENT BOOK WORLD...
SURELY THERE'S NOTHING MORE FULFILLING THAN THAT.

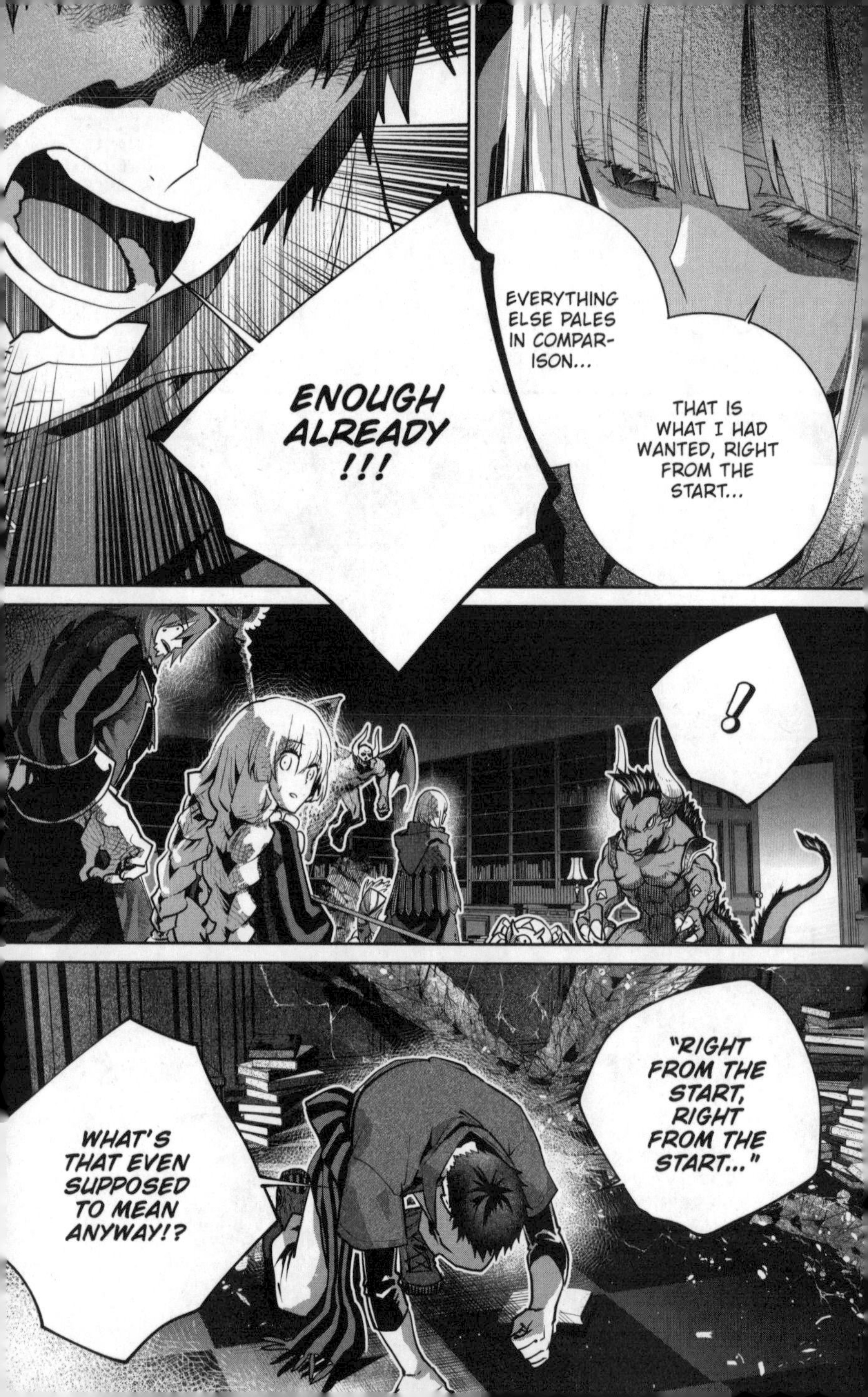
EVERYTHING ELSE PALES IN COMPARISON...
THAT IS WHAT I HAD WANTED, RIGHT FROM THE START...
ENOUGH ALREADY!!!
!
"RIGHT FROM THE START, RIGHT FROM THE START..."
WHAT'S THAT EVEN SUPPOSED TO MEAN ANYWAY!?

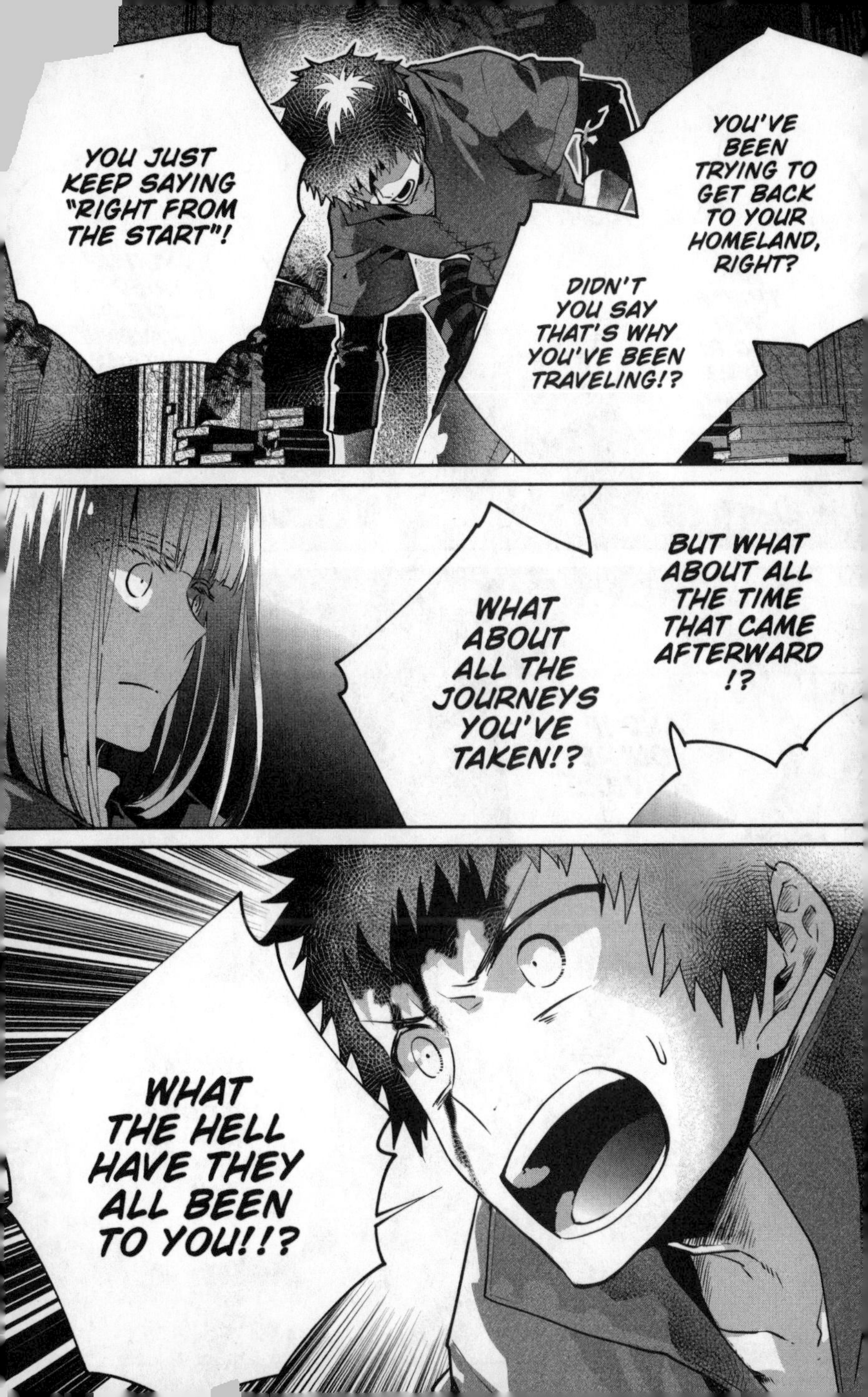
YOU'VE BEEN TRYING TO GET BACK TO YOUR HOMELAND, RIGHT?
DIDN'T YOU SAY THAT'S WHY YOU'VE BEEN TRAVELING!?
YOU JUST KEEP SAYING "RIGHT FROM THE START"!
BUT WHAT ABOUT ALL THE TIME THAT CAME AFTERWARD!?
WHAT ABOUT ALL THE JOURNEYS YOU'VE TAKEN!?
WHAT THE HELL HAVE THEY ALL BEEN TO YOU!!?

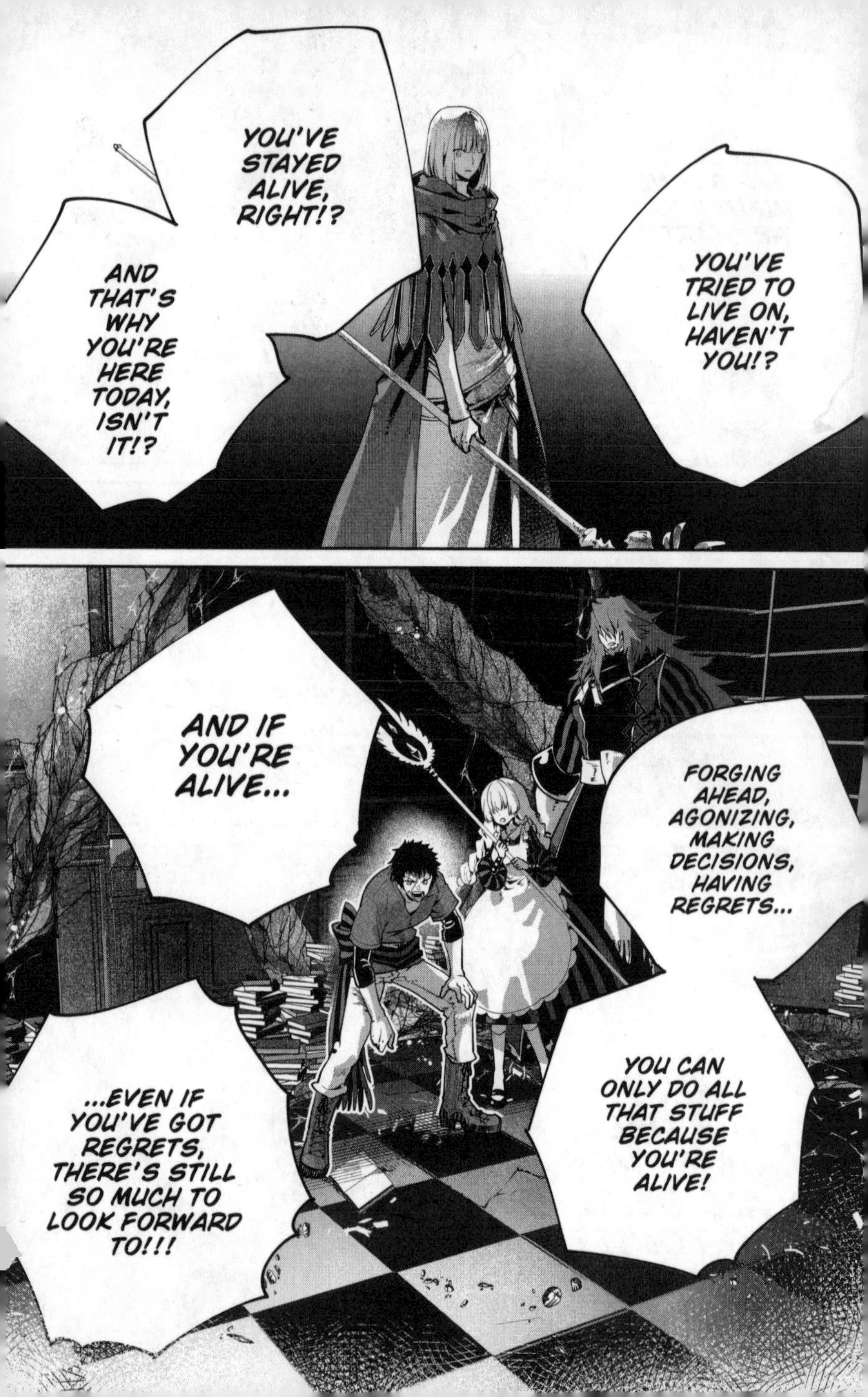
YOU'VE TRIED TO LIVE ON, HAVEN'T YOU!?
YOU'VE STAYED ALIVE, RIGHT!?
AND THAT'S WHY YOU'RE HERE TODAY, ISN'T IT!?
FORGING AHEAD, AGONIZING, MAKING DECISIONS, HAVING REGRETS...
YOU CAN ONLY DO ALL THAT STUFF BECAUSE YOU'RE ALIVE!
AND IF YOU'RE ALIVE...
...EVEN IF YOU'VE GOT REGRETS, THERE'S STILL SO MUCH TO LOOK FORWARD TO!!!

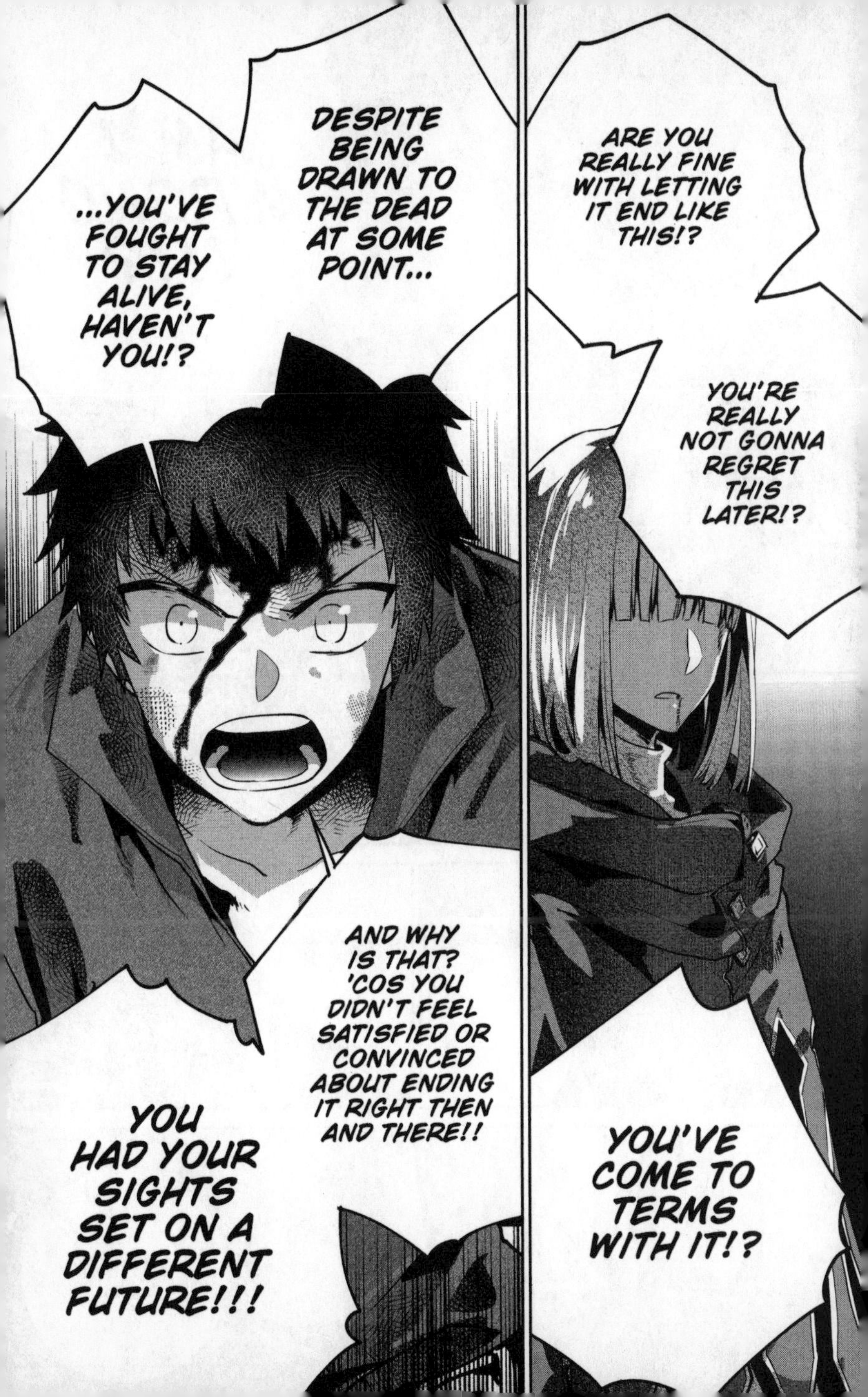
ARE YOU REALLY FINE WITH LETTING IT END LIKE THIS!?
YOU'RE REALLY NOT GONNA REGRET THIS LATER!?
YOU'VE COME TO TERMS WITH IT!?
DESPITE BEING DRAWN TO THE DEAD AT SOME POINT...
...YOU'VE FOUGHT TO STAY ALIVE, HAVEN'T YOU!?
AND WHY IS THAT? 'COS YOU DIDN'T FEEL SATISFIED OR CONVINCED ABOUT ENDING IT RIGHT THEN AND THERE!!
YOU HAD YOUR SIGHTS SET ON A DIFFERENT FUTURE!!!

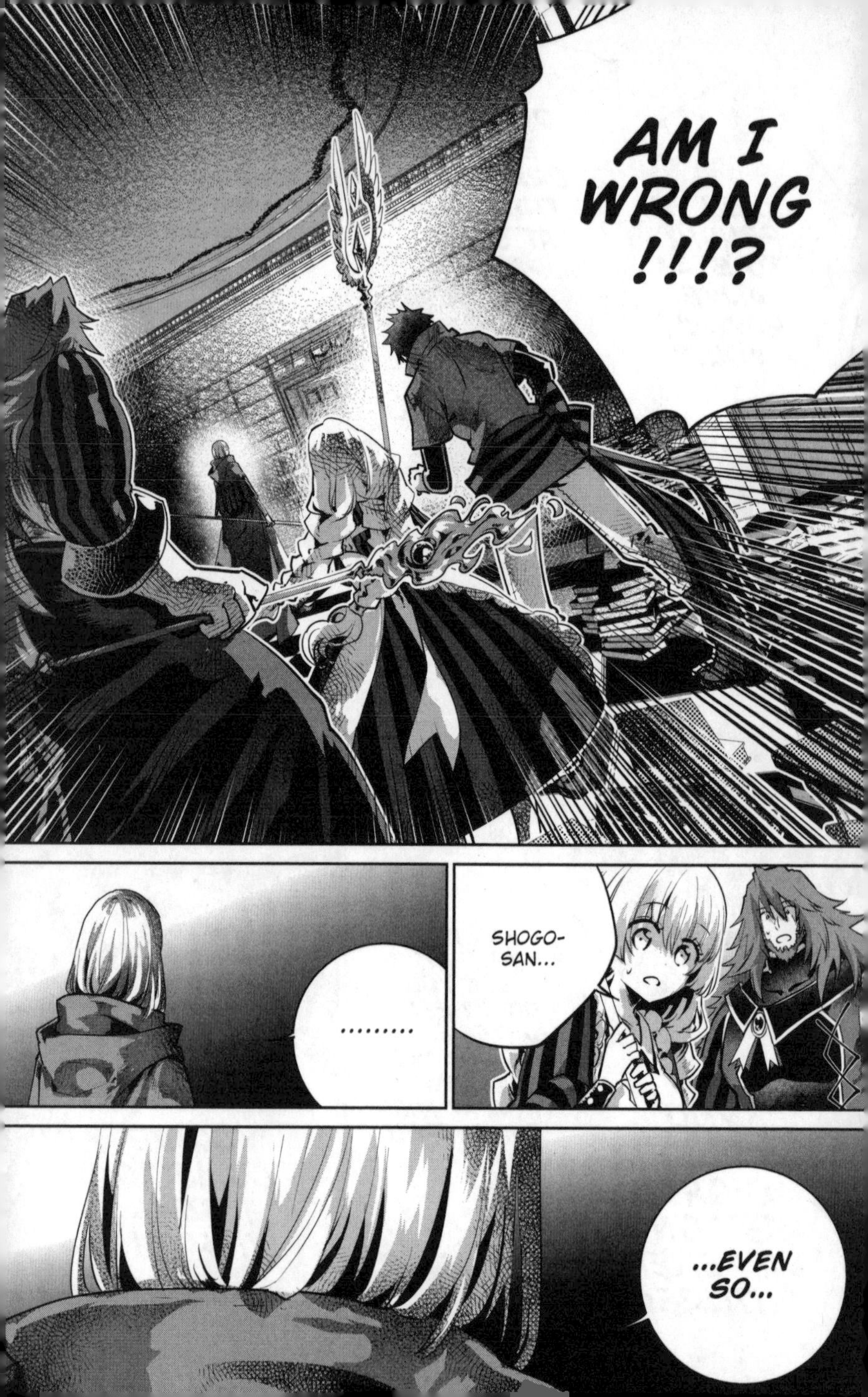
AM I WRONG !!!?
SHOGO-SAN...
.........
...EVEN SO...

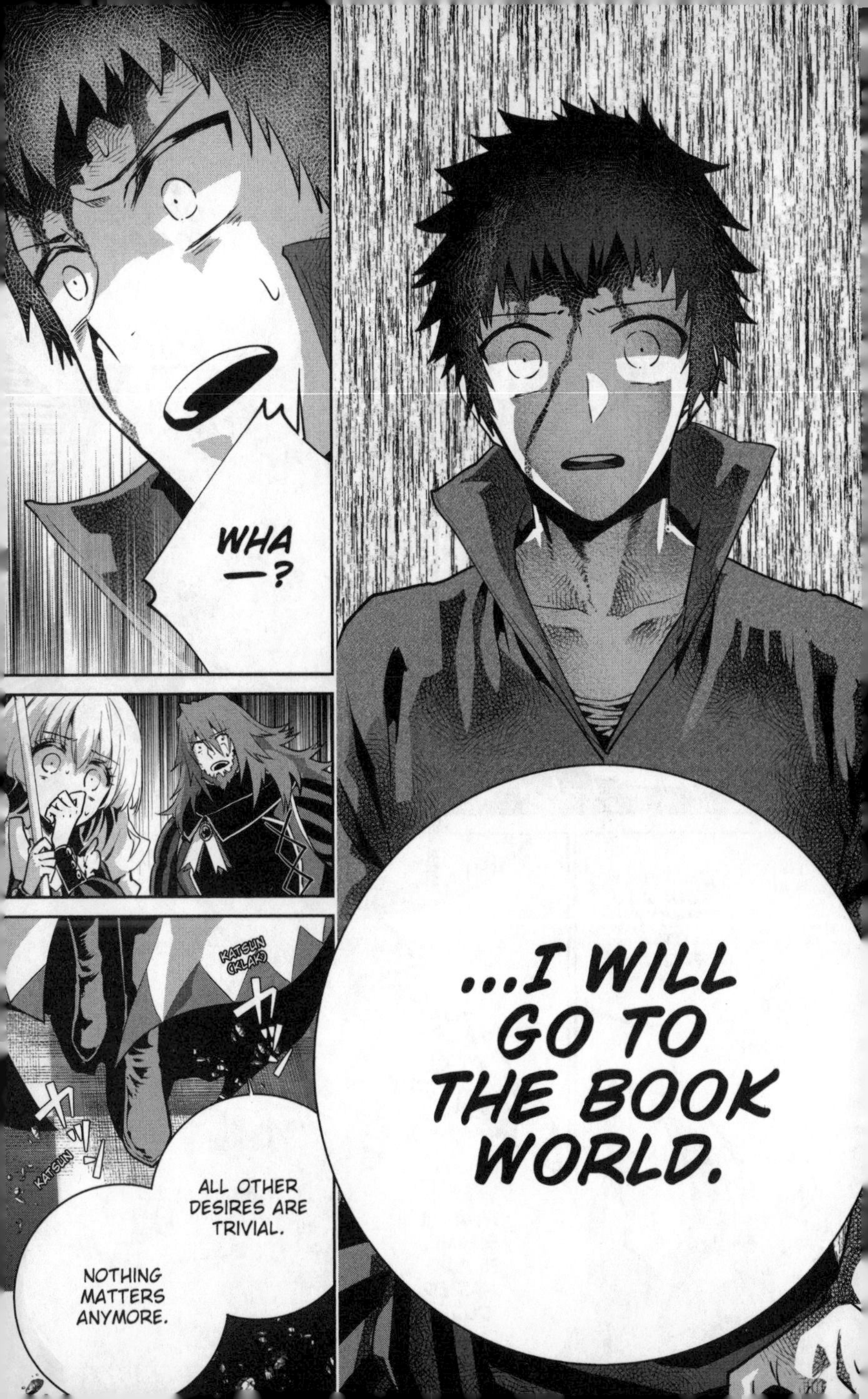
...I WILL GO TO THE BOOK WORLD.
WHA—?
KATSUN (KLAK)
KATSUN
ALL OTHER DESIRES ARE TRIVIAL.
NOTHING MATTERS ANYMORE.

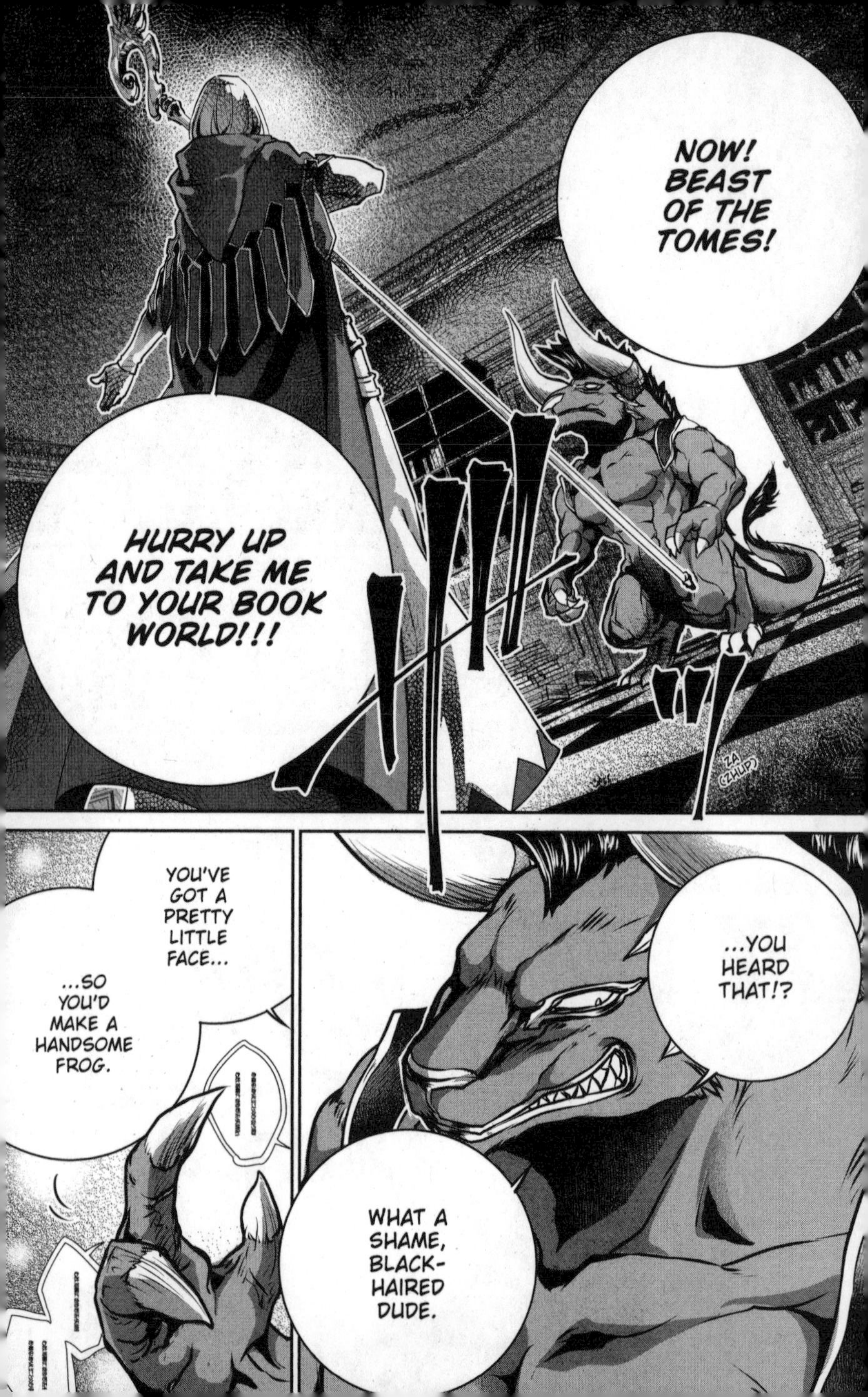
NOW! BEAST OF THE TOMES!
HURRY UP AND TAKE ME TO YOUR BOOK WORLD!!!
ZA (ZHUP)
...YOU HEARD THAT!?
WHAT A SHAME, BLACK-HAIRED DUDE.
YOU'VE GOT A PRETTY LITTLE FACE...
...SO YOU'D MAKE A HANDSOME FROG.

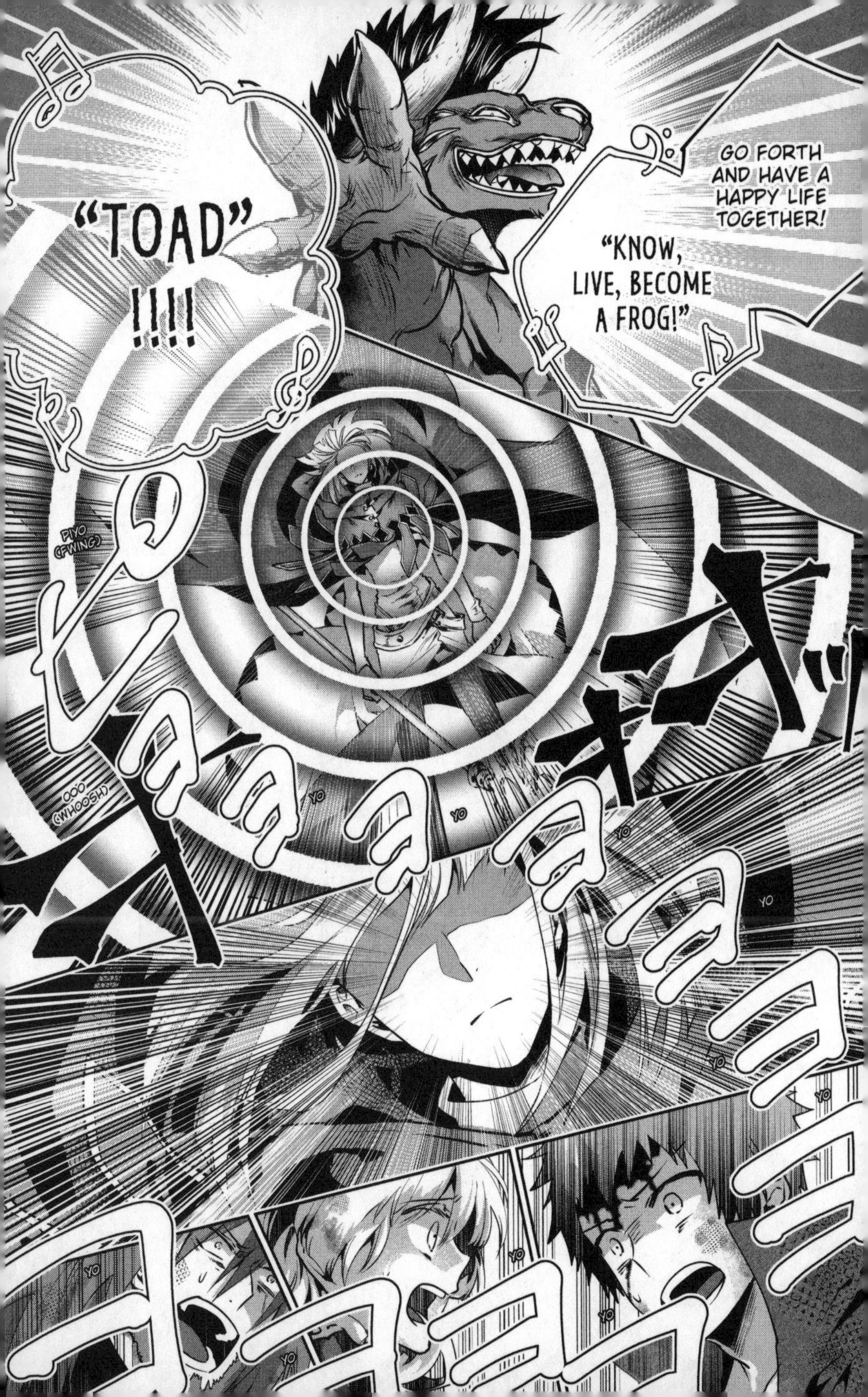
GO FORTH AND HAVE A HAPPY LIFE TOGETHER!
"KNOW, LIVE, BECOME A FROG!"
"TOAD" !!!!
PIYO (FWING)
OOO (WHOOSH)
YO

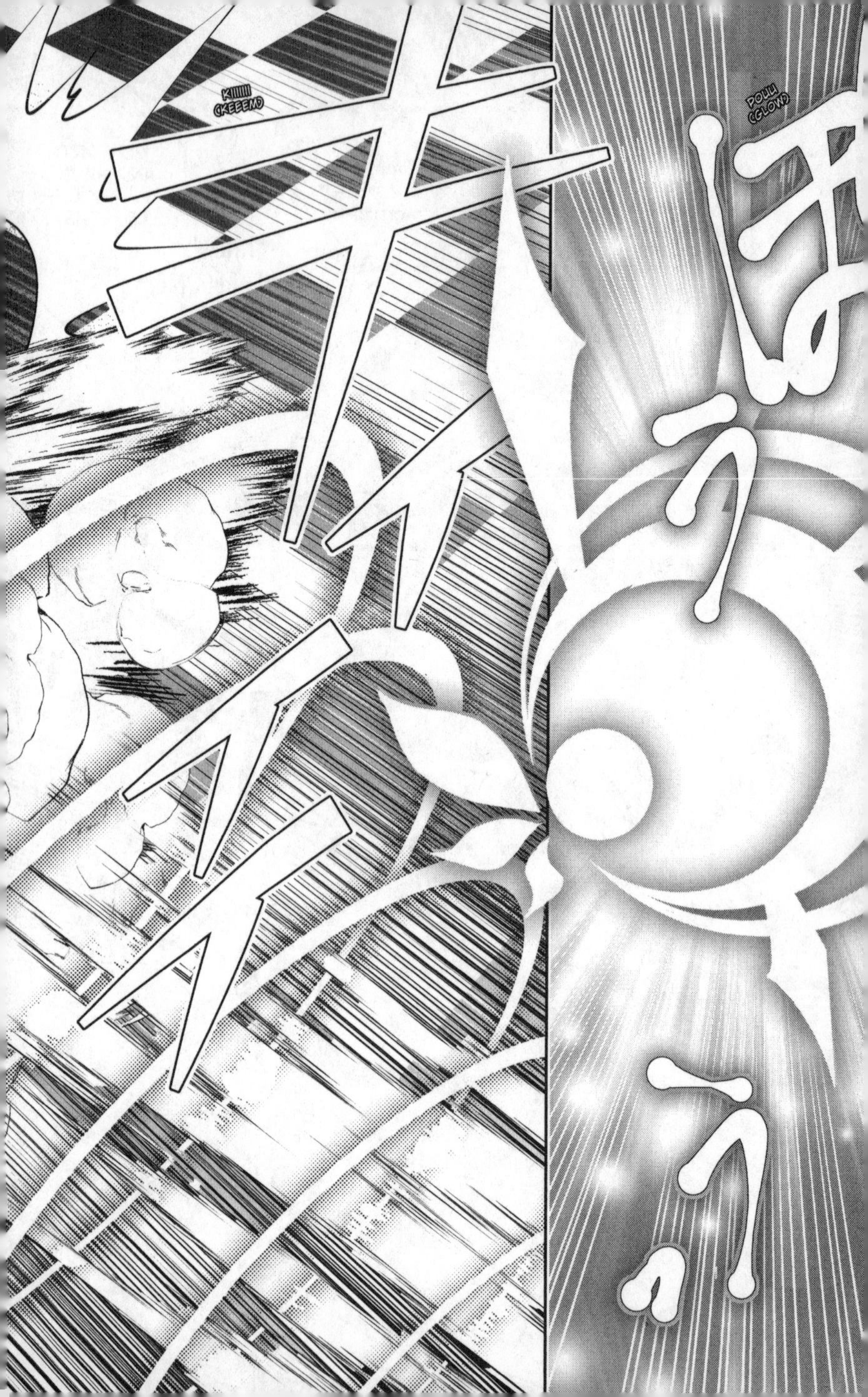
POUU
(GLOW)
KIIIIII
(KEEEN)

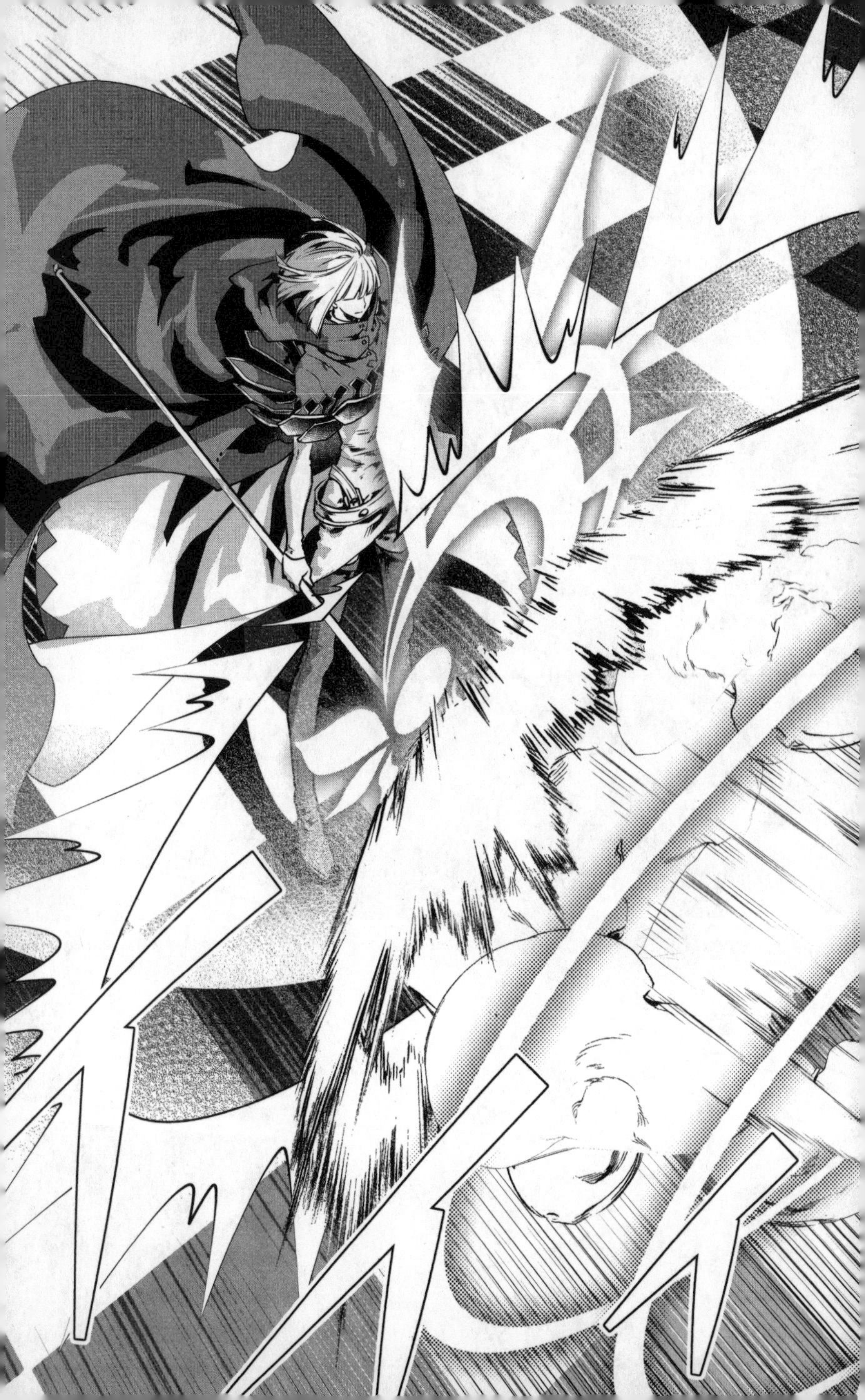

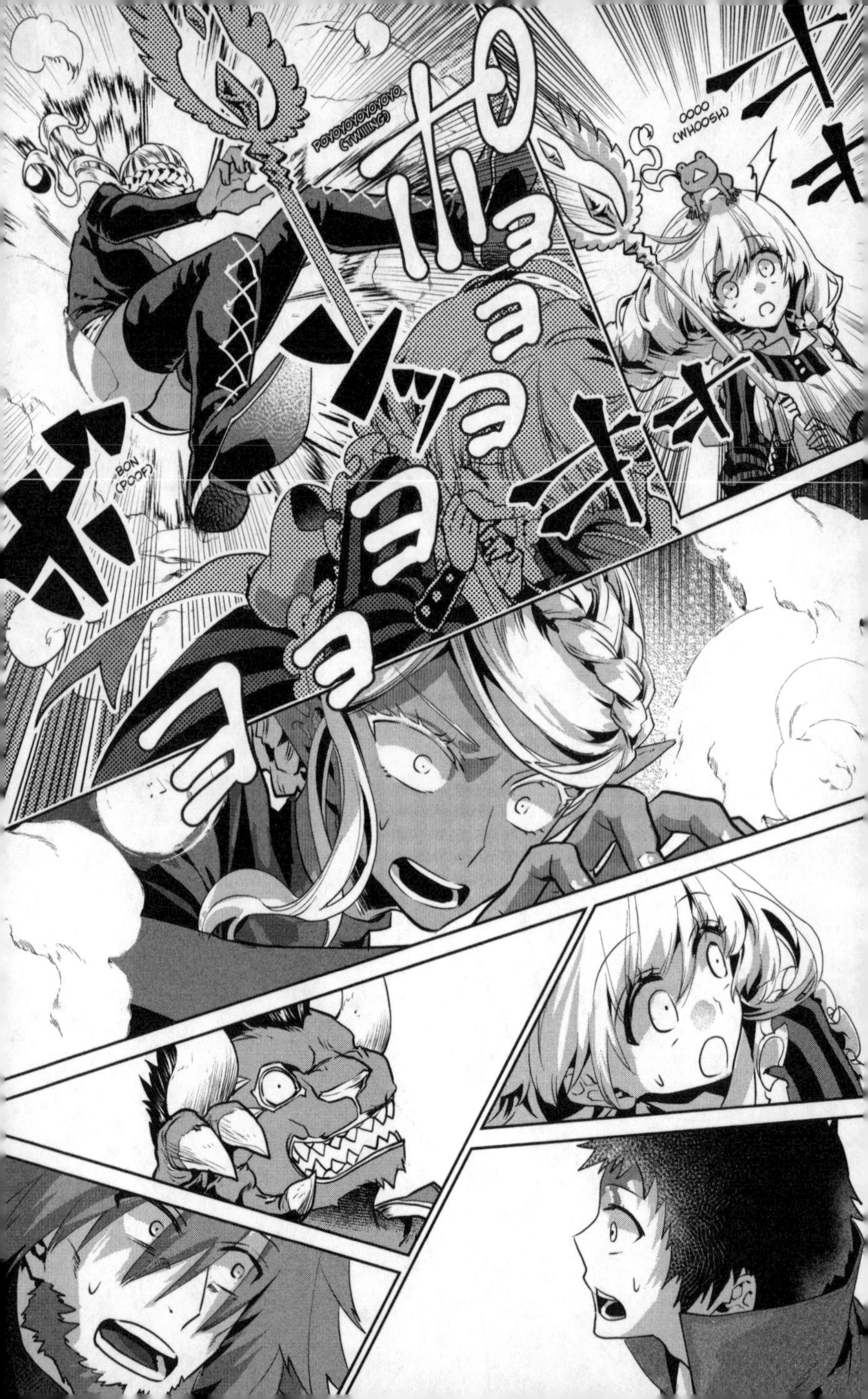
OOOO (WHOOSH)
POYOYOYOYOYOYO (TWIIIING)
BON (POOF)

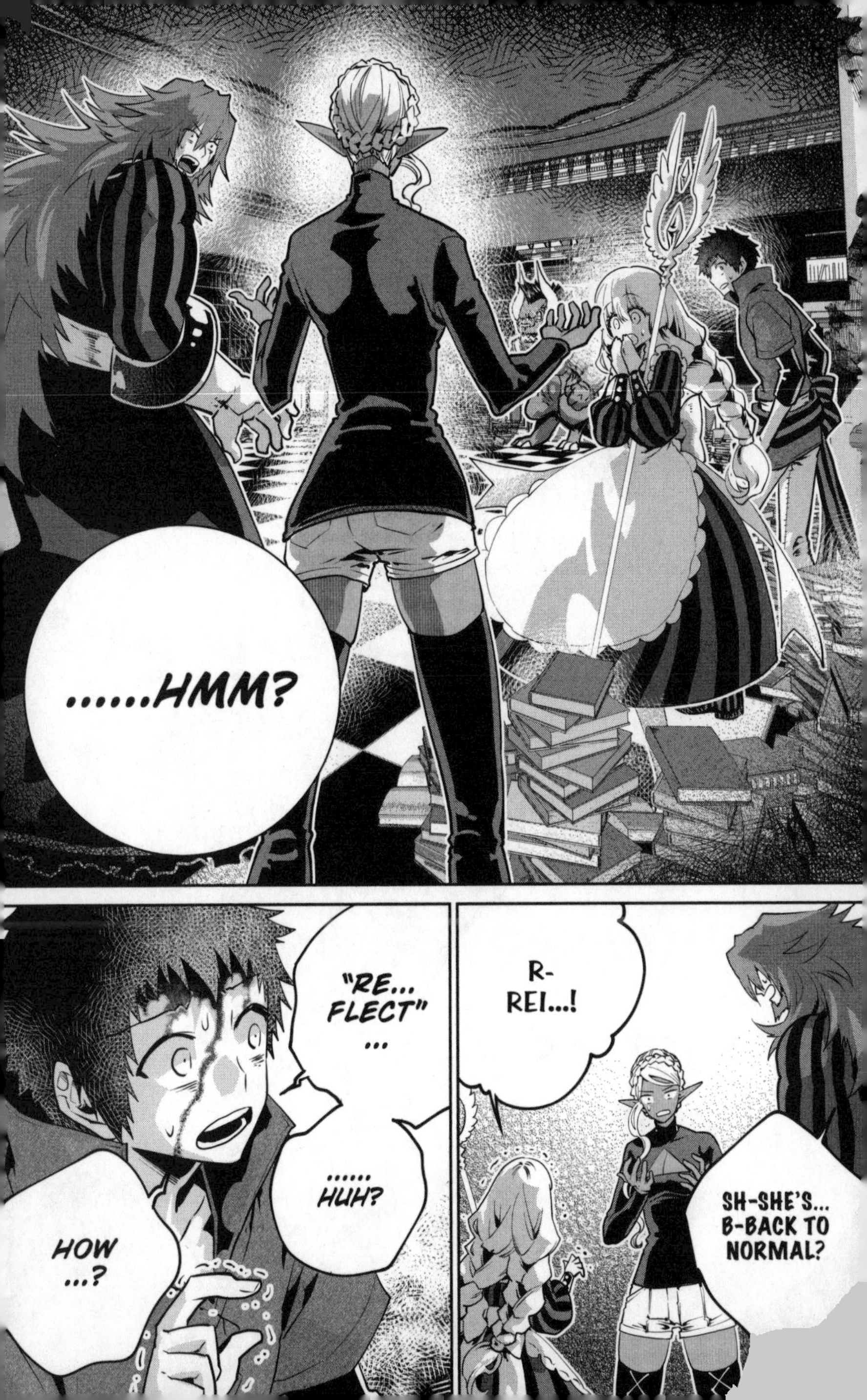
......HMM?
R-REI...!
SH-SHE'S... B-BACK TO NORMAL?
"RE... FLECT" ...
...... HUH?
HOW ...?

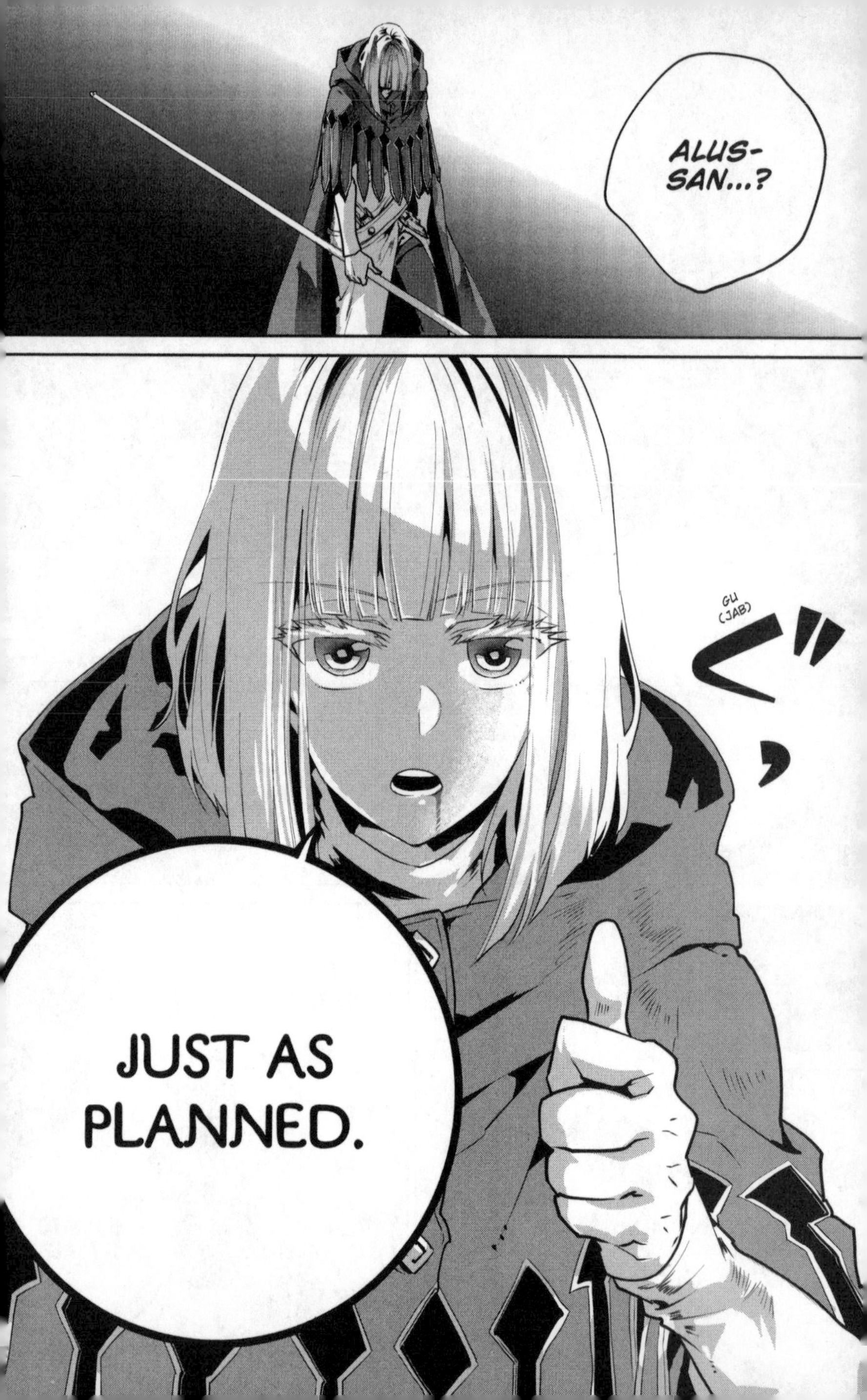
ALUS-SAN...?
GU (JAB)
JUST AS PLANNED.

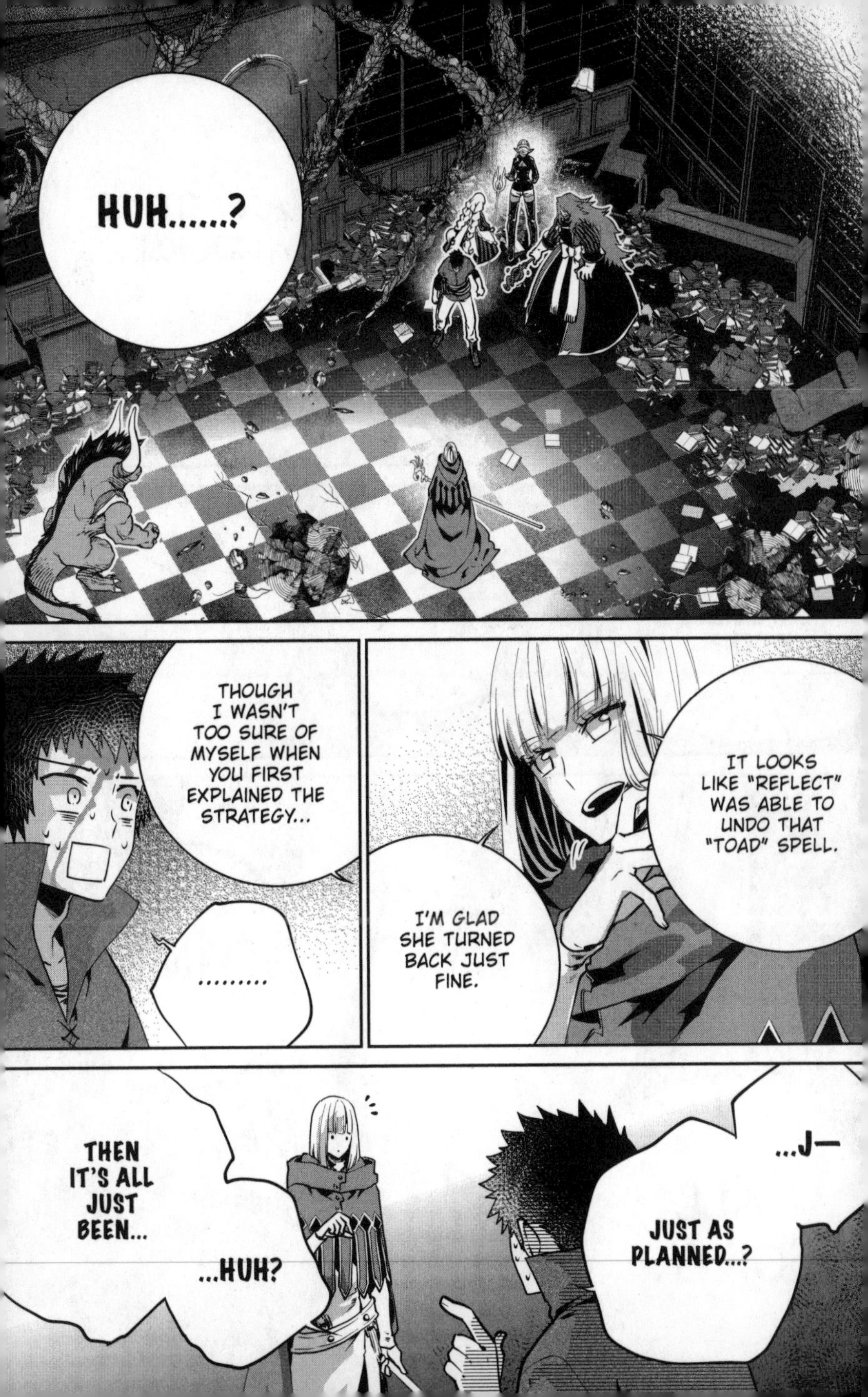
HUH......?
IT LOOKS LIKE "REFLECT" WAS ABLE TO UNDO THAT "TOAD" SPELL.
I'M GLAD SHE TURNED BACK JUST FINE.
THOUGH I WASN'T TOO SURE OF MYSELF WHEN YOU FIRST EXPLAINED THE STRATEGY...
.........
...J—
JUST AS PLANNED...?
THEN IT'S ALL JUST BEEN...
...HUH?

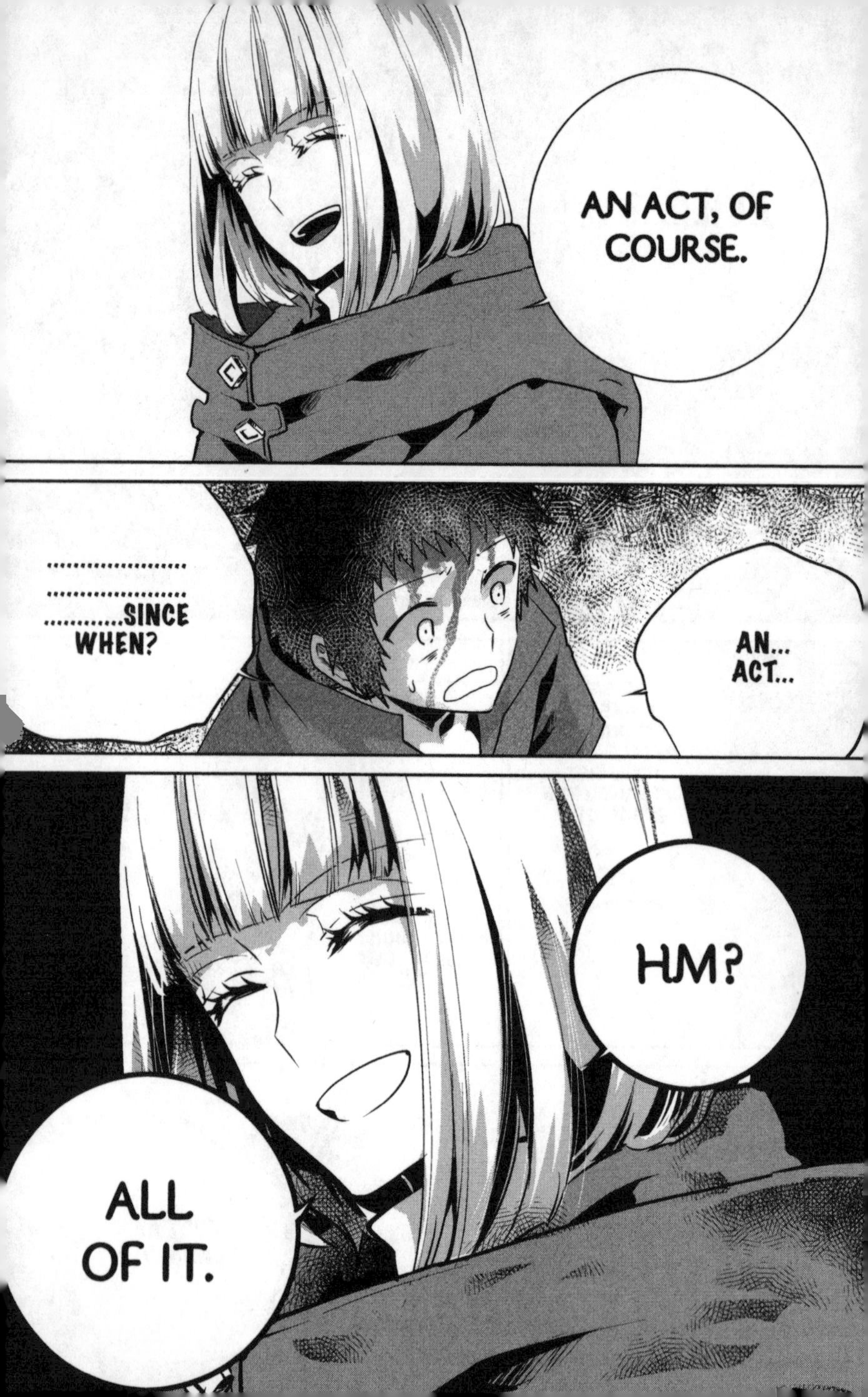
AN ACT, OF COURSE.
AN... ACT...
........................ ........................ ............SINCE WHEN?
HM?
ALL OF IT.

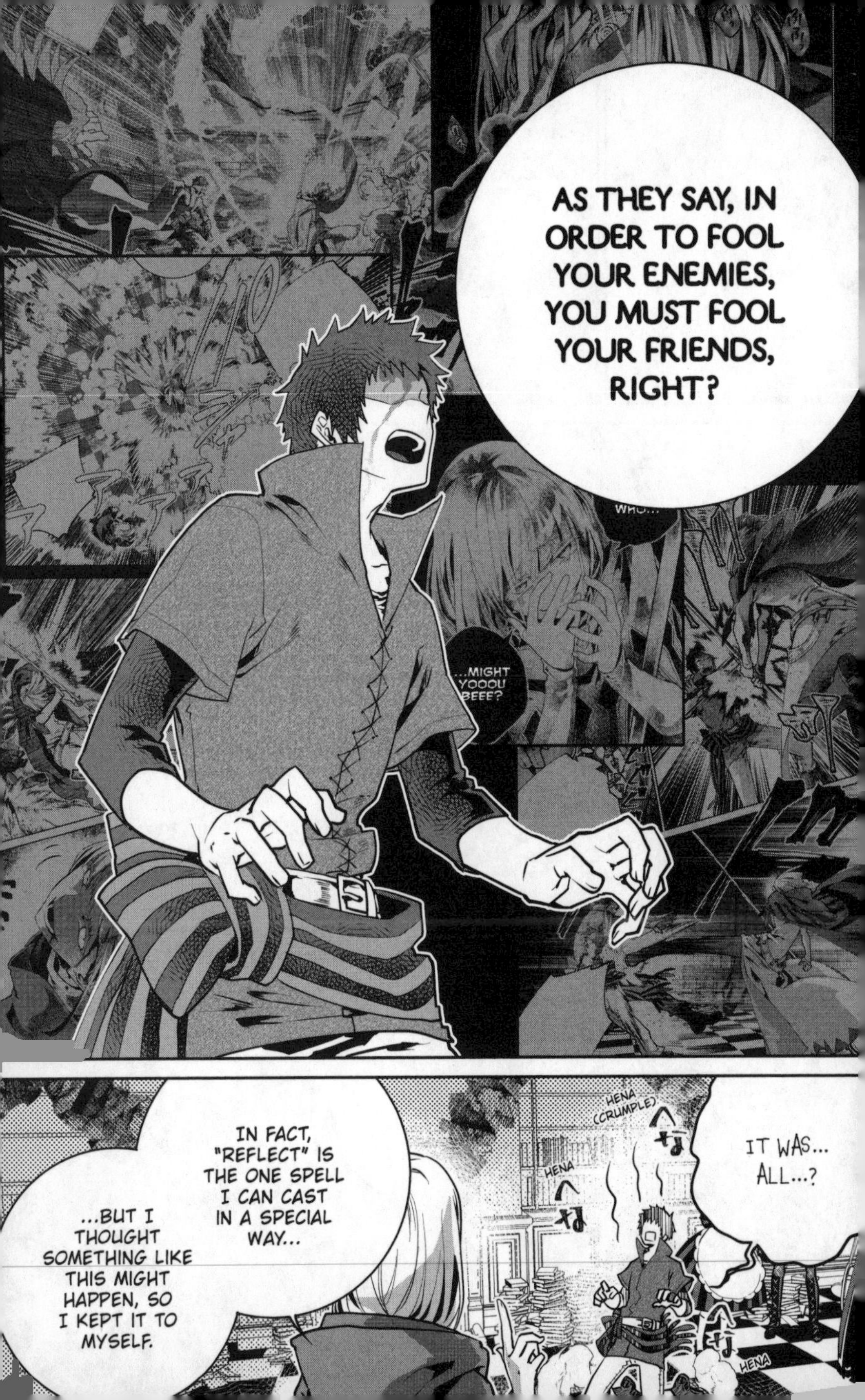
AS THEY SAY, IN ORDER TO FOOL YOUR ENEMIES, YOU MUST FOOL YOUR FRIENDS, RIGHT?
WHO...
...MIGHT YOOOU BEEE?
IT WAS... ALL...?
HENA (CRUMPLE)
HENA
HENA
IN FACT, "REFLECT" IS THE ONE SPELL I CAN CAST IN A SPECIAL WAY...
...BUT I THOUGHT SOMETHING LIKE THIS MIGHT HAPPEN, SO I KEPT IT TO MYSELF.

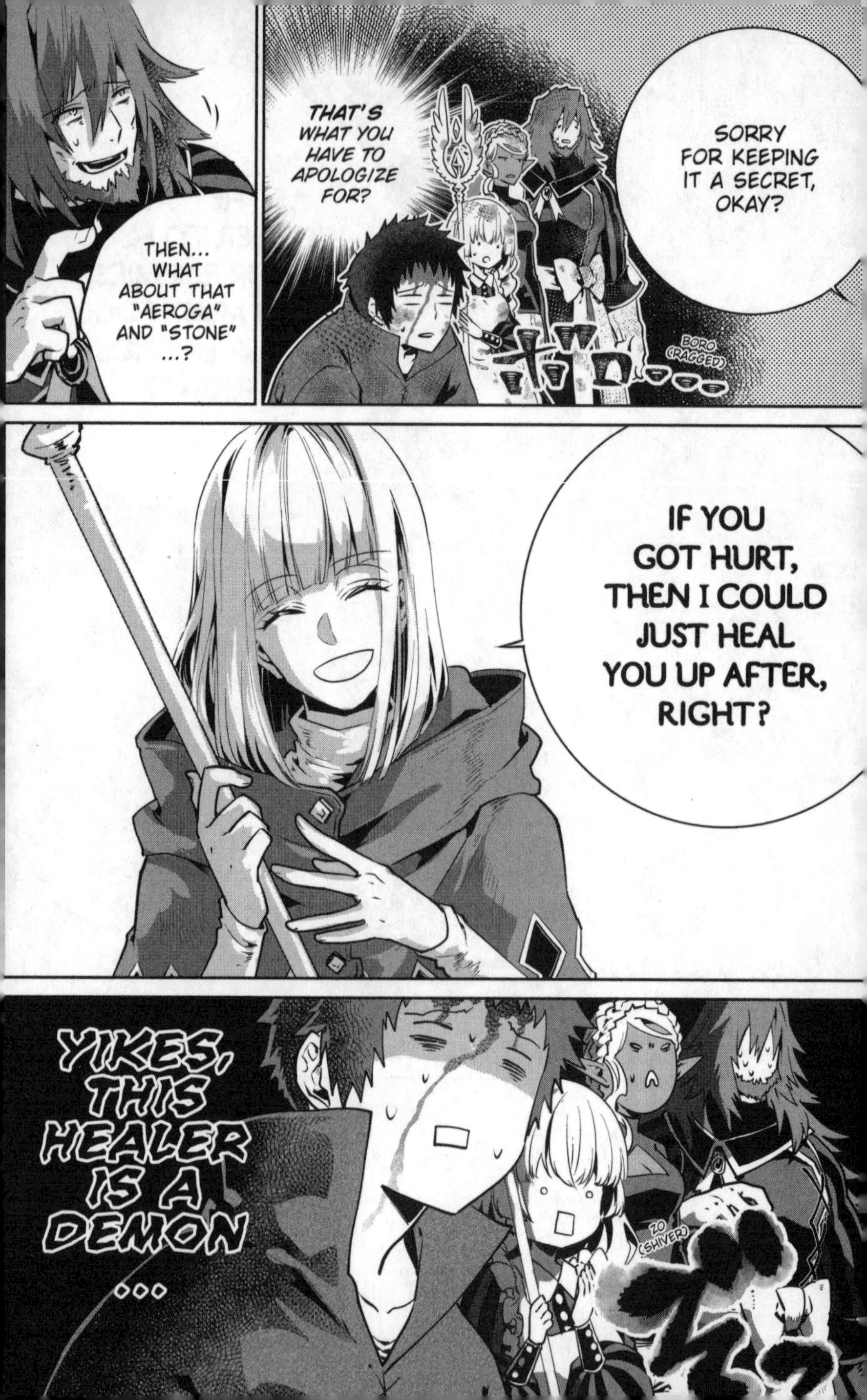
SORRY FOR KEEPING IT A SECRET, OKAY?
THAT'S WHAT YOU HAVE TO APOLOGIZE FOR?
BORO (RAGGED)
THEN... WHAT ABOUT THAT "AEROGA" AND "STONE" ...?
IF YOU GOT HURT, THEN I COULD JUST HEAL YOU UP AFTER, RIGHT?
YIKES, THIS HEALER IS A DEMON...
ZO (SHIVER)

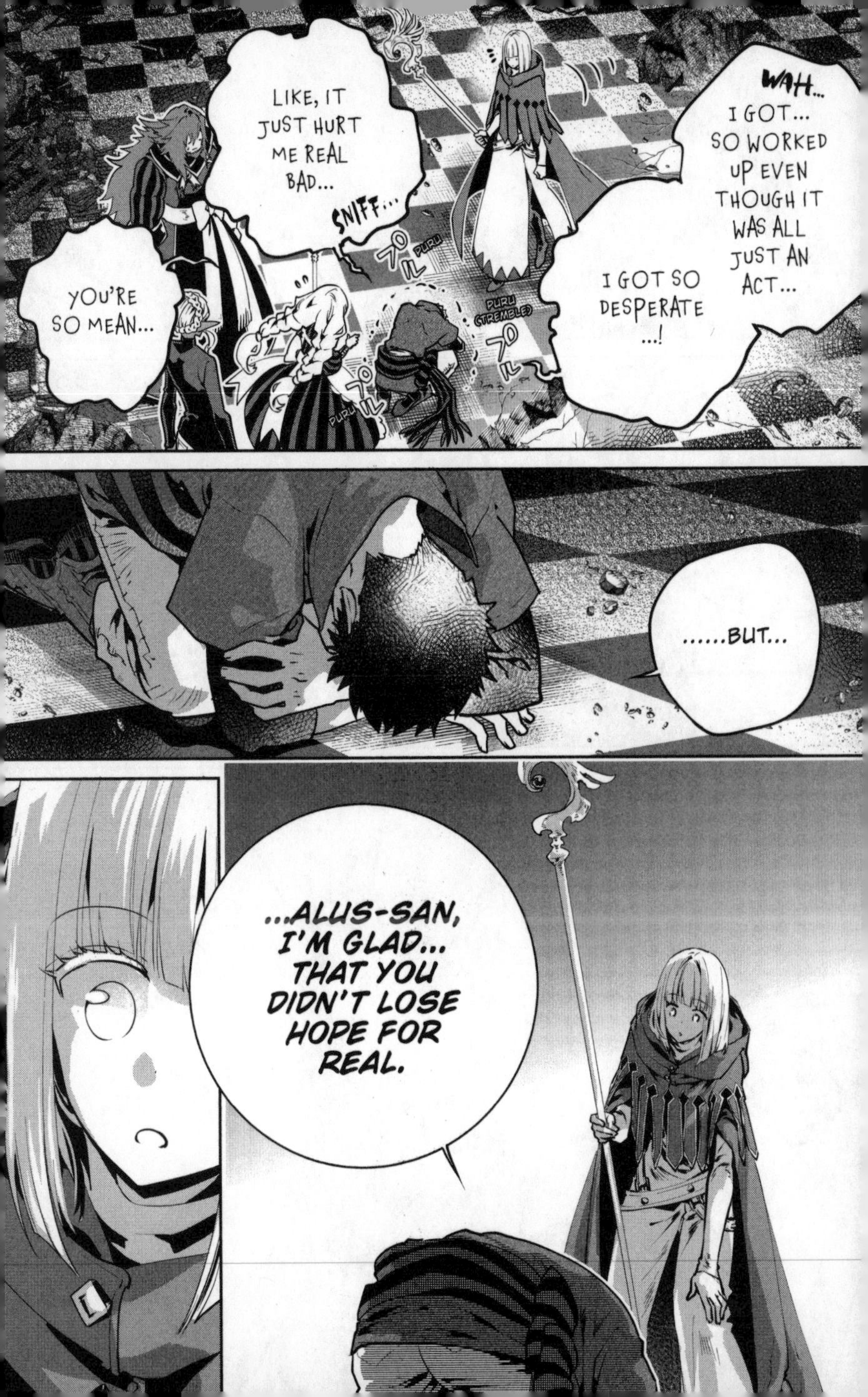

WAH... I GOT... SO WORKED UP EVEN THOUGH IT WAS ALL JUST AN ACT...
I GOT SO DESPERATE...!
PURU (TREMBLE)
PURU
LIKE, IT JUST HURT ME REAL BAD...
SNIFF...
PURU
YOU'RE SO MEAN...
......BUT...
...ALUS-SAN, I'M GLAD... THAT YOU DIDN'T LOSE HOPE FOR REAL.

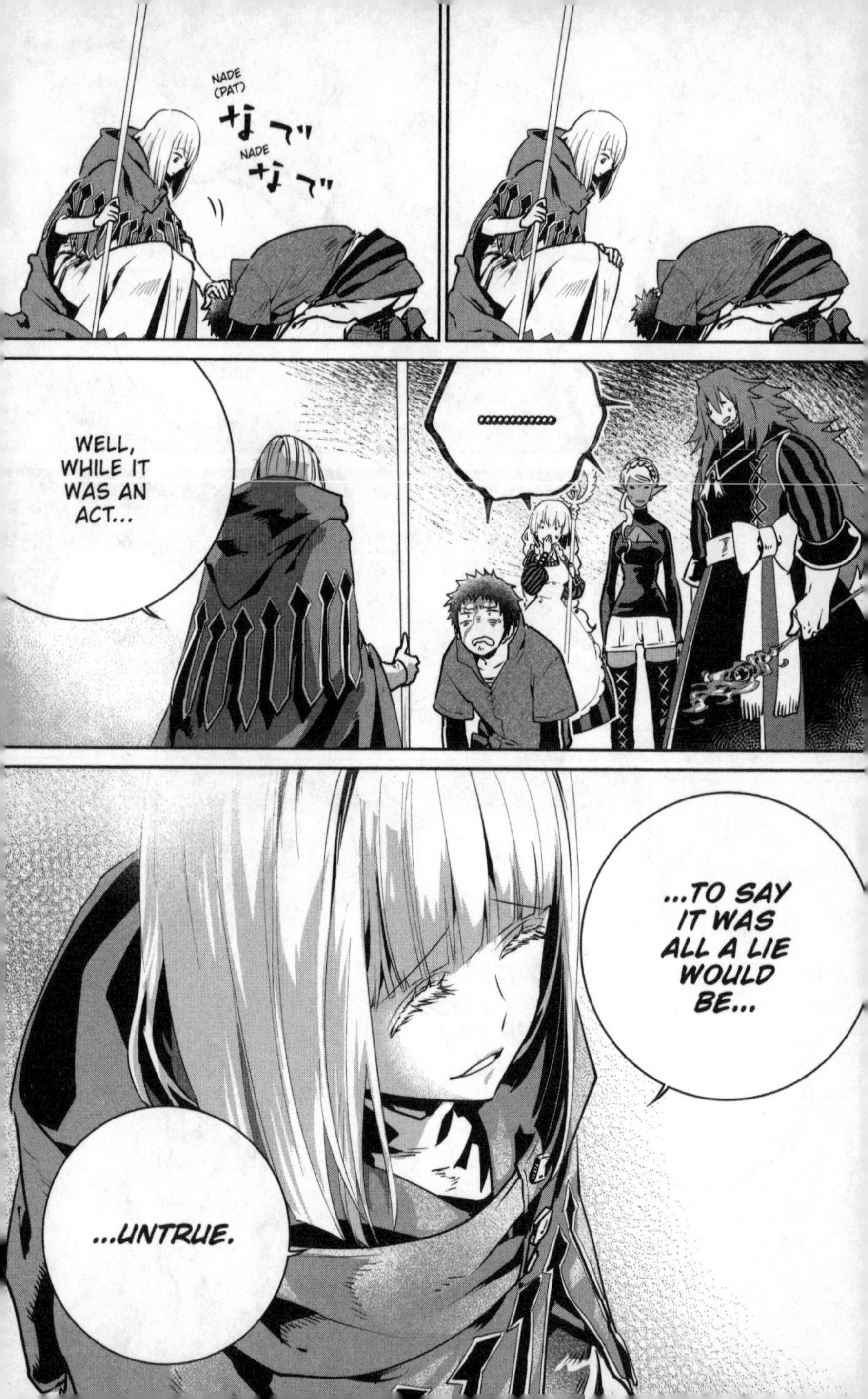
NADE (PAT)
なで
NADE
なで
............
WELL, WHILE IT WAS AN ACT...
...TO SAY IT WAS ALL A LIE WOULD BE...
...UNTRUE.

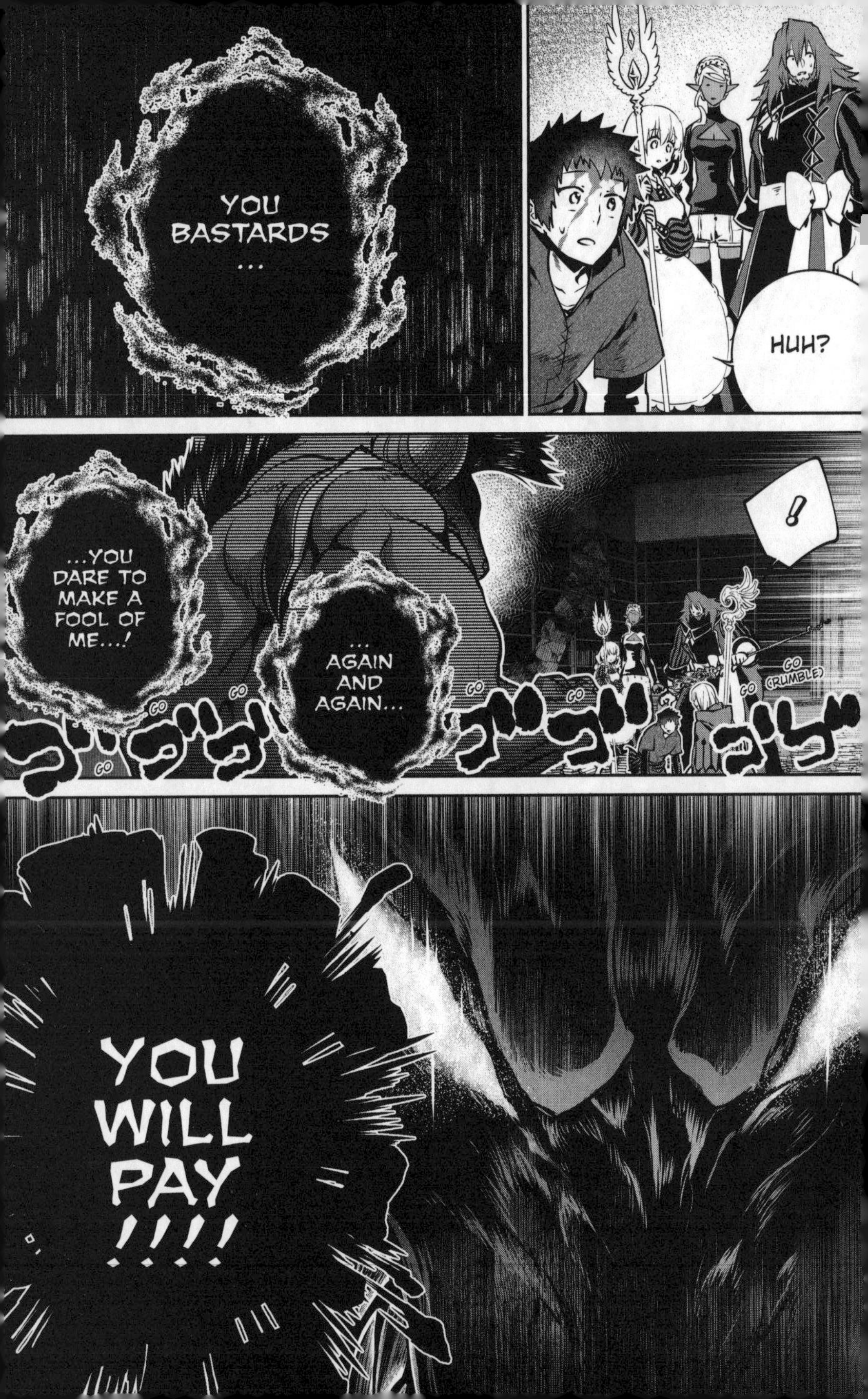
HUH?
YOU BASTARDS ...
!
...YOU DARE TO MAKE A FOOL OF ME...!
... AGAIN AND AGAIN...
GO GO GO GO GO GO GO (RUMBLE)
YOU WILL PAY !!!!

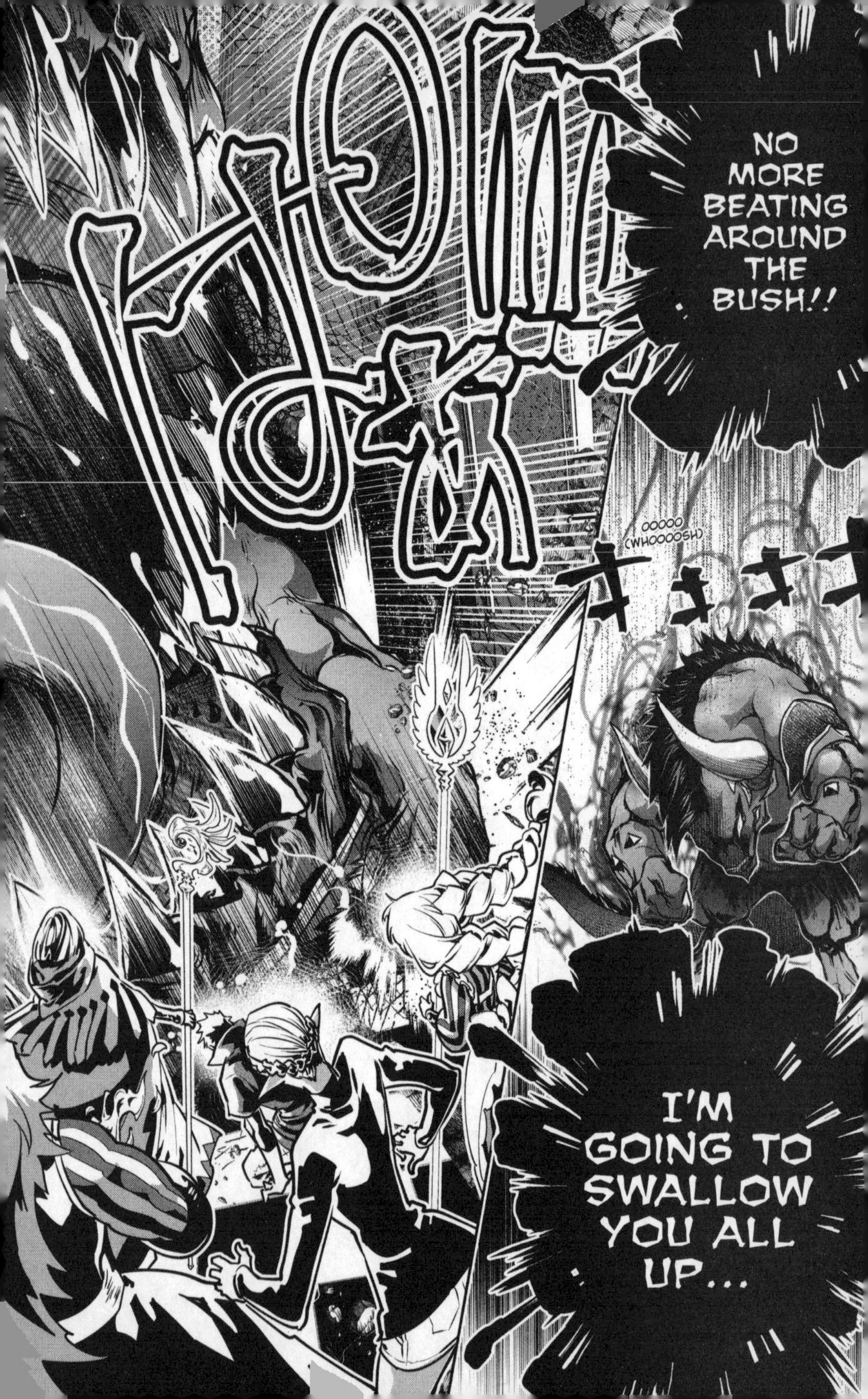
NO MORE BEATING AROUND THE BUSH!!
OOOOO (WHOOOOSH)
I'M GOING TO SWALLOW YOU ALL UP...

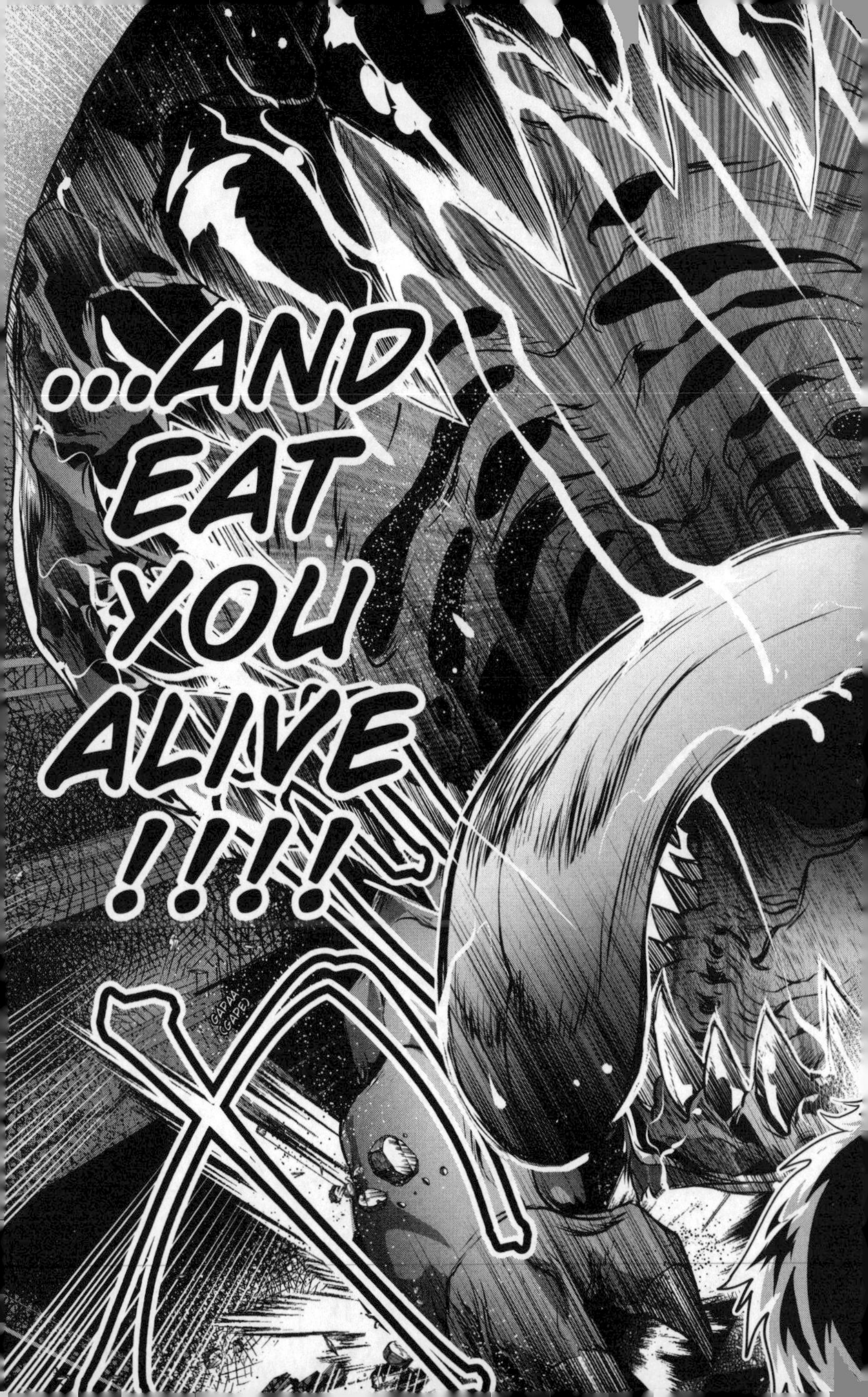
...AND EAT YOU ALIVE !!!!
GAPAA (GAPE)

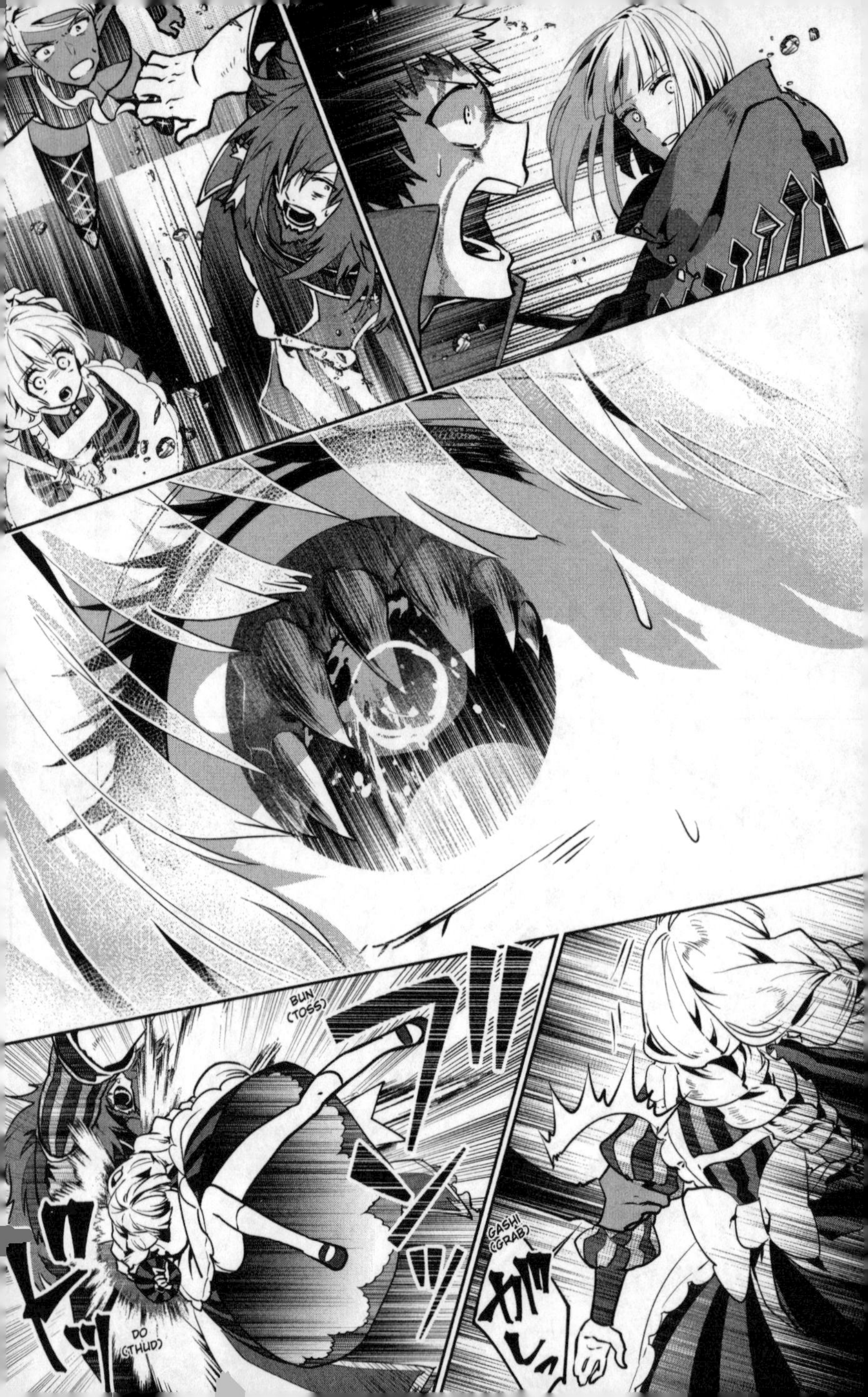
GASHI
(GRAB)
BUN
(TOSS)
DO
(THUD)

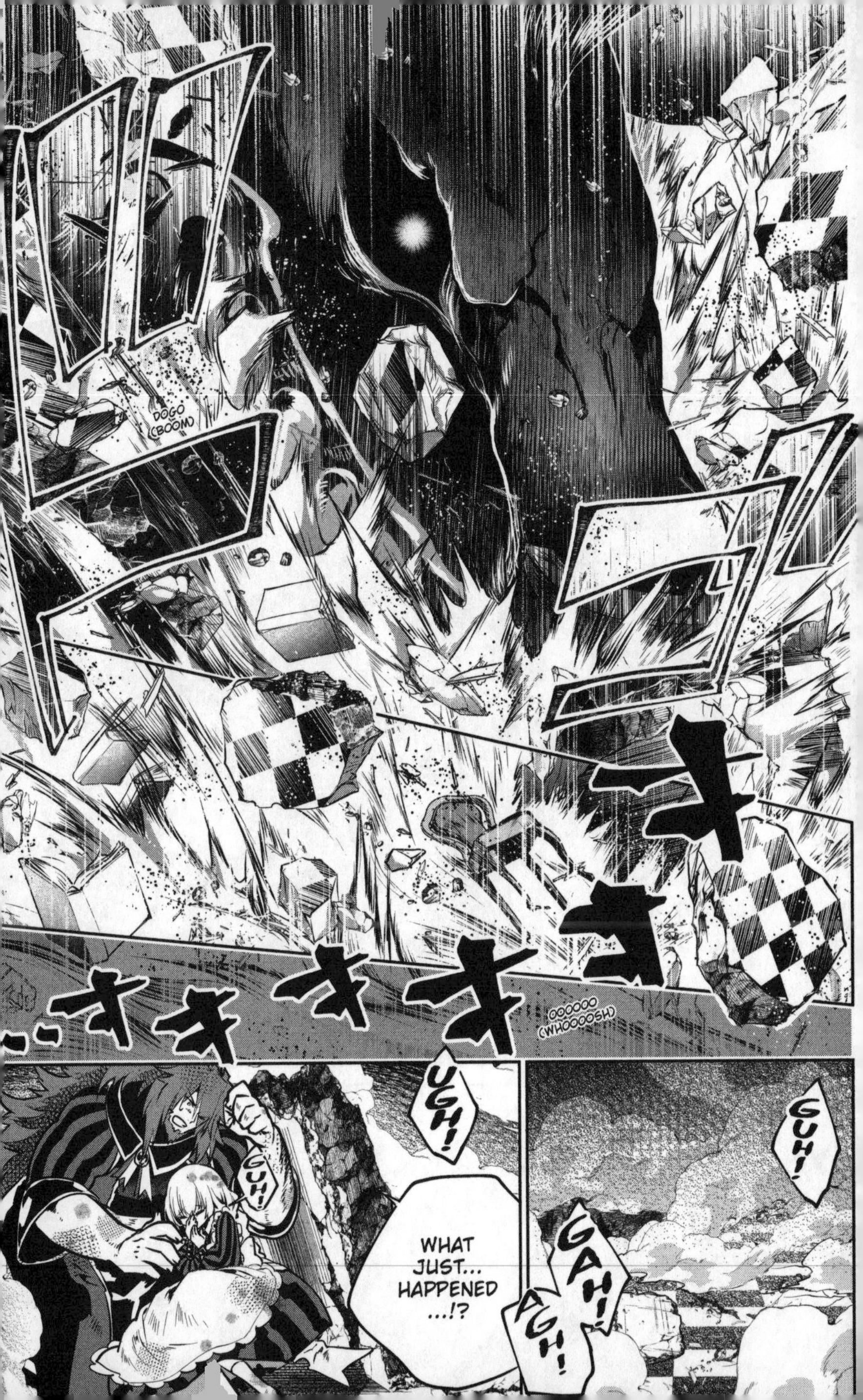
DOGO (BOOM)
OOOOOO (WHOOOOSH)
GUH!
GAH!
AGH!
UGH!
GUH!
WHAT JUST... HAPPENED ...!?

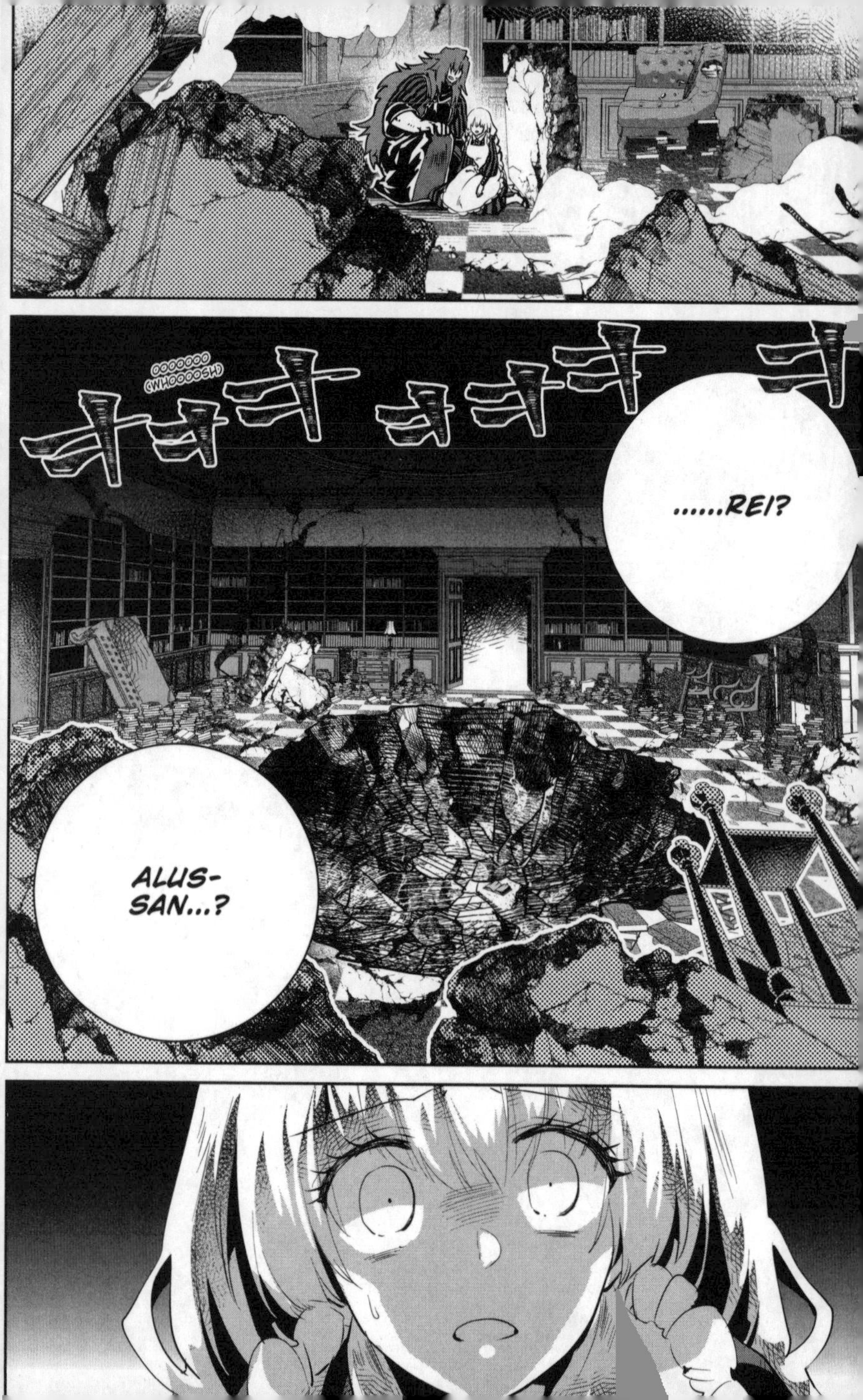
OOOOOOO (WHOOOOSH)
......REI?
ALUS-SAN...?

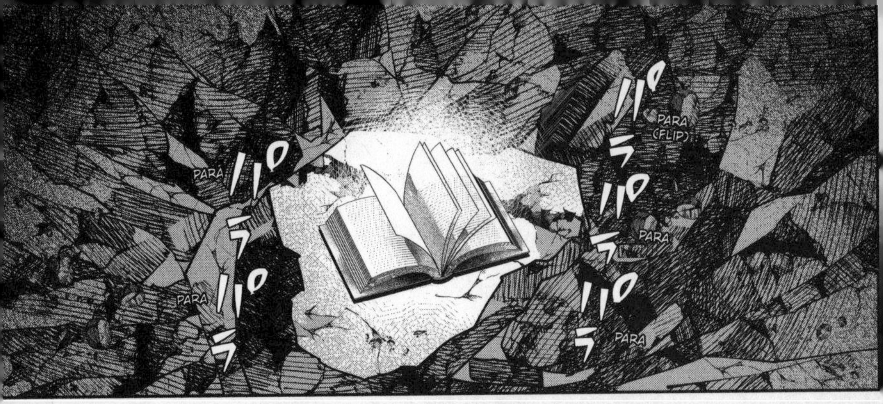
PARA (FLIP)
PARA
PARA
PARA
PARA

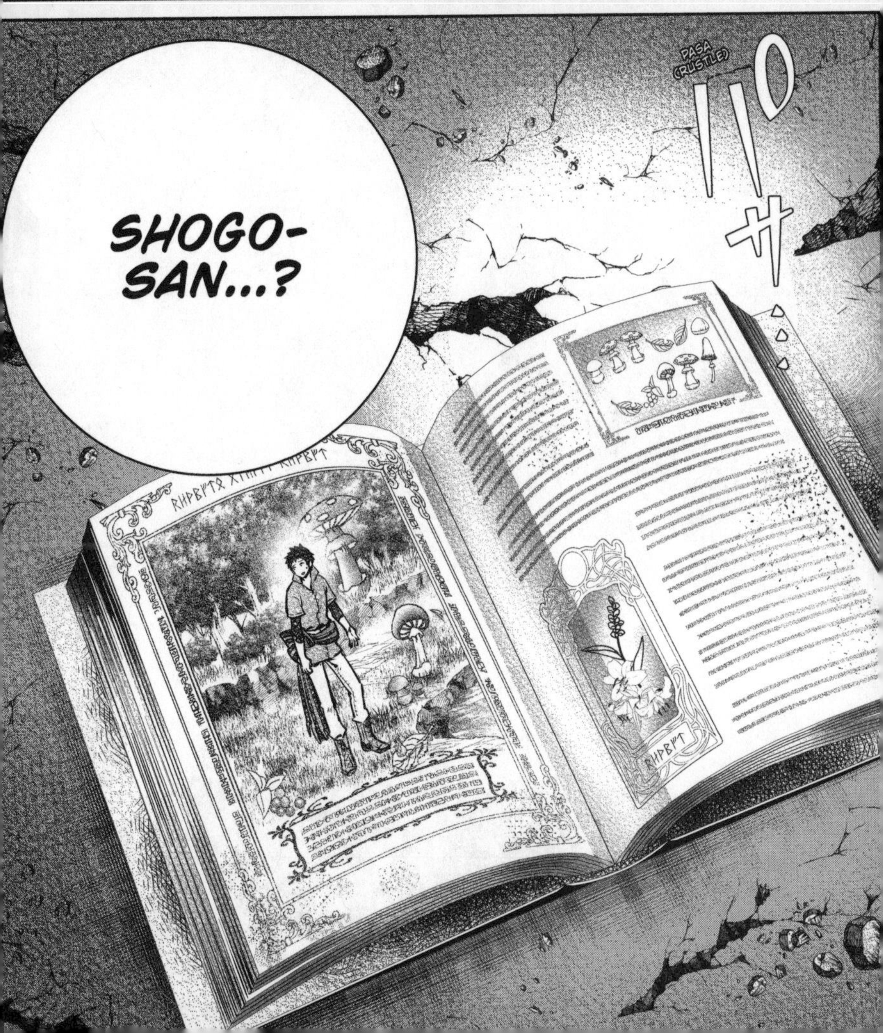
PASA (RUSTLE)
SHOGO-SAN...?

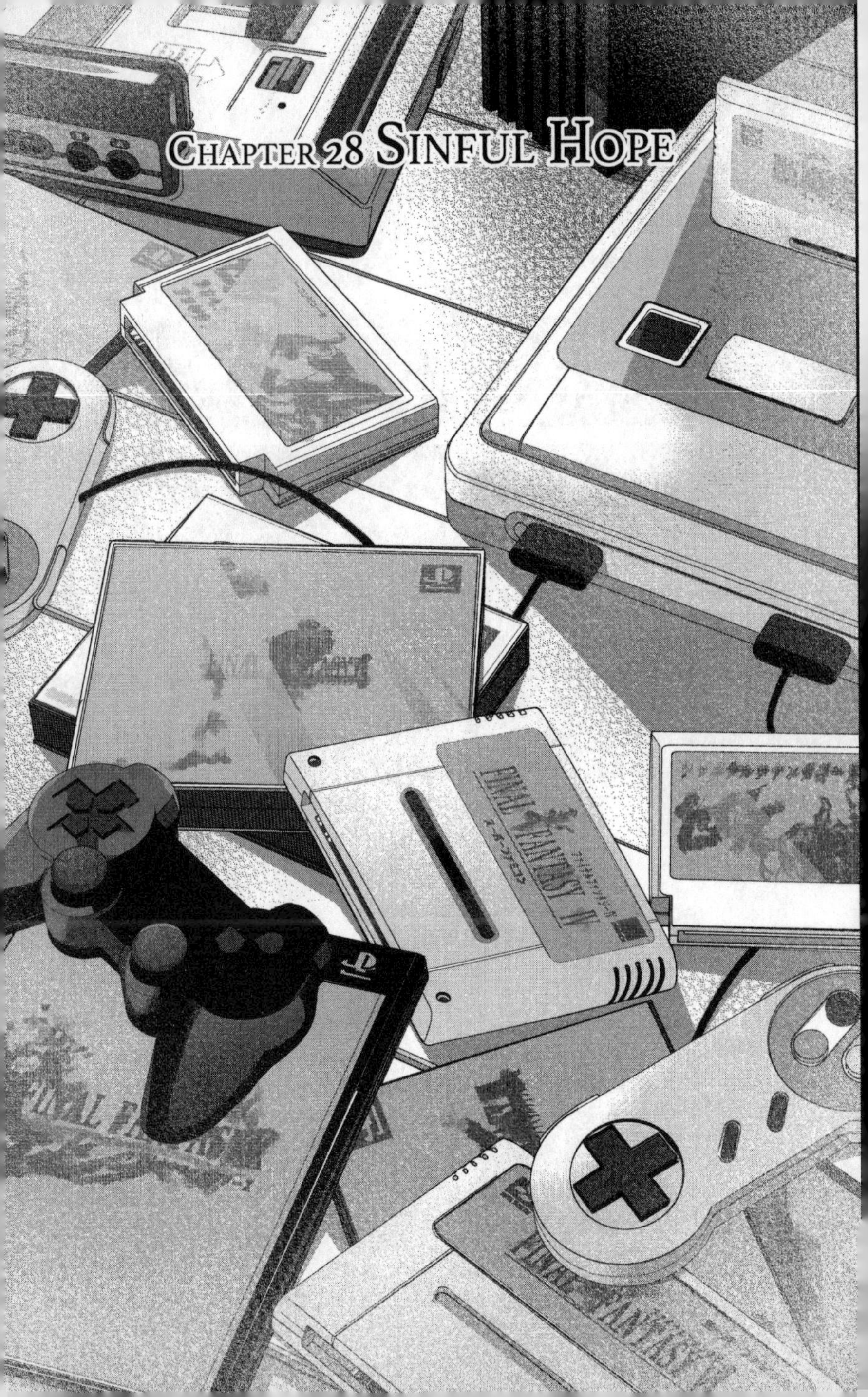
CHAPTER 28 SINFUL HOPE
FINAL FANTASY IV

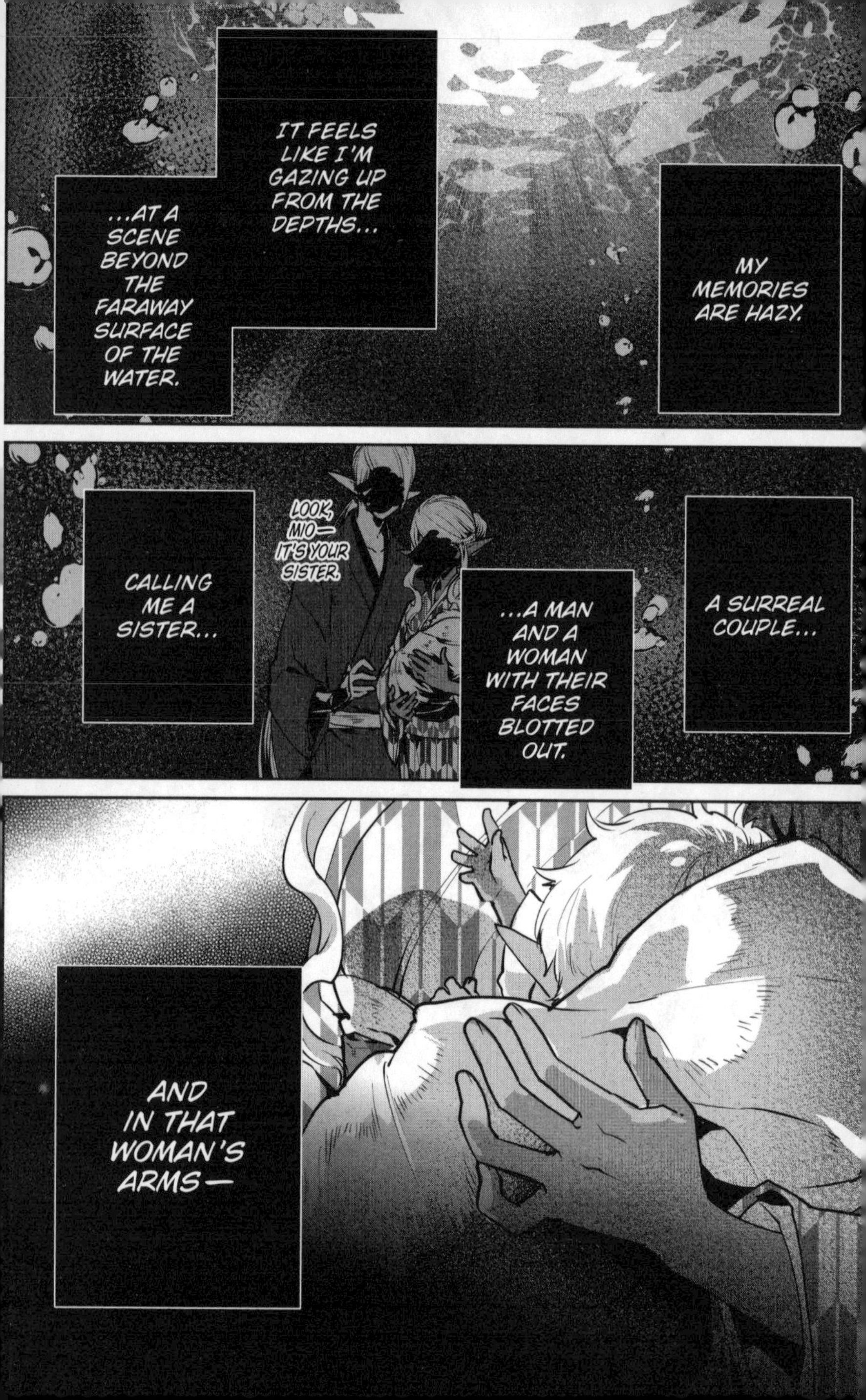
MY MEMORIES ARE HAZY.
IT FEELS LIKE I'M GAZING UP FROM THE DEPTHS...
...AT A SCENE BEYOND THE FARAWAY SURFACE OF THE WATER.
A SURREAL COUPLE...
...A MAN AND A WOMAN WITH THEIR FACES BLOTTED OUT.
LOOK, MIO— IT'S YOUR SISTER.
CALLING ME A SISTER...
AND IN THAT WOMAN'S ARMS—

PICHI
ピチ

PICHICHICHICHI
(CHIRRRP)
ピチチチチ

PICHICHICHICHICHICHI
ピチチチチチチ

・・・・・・・・・・・

SAAAAA
(SWOOSH)
サァァァァ

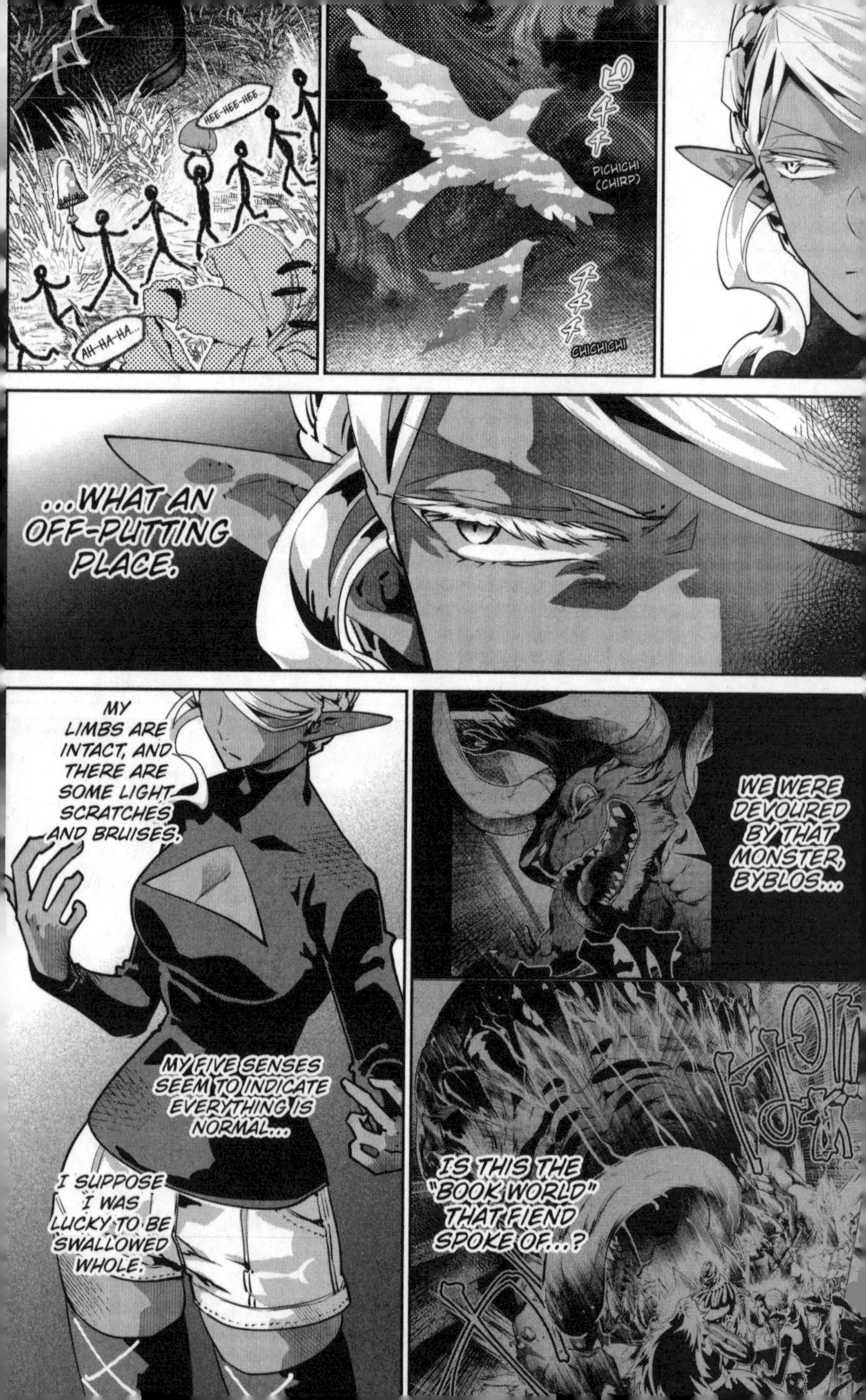
ピチチ
PICHICHI (CHIRP)
チチチ
CHICHICHI
HEE-HEE-HEE...
AH-HA-HA...
...WHAT AN OFF-PUTTING PLACE.
WE WERE DEVOURED BY THAT MONSTER, BYBLOS...
IS THIS THE "BOOK WORLD" THAT FIEND SPOKE OF...?
MY LIMBS ARE INTACT, AND THERE ARE SOME LIGHT SCRATCHES AND BRUISES.
MY FIVE SENSES SEEM TO INDICATE EVERYTHING IS NORMAL...
I SUPPOSE I WAS LUCKY TO BE SWALLOWED WHOLE.

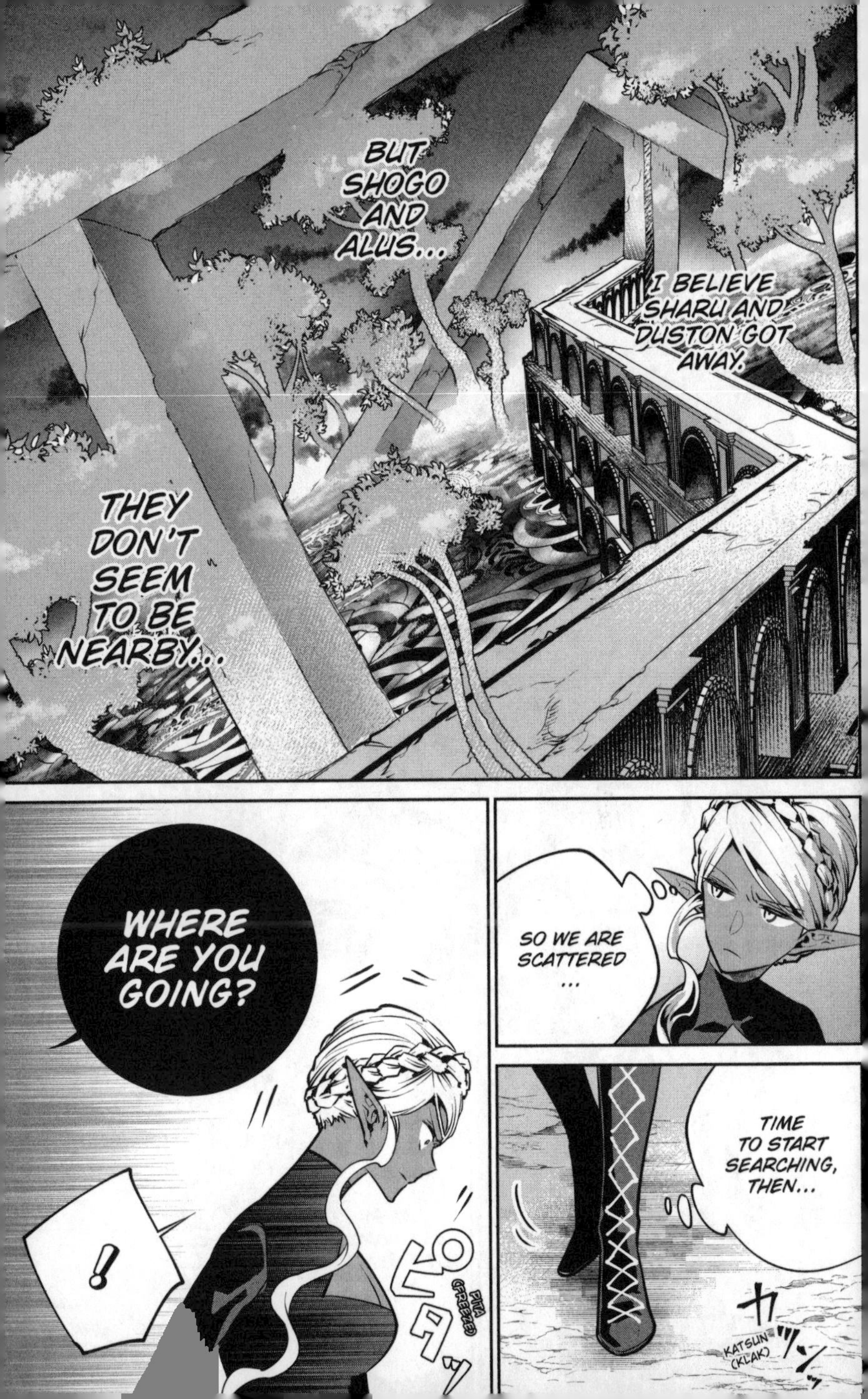
I BELIEVE SHARU AND DUSTON GOT AWAY.
BUT SHOGO AND ALUS...
THEY DON'T SEEM TO BE NEARBY...
SO WE ARE SCATTERED ...
TIME TO START SEARCHING, THEN...
KATSUN (KLAK)
WHERE ARE YOU GOING?
!
PITA (FREEZE)

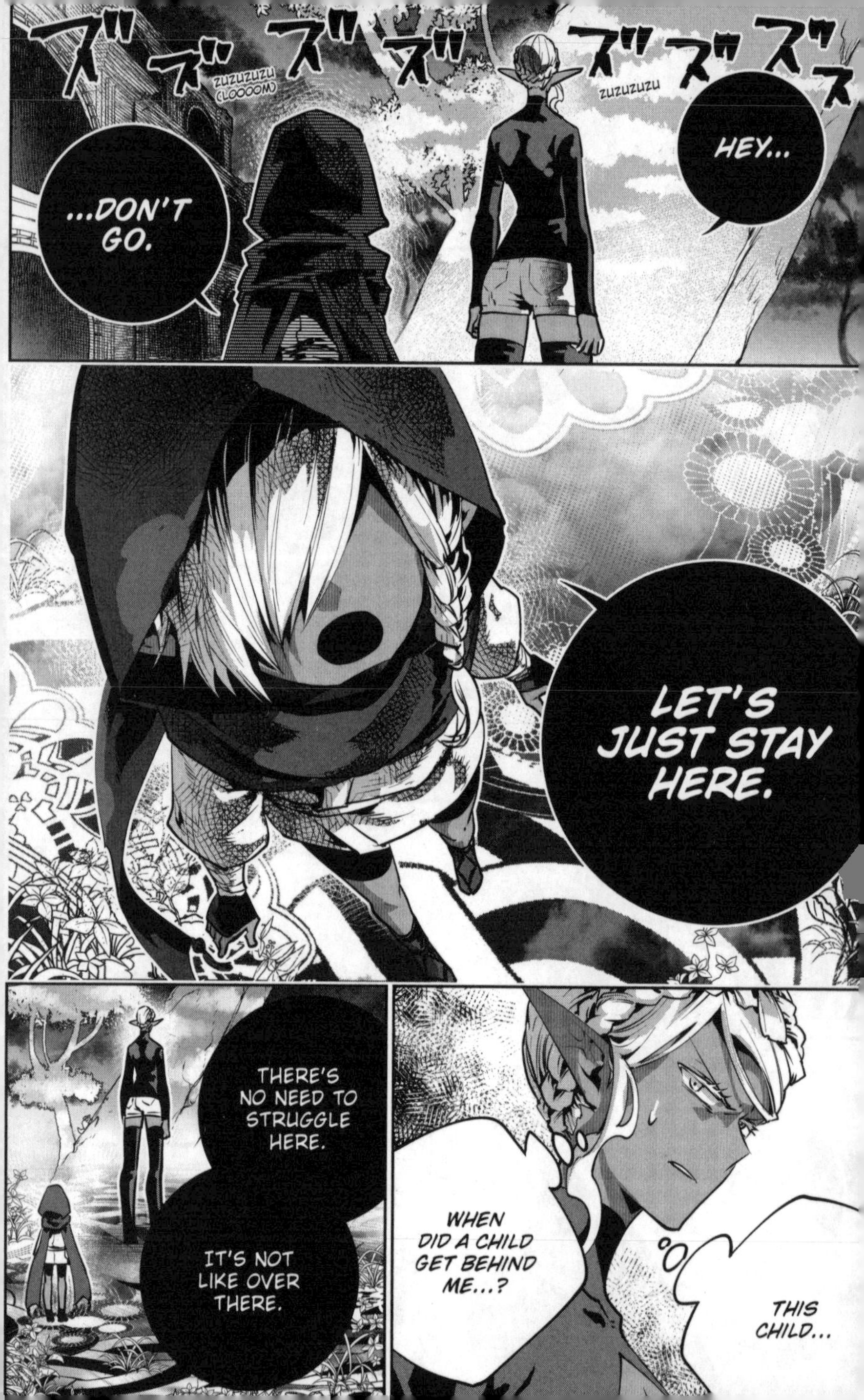
ZUZUZUZU
HEY...
ZUZUZUZU (LOOOOM)
...DON'T GO.
LET'S JUST STAY HERE.
WHEN DID A CHILD GET BEHIND ME...?
THIS CHILD...
THERE'S NO NEED TO STRUGGLE HERE.
IT'S NOT LIKE OVER THERE.

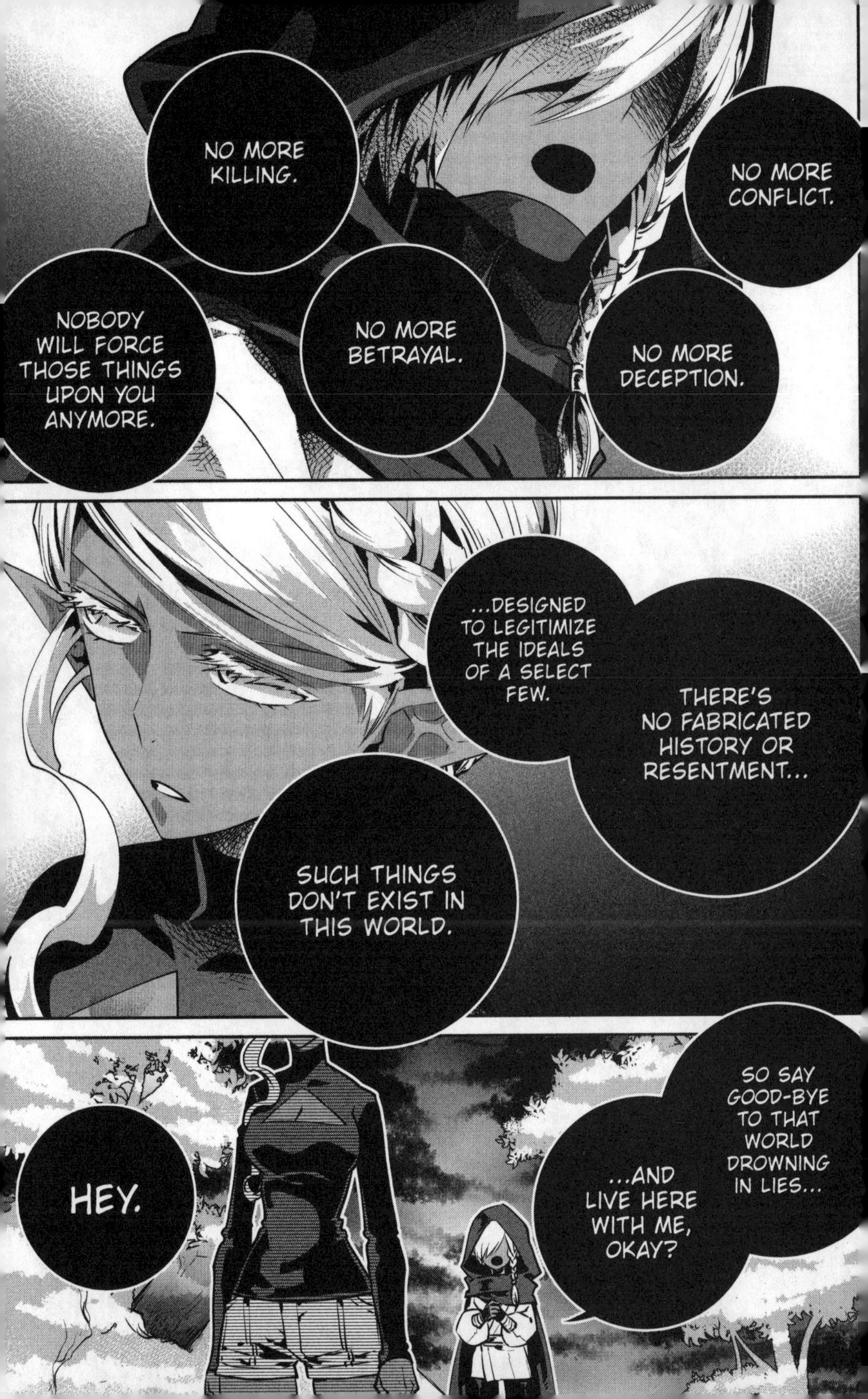
NO MORE CONFLICT.
NO MORE KILLING.
NO MORE DECEPTION.
NO MORE BETRAYAL.
NOBODY WILL FORCE THOSE THINGS UPON YOU ANYMORE.
THERE'S NO FABRICATED HISTORY OR RESENTMENT...
...DESIGNED TO LEGITIMIZE THE IDEALS OF A SELECT FEW.
SUCH THINGS DON'T EXIST IN THIS WORLD.
SO SAY GOOD-BYE TO THAT WORLD DROWNING IN LIES...
...AND LIVE HERE WITH ME, OKAY?
HEY.

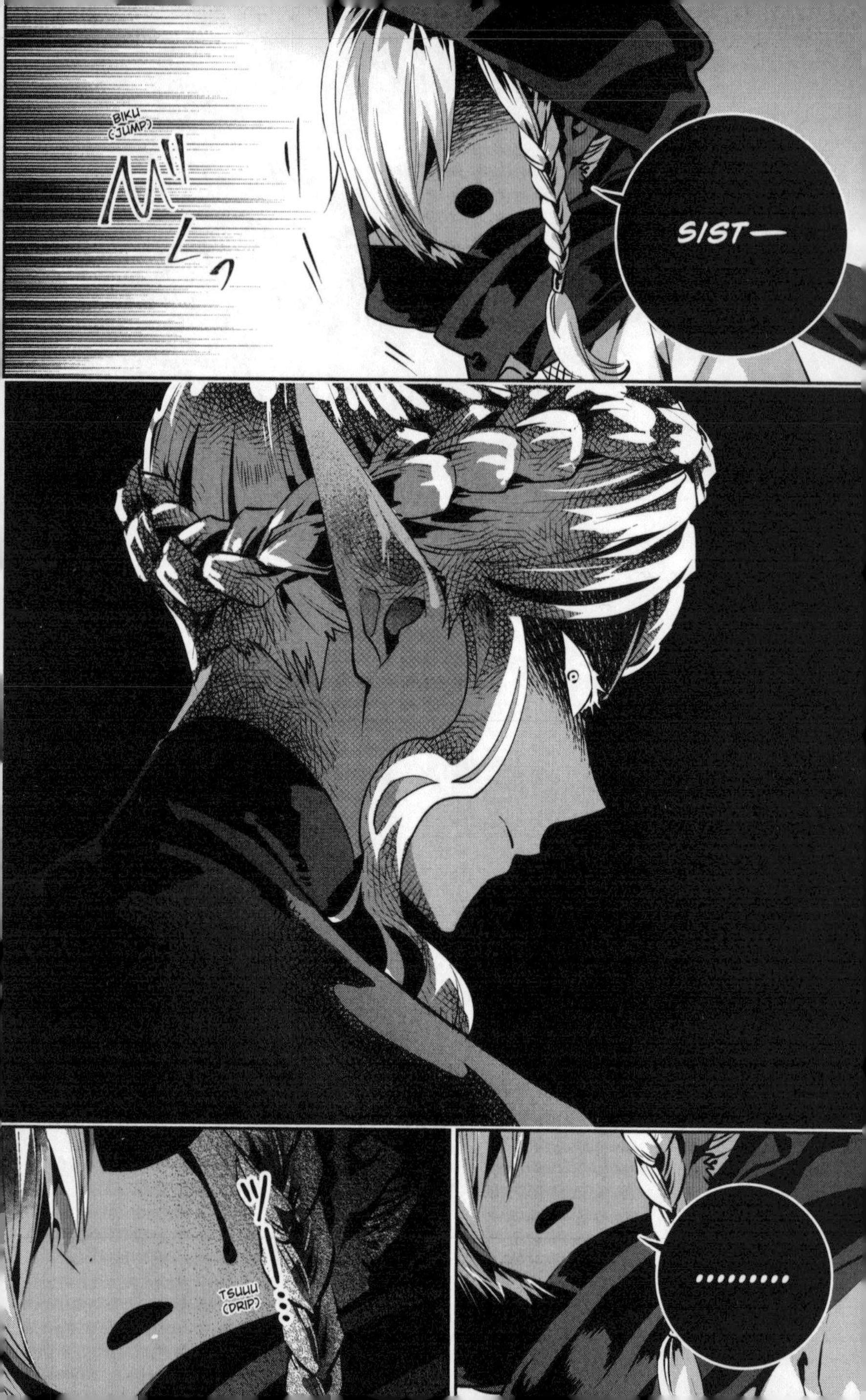
SIST—
BIKU (JUMP)
..........
TSUUU (DRIP)

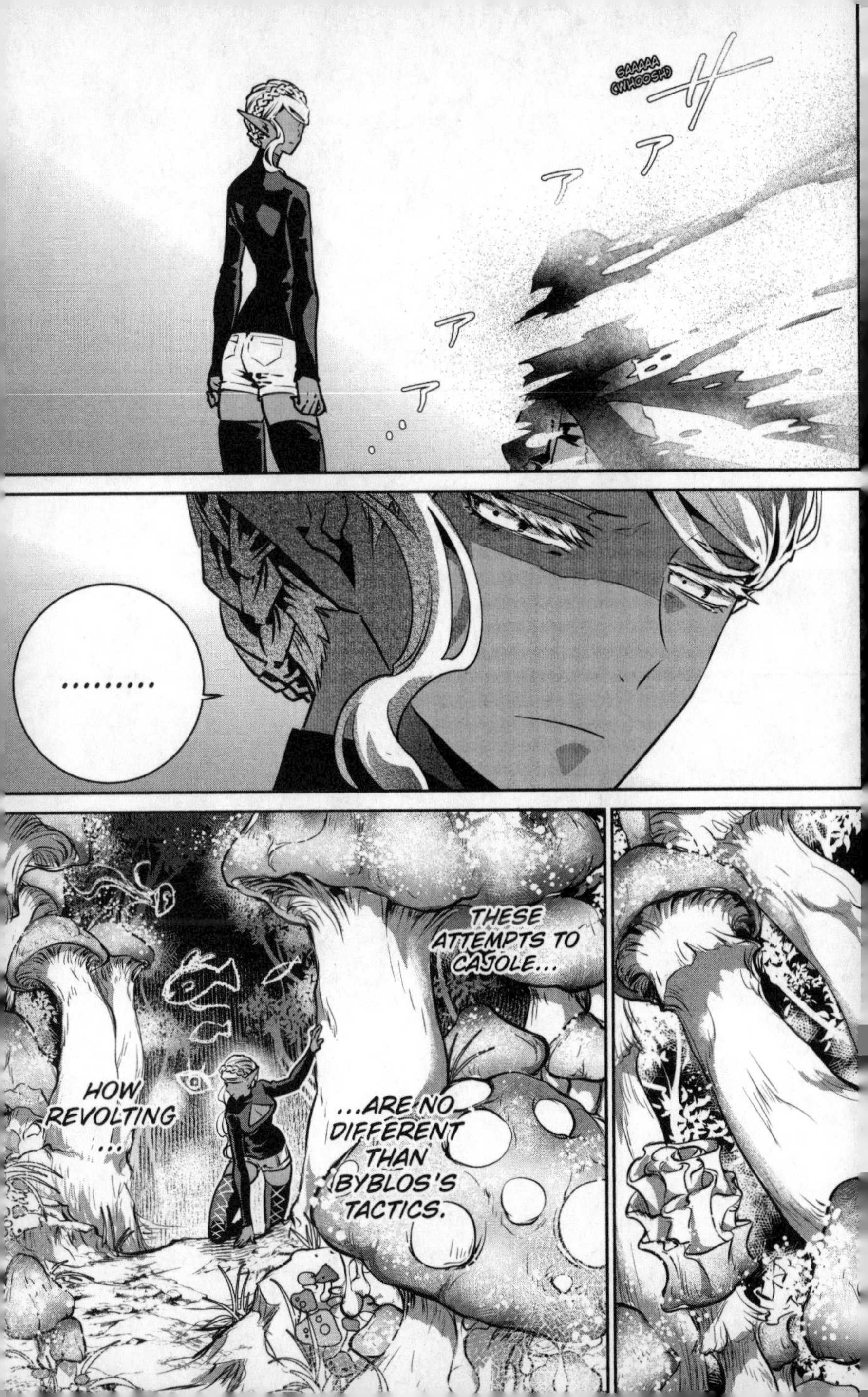
SAAAAA (WHOOSH)
サアアアア
.........
THESE ATTEMPTS TO CAJOLE...
...ARE NO DIFFERENT THAN BYBLOS'S TACTICS.
HOW REVOLTING...

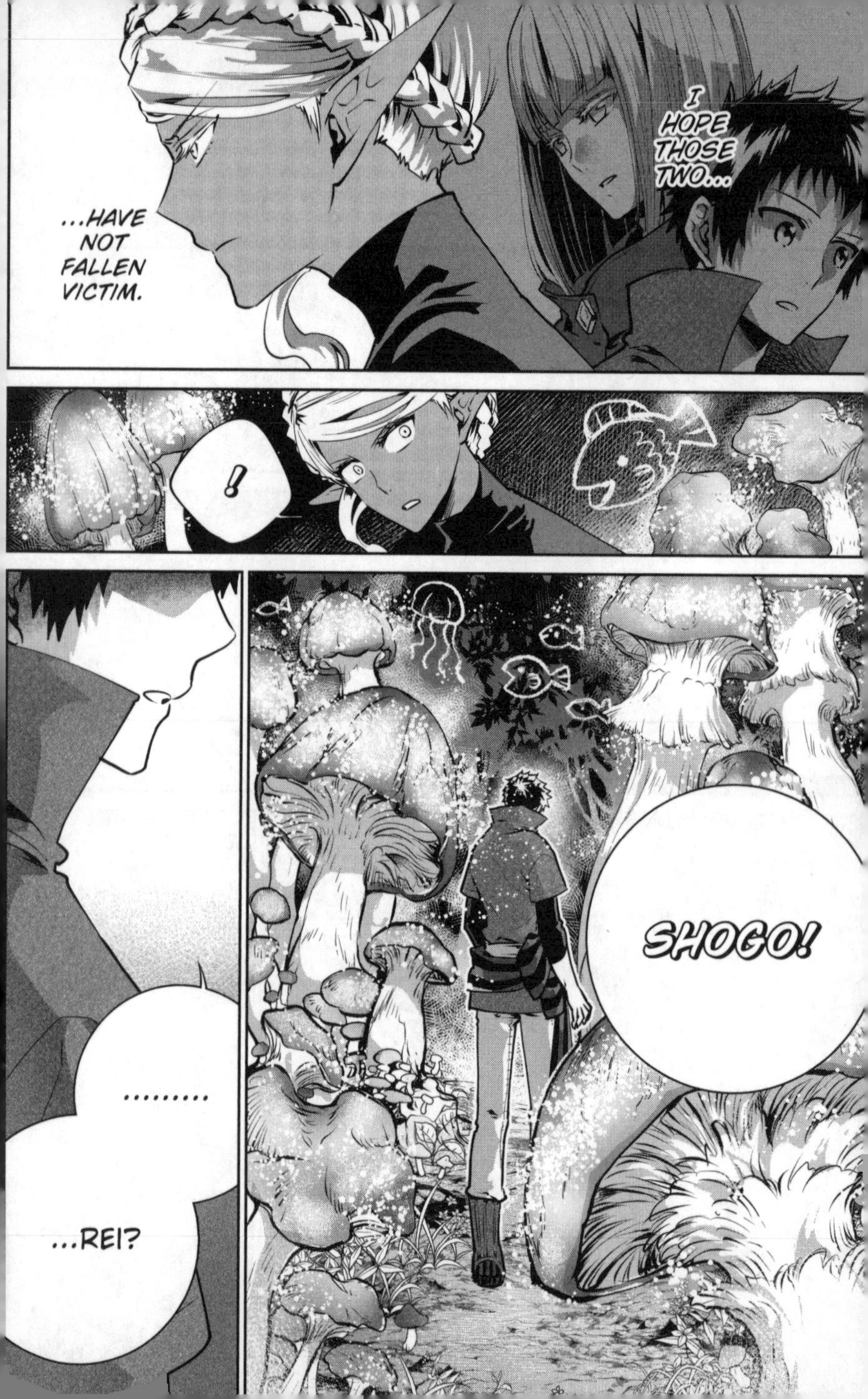
I HOPE THOSE TWO...
...HAVE NOT FALLEN VICTIM.
!
SHOGO!
.........
...REI?

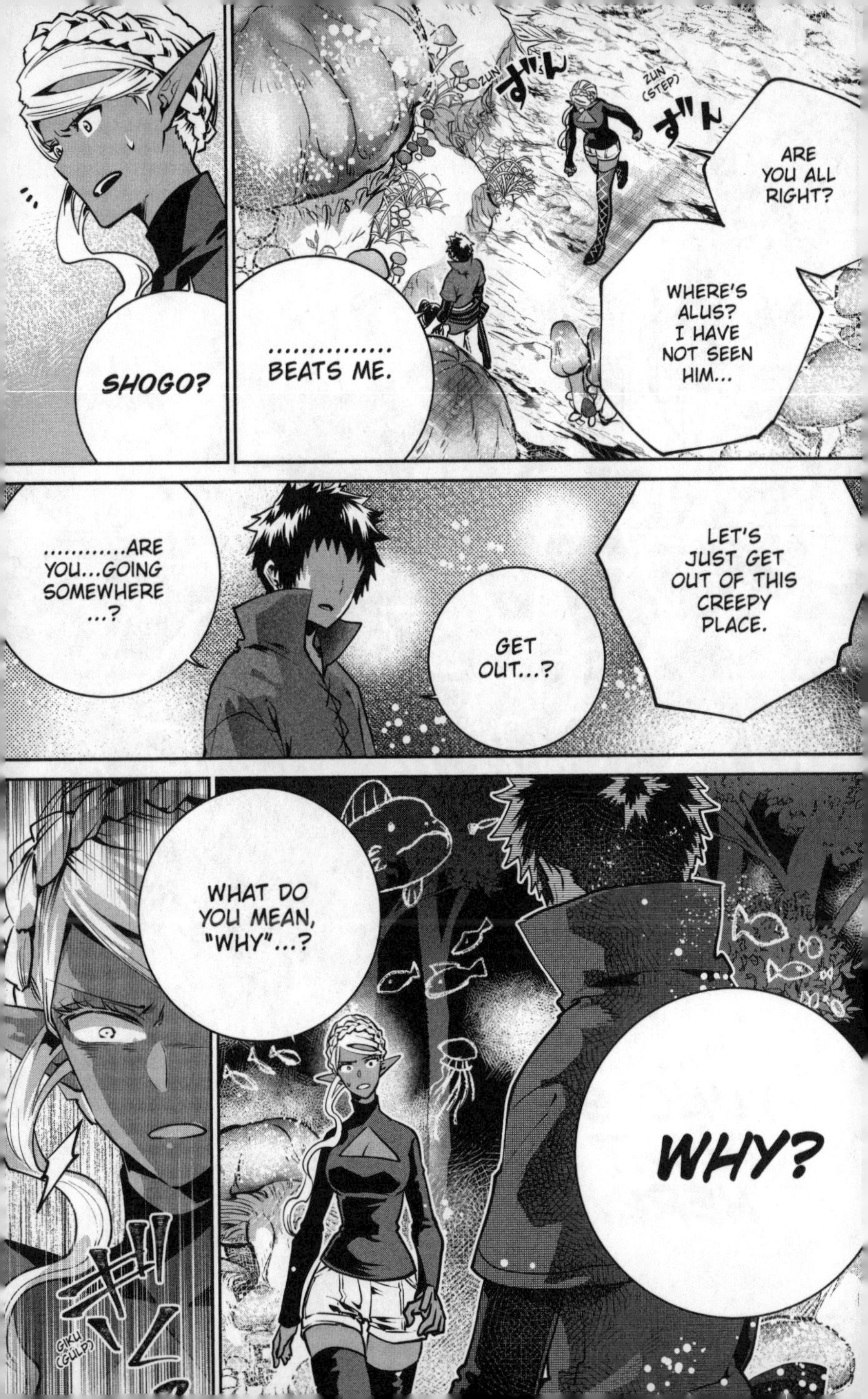
ずん
ZUN
ずん
ZUN (STEP)
ARE YOU ALL RIGHT?
WHERE'S ALUS? I HAVE NOT SEEN HIM...
............... BEATS ME.
...
SHOGO?
LET'S JUST GET OUT OF THIS CREEPY PLACE.
GET OUT...?
...........ARE YOU...GOING SOMEWHERE ...?
WHY?
WHAT DO YOU MEAN, "WHY"...?
ギクッ
GIKU (GULP)

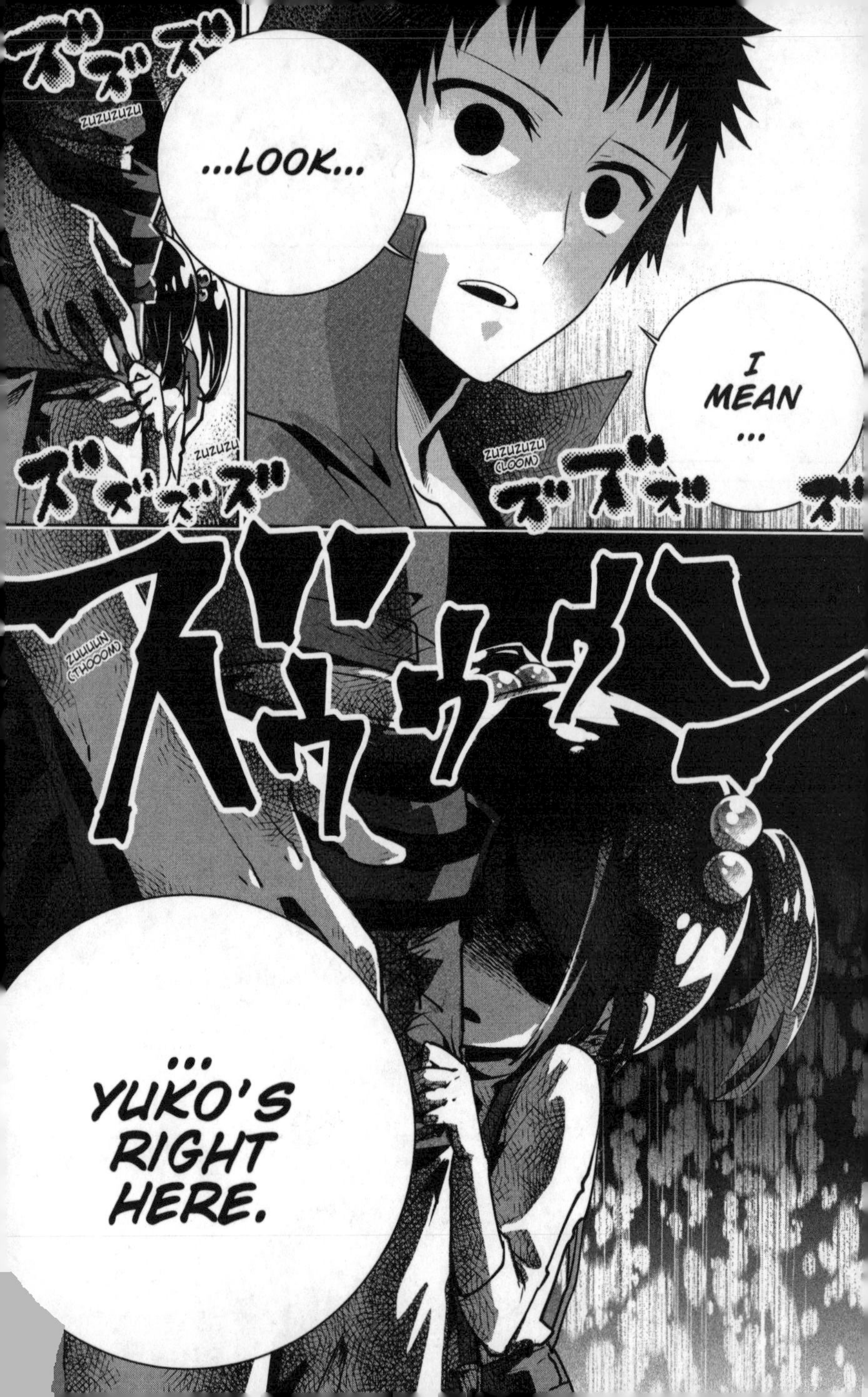
...LOOK...
I MEAN ...
ZUZUZUZU (LOOM)
ZUZUZUZU
ZUZUZU
ZUUUUN (THOOOM)
...YUKO'S RIGHT HERE.

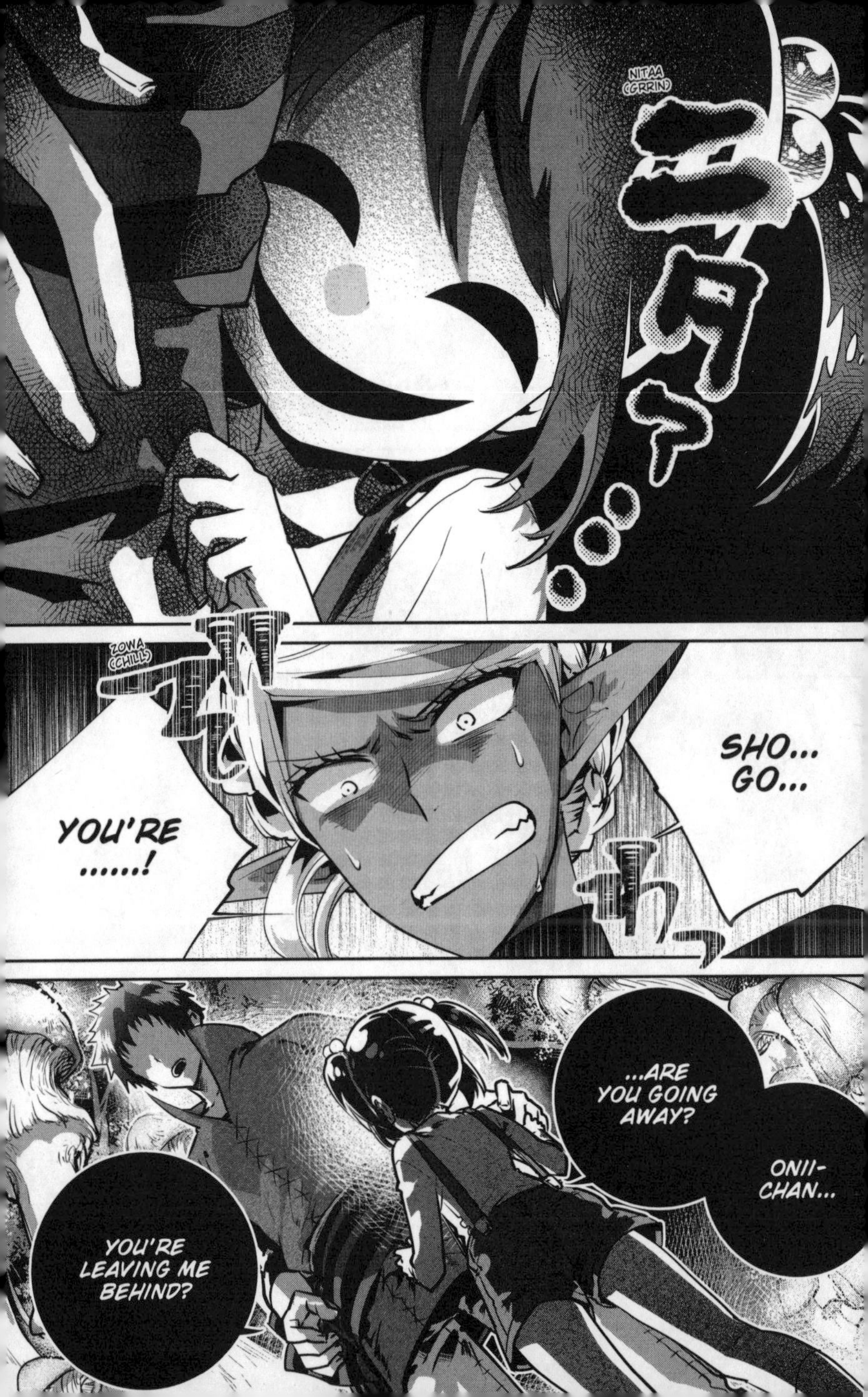

ニタァ…
NITAA (GRRIN)
SHO... GO...
YOU'RE ......!
ZOWA (CHILL)
ONII-CHAN...
...ARE YOU GOING AWAY?
YOU'RE LEAVING ME BEHIND?

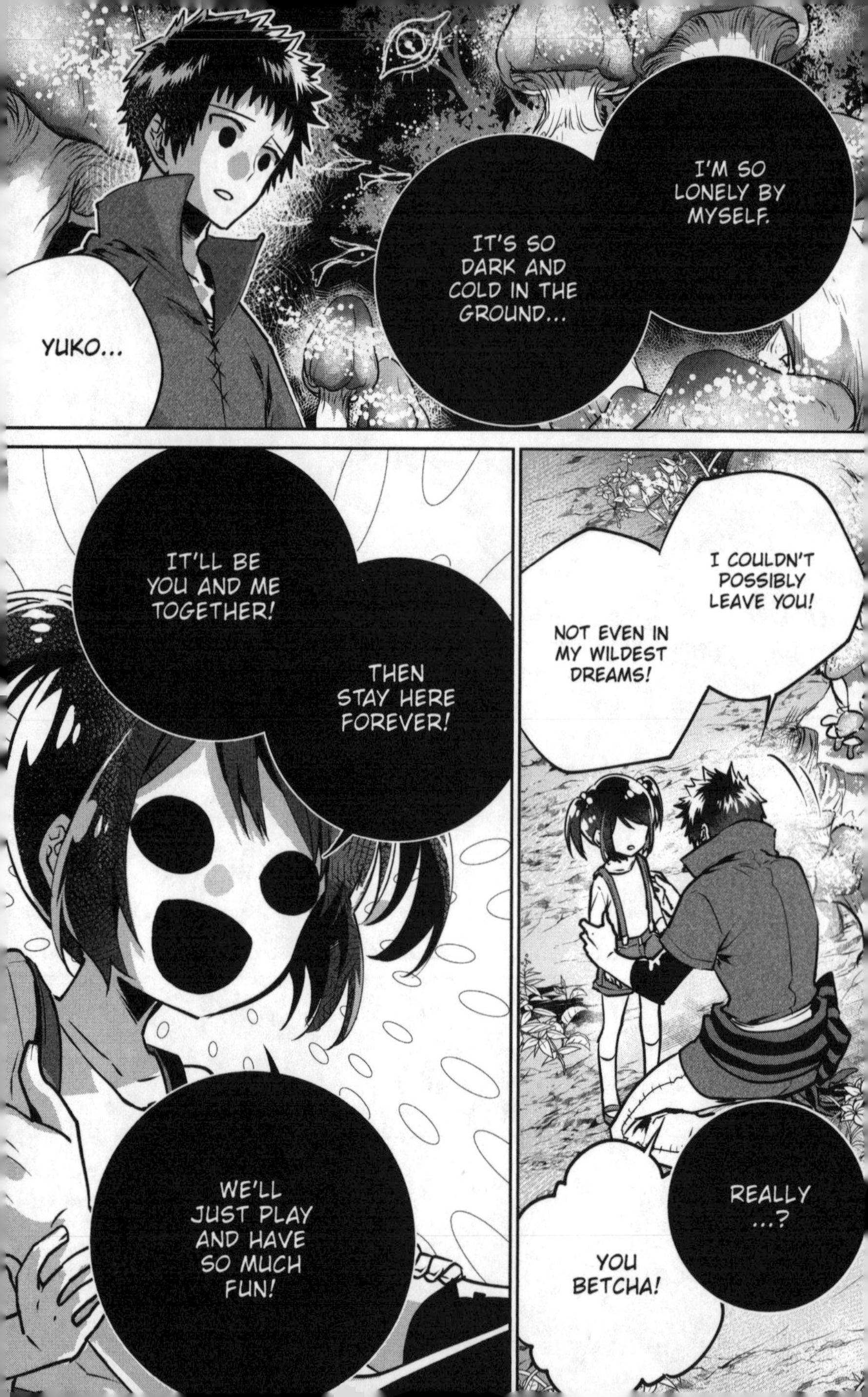
I'M SO LONELY BY MYSELF.
IT'S SO DARK AND COLD IN THE GROUND...
YUKO...
I COULDN'T POSSIBLY LEAVE YOU!
NOT EVEN IN MY WILDEST DREAMS!
REALLY ...?
YOU BETCHA!
THEN STAY HERE FOREVER!
IT'LL BE YOU AND ME TOGETHER!
WE'LL JUST PLAY AND HAVE SO MUCH FUN!

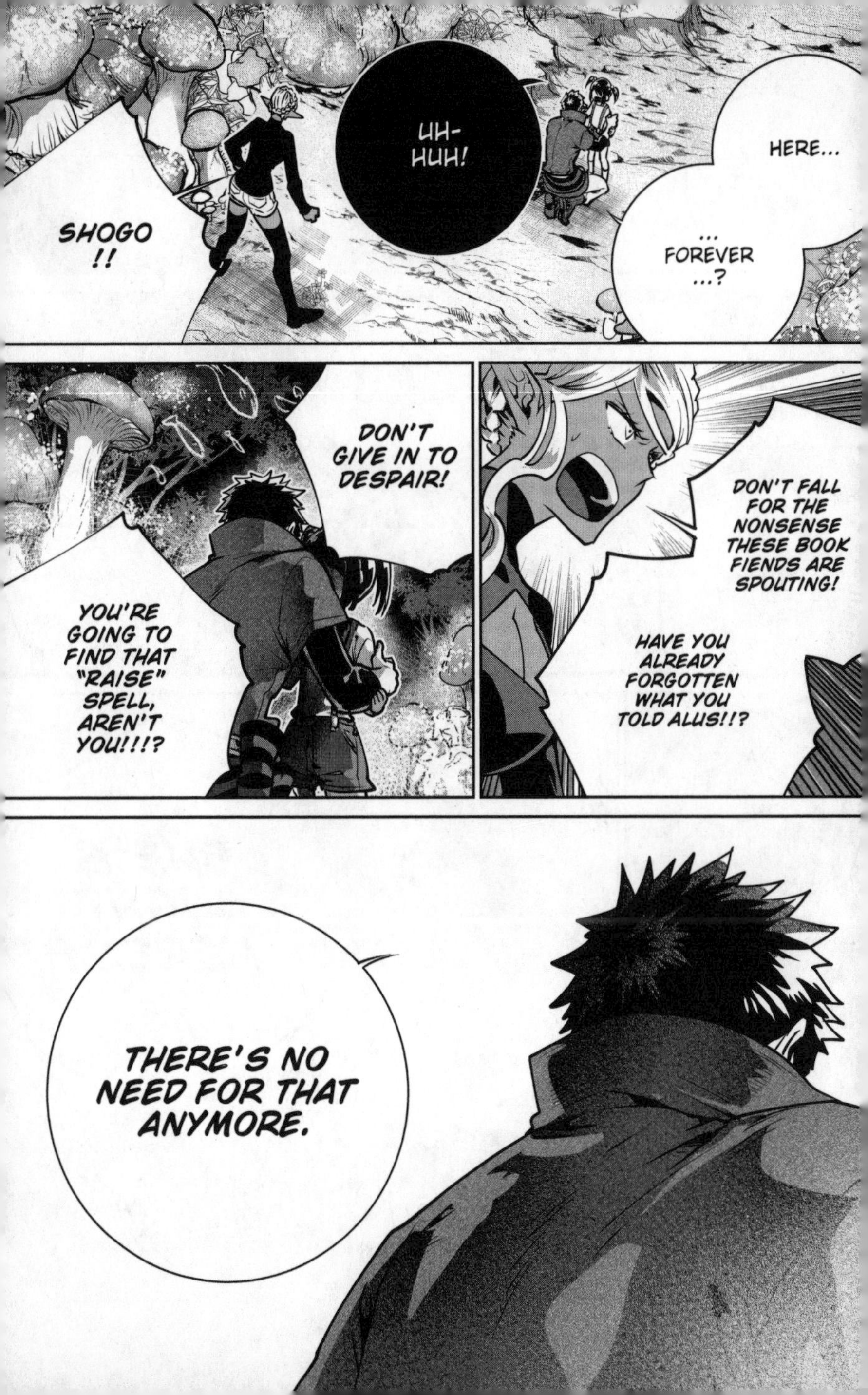
HERE...
...FOREVER...?
UH-HUH!
SHOGO!!
DON'T FALL FOR THE NONSENSE THESE BOOK FIENDS ARE SPOUTING!
HAVE YOU ALREADY FORGOTTEN WHAT YOU TOLD ALUS!!?
DON'T GIVE IN TO DESPAIR!
YOU'RE GOING TO FIND THAT "RAISE" SPELL, AREN'T YOU!!!?
THERE'S NO NEED FOR THAT ANYMORE.

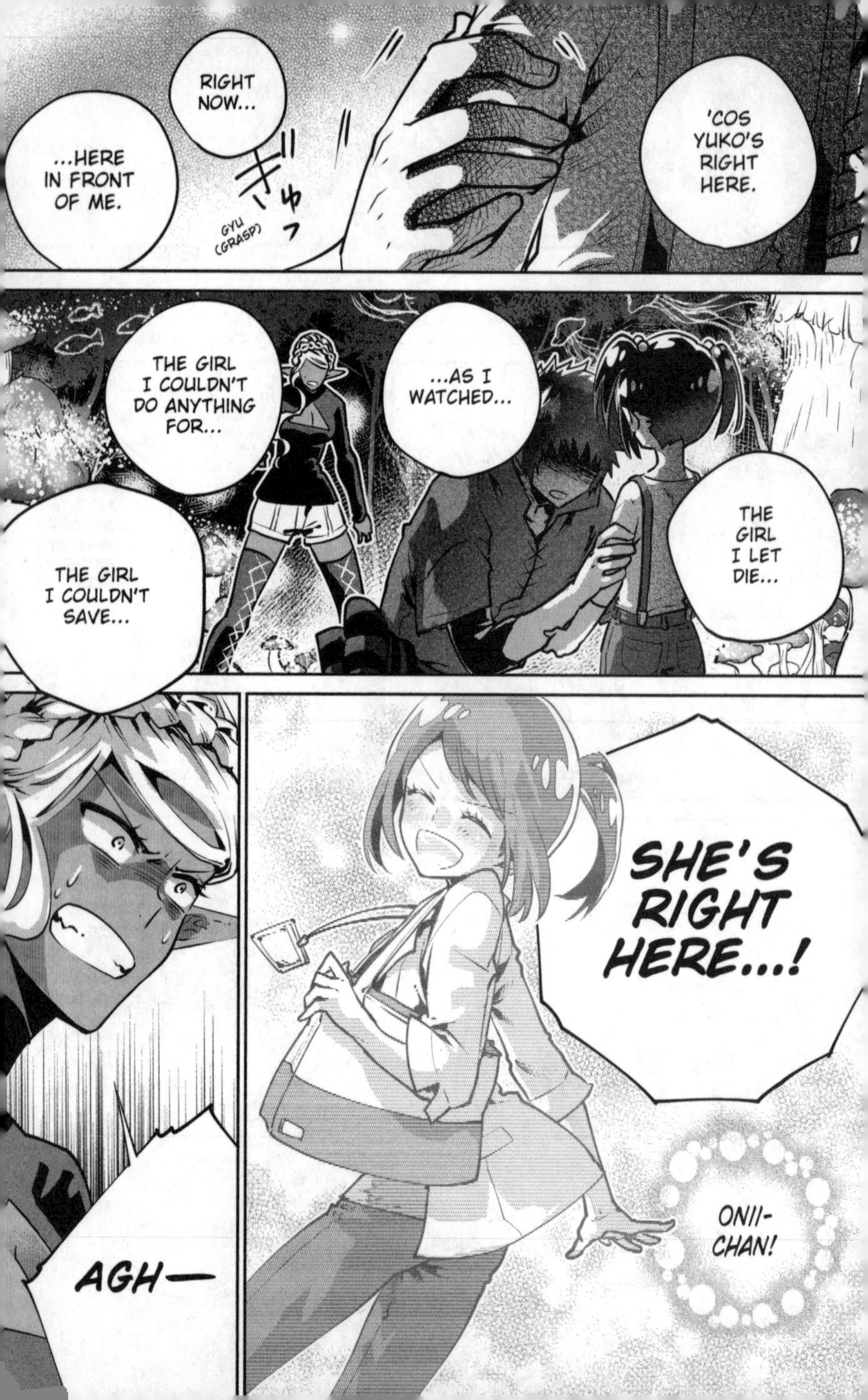
'COS YUKO'S RIGHT HERE.
RIGHT NOW...
GYU (GRASP)
...HERE IN FRONT OF ME.
THE GIRL I LET DIE...
...AS I WATCHED...
THE GIRL I COULDN'T DO ANYTHING FOR...
THE GIRL I COULDN'T SAVE...
SHE'S RIGHT HERE...!
ONII-CHAN!
AGH—

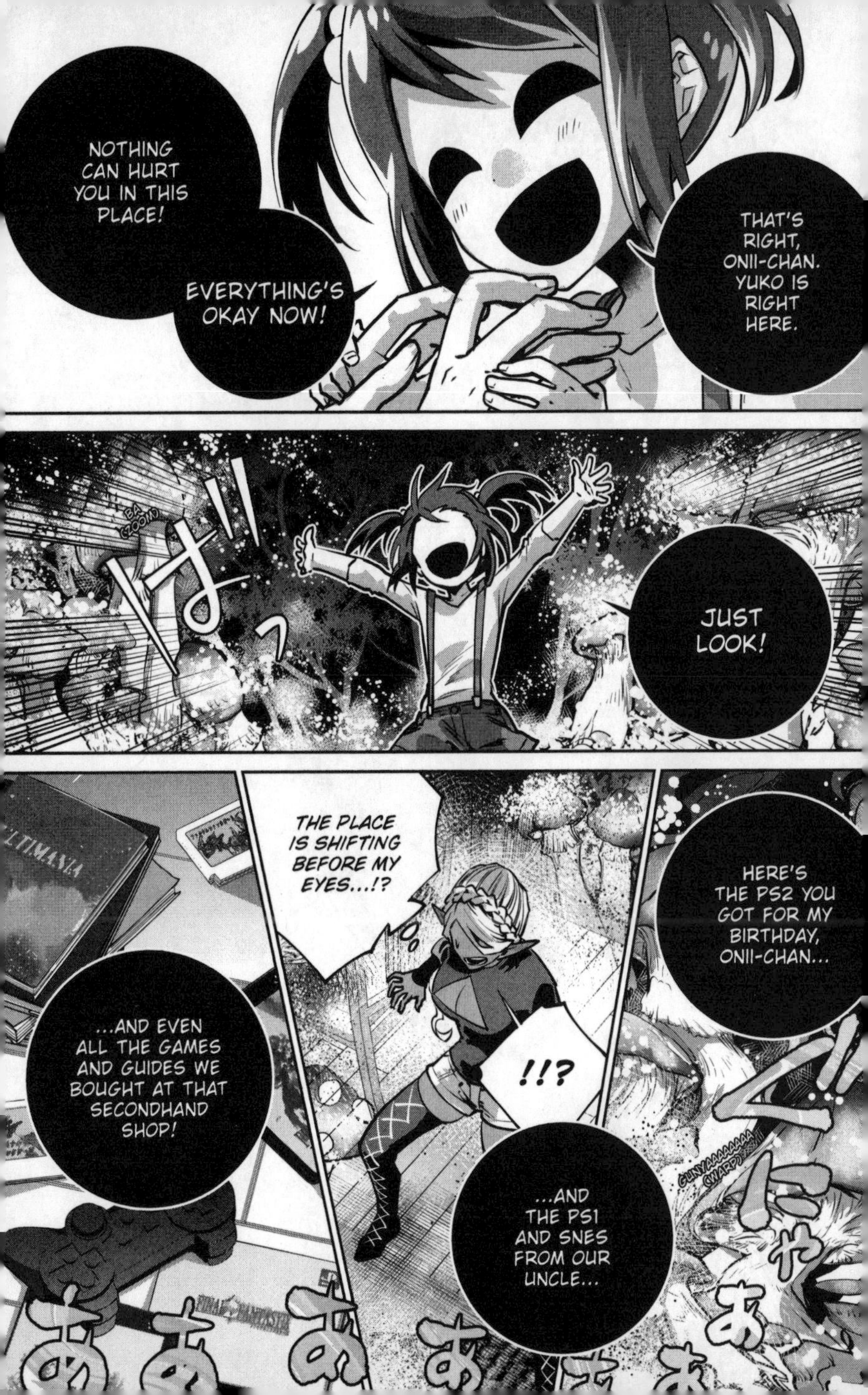
THAT'S RIGHT, ONII-CHAN. YUKO IS RIGHT HERE.
NOTHING CAN HURT YOU IN THIS PLACE!
EVERYTHING'S OKAY NOW!
JUST LOOK!
BA (ZOOM)
HERE'S THE PS2 YOU GOT FOR MY BIRTHDAY, ONII-CHAN...
GUNYAAAAAAAA (WARP)
...AND THE PS1 AND SNES FROM OUR UNCLE...
THE PLACE IS SHIFTING BEFORE MY EYES...!?
!!?
...AND EVEN ALL THE GAMES AND GUIDES WE BOUGHT AT THAT SECONDHAND SHOP!

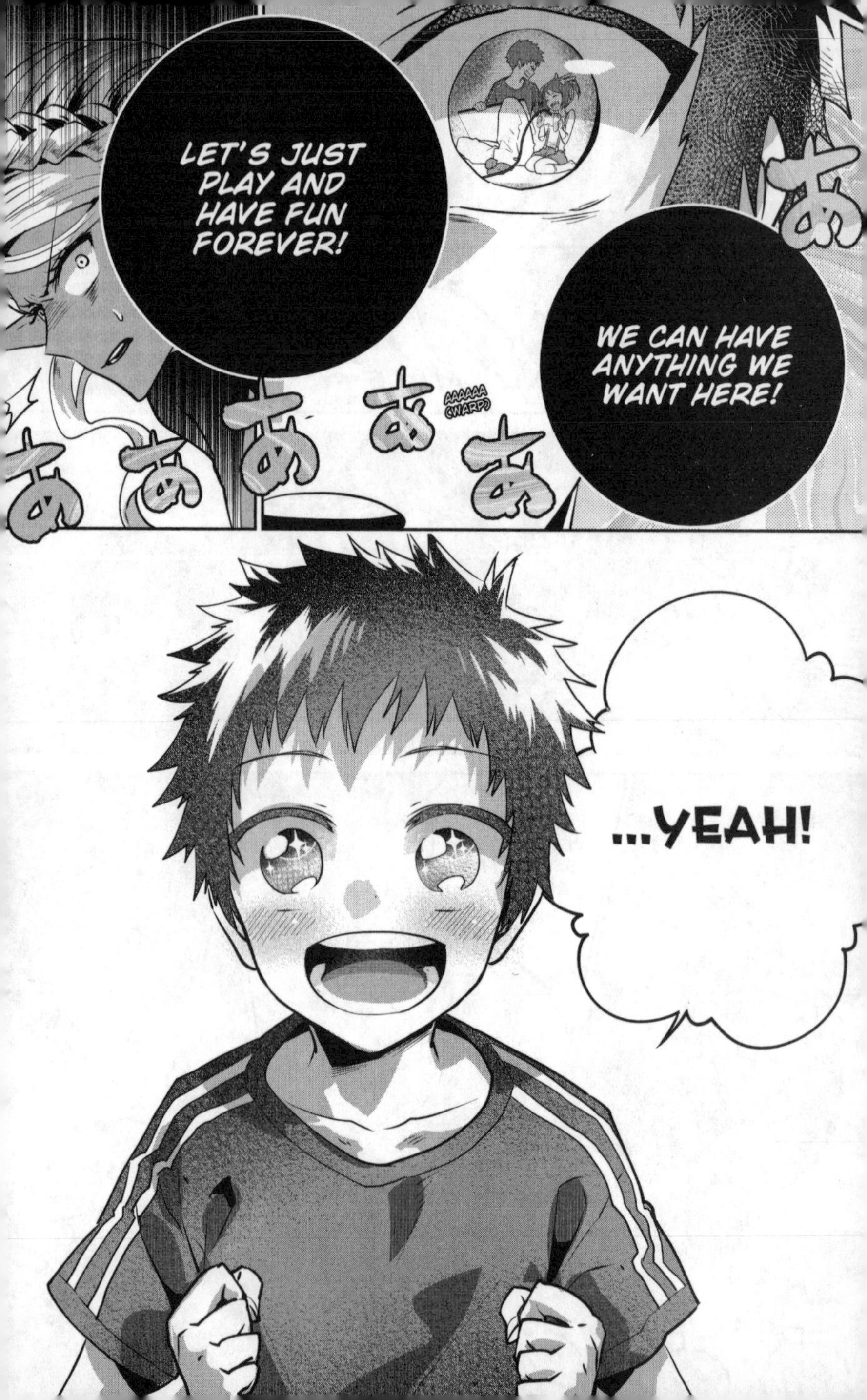
WE CAN HAVE ANYTHING WE WANT HERE!
LET'S JUST PLAY AND HAVE FUN FOREVER!
AAAAAA (WARP)
あ あ あ あ あ あ
...YEAH!

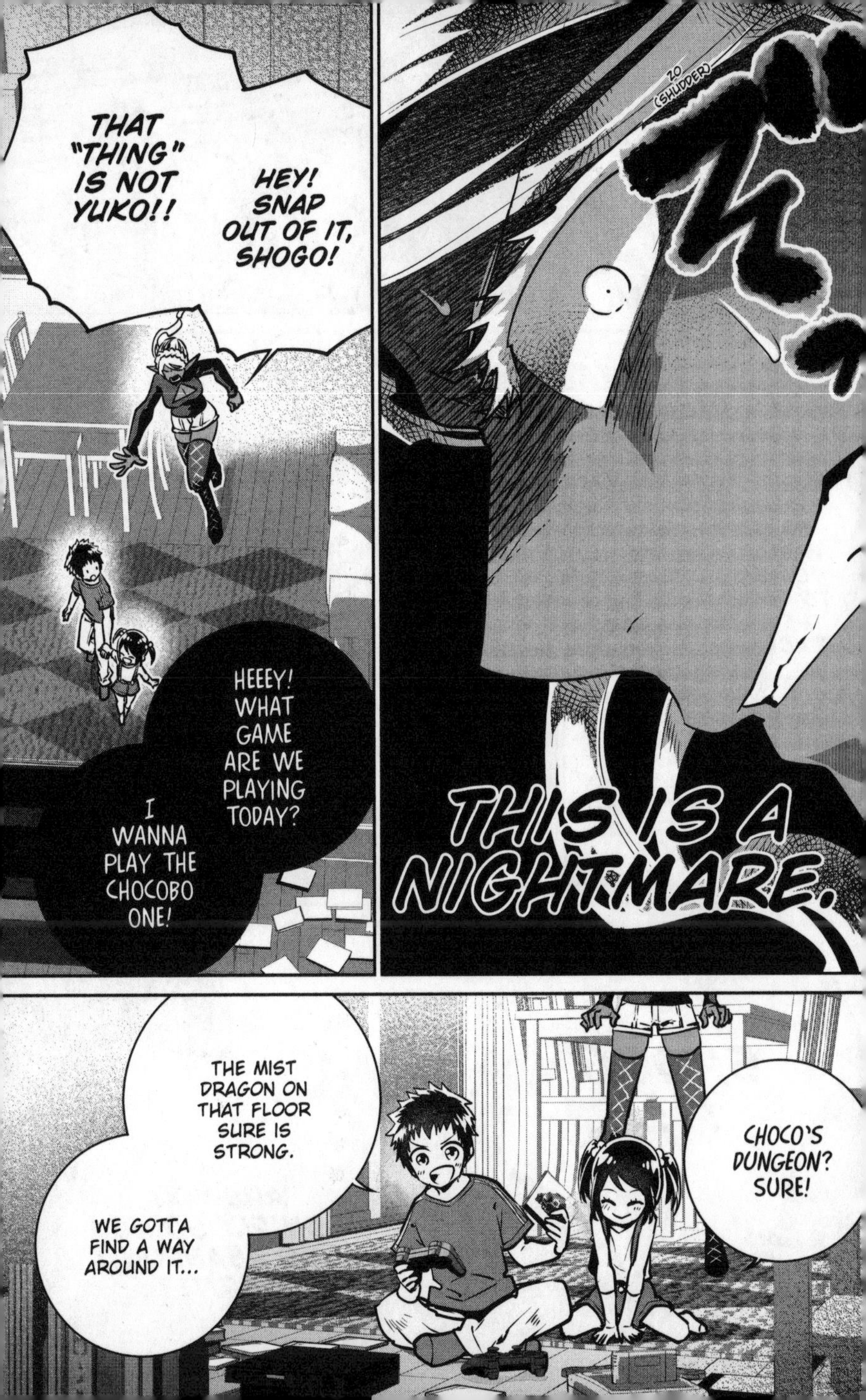
ZO (SHUDDER)
THIS IS A NIGHTMARE.
HEY! SNAP OUT OF IT, SHOGO!
THAT "THING" IS NOT YUKO!!
HEEEY! WHAT GAME ARE WE PLAYING TODAY?
I WANNA PLAY THE CHOCOBO ONE!
CHOCO'S DUNGEON? SURE!
THE MIST DRAGON ON THAT FLOOR SURE IS STRONG.
WE GOTTA FIND A WAY AROUND IT...

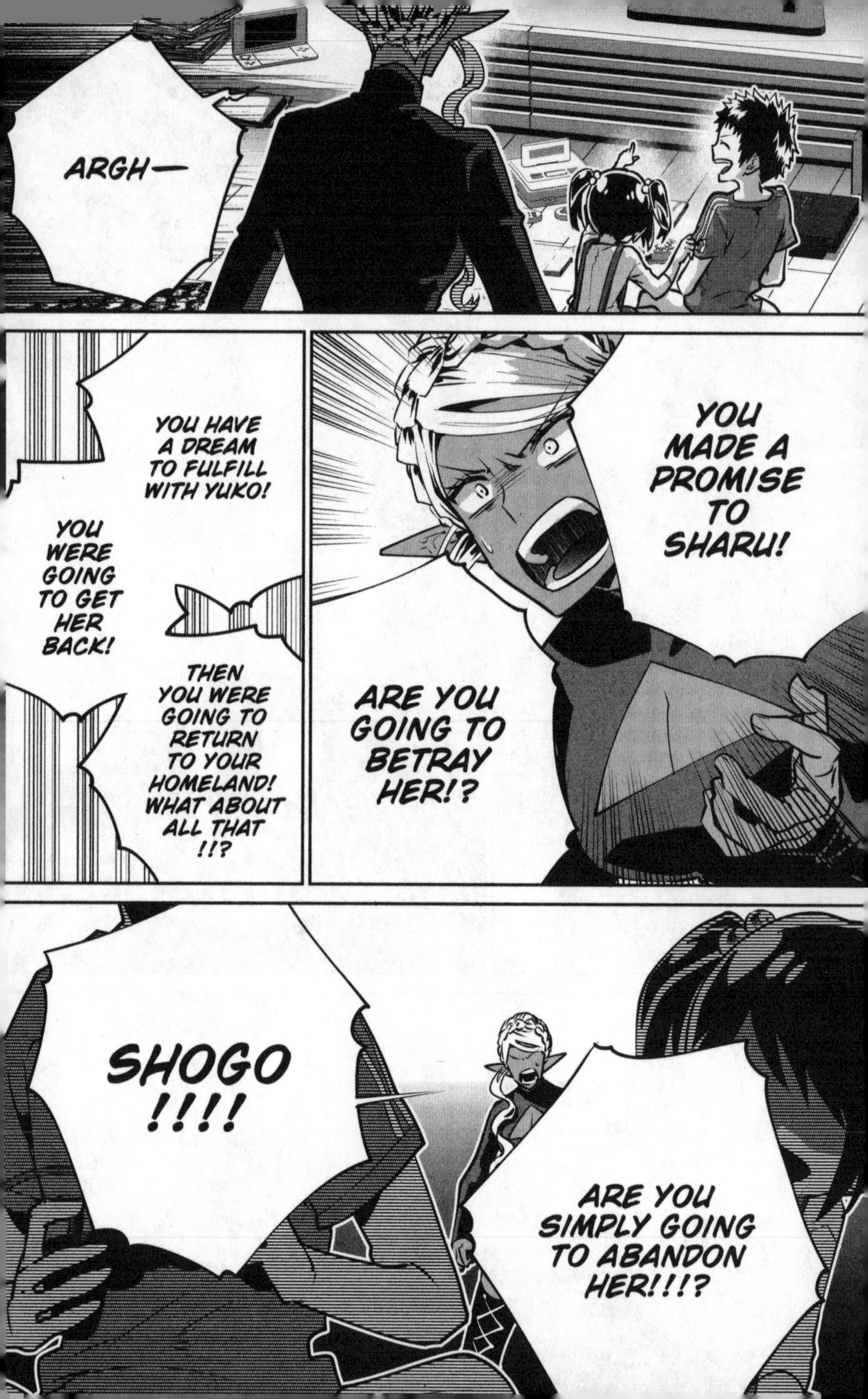
ARGH—
YOU MADE A PROMISE TO SHARU!
ARE YOU GOING TO BETRAY HER!?
YOU HAVE A DREAM TO FULFILL WITH YUKO!
YOU WERE GOING TO GET HER BACK!
THEN YOU WERE GOING TO RETURN TO YOUR HOMELAND! WHAT ABOUT ALL THAT!!?
SHOGO!!!!
ARE YOU SIMPLY GOING TO ABANDON HER!!!?

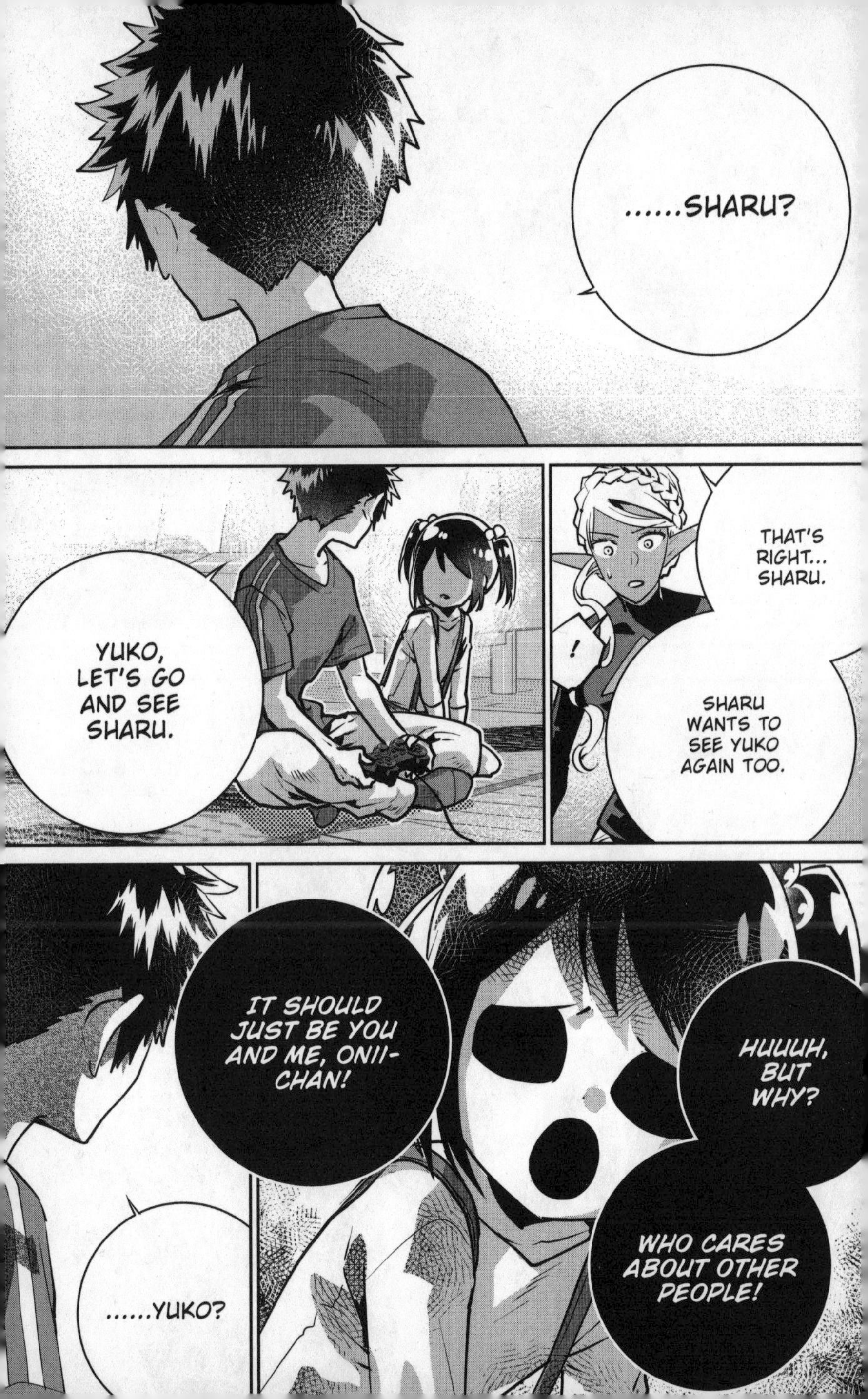

......SHARU?
THAT'S RIGHT... SHARU.
!
SHARU WANTS TO SEE YUKO AGAIN TOO.
YUKO, LET'S GO AND SEE SHARU.
HUUUH, BUT WHY?
WHO CARES ABOUT OTHER PEOPLE!
IT SHOULD JUST BE YOU AND ME, ONII-CHAN!
......YUKO?

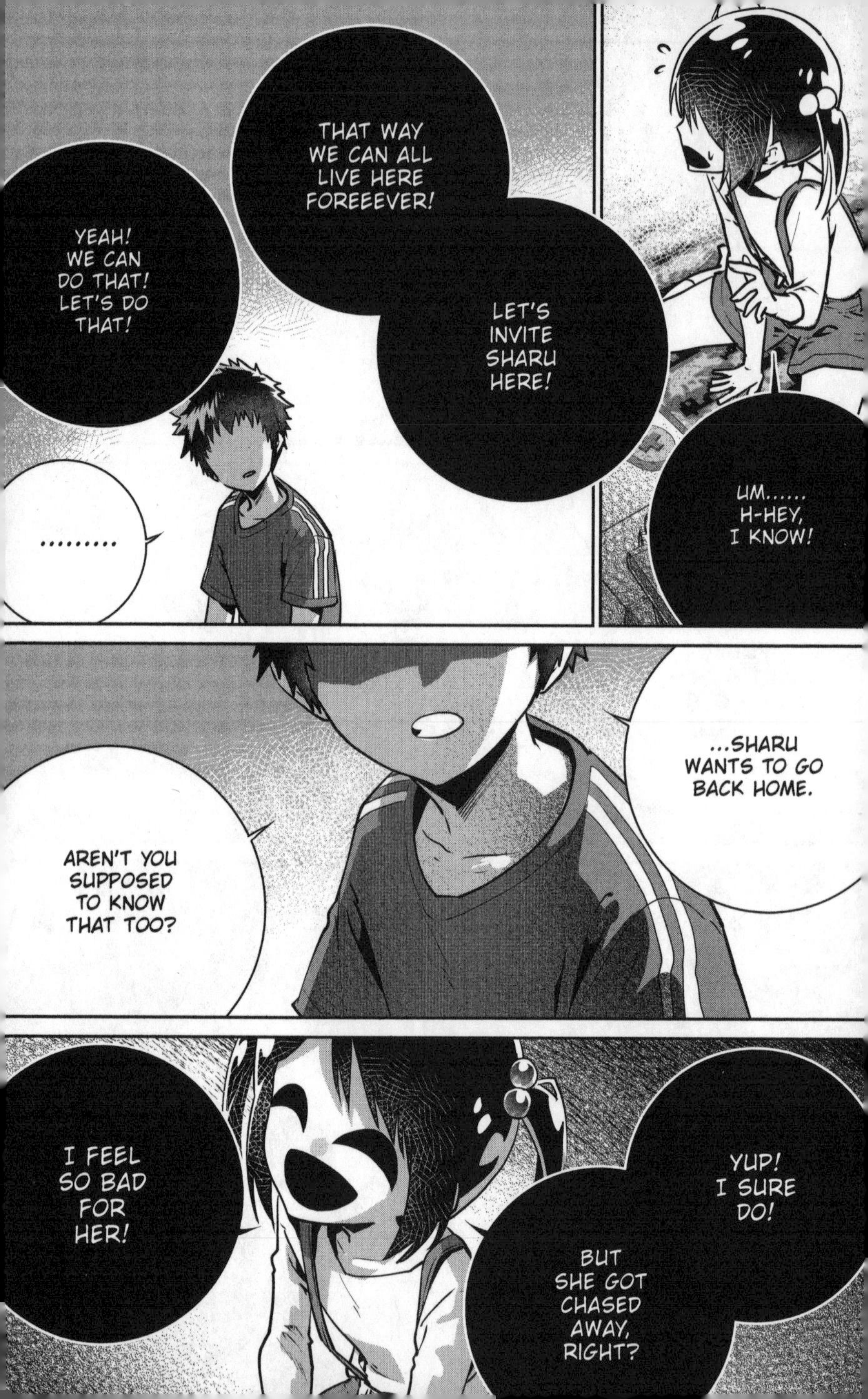
UM...... H-HEY, I KNOW!
LET'S INVITE SHARU HERE!
THAT WAY WE CAN ALL LIVE HERE FOREEEVER!
YEAH! WE CAN DO THAT! LET'S DO THAT!
.........
...SHARU WANTS TO GO BACK HOME.
AREN'T YOU SUPPOSED TO KNOW THAT TOO?
YUP! I SURE DO!
BUT SHE GOT CHASED AWAY, RIGHT?
I FEEL SO BAD FOR HER!

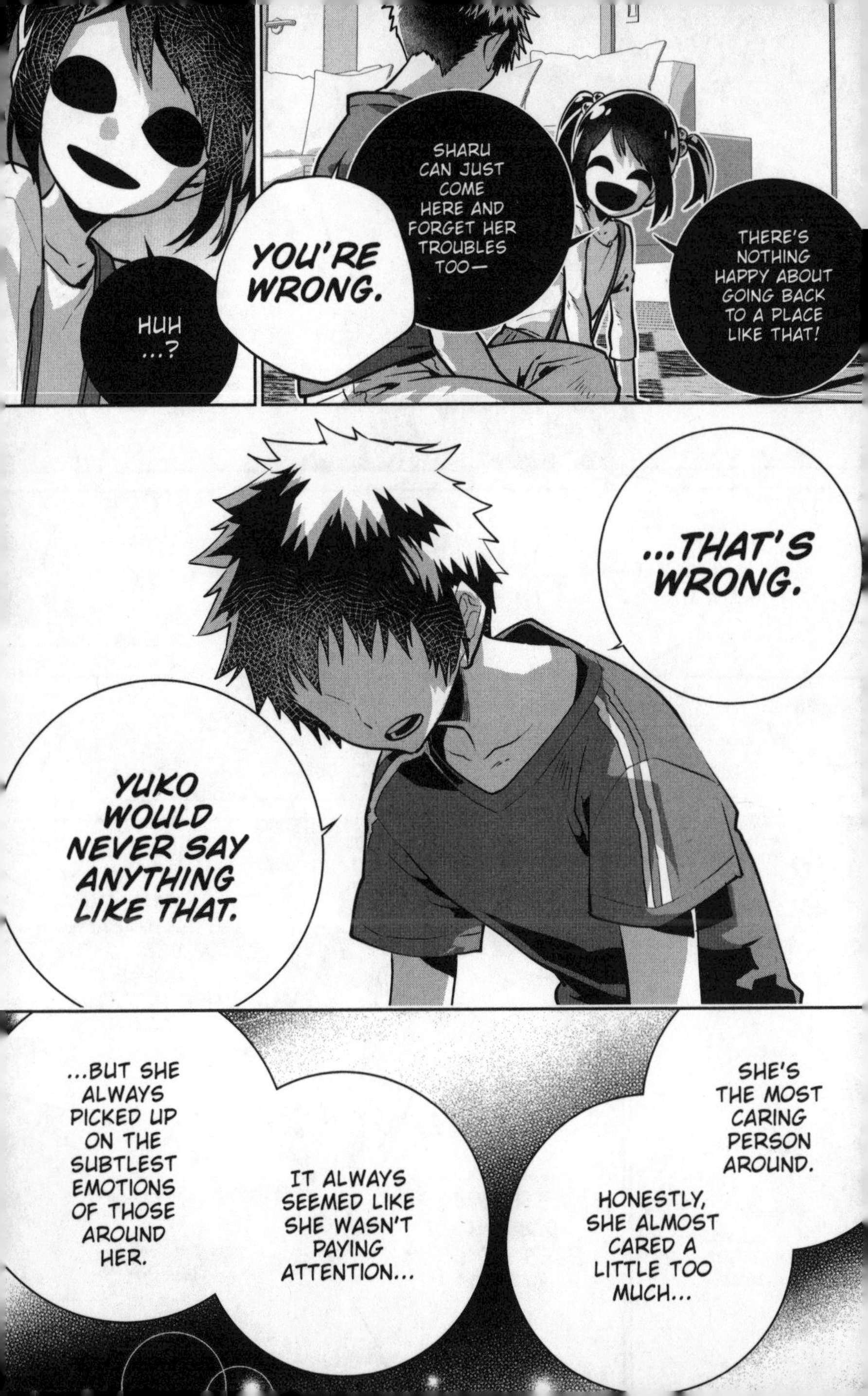
THERE'S NOTHING HAPPY ABOUT GOING BACK TO A PLACE LIKE THAT!
SHARU CAN JUST COME HERE AND FORGET HER TROUBLES TOO—
YOU'RE WRONG.
HUH ...?
...THAT'S WRONG.
YUKO WOULD NEVER SAY ANYTHING LIKE THAT.
SHE'S THE MOST CARING PERSON AROUND.
HONESTLY, SHE ALMOST CARED A LITTLE TOO MUCH...
IT ALWAYS SEEMED LIKE SHE WASN'T PAYING ATTENTION...
...BUT SHE ALWAYS PICKED UP ON THE SUBTLEST EMOTIONS OF THOSE AROUND HER.

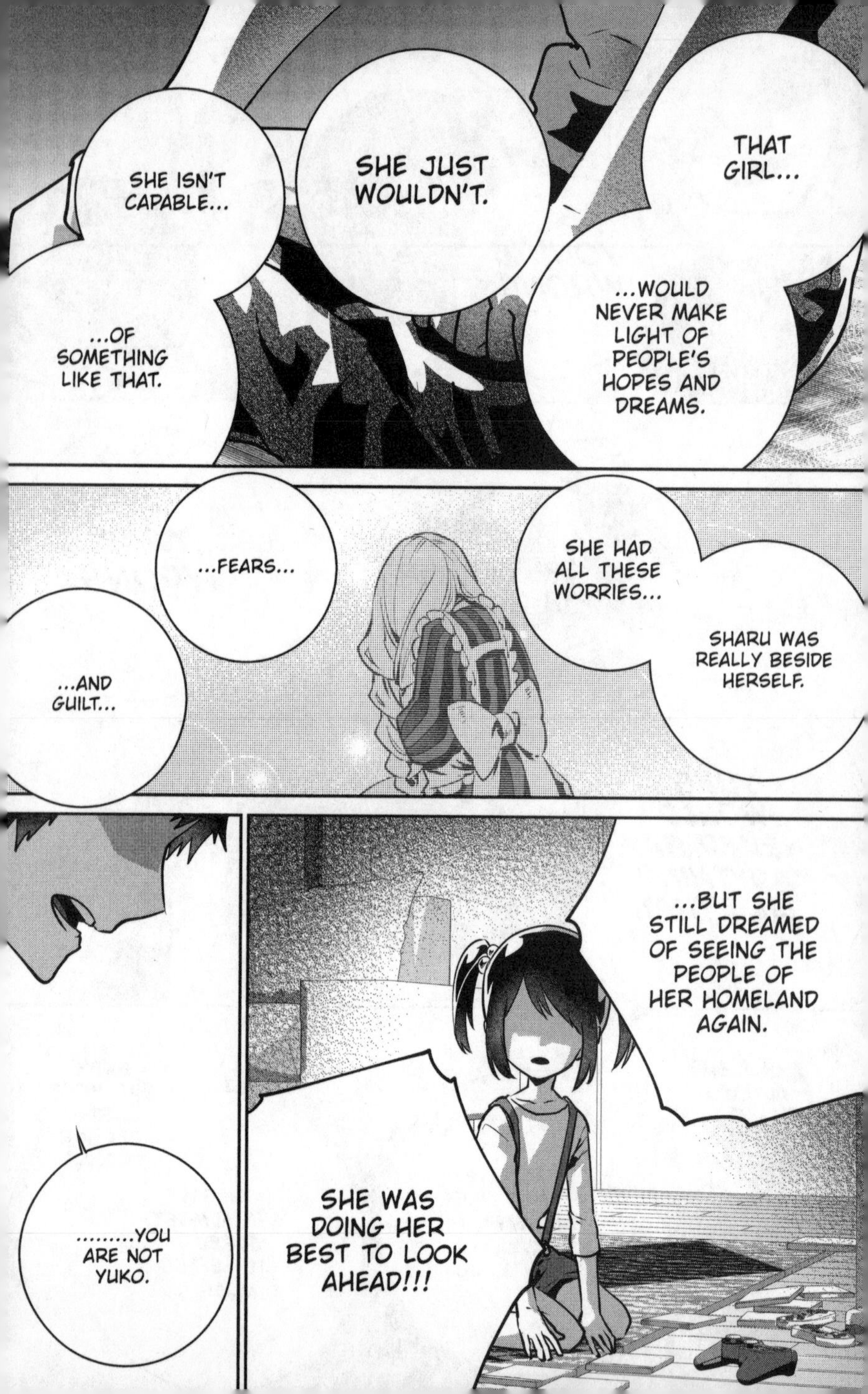
THAT GIRL...
...WOULD NEVER MAKE LIGHT OF PEOPLE'S HOPES AND DREAMS.
SHE JUST WOULDN'T.
SHE ISN'T CAPABLE...
...OF SOMETHING LIKE THAT.
SHARU WAS REALLY BESIDE HERSELF.
SHE HAD ALL THESE WORRIES...
...FEARS...
...AND GUILT...
...BUT SHE STILL DREAMED OF SEEING THE PEOPLE OF HER HOMELAND AGAIN.
SHE WAS DOING HER BEST TO LOOK AHEAD!!!
.........YOU ARE NOT YUKO.

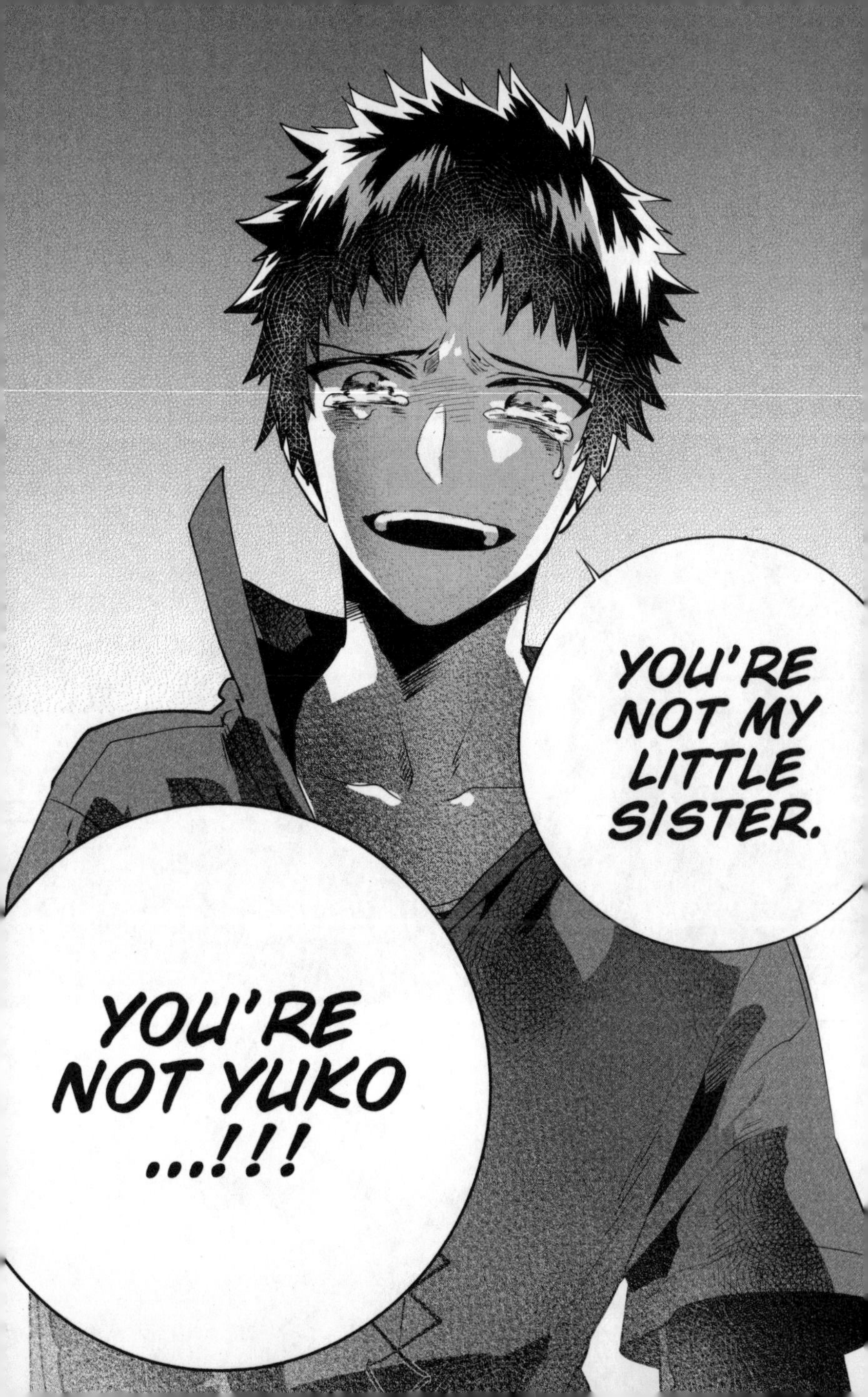
YOU'RE NOT MY LITTLE SISTER.
YOU'RE NOT YUKO ...!!!

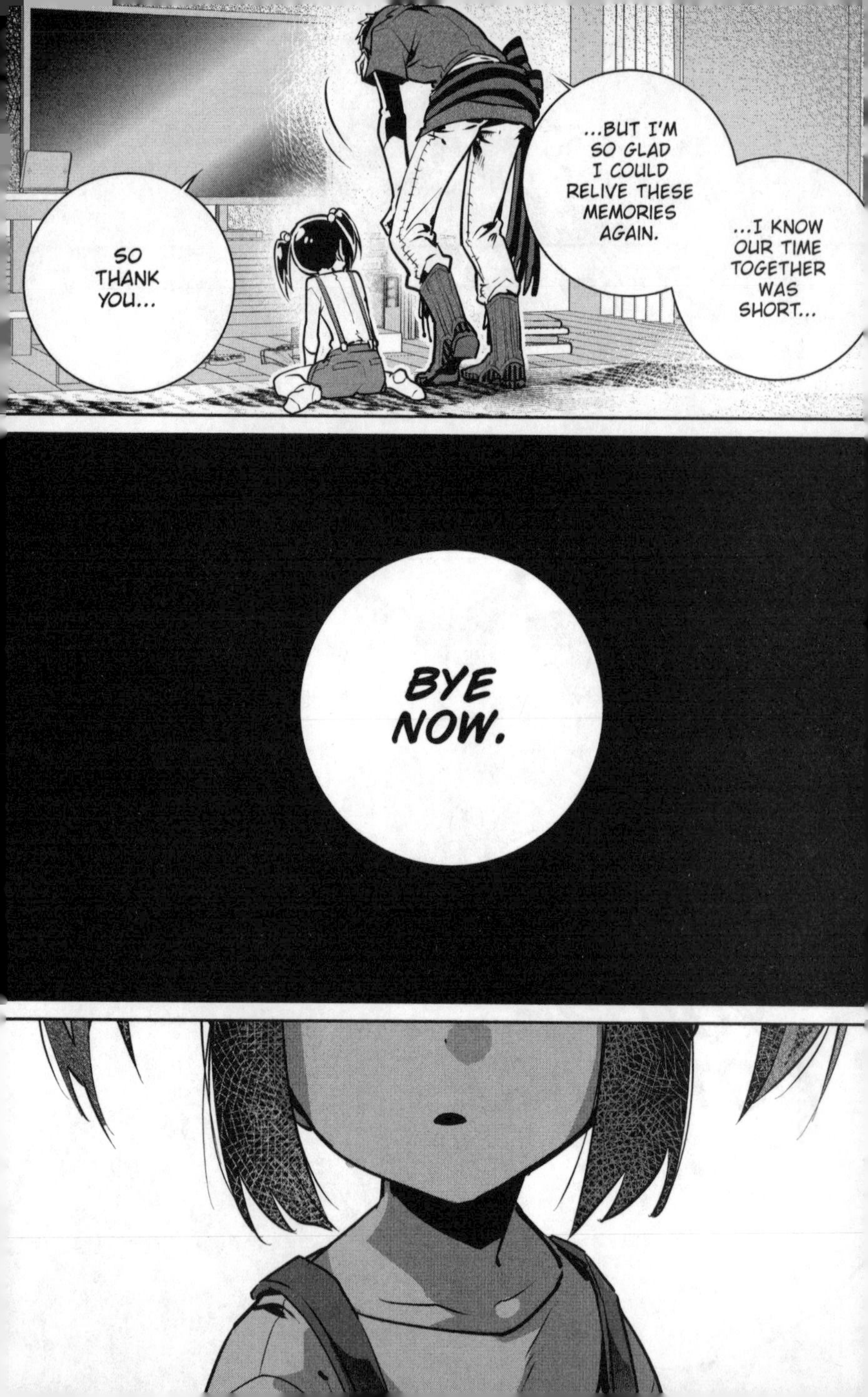
...I KNOW OUR TIME TOGETHER WAS SHORT...
...BUT I'M SO GLAD I COULD RELIVE THESE MEMORIES AGAIN.
SO THANK YOU...
BYE NOW.

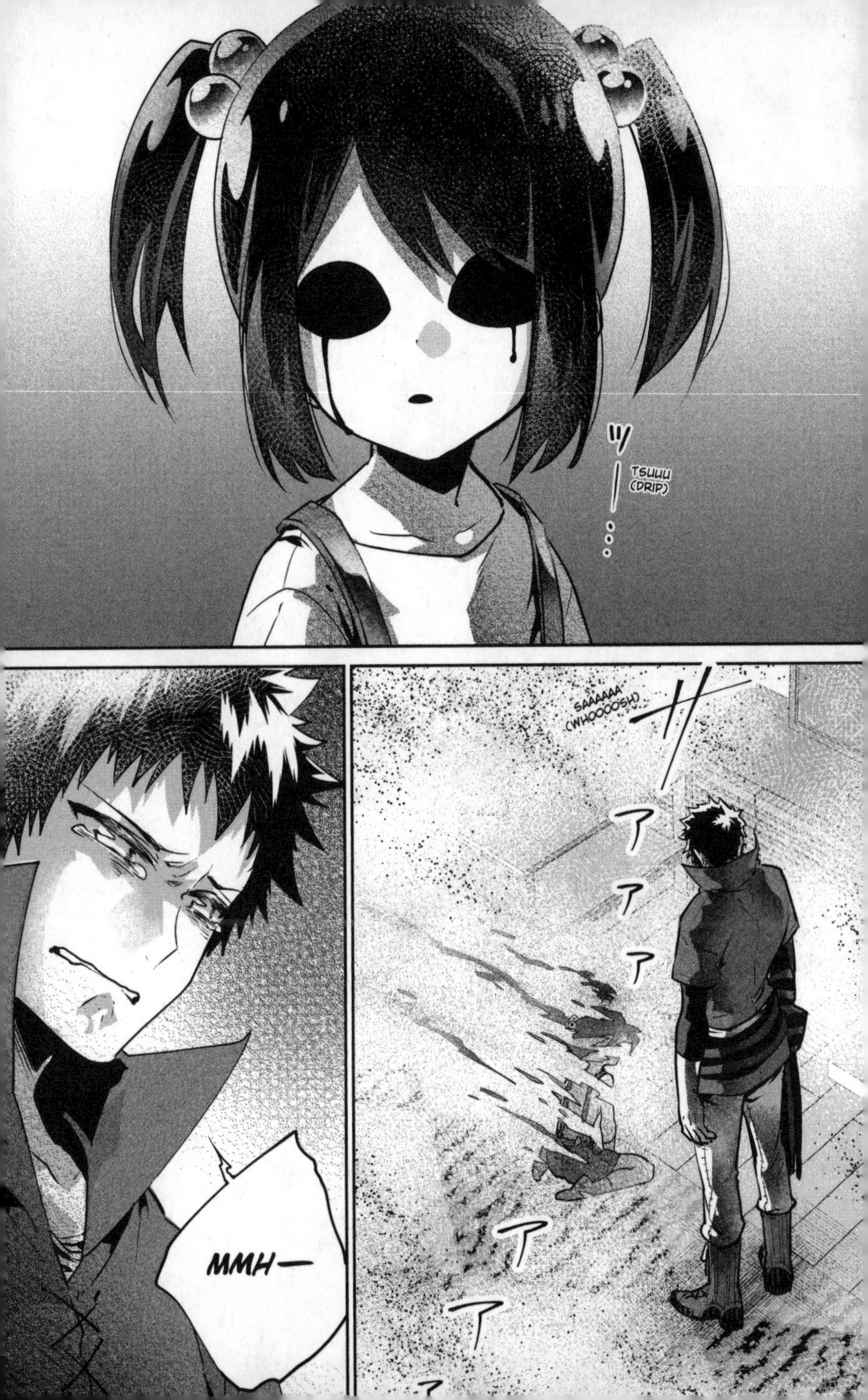
ツー…
TSUUU (DRIP)
ザァァァァァ
SAAAAAA (WHOOOOOSH)
MMH—

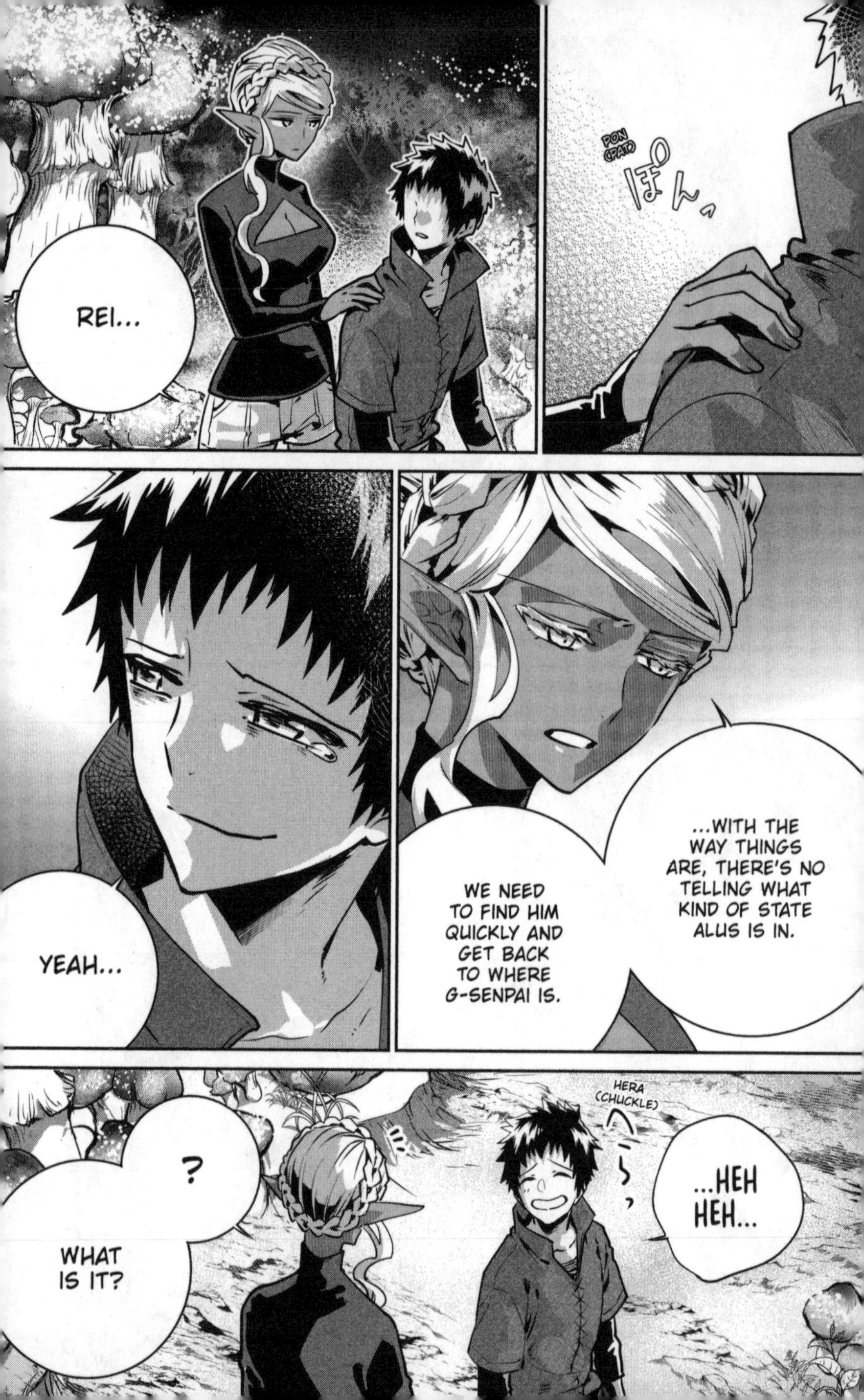
PON (PAT)
ぽん
REI...
...WITH THE WAY THINGS ARE, THERE'S NO TELLING WHAT KIND OF STATE ALUS IS IN.
WE NEED TO FIND HIM QUICKLY AND GET BACK TO WHERE G-SENPAI IS.
YEAH...
HERA (CHUCKLE)
...HEH HEH...
?
WHAT IS IT?

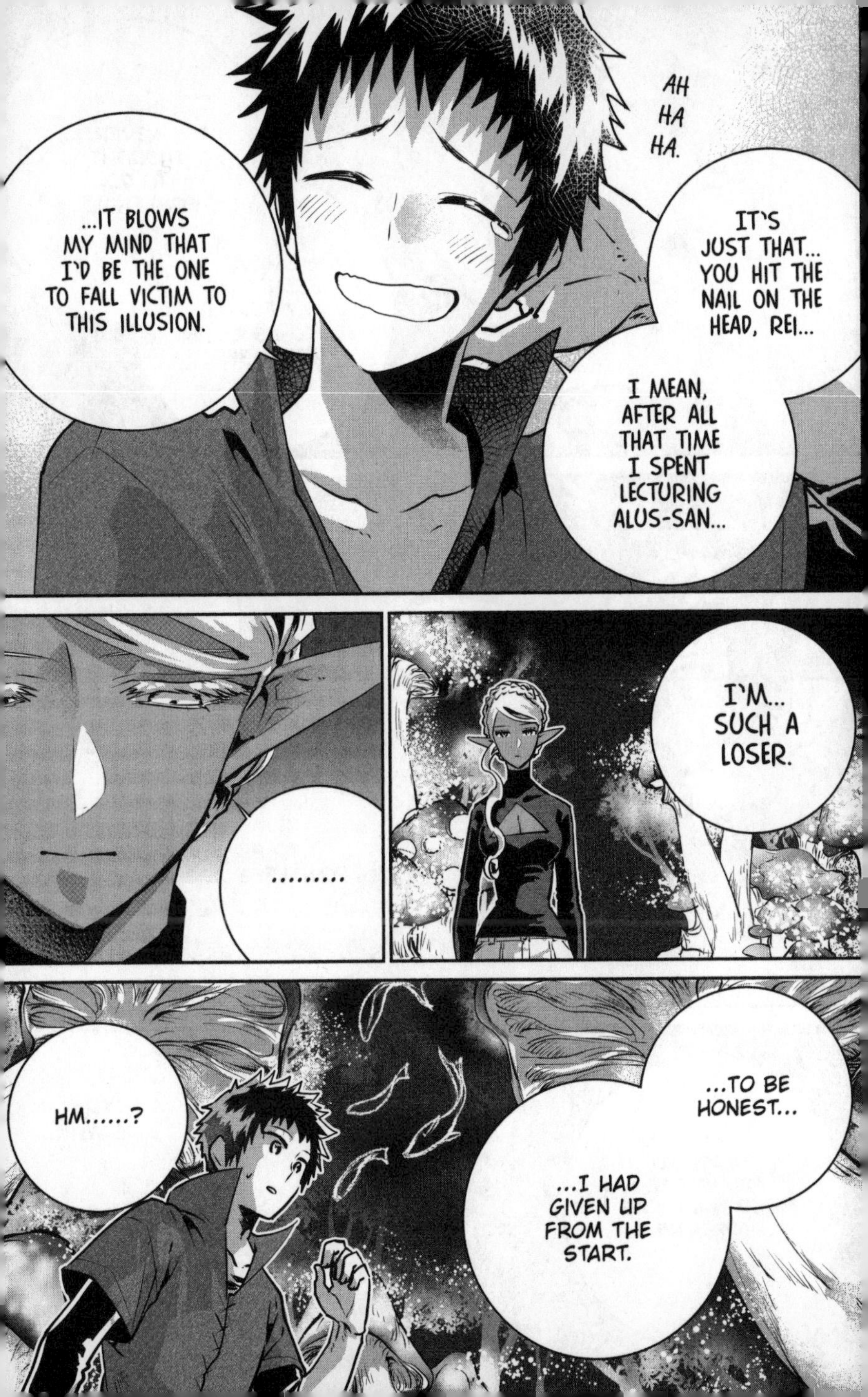
AH HA HA.
IT'S JUST THAT... YOU HIT THE NAIL ON THE HEAD, REI...
I MEAN, AFTER ALL THAT TIME I SPENT LECTURING ALUS-SAN...
...IT BLOWS MY MIND THAT I'D BE THE ONE TO FALL VICTIM TO THIS ILLUSION.
I'M... SUCH A LOSER.
.........
...TO BE HONEST...
...I HAD GIVEN UP FROM THE START.
HM......?

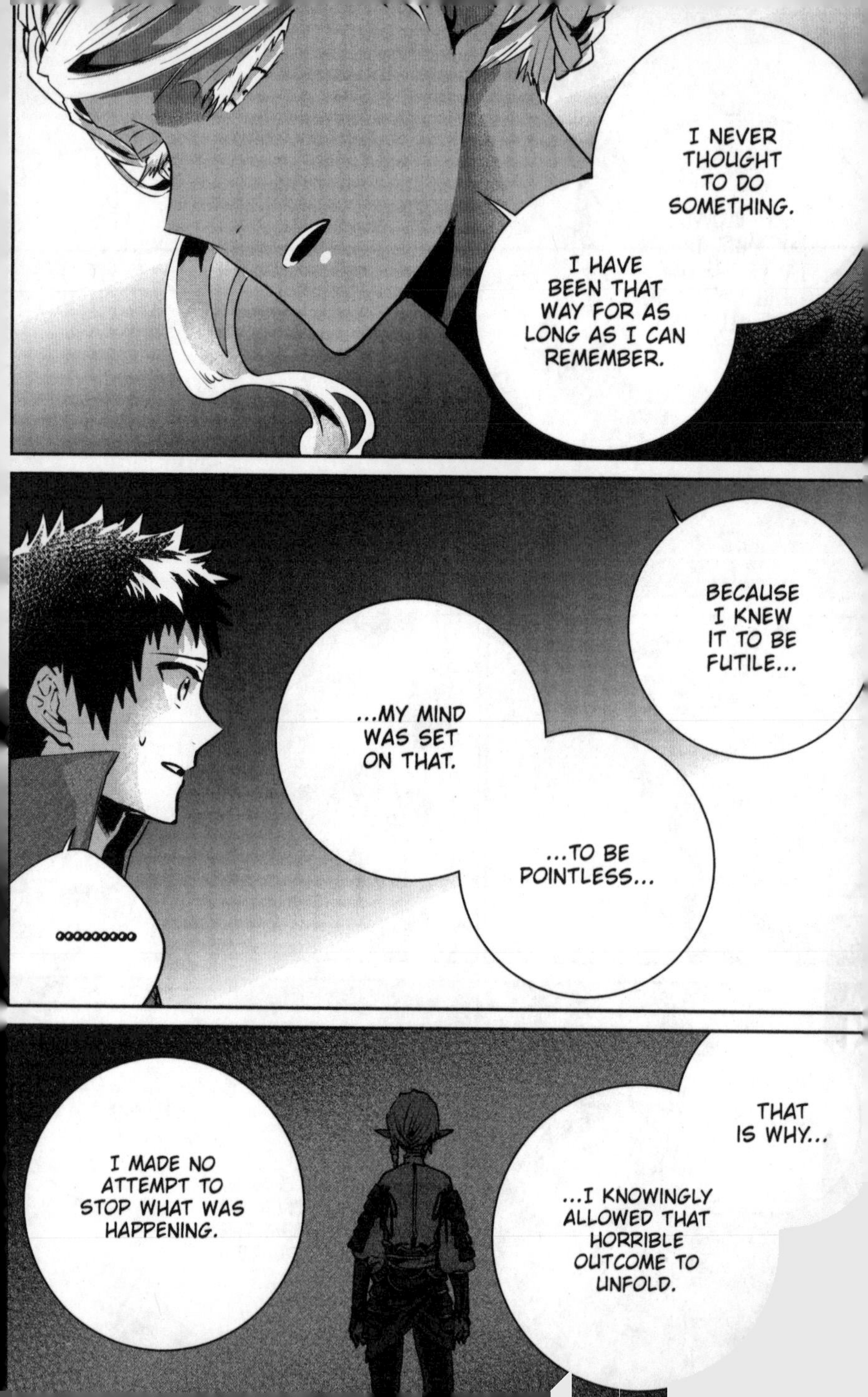
I NEVER THOUGHT TO DO SOMETHING.
I HAVE BEEN THAT WAY FOR AS LONG AS I CAN REMEMBER.
BECAUSE I KNEW IT TO BE FUTILE...
...TO BE POINTLESS...
...MY MIND WAS SET ON THAT.
.........
THAT IS WHY...
...I KNOWINGLY ALLOWED THAT HORRIBLE OUTCOME TO UNFOLD.
I MADE NO ATTEMPT TO STOP WHAT WAS HAPPENING.

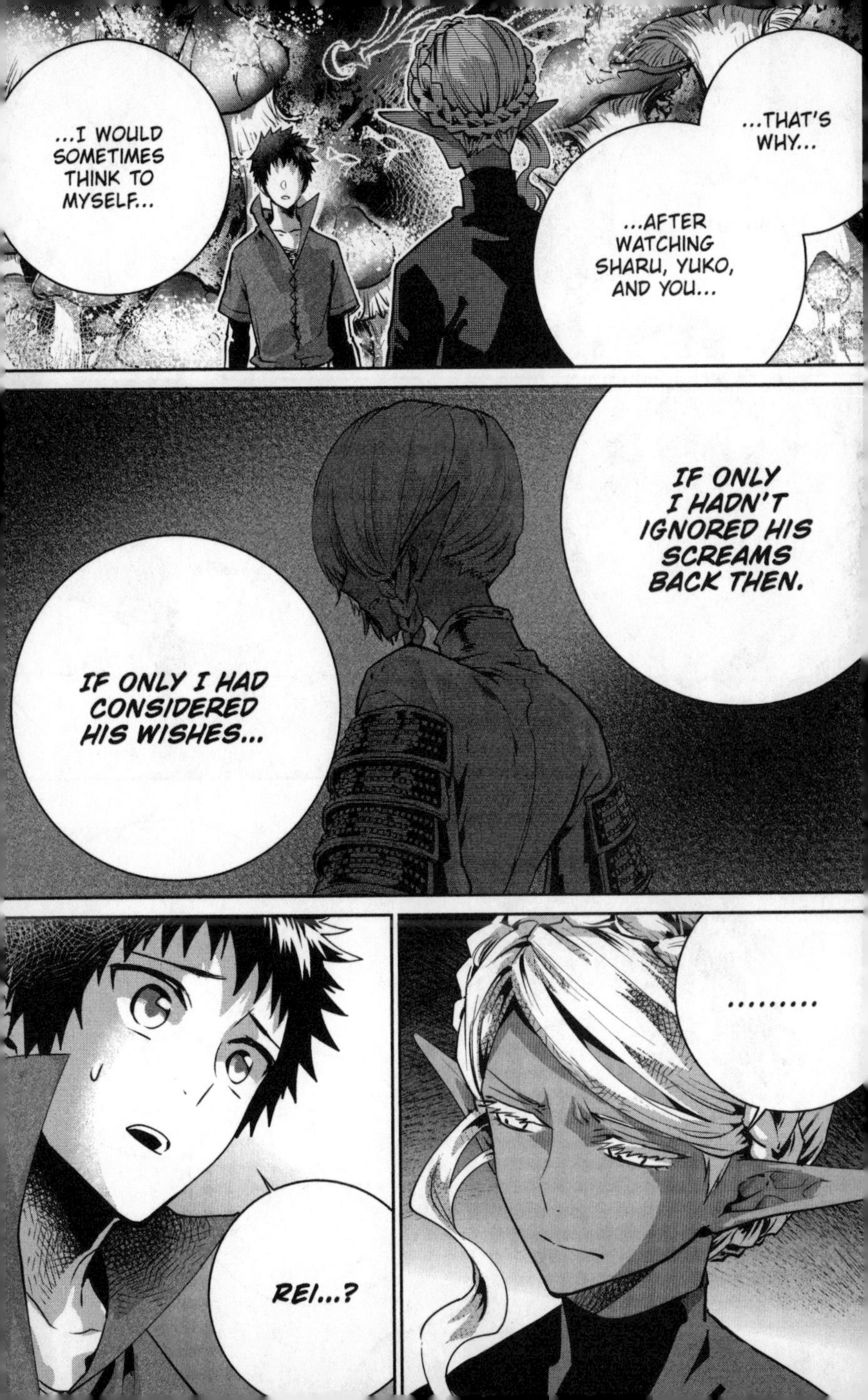
...THAT'S WHY...
...AFTER WATCHING SHARU, YUKO, AND YOU...
...I WOULD SOMETIMES THINK TO MYSELF...
IF ONLY I HADN'T IGNORED HIS SCREAMS BACK THEN.
IF ONLY I HAD CONSIDERED HIS WISHES...
.........
REI...?

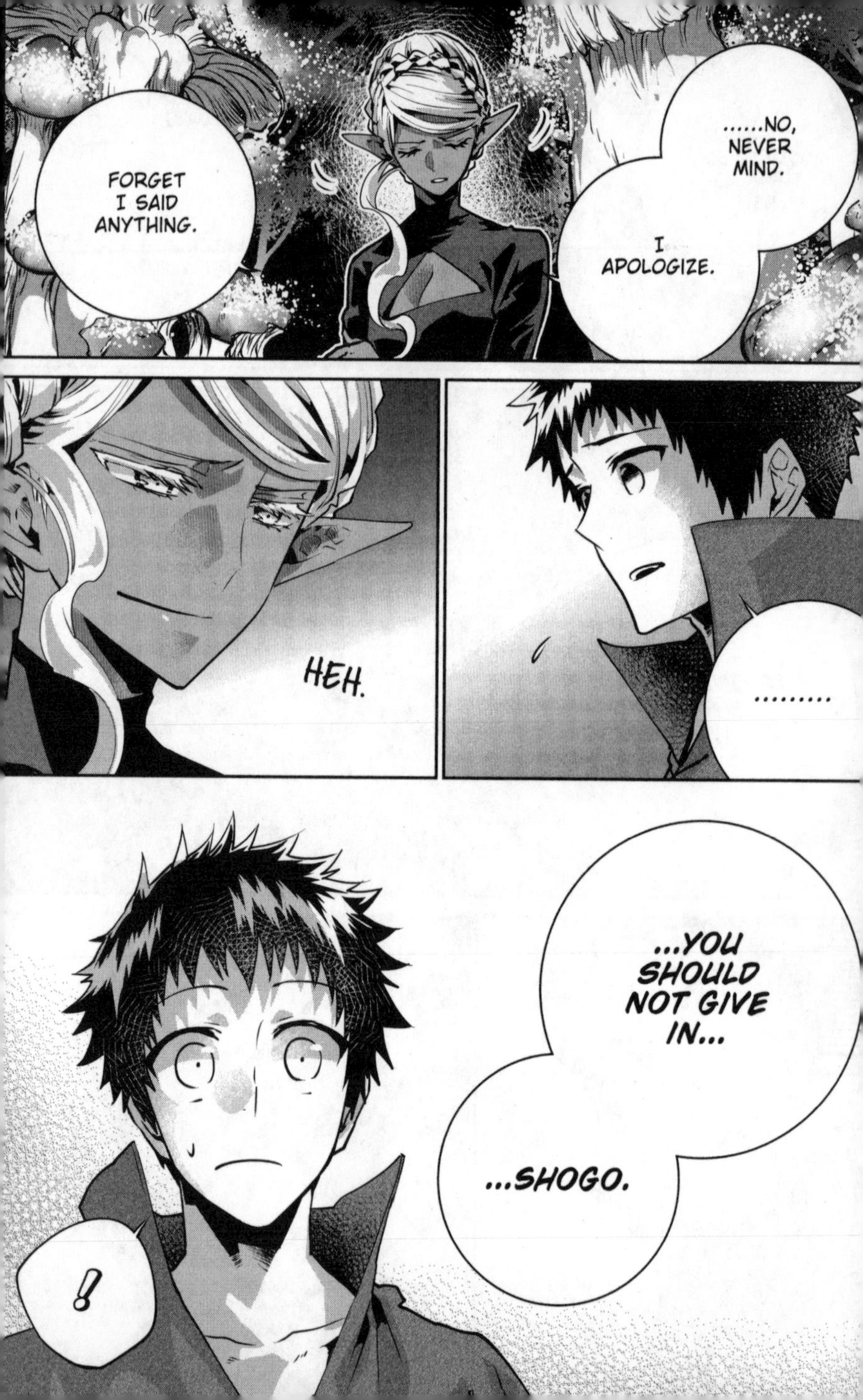
......NO, NEVER MIND.
I APOLOGIZE.
FORGET I SAID ANYTHING.
.........
HEH.
...YOU SHOULD NOT GIVE IN...
...SHOGO.
!

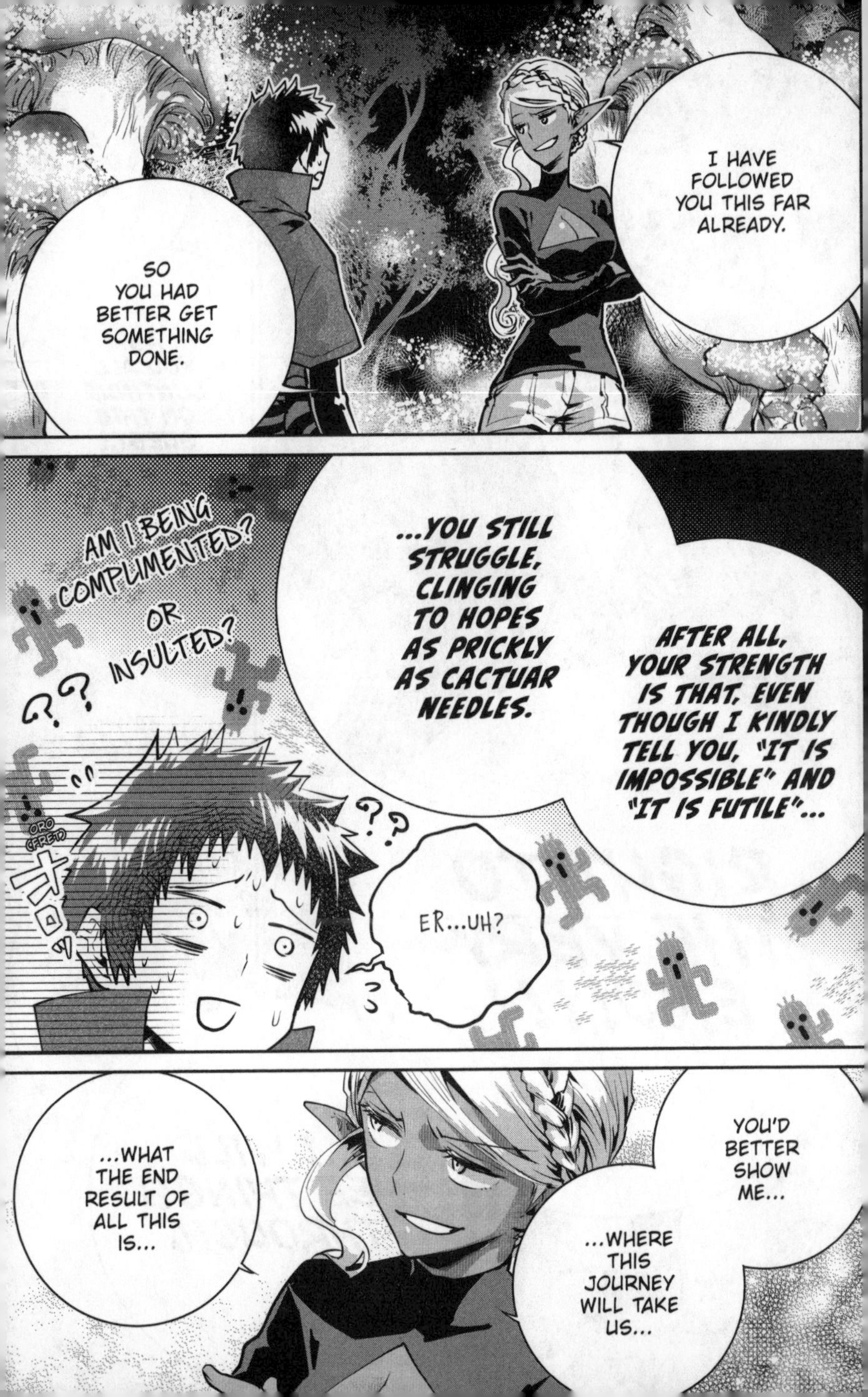
I HAVE FOLLOWED YOU THIS FAR ALREADY.
SO YOU HAD BETTER GET SOMETHING DONE.
AFTER ALL, YOUR STRENGTH IS THAT, EVEN THOUGH I KINDLY TELL YOU, "IT IS IMPOSSIBLE" AND "IT IS FUTILE"...
...YOU STILL STRUGGLE, CLINGING TO HOPES AS PRICKLY AS CACTUAR NEEDLES.
ER...UH?
AM I BEING COMPLIMENTED? OR INSULTED?
ORO (FRET)
YOU'D BETTER SHOW ME...
...WHERE THIS JOURNEY WILL TAKE US...
...WHAT THE END RESULT OF ALL THIS IS...

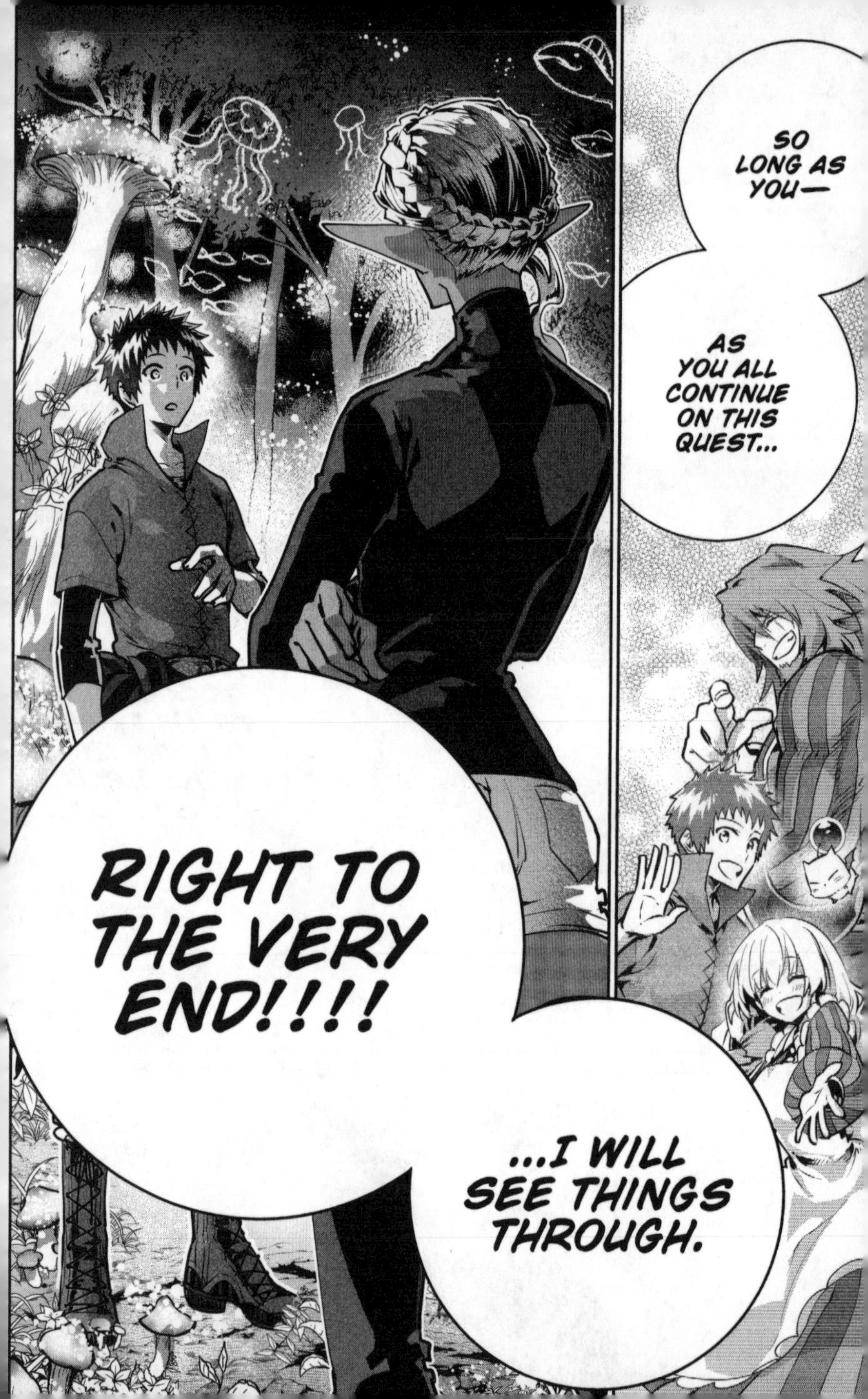
SO LONG AS YOU—
AS YOU ALL CONTINUE ON THIS QUEST...
...I WILL SEE THINGS THROUGH.
RIGHT TO THE VERY END!!!!

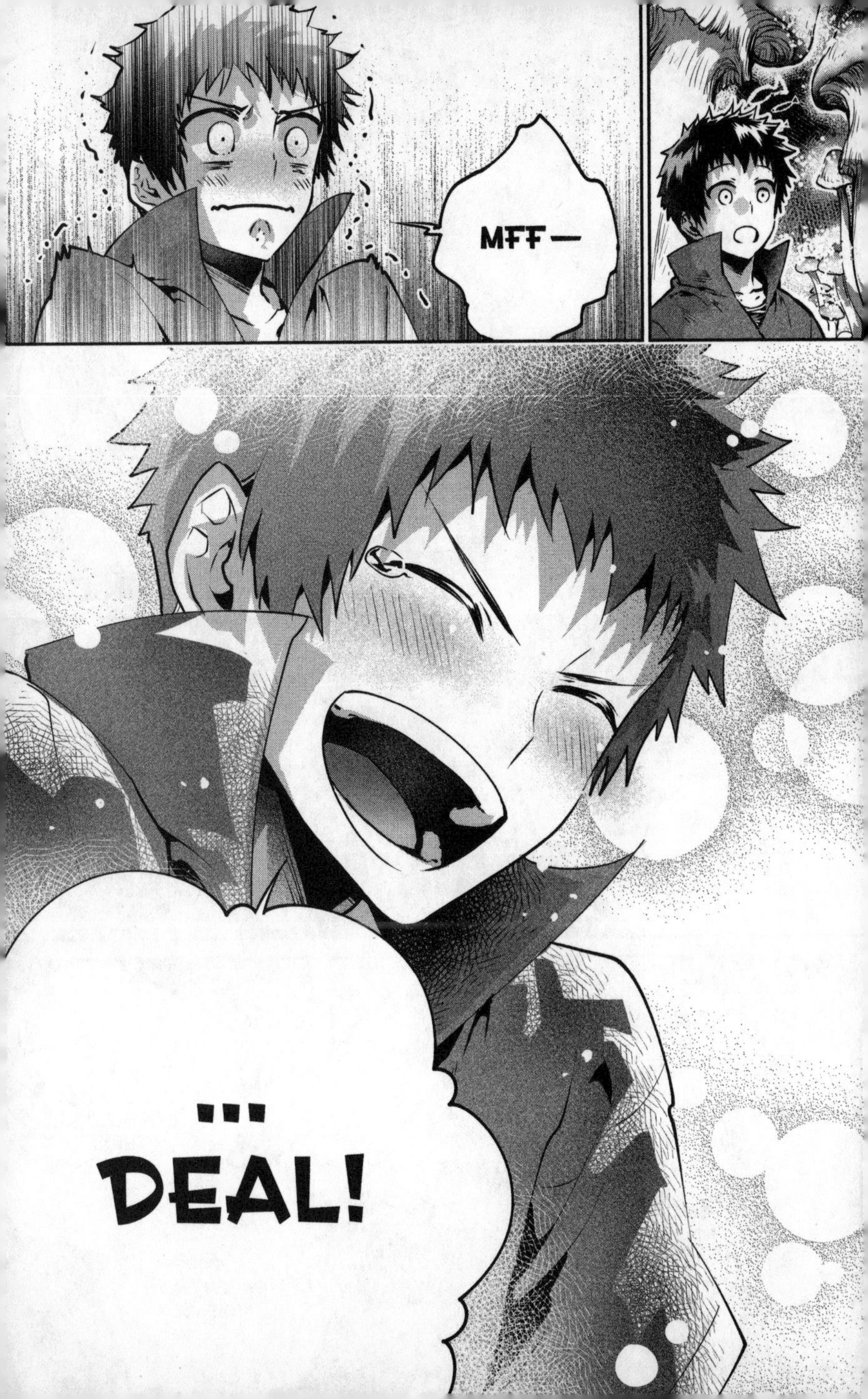
MFF—
...DEAL!

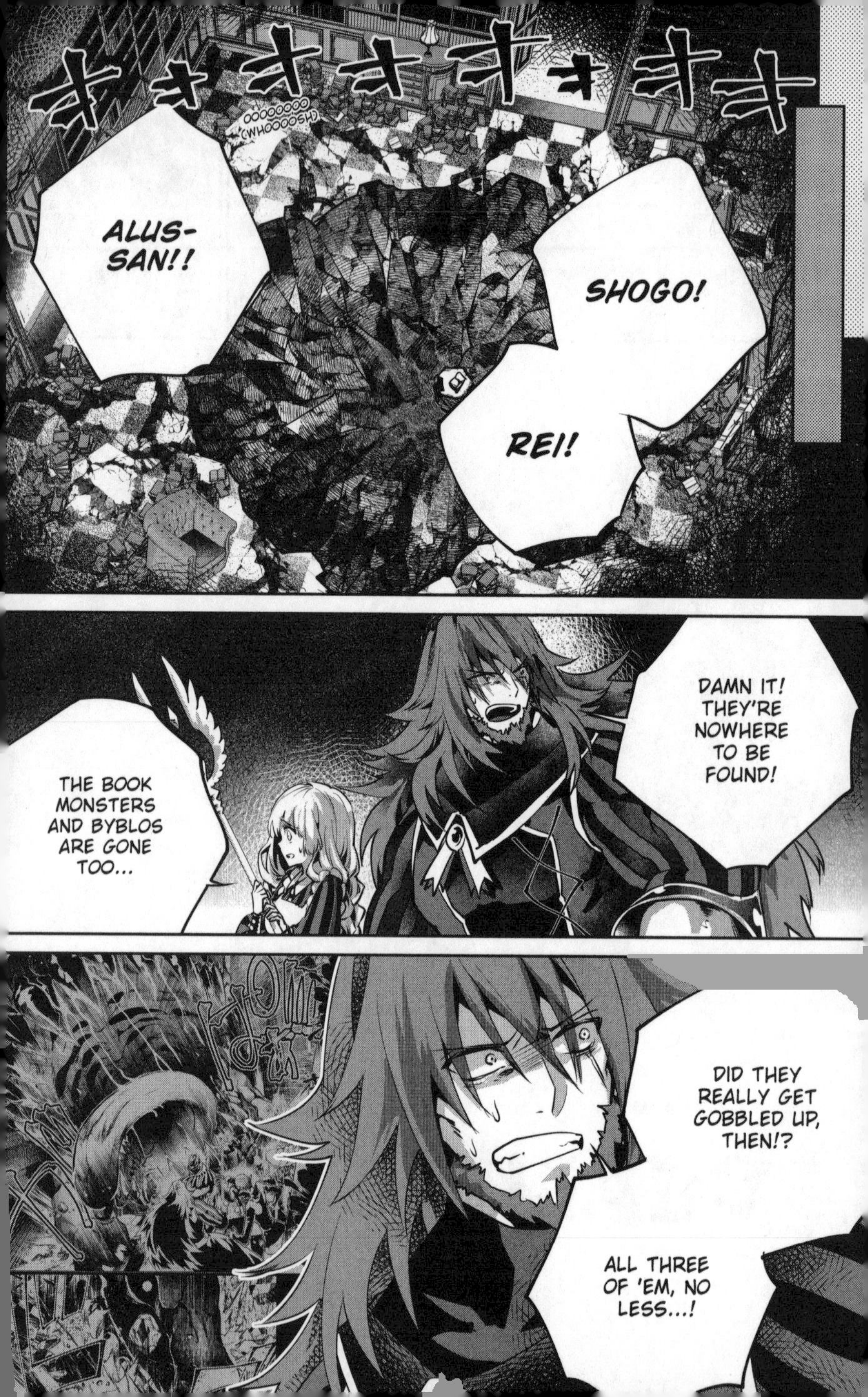
(WHOOOOSH)
SHOGO!
REI!
ALUS-SAN!!
DAMN IT! THEY'RE NOWHERE TO BE FOUND!
THE BOOK MONSTERS AND BYBLOS ARE GONE TOO...
DID THEY REALLY GET GOBBLED UP, THEN!?
ALL THREE OF 'EM, NO LESS...!

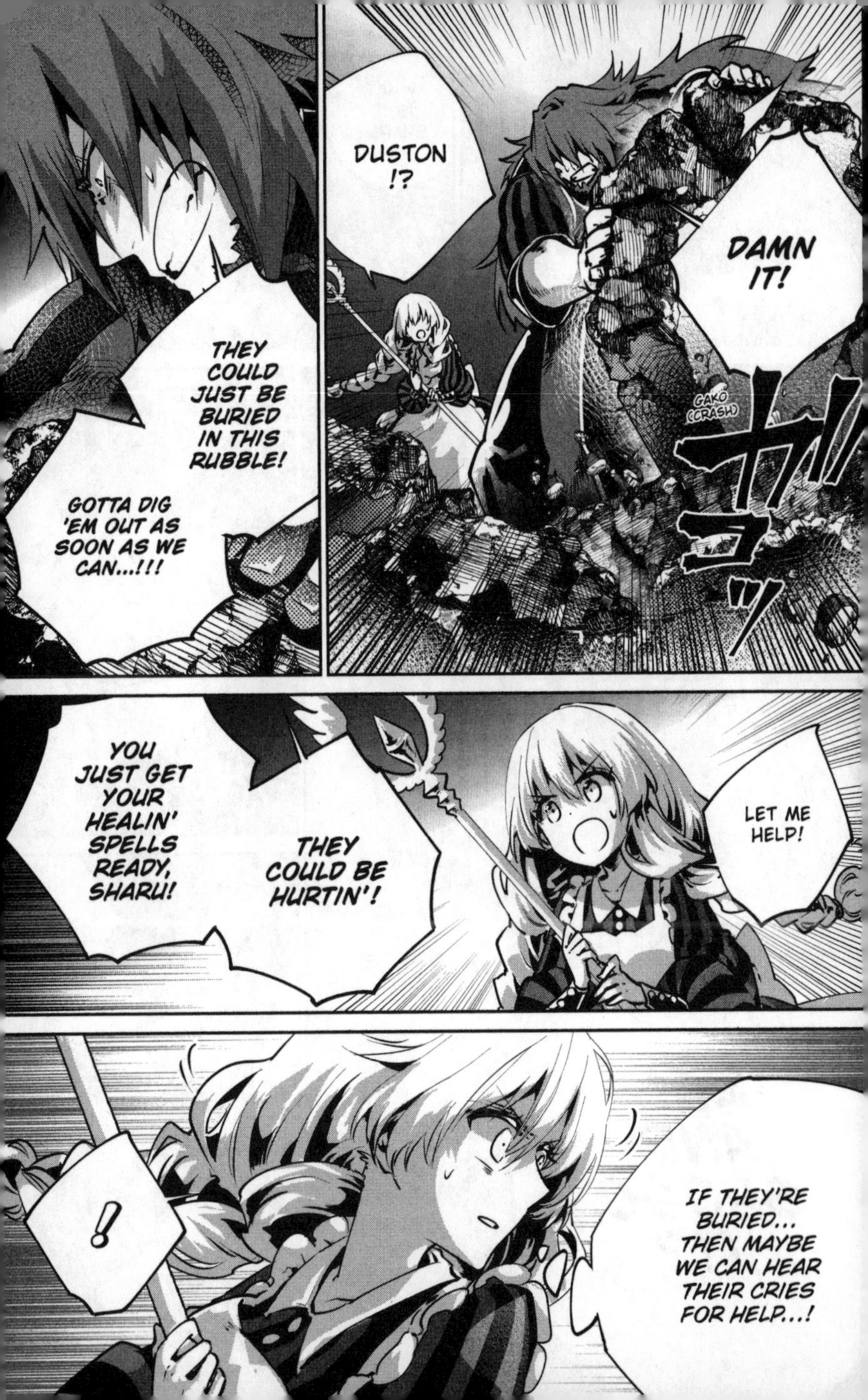
DUSTON !?
DAMN IT!
GAKO (CRASH)
THEY COULD JUST BE BURIED IN THIS RUBBLE!
GOTTA DIG 'EM OUT AS SOON AS WE CAN...!!!
LET ME HELP!
THEY COULD BE HURTIN'!
YOU JUST GET YOUR HEALIN' SPELLS READY, SHARU!
IF THEY'RE BURIED... THEN MAYBE WE CAN HEAR THEIR CRIES FOR HELP...!
!

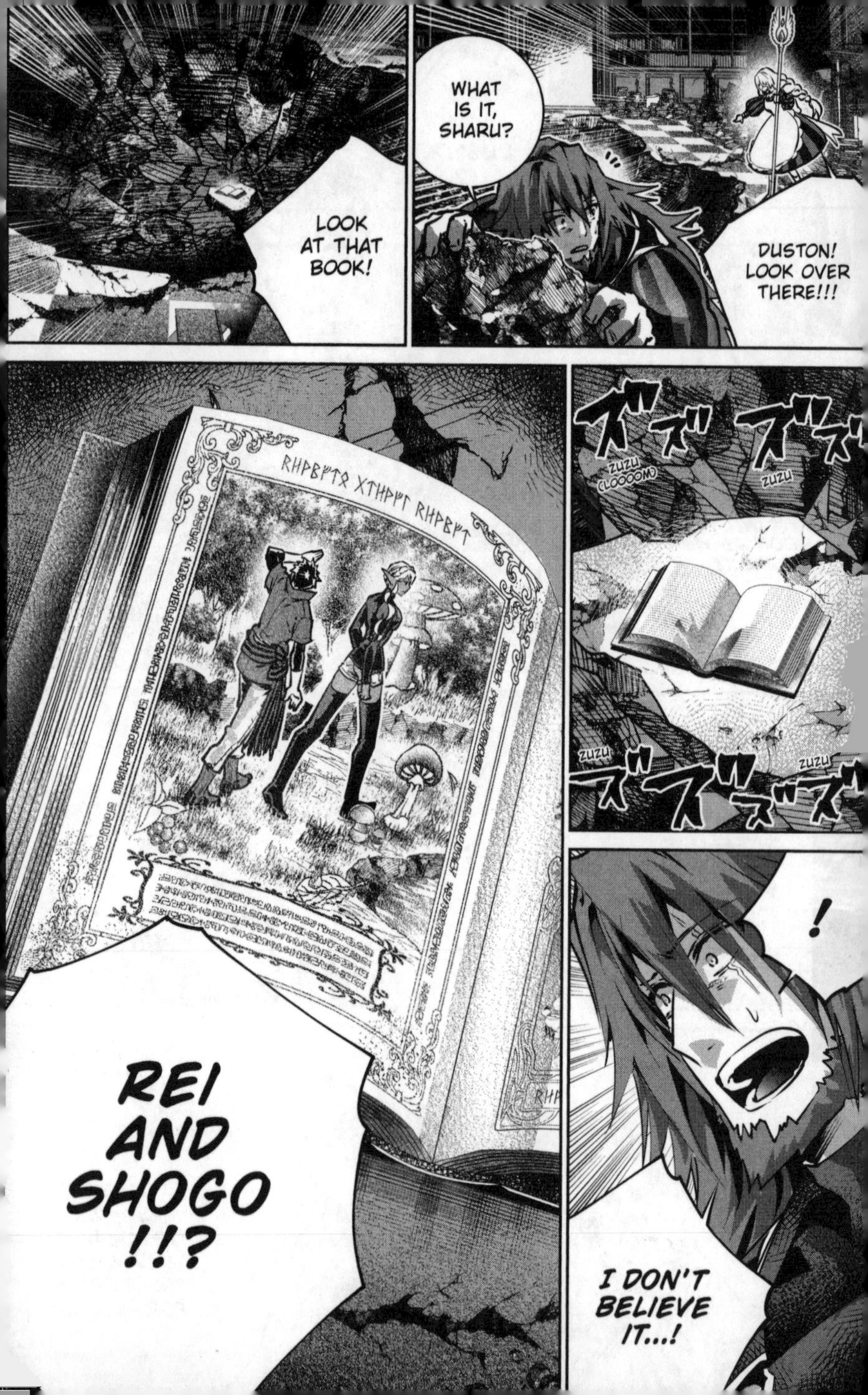
DUSTON! LOOK OVER THERE!!!
WHAT IS IT, SHARU?
LOOK AT THAT BOOK!
ZUZU (LOOOOM)
ZUZU
ZUZU
ZUZU
!
I DON'T BELIEVE IT...!
REI AND SHOGO!!?

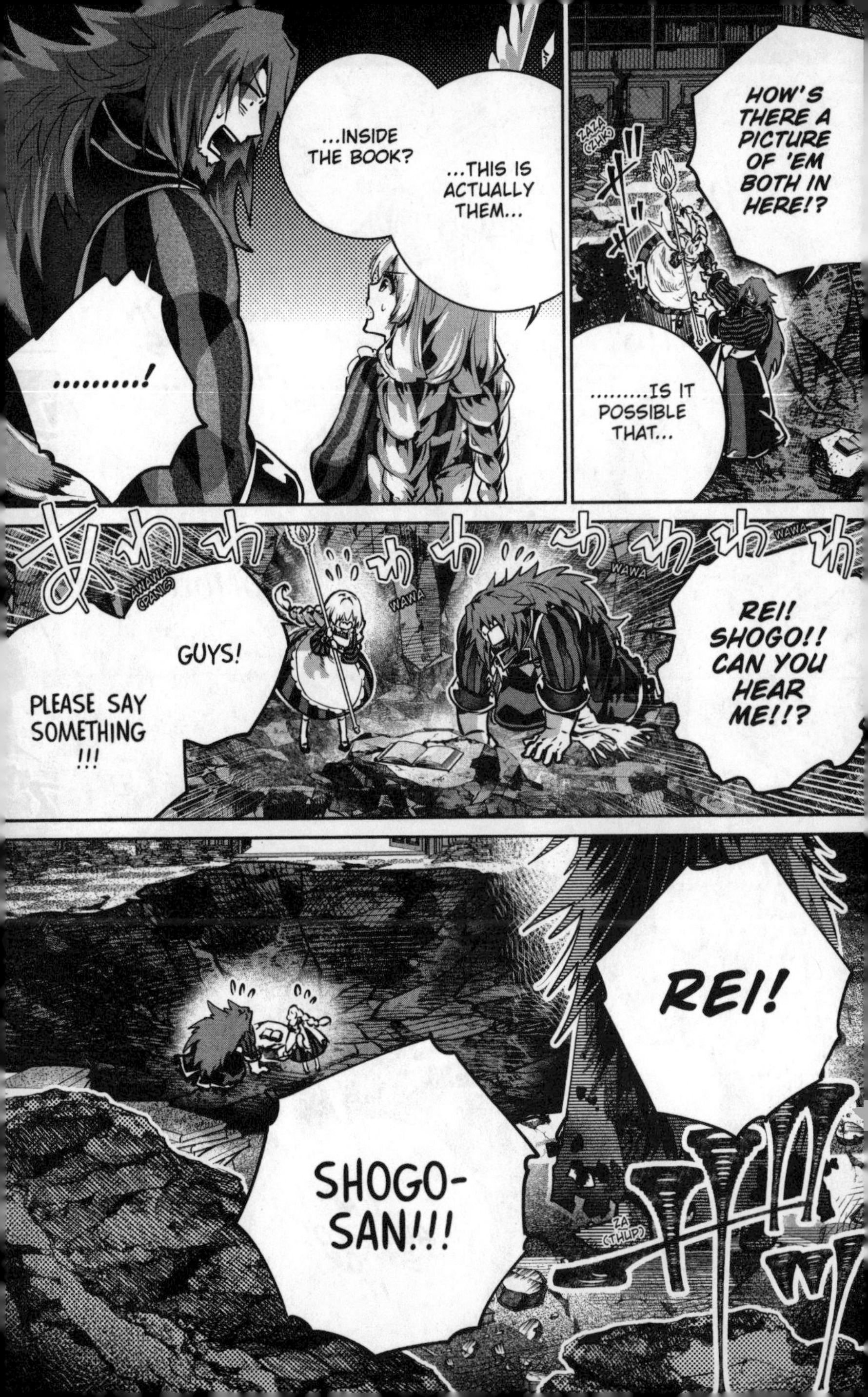
HOW'S THERE A PICTURE OF 'EM BOTH IN HERE!?
.........IS IT POSSIBLE THAT...
...THIS IS ACTUALLY THEM...
...INSIDE THE BOOK?
.........!
REI! SHOGO!! CAN YOU HEAR ME!!?
WAWA
WAWA
WAWA
GUYS!
PLEASE SAY SOMETHING!!!
AWAWA
REI!
SHOGO-SAN!!!

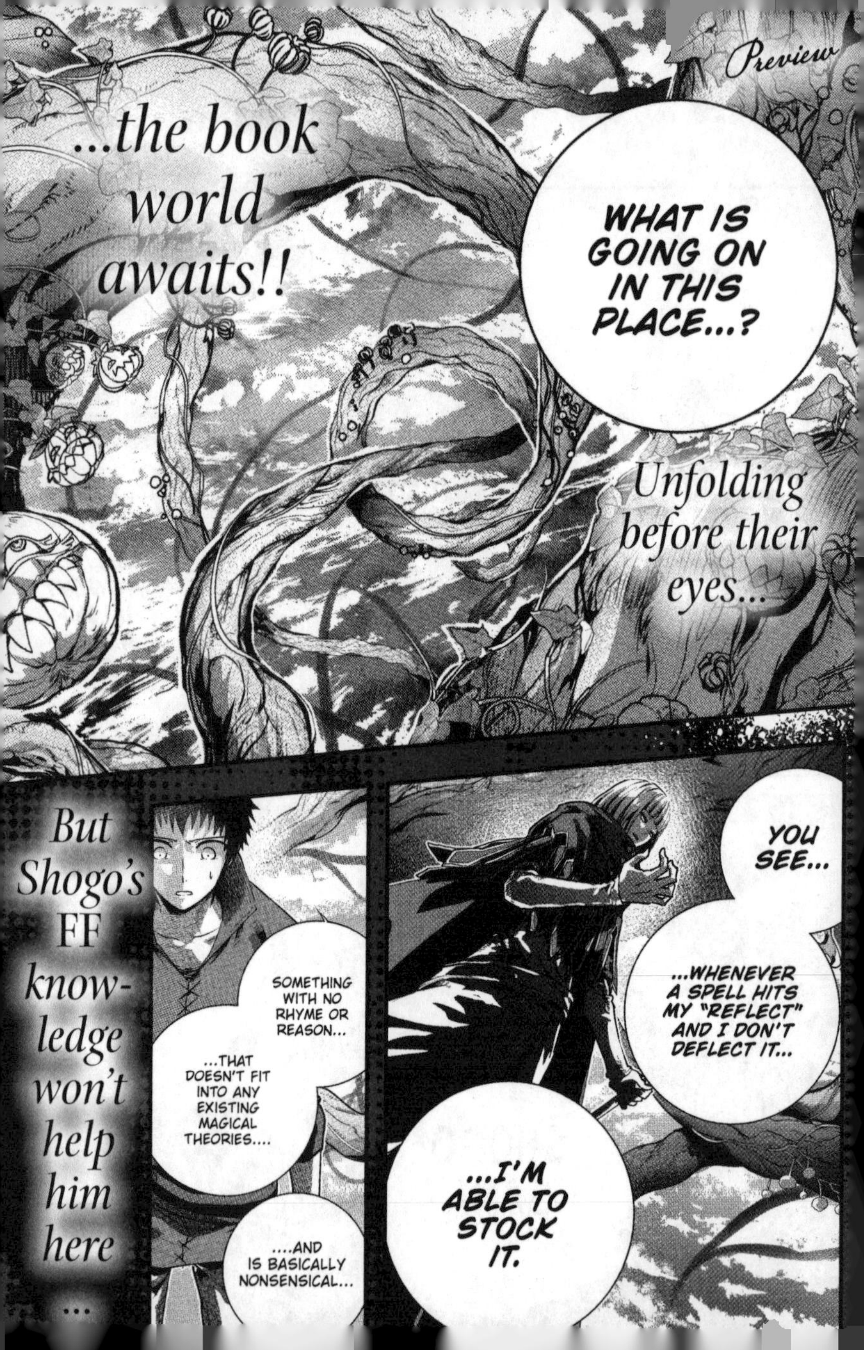
Preview
WHAT IS GOING ON IN THIS PLACE...?
Unfolding before their eyes...
...the book world awaits!!
YOU SEE...
...WHENEVER A SPELL HITS MY "REFLECT" AND I DON'T DEFLECT IT...
...I'M ABLE TO STOCK IT.
SOMETHING WITH NO RHYME OR REASON...
...THAT DOESN'T FIT INTO ANY EXISTING MAGICAL THEORIES....
....AND IS BASICALLY NONSENSICAL...
But Shogo's FF know-ledge won't help him here ...

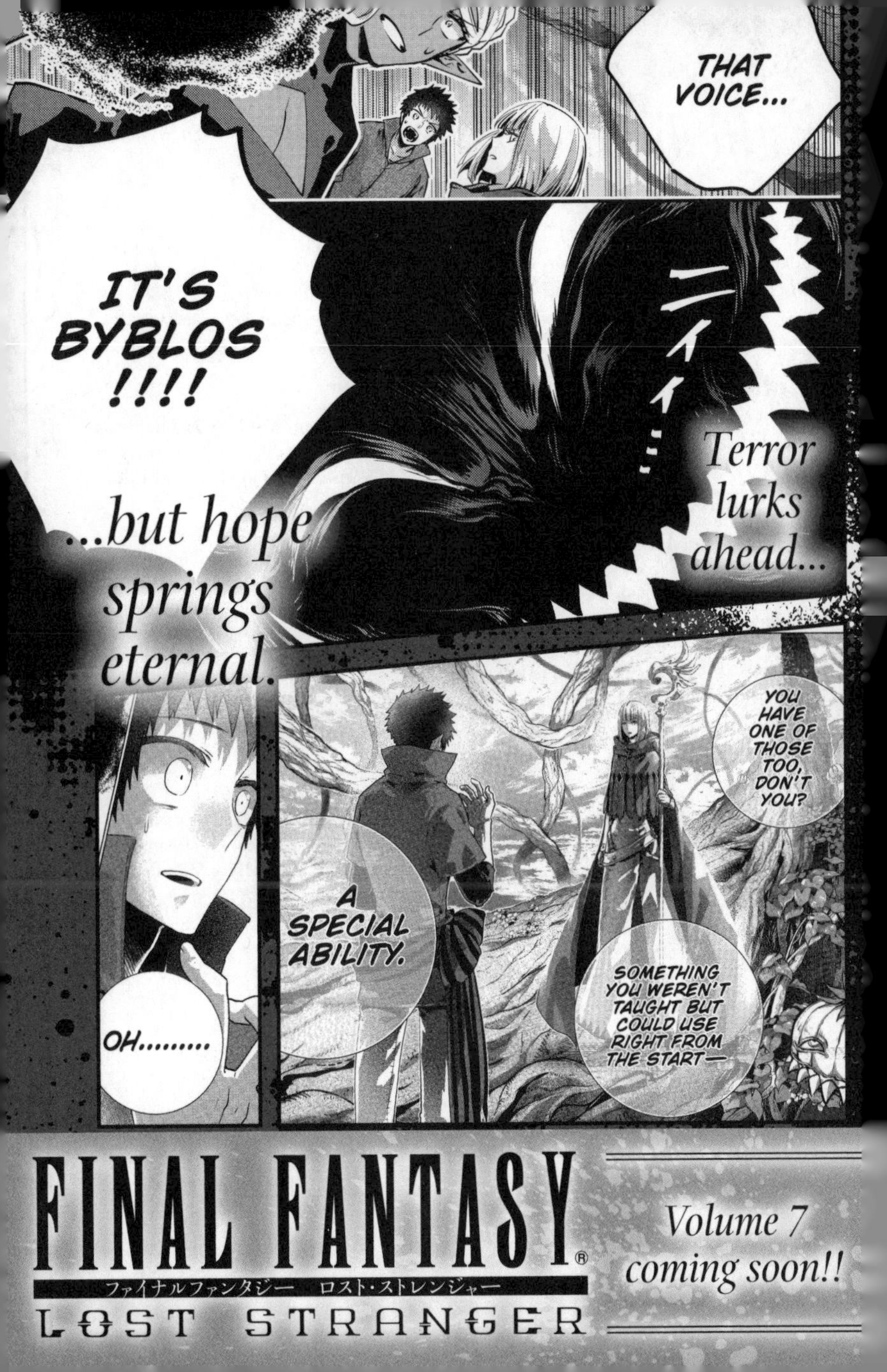
THAT VOICE...
IT'S BYBLOS !!!!
Terror lurks ahead...
...but hope springs eternal.
YOU HAVE ONE OF THOSE TOO, DON'T YOU?
SOMETHING YOU WEREN'T TAUGHT BUT COULD USE RIGHT FROM THE START—
A SPECIAL ABILITY.
OH.........

# FINAL FANTASY®

ファイナルファンタジー　ロスト・ストレンジャー

## LOST STRANGER

Volume 7 coming soon!!

# TRANSLATION NOTES

## COMMON HONORIFICS

no honorific: Indicates familiarity or closeness; if used without permission or reason, addressing someone in this manner would constitute an insult.

-san: The Japanese equivalent of Mr./Mrs./Miss. If a situation calls for politeness, this is the fail-safe honorific.

-kun: Used most often when referring to boys, this indicates affection or familiarity. Occasionally used by older men among their peers, but it may also be used by anyone referring to a person of lower standing.

-chan: An affectionate honorific indicating familiarity used mostly in reference to girls; also used in reference to cute persons or animals of either gender.

-sensei: A respectful term for teachers, artists, or high-level professionals.

onii-chan: An affectionate term used for older brothers or brother figures.

-senpai: An honorific used for upperclassmen and older, more knowledgeable colleagues.

### ◆ PAGE 4
The "Great Library" is a reference to the "Great Gubal Library" in FF14.

### ◆ PAGE 5
The Japanese title of this chapter translates to "Desired Power," but it's also the name of the FF12 track "Seeking Power."

### ◆ PAGE 19
The Remedy and Maiden's Kiss items, as well as the "Esuna" spell, are all ways to cure the Frog status in various FF titles.

### ◆ PAGE 26
In Japanese, there is no spelling or pronunciation distinction between "aether" and "ether," which is why Sharu is so quick to equate the two.

Spirit energy shows up in FF7 as the Lifestream, and "natural energy" appears in FF12 as Mist.

### ◆ PAGE 41
The title of this chapter appears in the soundtrack of a number of FF games—Final Fantasy Tactics, Final Fantasy 3, and Final Fantasy 5.

### ◆ PAGE 66
The Japanese title of this chapter translates to "The Flow of Life," but it's also the name of the FF7 track "Lifestream."

### ◆ PAGE 87
"Know, live, become a frog!" is an incantation recited when casting "Toad" in Final Fantasy Tactics.

**◆ PAGE 102**
While it never appeared in the final game, "Infuse a bug's mind into the soul! Confuse!" is a quote tied to the "Confuse" spell in the game files of *Final Fantasy Tactics*. Oddly enough, the quote for "Confuse2" actually does appear in the game.

**◆ PAGE 111**
The Japanese title of this chapter translates to "Transience," but it's also the name of the *FF Type-0* track "Utakata."

**◆ PAGE 114**
"Stone" is a weak earth elemental spell featured in many *Final Fantasy* games.

**◆ PAGE 118**
A Phoenix Down is a consumable item that revives KO'd characters. It is found in almost all *Final Fantasy* games.

**◆ PAGE 122**
"Fluid Aura" is a nondamaging White Magic spell that used to knock back and briefly bind an opponent up until the *Stormblood* expansion. As of the *Shadowbringers* expansion, the spell only binds an opponent.

**◆ PAGE 169**
The title of this chapter gets its name from the *FF13* track "Sinful Hope."

**◆ PAGE 187**
*Choco's Dungeon* is short for *Chocobo's Mysterious Dungeon*, a PS1 game released exclusively in Japan. Players must safely guide a chocobo hero named Poulet through dungeons with many floors. The gameplay is similar to that of its sequel, *Chocobo's Dungeon 2* (PS1), which did receive an English release.

Translation: Melody Pan    Lettering: Phil Christie

This book is a work of fiction. Names, characters, places, and incidents are the product of the author's imagination or are used fictitiously. Any resemblance to actual events, locales, or persons, living or dead, is coincidental.

FINAL FANTASY LOST STRANGER Volume 6 ©2020 Hazuki Minase, Itsuki Kameya/SQUARE ENIX CO., LTD. ©2020 SQUARE ENIX CO., LTD. All Rights Reserved. First published in Japan in 2020 by SQUARE ENIX CO., LTD. English translation rights arranged with SQUARE ENIX CO., LTD. and Yen Press, LLC through Tuttle-Mori Agency, Inc., Tokyo.

English translation © 2021 by SQUARE ENIX CO., LTD.

Yen Press
150 West 30th Street, 19th Floor
New York, NY 10001

Visit us at yenpress.com
facebook.com/yenpress
twitter.com/yenpress
yenpress.tumblr.com
instagram.com/yenpress

First Yen Press Edition: August 2021
The chapters in this volume were originally published as ebooks by Yen Press.

Yen Press is an imprint of Yen Press, LLC.
The Yen Press name and logo are trademarks of Yen Press, LLC.

The publisher is not responsible for websites (or their content) that are not owned by the publisher.

Library of Congress Control Number: 2018948073

ISBNs: 978-1-9753-3575-5 (paperback)
978-1-9753-3576-2 (ebook)

10 9 8 7 6 5 4 3 2 1

BVG

Printed in the United States of America